The Philosophical Quest
Of Philosophy, Ethics, Law and Halakhah

MAGGID

Michael Scharf
Publication Trust
Yeshiva University Press

Rabbi J. David Bleich

THE PHILOSOPHICAL QUEST

OF PHILOSOPHY, ETHICS, LAW AND HALAKHAH

The Michael Scharf Publication Trust of
Yeshiva University Press
Rabbi Isaac Elchanan Theological Seminary

The RIETS Hashkafah Series
Rabbi Daniel Z. Feldman, Series Editor

Maggid Books

The Philosophical Quest:
Of Philosophy, Ethics, Law and Halakhah

First Edition, 2013

The Michael Scharf Publication Trust
of Yeshiva University Press

Maggid Books
An imprint of Koren Publishers Jerusalem Ltd.

POB 8531, New Milford, CT 06776-8531, USA
& POB 4044, Jerusalem 91040, Israel
www.korenpub.com

© J. David Bleich 2013

Cover Design: Tani Bayer

ISBN 978-1-59264-343-1, *hardcover*

A CIP catalogue record for this title is
available from the British Library

Printed and bound in the United States

Table of Contents

Foreword

We are proud to inaugurate the English language *hashka-fah* (Jewish philosophy) series of the Rabbi Isaac Elchanan Theological Seminary (RIETS) division of the Michael Scharf Publication Trust of Yeshiva University Press (the "RIETS Press") with this volume of essays by Rabbi J. David Bleich on a variety of topics relating to Jewish philosophical thought.

Rabbi Bleich serves as a Rosh Yeshiva and the *Rosh Kollel Le-Hora'ah* at RIETS, Professor of Law at the Benjamin N. Cardozo School of Law, and Herbert and Florence Tenzer Professor of Law and Ethics at Yeshiva University. He is a towering figure in the areas of Jewish law and Jewish philosophy, and our students are privileged to be the beneficiaries of his wisdom and erudition.

It is extremely important, particularly in the modern age of skepticism, to provide a sophisticated analysis of Jewish beliefs, dogmas and epistemology. Ultimately, the Jewish credo is *"tamim tihyeh im Hashem E-lokekha"* (*Devarim* 18:13), that one should adopt a simple and wholesome faith. At the same time, the imperative of "wholesomeness" also denotes that it is essential to have an understanding of the fundamental components of an *"emuna sheleima"* – of a complete and comprehensive faith system. Based on these considerations, the rabbinical training program at RIETS features a constellation of courses in Jewish theology and philosophy, including a year-long survey course in Jewish thought for all rabbinical students.

In fact, Maimonides went so far as to write in his Commentary to the Mishnah (*Sanhedrin*, Chapter 10) that a Jew who does not believe in the thirteen principles of faith (as articulated by Maimonides) is not considered to be a member of the community of Israel. Along similar lines, the Chazon Ish (Reb Avraham Yeshayahu Karelitz) wrote that a prospective convert, in addition to accepting the yoke of all of the mitzvot of the Torah, must possess a firm belief in the fundamental principles of Jewish faith (*Yoreh Deah* 119:2). Clearly, Judaism is a religion of both deed and creed.

We are thus exceedingly grateful to Rabbi Bleich for sharing his first rate scholarship in Jewish philosophy with the broader community. It is our hope that his clear and cogent manner of presentation will edify scholars and laypeople alike with respect to the tenets and telos of the Jewish religion.

In addition, we extend our appreciation to Rabbi Daniel Feldman, who, in his role as executive editor of the RIETS Press, has enabled the publication of this volume in accordance with his customary standard of editorial excellence.

Finally, we gratefully acknowledge the encouragement of our *Nasi HaYeshiva*, President Richard Joel, our *Rosh HaYeshiva* Rabbi Dr. Norman Lamm, and our Dean Emeritus Rabbi Zevulun Charlop, in building a cadre of luminous faculty and supporting the Torah scholarship that permeates our study halls and classrooms. "*Ashreikhem talmidei ḥakhamim shedivrei Torah ḥavivin aleikhem beyoter*" – fortunate are Torah scholars for whom the greatest joy is Torah scholarship (*Menaḥot* 18a).

Rabbi Yona Reiss
Max and Marion Grill Dean of RIETS
5 Kislev 5773

Editor's Preface

With gratitude tendered to the *Ribbono Shel Olam*, we present before the learning public the first volume of the RIETS Series of Hashkafah. This series is one of many initiatives currently being undertaken at Rabbi Isaac Elchanan Theological Seminary (RIETS), an affiliate of Yeshiva University, as a new stage in our yeshiva's efforts to extend the teaching of Torah at a level that is both deep and wide: advanced and uncompromised in its content and substance, and broad in its accessibility and availability. In recent years, we have seen the release of a growing number of volumes of this initiative, both works written in the classical Hebrew style of the *beit ha-medrash* and in the modern English idiom that allows for an expanded range of communication.

This series, the RIETS Series of Hashkafah, endeavors to publish volumes, authored by the *rashei yeshiva* of RIETS, which will present detailed and sophisticated analysis and elucidation of the principles of Jewish belief. The practice of Judaism is premised upon its foundational creeds; the belief system of Judaism is given an audible voice through the observance of the commandments of the Torah. It is a fitting expression of Yeshiva's mission that with the inauguration of this new series, we now present multi-volume expressions of studies of both realms in tandem.

It is particularly appropriate and a tremendous honor to launch the RIETS Hashkafah series with a volume of writings by Rabbi J. David Bleich, who has long been recognized as an international authority in both Jewish law and Jewish thought. This work contains essays that have been previously published elsewhere but are for the first time being brought together in one volume. The very nature of the diverse venues of their initial appearances, from law school journals to philosophical tomes to journals of Orthodox Jewish thought, is itself a testament to the breadth and depth of their distinguished author, who is at once a Rosh Kollel and a law professor, a world-renowned halakhic authority and an accomplished scholar of Jewish philosophy. His works, both in Jewish law and in Jewish thought, have for decades filled the shelves of libraries, *batei midrash,* and homes in which a serious and mature understanding of Torah beliefs and practices is a priority. Throughout these decades, Yeshiva University has benefited by his presence and active involvement, as he serves as Rosh Yeshiva and the *Rosh Kollel Le-Hora'ah* at RIETS, Professor of Law at the Benjamin N. Cardozo School of Law, and Herbert and Florence Tenzer Professor of Law and Ethics at Yeshiva University.

We are grateful to Willie Roth, whose diligence, scholarship and acumen belie his young years and who graciously brought these attributes to bear in facilitating and preparing of these articles for publication in this volume.

We are profoundly grateful to the administration of RIETS for their stalwart guidance of our Yeshiva, and for their dedication in making Yeshivat Rabbenu Yitzchak Elchanan the magnificent center of Torah study and rabbinic training that it is. Rav Yona Reiss, the Max and Marion Grill Dean of RIETS, consistently provides his wisdom and guidance to all of the functions of the yeshiva, including the insight and direction he has provided to the projects of the RIETS initiative of YU Press. We are the fortunate beneficiaries of the tireless efforts of President Richard Joel; Rosh Hayeshiva and Chancellor Rav Norman Lamm; Dean Emeritus Rav Zevulun Charlop, and Rav Chaim Bronstein.

This volume is being published through the generosity of the Michael Scharf Publication Trust of Yeshiva University Press, and we express gratitude to Michael and Fiona Scharf for all of their work in bringing Torah literature to print under the auspices of Yeshiva University.

Finally, a tremendous thank you to Matthew Miller, Rabbi Reuven Ziegler and the wonderful staff at Maggid Books for all of their work in ensuring that the volume is brought to print in the most beautiful way possible.

It is our fervent wish that this volume and those that follow it will add to the realization of our yeshiva's mission, to study, teach, clarify and spread *HaKadosh Barukh Hu*'s holy Torah, *le-hagdilah u-le-ha'adirah*.

Daniel Z. Feldman
Shevat, 5773

Author's Preface

The present volume is a collection of papers and essays that have appeared in a wide variety of publications over a span of years. They are presented here with some additions and relatively minor revisions. Separate chapters are devoted to axiological principles of faith that define the essence of Jewish belief, philosophical concepts reflected in the halakhic system, Jewish responsibilities in a non-Jewish society as well as ethical values as they relate to resolution of societal problems.

Discrepancies in matters of style reflect the different venues in which this material was originally published. That is most apparent in chapters that were adapted from Law Review articles in which Blue Book style has been retained. I wish to express my gratitude to the publishers of the journals and books in which these papers were originally featured. The following is a list of those essays and the publications in which they appeared: "Faith and Dogma in Judaism" and "The Thirteen Principles of Faith," *With Perfect Faith: The Foundations of Jewish Belief*, ed. J. David Bleich, New York: Ktav Publishing House, Inc., 1983; "Divine Unity in Maimonides, the Tosafists and Me'iri," *Neoplationism and Jewish Thought*, ed. Lenn E. Goodman, Stony Brook, N.Y.: State University of New York Press, 1992; "Was Spinoza a Jewish Philosopher?" *Cardozo Law Review*, vol. 25, no. 2, December 2003; *"Lo Ba-Shamayim Hi*: A Philosophical *Pilpul*," *Tradition and Transition: Essays Presented to Chief Rabbi Sir Immanuel Jakobovits to celebrate twenty years in office*, ed. Jonathan Sacks, London: Jews' College Publications, 1986; "Judaism and Natural Law," *Jewish Law Annual*, vol. VII, 1988; "Is there an Ethic Beyond Halakhah?" *Proceedings of the Ninth World Congress of Jewish Studies, Division C*, Jerusalem: World Union of Jewish Studies, 1986; "Duran's View of Providence," *Jewish Quarterly Review*, new series, vol. 69, April, 1979, "Providence in the Philosophy of Hasdai Crescas and Joseph Albo," *Ḥazon Naḥum: Studies in Jewish Law, Thought, and History Presented to Dr. Norman Lamn on the Occasion of his Seventieth Birthday*, ed. Yaakov Elman and Jeffrey S. Gurock, New York: Yeshiva University Press, 1997; "*Tikkun Olam*: Jewish Obligations to Non-Jewish Society," *Tikkun Olam: Social Responsibility in Jewish Thought and Law*, ed. David Shatz, Chaim Waxman and Nathan Diament, Northvale, N.J.: Jason Aaronson, Inc., 1997; "Maimonides on the Distinction between Science and Pseudoscience," *Moses Maimonides, Physician, Scientist, and Philosopher*, ed. Fred Rosner and Samuel S. Kottek, Northvale, N.J.: Jason Aaronson Inc., 1993; "The Problem of Identity in Rashi, Rambam and the Tosafists," *Between Rashi and Maimonides: Themes in Medieval Jewish Thought, Literature and Exegesis*, ed. Ephraim Kanarfogel and Moshe Sokolow, New York: Yeshiva University Press, 2010;" Resurrection and Personal Identity," *Tradition*, vol. 45, no. 3, Fall, 2012; "The Metaphysics of Property Interests in Jewish Law: An Analysis of *Kinyan*," *Tradition*, vol. 42, no. 2, Summer, 2010; "Is There a Right to Physician-Assisted Suicide?" *Fordham Urban Law Review Journal*, vol. 24, no. 4, November, 1997; "The Physician as a Conscientious Objector," *Fordham Urban Law Review Journal*, vol. 30, no. 1, November, 2002; and "Godtalk: Should Religion Inform Public Debate?" *Loyola of Los Angeles Law Review*, vol. 29, no. 4, June, 1996.

My thanks as well to Rabbi Moshe Schapiro, Mr. Zalman Alpert and Mr. Zvi Erenyi of the Mendel Gottesman Library of Yeshiva University for their constant helpfulness; to my secretary at the Benjamin N. Cardozo School of Law, Miss Kaaron Saphir, for her patience and understanding; and most especially to my granddaughter Hadassah Gurwitz whose thorough and meticulous proofreading and incisive observations have spared this work from many inadvertent errors. My gratitude also to Rabbi Daniel Feldman, the editor of the RIETS Hashkafah Series, for his dedication and diligence; to Mr. Willie Roth of The Rabbi Isaac Elchanan Theological Seminary for his meticulous work related to the technical aspects of preparing the material; as well as to Mr. Matthew Miller, Rabbi Reuven Ziegler and the staff of Maggid Books (an imprint of Koren Publishers Jerusalem) for their painstaking efforts in shepherding the manuscript through the various stages of publication.

Above all, I am grateful to the Almighty for my cherished collaborators – the members of my family. Our prayer to the Almighty is that we continue to be numbered among the *mashkimim le-divrei Torah* and, to paraphrase the words of the *hadran*, *ke-shem she-'azartanu le-sayyem sefer zeh, ken ta'azrenu le-hathil sefarim aherim u-le-sayyemam, lilmod u-le-lamed, lishmor ve-la'asot u-le-kayyem.*

.

Introduction

The Challenge of
Faith Commitment

T he thirst for knowledge, the desire for understanding and
the yearning for meaning are present in every thinking individual. For
people of faith the quest for a deeper appreciation of the fundamentals
of their belief system is compelling. For Jews that quest is integral to the
mitzvah of *talmud Torah*.

During roughly the first half of the twentieth century, laxity in
religious observance posed the major challenge to the continuity of
Jewish tradition in Western society. Economic conditions combined
with a desire for social acceptance within the dominant culture to
create a milieu in which the Jewish community became increasingly
tolerant of relaxed religious norms. Even in observant circles compromise of a greater or lesser degree, ofttimes born of expedience but not
infrequently motivated by a sincere desire to preserve the preservable,
became prevalent.

Within the Orthodox community, by the grace of God, that has
changed. A shifting social climate, ethnic pride, the emergence of cultural
diversity as a desideratum, a new economic reality and, above all, higher

standards of Jewish education which inevitably dispel inconsistencies and raise standards of commitment, have all coalesced to produce on these shores a generation of observant Jews whose standards of religiosity are superior to those of their parents and, with increasing frequency, of their grandparents as well. *Akhshar dara* – How the generation has progressed! And for that we must be thankful.

Would that such were the case with regard to ideological commitment, ethical values and social mores as well. In generations past, the Thirteen Principles of Faith were not the subject matter of instruction in the curriculum of either the *ḥeder* or the yeshiva. They were transmitted with mother's milk and absorbed through the osmotic fabric of the Jewish family. Observance, at some times and in some places, may have been less than meticulous, but ideological vacillation was far more rare.

The "*Ketzos Yid*" of Jewish folklore, an individual depicted as sitting at a table on *Shabbat* hunched over a rabbinic tome with a cigarette between his fingers, if he ever existed, was a rare bird indeed. But even he recognized that the Thirteen Principles constitute the bedrock of Judaism. For the immigrant generation, even in non-observant sectors of the community, the synagogue one did not attend was the Orthodox synagogue and the only Judaism to be embraced or rejected was the Judaism of unequivocal belief.

With the passage of time, a different form of Judaism began to gain ascendancy – a Judaism based upon practice rather than belief. Orthopraxy became a socio-religious phenomenon. Identification of motivating forces are the domain of the historian; to students of philosophy or of Halakhah they are of scant interest. But it is certainly likely that such an ideological metamorphosis must be attributed either to a desire for intellectual justification of certain antinomian tendencies or as an adaptation and internalization of liberal theological beliefs prevalent in the dominant society. The latter phenomenon represents a limited form of intellectual assimilation. From the vantage point of Jewish tradition, the result, to a greater or lesser degree, is a form of cultural Judaism rather than espousal of a faith commitment. And yes, particularly when observance is intense and consistent, it is quite possible that the undiscerning may be incapable of identifying a peer as a cultural Jew rather than as an ideologically committed Jew.

Cognoscenti, few as they may be, are all too aware that while a generation ago the phenomenon of the non-observant Orthodox was the focus of consternation, in our time, it is the observant non-Orthodox that should be our concern. It may well be the case that, presently, the base level of educational attainment among Orthodox laity in the diaspora is greater than at any identifiable period of Jewish history. In that sense our educational endeavors have been crowned with unanticipated success. Not so with regard to transmission of Jewish belief. Western society is strongly materialistic and lacking in rigorously defined and firmly held dogmatic beliefs. For reasons best left to analysis on the part of others, but undoubtedly due, at least in part, to interruption of a cultural continuum resulting from a wrenching adjustment to Western society and a Western way of life, currently, the dominant influences brought to bear upon a developing adolescent are not the traditions transmitted through the medium of the home but the intellectual trends and mores of society at large. Our educational institutions, by and large, have not risen to the challenge. Matters of belief and ideology are simply not stressed in our schools. Not surprisingly, products of such an educational system who have grown to intellectual maturity while continuing to identify themselves as Orthodox seek to justify that appellation by challenging norms of Jewish faith accepted throughout the ages as fundamental to Judaism.

The revered R. Abraham I. Kook, of blessed memory, *Iggerot Re'iyah*, I, no. 138, wrote with sensitivity about youth who have been led astray by "the raging current of the times" and eloquently portrayed the intellectual blandishments of our age as an evil maidservant who makes use of "all her enchantments to persuade our children" to accept alien ideologies. As a result, he asserted, "They are absolute victims of duress and heaven forefend that we judge the compelled as we do the self-willed." Whether such doctrinal error be categorized as heresy or invincible ignorance, the contemporary state of disbelief should not be tacitly accepted. As educators we have been sorely remiss. At the very minimum, it is the manifest duty of rabbinic scholars to define the fundamental dogmas of Judaism, to delineate areas of legitimate disagreement, to acknowledge what may appear to be contradictory texts and to place them in proper perspective.

Hardly less significant are issues that do not reflect matters of dogma, but which should be resolved in light of a system of ethics and values that must inform public policy. Here, too, in an age gone by, Jewish reactions would have been almost Pavlovian. Ethical norms and values were deeply engrained in the Jewish psyche. Not infrequently, the Jewish response was unique and at variance from that of other religious or cultural groups. Such values were transmitted from generation to generation and became virtually intuitive.

That, too, has changed. Religious toleration and social acceptance have had a pernicious effect. It has become a common assumption that humanistic values are universal and hence must be integral to the teachings of Judaism. Thus, the Jewish position on virtually any social or political issue is presumed to be no different than that of any intelligent, enlightened and ethical member of society. Many are shocked to discover that this is not always the case. Jewish responses to such issues are predicated upon timeless Jewish teachings not always readily grasped by the uninitiated. Here, too, rabbinic scholars have all too often been remiss in failing to formulate authentic Jewish responses to the problems of the day based upon sacred texts and hallowed traditions.

Indeed, transmission of fundamental beliefs is integral to the *mitzvah* of *talmud Torah* incumbent upon us. Instruction in basic doctrines of Judaism is coextensive with teaching love of God. "And you shall love the Lord your God" (Deuteronomy 6:5) is one of the 613 commandments incumbent upon Jews. Yet, emotions can no more be commanded than can sensory perceptions. A person might be ordered to be present at a certain place at a certain time, but, once there, it makes little sense to demand of him that he see certain images or hear certain sounds. Sensory perceptions are essentially involuntary and hence not subject to command. What can be commanded is that a person engage in the requisite antecedent activities that make such perceptions possible. Thus, "And it shall be to you as fringes and you shall see them" (Numbers 15:39) is more accurately rendered as "And it shall be to you as fringes *so that* you shall see them." The commanded act is placement of the fringes in the garment; seeing them is the purpose of the act but is a resultant visual phenomenon that is virtually compelled.

"And you shall love your neighbor as yourself" (Leviticus 19:18). How can love be commanded? Either one experiences love for one's fellow or one does not. If such an emotion is present, the commandment is superfluous; if absent, the commandment is vacuous. Rambam, in his *Sefer ha-Mitzvot, mitzvot aseh*, no. 206, readily grasped that it is not human emotion that is the subject of the commandment but it is acts that are associated with the commandment – and indeed causally related to developing the emotions – that are commanded. The essence of the commandment is that a person have "love and compassion for his brother just as he has love and compassion for himself with regard to his fortune and his person... [and] all that I desire for myself I shall desire for him." Love, declares Rambam, is expressed in concrete acts. The commandment "and you shall love the proselyte" (Deuteronomy 10:19) which follows immediately in the *Sefer ha-Mitzvot* as *mitzvot aseh*, no. 207, is understood by Rambam as having exactly the same ambit and hence as constituting nothing other than imposition of an additional duty *vis-à-vis* the convert encompassing precisely the same norms of conduct. [1]

How does one love God? Rambam, *Sefer ha-Mitzvot, mitzvot aseh*, no. 3; *Hilkhot Yesodei ha-Torah* 2:2; and *Guide of the Perplexed*, Part III, chap. 28, defines the *mitzvah* in intellectual, rather than emotional, terms. As stated by Rambam in his *Sefer ha-Mitzvot, mitzvot aseh*, no. 3, with regard to the *mitzvah* commanding us to love God:

> That is, that we reflect upon and ponder His *mitzvot* and dicta and His works until we apprehend Him and delight in the ultimate degree of pleasure in apprehending Him. This is the mandatory love. In the words of *Sifri*: "For it says, 'And you shall love the Lord your God' (Deuteronomy 6:5). I do not know how to love God. Therefore, [Scripture] teaches, 'And these matters which I command you this day shall be upon your heart' (Deuteronomy

---

1. Rambam reiterates this point in *Hilkhot De'ot* 6:3-4. Cf., R. Yitzchak Hutner, *Paḥad Yitzḥak, Pesaḥ*, no. 29, reprinted in *Netzaḥ Yisra'el*, no. 4 (Nisan 5769), pp. 295-297, who endeavors to show the distinctive purpose and intrinsic nature of each of the two commandments.

6:6). From that you will recognize He who spoke and the universe came into being." Behold we have explained to you that through reflection you will succeed in apprehension and achieve pleasure, and love will come necessarily.

Significantly, Rambam introduces that exposition by declaring that the *mitzvah* "And you shall love the Lord your God" requires first and foremost "that we reflect upon and ponder His *mitzvot* and dicta." The phrase "*she-neḥashev ve-nitbonen be-mitzvotav u-ma'amarav* – that we reflect upon and ponder His *mitzvot* and dicta" is crafted with precision. The content of His *mitzvot* and dicta is the corpus of the Torah in its entirety. We must "reflect upon and ponder," i.e., understand the depths of meaning inherent in the words of Torah. Such understanding is integral to, and indeed synonymous with, knowledge and hence love, of God. In his *Guide*, Part III, chap. 26, Rambam insists that *mitzvot* are the product of divine reason. Accordingly, Torah, as the manifestation of divine reason, emanates directly from the essence of the Deity. It necessarily follows that knowledge of Torah is, *ipso facto*, knowledge of God.

Knowledge of Torah can be knowledge of God only because the Torah in our possession is, in its entirety, the product of divine revelation. In revealing the Torah at Mount Sinai God revealed Himself to the extent that He can be apprehended by the human intellect. Were it otherwise, knowledge of Torah could not be equated with love of God. Mastery of any of the myriad facets of Torah constitutes at least partial fulfillment of the *mitzvah*. Thus, Rambam's insistence that the Torah in its entirety, both the Oral as well as the Written Law, are the revealed word of God and that denial of the authenticity of the *mesorah* originating at Sinai and transmitted by Torah scholars from generation to generation is tantamount to renunciation of God Himself.

Man is not endowed with knowledge upon birth. One can no more be commanded to know than one can be commanded to love. Knowledge is acquired through a long and arduous process of study. An admonition to be proficient in Torah is a commandment to study Torah – an endeavor entirely within the scope of human capacity. To know God is to know His Torah; one masters Torah only by studying

Torah. Mastering Torah is the *sine qua non* of loving God. Little wonder, then, that Rambam posits penetrating and intense study of Torah as the very first element in the fulfillment of the commandment "And you shall love the Lord your God."

A person fulfills the *mitzvah* "and you shall love the Lord your God" by intellectually recognizing the majesty of the Deity and the grandeur of His creation. Moreover, as elucidated by R. Ovadiah ben David, author of the unidentified commentary published together with that section of the *Mishneh Torah*, love is directly commensurate with knowledge: the greater the intellectual apprehension, the greater the love. *Ahavah* and *yedi'ah*, love and knowledge, become conflated into a single concept. As Rambam, *Hilkhot Teshuvah* 10:6, declares:

> One loves the Holy One, blessed be He, only through the knowledge with which one knows Him. According to the knowledge is the love, if little, little and if great, great.

Rambam, *Hilkhot Teshuvah* 10:3, followed by *Sefer Ḥaredim* 1:5, declares that such intellectual awareness generates an emotional state akin to lovesickness as described by King Solomon, Song of Songs 2:5. As stated earlier, in his *Sefer ha-Mitzvot* Rambam writes, "Behold we have explained to you that through reflection you will succeed in apprehension and achieve pleasure, and love will come necessarily." Rambam declares that it is not simply belief in the existence of God or of His majesty and glory on the basis of faith that constitutes fulfillment of the commandment "And you shall love the Lord your God"; rather, it is the intellectual pleasure that is born of rational apprehension in which lies fulfillment of the *mitzvah*. In his *Guide*, Part III, chap. 28, Rambam reiterates that acceptance of basic truths concerning the nature of God is inferred from the words "And you shall love the Lord your God with all your heart and with all your soul and with all your might." It is comprehensive understanding, internalization and its attendant intellectual exhilaration that constitute love of God.

The challenge facing our generation is authentic transmission of the essence of the commandment "And you shall love the Lord your God" to convey the message that Judaism is not only a religion of law and ritual but fundamentally a religion of particular beliefs and that those beliefs dictate uniquely Jewish responses to many contemporary issues. Our endeavors on behalf of *talmud Torah* must extend to elucidation of principles of faith. In repairing breaches of the *mesorah* we will, please God, assure generations of *ma'aminim bnei ma'aminim*.

1

Faith and Dogma in Judaism

One widespread misconception concerning Judaism is the notion that Judaism is a religion which is not rooted in dogma. The view that Judaism has no dogmas originated with Moses Mendelssohn[1] and subsequently gained wide currency. In some circles this idea has been maintained with such vigor that it has been somewhat jocularly described as itself constituting the "dogma of dogmalessness." Nevertheless, even a superficial acquaintance with the classical works of Jewish philosophy is sufficient to dispel this misconceived notion. To be sure, membership in the community of Israel is not contingent upon a formal creedal affirmation. This, however, does not imply that members of the community of Israel are free to accept or to reject specific articles of faith. Birth as a Jew carries with it unrenounceable obligations and responsibilities, intellectual as well as ritual.

---

1. See his "Betrachtungen über Bonnets Palingenesie," *Gesammelte Schriften*, III (Berlin, 1843), 159-166.

9

While great stress is placed upon fulfillment of commandments and performance of good deeds, it is a gross error to assume that this stress is accompanied by a diminution of obligations with regard to belief. It is certainly true that lessened concern with explication of the dogmas of Judaism was evidenced during certain periods of Jewish history. This, however, was the result of an unquestioning acceptance of basic principles of faith rather than of disparagement of the role of dogma. In some epochs formulations of essential beliefs were composed by foremost thinkers as a corrective measure designed to rectify this lack of attention; in other ages endeavors designed to explicate the dogmas of Judaism constituted a reaction to creedal formulations on the part of other religions.

The importance of correct belief as a religious obligation is stressed in particular in the writings of Bahya ibn Pakuda. In the introduction to his widely acclaimed *Hovot ha-Levavot* (properly translated as *Duties of the Intellect* rather than *Duties of the Heart*),[2] Bahya wrote that the Torah demands of man that he acquire the knowledge requisite for fulfillment of the obligations of the intellect, just as it makes demands of him with regard to fulfillment of the obligations of the physical organs. Nevertheless, he found that his predecessors had devoted themselves in their writings to the discussion and detailed clarification of "duties of the organs" but had neglected to set forth systematically the principles pertaining to the "duties of the intellect" and their ramifications. *Hovot ha-Levavot* was composed to fill this lacuna.

The role of dogma as the fulcrum of Judaism was most dramatically highlighted by Maimonides. His *magnum opus*, the *Mishneh Torah*, is devoted to a codification of Jewish law. Yet the opening section of this work is entitled *Hilkhot Yesodei ha-Torah* ("Laws of the Foundations of the Torah") and includes a detailed presentation of Jewish belief together with unequivocal statements declaring acceptance of those beliefs to be binding upon all Jews. Dogma, then, does not stand apart from the normative demands of Judaism but is the *sine qua non* without which other values and practices are bereft of meaning. By incorporating this

---

2. In medieval usage the heart is frequently spoken of as the seat of knowledge and the word *lev* is used as a synonym for "intellect."

material in his *Mishneh Torah*, Maimonides demonstrated that basic philosophical beliefs are not simply matters of intellectual curiosity but constitute a branch of Halakhah. By placing them at the very beginning of this monumental work he demonstrated that they constitute the most fundamental area of Jewish law. In Judaism, profession of faith is certainly no less significant than overt actions. Contrary to the dictum of Moses Mendelssohn, Judaism imposes obligations not only with regard to action but with regard to religious belief as well.

Bahya demonstrates the existence and the binding nature of obligations incumbent upon the intellect, not simply on the basis of Scripture and tradition, but on the basis of reason as well. Reason dictates that the heart and mind, the choicest and most unique elements of human existence, should not be exempt from obligations imposed in the service of God. The manifold references in Scripture to man's duty to love God and, moreover, the very existence of a biblical code establishing rules of conduct for mankind implies the existence of a divine lawgiver. While in his *Sefer ha-Mitzvot* Maimonides cites the verse "I am the Lord your God who has brought you out of the land of Egypt" (Exodus 20:2) as constituting the first in his list of 613 commandments, i.e., belief in the existence of a Deity, others among his predecessors failed to do so, not because they did not feel belief in God to be incumbent upon each Jew, but because they viewed such belief to be already assumed by, and hence outside of, a system of commandments. There can be no commandment without one who commands. As Bahya puts it, there can be no fulfillment of physical duties without assent of the mind. Accordingly, acceptance of obligatory commandments presumes antecedent acceptance of the existence and authority of God.

Nahmanides pursues this argument to its logical conclusion by declaring that a heretic need not anticipate reward even for meritorious deeds which he has performed. In the introduction to his commentary on the Book of Job, Nahmanides writes, "There is no merit in the actions of the evil persons who deny God… even if they comport themselves in accordance with beautiful and good traits all their days," and proceeds to query how it is possible for them to be the recipients of any form of beneficence. A noted talmudic scholar, the late Rabbi Elchanan Wasserman, although apparently unaware of Nahmanides' comments, categorizes the fulfillment of a commandment on the part of an unbeliever as *mitasek*, an unmeditated, thoughtless performance devoid of religious significance.[3] Commandments, regardless of their intrinsic rationality, are binding and significant in the theological sense only because they constitute the fulfillment of a divine command. Thus, not only the existence of God but also the authenticity of revelation as a historical event and the divinity of the entire corpus of Torah are inherent even in those moments of Judaism which concern themselves with action and conduct rather than belief.

To be sure, the formal promulgation of a creed of faith is unknown in Judaism. By the same token, official synods for the comprehensive codification of the laws and regulations governing ceremonial obligations or other areas of human conduct are also virtually unknown to Judaism. Within Judaism, Halakhah is hardly monolithic in nature. "Judges and bailiffs shall you appoint for yourselves in all your gates" (Deuteronomy 16:18), commands the Torah. Each community possesses not only the authority but also the obligation to appoint ecclesiastical authorities. In all matters of doubt or dispute their decisions are binding upon all who are subject to their authority. Only when local authorities were unable to resolve a complex question was the question referred to the Great Court sitting in Jerusalem, whose decision was binding upon all of Israel. Inevitably, divergent practices arose in different locales. With the redaction of the Mishnah, and later of the Gemara, binding decisions were promulgated with regard to any matters of Halakhah which served to establish normative practices in areas which previously had been marked by diversity born of dispute. This, of course, did not preclude subsequent disagreement with regard to other questions which had not been expressly resolved.

Since matters of belief are inherently matters of Halakhah, it is not at all surprising that disagreements exist with regard to substantive matters of belief just as is the case in other areas of Jewish law. Thus, while there is unanimity among all rabbinic authorities with regard to the existence of a body of Jewish law that is binding in nature with respect to matters of faith, there is considerable disagreement of opinion with

---

3. *Kovetz Ma'amarim* (Jerusalem, 1963), no. 11, sec. 14.

regard to precisely which beliefs are binding and which are not, as well as, in some instances regarding substantive matters of faith.

The concept of the Messiah is one example of a fundamental principle of belief concerning which, at one point in Jewish history, there existed a legitimate divergence of opinion, since resolved normatively. The Gemara, *Sanhedrin* 99a, cites the opinion of the Amora, Rav Hillel, who asserted, "There is no Messiah for Israel." Rashi modifies the literal reading of this dictum by explaining that Rav Hillel did not deny the ultimate redemption of Israel but asserted, rather, that the redemption will be the product of direct divine intervention without the intermediacy of a human agent. Nevertheless, Rav Hillel certainly denied that reestablishment of the monarchy and restoration of the Davidic dynasty are essential components of the process of redemption. Rabbi Moses Sofer quite cogently points out that were such views to be held by a contemporary Jew he would be branded a heretic.[4] Yet, the advancement of this opinion by one of the sages of the Talmud carried with it no theological odium. The explanation is quite simple. Before the authoritative formulation of the Halakhah with regard to this belief, Rav Hillel's opinion could be entertained. Following the resolution of the conflict in a manner which negates this theory, normative Halakhah demands acceptance of the belief that the redemption will be effected through the agency of a mortal messiah. As is true with regard to other aspects of Jewish law, the Torah "is not in Heaven" (Deuteronomy 30:12) and hence halakhic disputes are resolved in accordance with canons of law which are themselves part of the Oral Law.

Certainly, there remain many points regarding various articles of faith which have not been formally resolved by the sages of the Talmud. Indeed, in subsequent periods controversies did arise with regard to significant theological issues, such as, for example, the nature of providence and freedom of the will. In the absence of a definitive ruling, the question which presents itself is, would the exponent of a certain view with regard to any of these matters consider an opponent and his followers simply to be in error, or would he view them as heretics as well? The

---

4. *Teshuvot Ḥatam Sofer, Yoreh De'ah* no. 356.

answer is itself a matter of Halakhah having many ramifications, and, as proves to be the case, is the subject of considerable dispute.

The Mishnah which forms the opening section of the last chapter of *Sanhedrin* posits that all Jews enjoy a share in the world-to-come, but proceeds to exclude from this ultimate reward those who espouse certain heretical doctrines which are then enumerated in the text of the Mishnah. Maimonides' understanding of the underlying principle expressed in the Mishnah is that denial of a share in the world-to-come is not in the nature of punishment for failure to discharge a religious duty, but rather that profession of certain creeds is a necessary condition of immortality. The reason which prompts an individual to deny any specific article of faith is irrelevant. The person who has been misled or who, through error in the syllogistic process, reaches false conclusions, fails to affirm the basic propositions of Jewish faith and hence cannot aspire to the ultimate intellectual reward. This is entirely consistent with Maimonides' view, as will be explained below, that development of the intellect in recognition of fundamental metaphysical truths culminates in the perfection of the intellect and leads naturally to the ability of the soul to participate in the intellectual pleasures of the world-to-come. The nature of these pleasures is such that they simply cannot be apprehended by the totally undeveloped intellect. Thus, attainment of a share in the world-to-come is more in the nature of development of potential than of reward and punishment. Accordingly, the causes and motivating forces which lead either to belief or to nonbelief are irrelevant.

Simon ben Zemah Duran, who was followed in this matter, by his pupil, Joseph Albo, adopted an opposing view. Duran asserts that intellectual rejection of any doctrine of revelation constitutes heresy. Scripture must be accepted as divinely revealed and the contents of Scripture in their entirety must be acknowledged as absolute truth. Conscious denial of the veracity of any biblical statement constitutes heresy. Nevertheless, for Duran, one who is ignorant or fails to interpret the details of a revealed doctrine correctly may be an unwitting transgressor, but is not to be considered a heretic. For example, it is possible to interpret the biblical narrative concerning the creation of the universe in a manner which assumes the existence of a primordial hylic substance and thus contradicts the doctrine of *creatio ex nihilo*. In fact, there are midrashic statements which, at least on the basis of a superficial reading, seem to support this view; Albo declares that some sages did indeed subscribe to a view akin to the Platonic doctrine of primordial substance.[5] Such an interpretation, while in error, is not heretical, so long as it is not advanced as a knowing contradiction of the biblical account. Thus, man is free to engage in philosophical speculation and is not held culpable if as a result of such endeavors he espouses a false doctrine. False beliefs, if sincerely held as the result of honest error, do not occasion loss of eternal bliss. This position is also assumed by Abraham ben David of Posquières (Ra'avad) in a gloss to Maimonides' *Mishneh Torah*[6] and received wide circulation through Albo's exposition in his *Sefer ha-Ikkarim*.[7]

In his introduction to Ḥovot ha-Levavot, Bahya seeks to establish, on the basis of reason, that it is entirely logical that God should impose duties upon the intellect. Man is a composite of body and soul, i.e., corporeal substance and intellect. As was to be stressed by later thinkers, it is the intellectual component which is uniquely human and which constitutes the essence of man. The corporeal aspect of man is consecrated to the service of God by virtue of commandments imposed upon, and fulfilled by means of, the physical organs of man. It is to be anticipated that the intellect should also be impressed into the service of God in a like manner through imposition of commandments specifically binding upon the mind.

It is axiomatic that God does not impose obligations which cannot be fulfilled. Quite apart from questions of theodicy which would arise from the imposition of such obligations, it simply does not make sense to speak of an obligation which cannot under any circumstances be discharged. Jewish philosophers have repeatedly stressed that God cannot command man to accept the illogical or the irrational. The human intellect, no matter how much it may desire to do so, cannot affirm the absurd. Man may, if prompted by a sufficiently compelling reason, postulate the existence of unicorns or mermaids, but he cannot affirm the existence of a geometric object which is at one and the same time

---

5. *Sefer ha-Ikkarim*, Book I, chap. 2.
6. *Hilkhot Teshuvah* 3:7.
7. Book I, chap. 2.

endowed with the properties of both a square and a circle. He cannot fathom the concept of a square circle, much less affirm the ontological existence of such an object.

Propositions which constitute objects of belief must, then, first and foremost do no violence to human credulity. They must be readily apprehended and accepted by human thought. Yet belief implies more than hypothesization. Belief connotes unequivocal affirmation of that which is regarded as certain, rather than speculative postulation of the contingent. The latter is compatible with a state of doubt; the former is not. And herein lies a dilemma: the intellect need not be commanded to recognize the possible. An open, honest, and inquiring mind must of necessity recognize the ontological contingency of that which is affirmed by any proposition which does not violate the canons of logic. Recognition of the contingent nature of such propositions need not at all be commanded and does not constitute belief. Belief, by virtue of its very nature, entails positive affirmation of the veracity of a proposition. But how can intellectual certainty be commanded? Certainty is a psychological state of mind. It would appear that such certainty is either present or it is absent. If present, the commandment to believe is superfluous; if absent, the commandment to believe poses an obligation which cannot be fulfilled.

This paradox is presented and discussed forthrightly in the essay by Rabbi Elchanan Wasserman cited above.[8] Rabbi Wasserman's thesis is that an unbiased and unimpeded mind cannot escape an awareness and affirmation of the existence of a Creator. The Midrash presents what is probably the oldest, and certainly one of the most eloquent, formulations of the argument from design. A heretic approached Rabbi Akiva and asked him, "Who created the universe?" R. Akiva answered, "The Holy One, blessed be He." Thereupon, the heretic demanded a demonstrative proof that this was indeed so. R. Akiva responded by posing a question of his own: "Who wove your coat?" he inquired of the heretic. "A weaver," replied the latter. "Present me a demonstrative proof!" demanded Rabbi Akiva. The exchange concludes with R. Akiva's simple but forceful formulation of the teleological argument. Addressing his

---

8. *Loc. cit.*, secs. 1-7.

students, he declared: "Just as the garment testifies to [the existence of] the weaver, just as the door testifies to [the existence of] the carpenter, and just as the house testifies to [the existence of] the builder, so does the universe testify to [the existence of] the Holy One, blessed be He, who created it."[9]

A different version of the teleological argument is recorded by Bahya with the comment that experience teaches that intelligent writing never results from overturning an inkwell onto a piece of paper.[10] To put it in a different idiom, the mathematical odds militating against the probability that a chimpanzee seated at a typewriter might peck at the keys in a random manner and in the process produce the collected works of Shakespeare are so great as to render the prospect preposterous. Bahya categorizes one who seriously entertains such a belief as either a simpleton or a lunatic. Yet, on the cosmic level, there are many who find it possible to dismiss evidence of intelligence and design and to attribute the ordered nature of the universe to random causes.

Rabbi Wasserman endeavors to explain this denial by pointing to the stated consideration underlying the prohibition against bribery. This prohibition is not limited to accepting a bribe for purposes of favoring one litigant over another. Such conduct is independently forbidden by the injunction "Thou shalt not bend judgment" (Deuteronomy 16:19). The prohibition against bribe-taking encompasses even instances in which the gift is presented on the express condition that a lawful and just verdict be issued. It also applies to situations in which both the plaintiff and the defendant present the judge with gifts of equal value. And the prohibition stands no matter how upright and incorruptible the judge might be. The reason for this extreme and all-encompassing ban is spelled out clearly in Scripture: "For a bribe blinds those who have sight and perverts the words of the righteous" (Exodus 23:8).

A judge, if he is to be entirely objective, must remain detached and emotionally uninvolved in the controversy between the litigants who appear before him. Justice is assured only when evidence can be

---

9. *Midrash Temurah*, chap. 3, published in *Bet ha-Midrash*, ed. Adolf Jellinek, I (Leipzig, 1853), 114, and in *Otzar ha-Midrashim*, ed. J.D. Eisenstein (New York, 1915), II, 583.
10. *Ḥovot ha-Levavot, Shaʿar ha-Yiḥud*, chap. 6.

examined in a cool and dispassionate manner. Human emotions cloud judgment. No matter how honest and objective a person may strive to be, once personal interests are introduced, objectivity is compromised. Receipt of a favor creates a bond of friendship. When a judge receives a gift from a litigant, the litigant's concern becomes, in a measure, that of the judge himself. When he accepts gifts from both parties, the concerns of both become his concerns, and he can no longer dispassionately adjudicate between competing claims solely on the basis of evidence and applicable law. The Torah testifies that all men are affected in this way at least to some extent.

All of mankind, points out Rabbi Wasserman, is subject to a subtle form of bribery. With the pleasure experienced in imbibing mother's milk, we begin to enjoy sensual gratification. Pleasure is addictive in nature; our desire for pleasure is, in a very real sense, insatiable. The need for gratification is very real, very human, and very constant.

Recognition of the existence of the Deity entails acknowledgment of His authority over us. Acceptance of other cardinal beliefs entails an awareness that our freedom to seek pleasure may be drastically curtailed. As beneficiaries of the gift of sensual gratification even before attaining the age of reason, human beings are never capable of entirely dispassionate analysis of the evidence substantiating basic religious beliefs. The sages put it succinctly in their statement, "Israel engaged in idol worship solely in order to permit themselves public licentiousness."[11] Worship of pagan gods surely involves an ideological commitment. Yet, psychologically speaking, the sages testify, intellectual conviction did not serve as the impetus for idolatry. Rather, the acknowledgment of pagan gods on the part of the worshippers of the golden calf was born of a desire for unbridled sexual gratification. Passion prevented a reasoned adjudication between the claims of idolatrous cults and monotheistic belief. Man is a logical animal; he finds it difficult to lead a life of self-contradiction. It is hard for him to accept certain concepts intellectually and then to act in a manner inconsistent with those affirmed principles. Denial of basic theological principles prevents such contradictions from arising. Certainly man has strong, albeit unconscious, motives for such denial.

---

11. *Sanhedrin* 63b.

It is Rabbi Wasserman's thesis that many non-believers close themselves off from faith-commitments in order to avoid tension between a desire for untrammeled sensual gratification and acknowledgment of divinely imposed restraints.

The notion of a commandment concerning belief can be understood in a different manner on the basis of a statement of Ḥananiah Kazis, contained in his *Kinat Soferim*, one of the classic commentaries on Maimonides' *Sefer ha-Mitzvot*.[12] *Kinat Soferim* understands the commandment affirming the existence of God as bidding us to disseminate knowledge of God's existence and to impart the knowledge upon which this belief is predicated to future generations. His argument is both conceptual and textual. The community of Israel that experienced a beatific vision of God at Mount Sinai did not need to be commanded to believe in Him; they *knew* Him. Moreover, the preamble to the Decalogue, "And God spoke all these words, *saying*" (Exodus 20:1), employs the Hebrew term *leimor*. In rabbinic exegesis, this term is customarily understood as meaning not simply "saying," but connoting that the person addressed is bidden "to say," that is, to convey to others the information which follows. Most frequently, this formula is employed in reporting that God addressed Moses bidding him to convey divine commandments to the Children of Israel. In light of the tradition which teaches that the first two commandments of the Decalogue were not transmitted to the assembled populace by Moses but were received by them directly from God,[13] the use of the term *leimor* in this context seems incongruous. *Kinat Soferim* argues that the connotation of the phrase in this instance is that those to whom the commandment was addressed were instructed to convey this information to succeeding generations for all of eternity. The commandment, then, is to *teach* in order that belief be possible.

Extending this concept, it certainly seems feasible to understand that the commandment as formulated delineates the *telos*, or goal, to which man is commanded to aspire. Although belief itself, while obligatory, cannot be commanded, nevertheless, activities through which belief is acquired may properly constitute the object of divine commandment.

---

12. *Mitzvot aseh*, no.1.
13. *Makkot* 24a.

Thus, in defining the commandment, "And you shall love the Lord, your God" (Deuteronomy 6:5), Maimonides writes:

> One only loves God with the knowledge with which one knows Him. According to the knowledge will be the love. If the former be little, the latter will be little; if the former be much, the latter will be much. Therefore, a person must devote himself to the understanding and comprehension of those sciences and studies which will inform him concerning his Master, as far as is the power within man to understand and comprehend, as indeed we have explained in the Laws of the Foundations of the Torah.[14]

Bahya also posits an obligation to engage in philosophical investigation directed to the rational demonstration of the objects of belief:

> ...Scripture expressly bids you to reflect and exercise your intellect on such themes. After you have attained knowledge of them by the method of tradition which covers all the precepts of the law, their principles and details, you should investigate them with your reason, understanding, and judgment, till the truth becomes clear to you and false notions dispelled; as it is written, "Know this day and lay it to your heart that the Lord, He is God" (Deuteronomy 4:39).[15]

Man is endowed with the capacity for knowledge and, hence, for belief. To state this is not at all to assume that the task is a facile one or that faith is immediately within the grasp of man. The hasidic sage, Rabbi Menaḥem Mendel of Kotzk, explained the matter by means of an allegory. God prepares a ladder by means of which souls descend from heaven to earth. The soul alights from the ladder and steps upon the ground. The ladder is immediately withdrawn and a voice calls out to the soul bidding it to return. Some souls do not even attempt what appears to be an impossible task. Some jump and fall; becoming disillusioned,

---

14. *Hilkhot Teshuvah* 10:6.
15. *Ḥovot ha-Levavot*, Introduction.

they make no further attempt. Others try and try again, leaping time after time, refusing to become discouraged, until God Himself draws them nigh to Him. "You must understand," concluded the Rabbi of Kotzk, "That God does not extend mercy on the basis of a single leap!"[16] Judaism does not teach that God requires of man a "leap of faith" in the Kierkegaardian sense, i.e., blind faith to the extent of acceptance of the absurd. It teaches, rather, that God's beneficence assures man that his diligence and perseverance will ultimately lead to understanding and intellectual satisfaction.

Every age has witnessed the presence of both believers and doubters. Intellectual doubt and the questioning of fundamental beliefs have always been present in one form or another. It is nevertheless axiomatic that man has the ability to rise above such inner conflict and to experience faith. A just and beneficent God could not demand belief without bestowing upon man the capacity for faith. Abiding belief must, however, be firmly rooted in knowledge. Study has the unique effect of dispelling doubt. There is a story of a group of Jewish students in Berlin during the *Haskalah* period who, as a result of their encounter with secular society, began to experience religious doubts. Questioning the faith claims of Judaism, they were on the verge of rejecting fundamental theological beliefs. But before making a final break with Judaism they resolved to send one of their company to the Yeshiva of Volozhin, which at the time was the foremost Torah center of the world, to determine whether or not there existed satisfactory answers to the questions which troubled them. The young man to whom they delegated this task spent a period of time as a student in the Yeshiva and immersed himself completely in that institution's program of studies. Upon his return to Berlin he was met by his friends, who eagerly awaited his report. The young man described his experiences and related that he had never before experienced such intellectual delight. "But," they demanded, "have you brought answers to the questions which we formulated?" "No," he replied. "I have brought no answers – but the questions no longer plague me."

Centuries ago the sages provided an explanation for this phenomenon. They depict the Almighty as declaring, "I have created an evil

---

16. See Yehudah Leib Lewin, *Bet Kotzk: Ha-Saraf* (Jerusalem, 1958), p. 98.

inclination but I have created the Torah as its antidote."[17] With acquisition of Torah knowledge doubt recedes and ultimately dissipates. This is the essence of Jewish belief with regard to the dilemma of faith. *"Ve'idakh perusha; zil gemor* – the rest is explanation; go and study!"

---

17. *Kiddushin* 30b; *Sifre, Parshat Eikev* 11:18; see also *Bava Batra* 16a.

2

The Thirteen
Principles of Faith

Maimonides' Thirteen Principles of Faith are widely regarded as a creedal formulation of Jewish belief. Widespread familiarity with the Thirteen Principles is due, in large measure, to their adaptation and inclusion in the daily prayerbook in two separate forms. Neither of these was composed by Maimonides himself. The *Yigdal* hymn, usually ascribed to Daniel ben Judah of Rome, who lived during the early part of the fourteenth century, occupies a position of prominence near the very beginning of the prayerbook. A second prose form of unknown authorship, composed in the early sixteenth century, is appended at the conclusion of the morning service in many prayerbooks. This addendum, expressed as a first-person affirmation, "I believe with perfect faith..." is designed as a personal confession of faith. Both formulations, designed for daily recitation, are necessarily briefer than Maimonides' original version. As abridged versions they not only lack in comprehensiveness but are, at times, inaccurate, insofar as felicity to the original is concerned.[1]

---

1. For an enumeration of the disparities between the *Ani Ma'amin* and Maimonides'

Maimonides' own formulation forms an integral part of his *Commentary on the Mishnah*, serving as an introduction to the final chapter of the tractate *Sanhedrin*. The initial Mishnah of this chapter lists the various classes of nonbelievers or heretics who are excluded from everlasting life.

Despite popular acceptance of the Thirteen Principles over the ages as *the* definitive creed of Judaism, Maimonides' endeavor remains a source of perplexity to philosophers and theologians.[2] Some, arguing that all teachings of the Torah are equally binding, contested the very notion of labeling certain specific propositions as "principles" of faith. This was Abarbanel's objection as well as that of the kabbalists. Indeed, Maimonides himself, in discussing the divine nature of Torah, the eighth of his Thirteen Principles, stresses that there is no difference between verses such as "And the sons of Ham were Gush and Mitzrayim and Put and Canaan" (Genesis 10:6), "And his wife's name was Mehetabel, daughter of Matred" (Genesis 36:39), or "And Timna was a concubine to Eliphaz" (Genesis 36:12) and verses such as "I am the Lord thy God" (Exodus 20:2) and "Hear O Israel the Lord our God the Lord is one" (Deuteronomy 6:4). Each is divinely revealed and incorporated in the Torah at the divine behest. Hence, denial of any of these truths is tantamount to rejection of the Torah itself. In his *Mishneh Torah, Hilkhot Teshuvah* 3:8, Maimonides declares that one who denies divine authorship of even a single word of the Torah or of its explanation and amplification in the Oral Law is a heretic. Thus every proposition embodied in either the Written or Oral Law is, in effect, a principle of faith. In positing the Thirteen Principles Maimonides could not conceivably have intended to convey the impression that Judaism mandates affirmation

---

own formulation see R. Eleazar Meir Preil, *Ha-Ma'or* (Jerusalem, 5689), p. 13-15. See also R. Chaim Hirschensohn, *Malki ba-Kodesh* (St. Louis, 5681), II, 238-242.

2. The notion that the creedal principles of faith are thirteen in number may well be an ancient tradition. R. Avraham ha-Levi Horowitz, *Shnei Luḥot ha-Brit, Sha'ar ha-Otiyyot*, sec. 1, p. 60a, cites a certain prayer ascribed to Rav Tavyomi, one of the talmudic sages, which contains a reference to thirteen principles. R. Avraham Horowitz himself sees an intrinsic connection between Maimonides' Thirteen Principles and the Thirteen Divine Attributes. He maintains that each of these principles may be derived from the corresponding Divine Attribute.

of only those enumerated articles of faith but permits denial or doubt with regard to others.

Others took exception to Maimonides' enumeration because they found his list to be too detailed and because it contains propositions which they did not regard as fundamental. Both Hasdai Crescas[3] and Simeon ben Zemah Duran[4] criticized Maimonides' formulation on this account. Crescas asserted that the list should be limited to six fundamentals, or beliefs, without which Judaism as a religious faith is inconceivable: (1) God's knowledge of all created things; (2) divine providence; (3) divine omnipotence; (4) prophecy; (5) freedom of the will; (6) the Torah leads man to his true goal and ultimate happiness. Crescas declared that the existence of God, a concept which includes the notion of unity and incorporeality as well, is in a class by itself and need not be included in this listing because it is logically prior to any enumeration of the fundamentals of Jewish belief.

Simon ben Zemah Duran maintained that the list can be reduced still further. According to Duran, whose views were adapted and popularized by Joseph Albo in the latter's widely known *Sefer ha-Ikkarim*, the principles of belief are three in number: (1) the existence of God; (2) revelation; (3) reward and punishment.[5] Duran and Albo both maintained that each of these dogmas entails a series of corollaries which can be derived from these three basic principles. The concept of revelation, for example, also includes God's knowledge of particulars; reward and punishment entails individual providence. One cannot deny the conclusion of a valid syllogism without denying the premise upon which it is based. Hence, denial of any of the corollaries implies a denial of the basic principle from which it is derived and is no less heretical than a denial of one of the three enumerated fundamental principles. Thus most of Maimonides' Thirteen Principles may be derived from the three principles to which they are reduced by Duran and Albo. Albo recognized still other beliefs which are a necessary and integral part of Jewish belief

---

3. *Or Ha-Shem* (Vienna, 1859), *Hatza'ah*, p. 3b; Second Treatise, introduction, p. 27b; Third Treatise, introduction, p.61a; and Fourth Treatise, introduction, p. 85a.

4. *Magen Avot* (Leghorn, 1785), p. 2b.

5. Book I, chap. 4.

and binding upon its adherents. Although these beliefs, which include among others the doctrine of creation, resurrection of the dead and the coming of the Messiah, cannot be derived from the basic principles in a vigorous and demonstrable fashion, they are included within the general framework of these principles. Albo's demonstration that most of the principles enumerated by Maimonides are reducible to three basic fundamental concepts makes it even more difficult to comprehend the purpose underlying Maimonides' formulation and enumeration.

The usual and most facile explanation of the considerations which prompted Maimonides' enumeration of these particular propositions is that he sought to delineate and emphasize those articles of faith which were most frequently subject to question and challenge in the historical period in which he lived. Thus, the doctrine of the unity of God had to be reiterated to counteract the polemics of Christians seeking to establish a scriptural basis for the doctrine of the Trinity; the supremacy of the prophecy of Moses needed to be underscored in order to emphasize the essential point of difference between Judaism and Islam. Formulation of the Thirteen Principles as a creed of faith served both a pedagogic and supportive function. It served to delineate and to teach beliefs which could not be renounced by a professing Jew. Publicization of the Thirteen Principles and their widespread acceptance as the *sine qua non* of Jewish faith meant that no believing Jew might be led astray by ignorance or confusion. Furthermore, their formulation in the nature of a creed served as reinforcement of faith for those finding themselves under relentless pressure to renounce the tenets of Judaism and to adopt the faith of the dominant culture. The Thirteen Principles, when placed against the professions of faith of other religious denominations, is an eloquent denial of religious and theological universalism. The oft-professed thesis that all men serve the same God and that differences of belief pale into insignificance against the backdrop of this underlying truism could no longer function as the opiate dulling the pain of apostasy. Widespread familiarity with the contents of the Thirteen Principles served to reinforce the simple faith of the Jewish populace and became a source of spiritual strength in deflecting theological assault.

Yet another thesis has been propounded which serves to explain Maimonides' motivation. This explanation has been offered independently by two such disparate personalities as Julius Guttmann, in his *Philosophies of Judaism*,[6] and the late Rabbi Isaac Ze'ev Soloveitchik, a prominent Talmudist popularly known as the *Brisker Rav*, in his unpublished lectures as recorded by his students.[7] For Maimonides, knowledge – but knowledge of a very special nature – is man's highest perfection and bliss. This knowledge, or at least a measure or approximation of this knowledge, is also a necessary condition for achieving immortality of the soul. Maimonides (*Guide*, I, 70 and III, 27) accepts the doctrine which teaches that immortality can be achieved only by virtue of actualization of man's intellectual power. Not only is achievement of this knowledge the human *telos*, contemplation of this knowledge in its supreme form is the exclusive activity of the soul in the world-to-come. The statement that "the righteous sit with crowns upon their heads and enjoy the splendor of the *Shekhinah*" (*Berakhot* 17a) is understood by Maimonides as a poetic description of the intellectual bliss associated with ultimate comprehension of the nature of God. Those in the requisite state of perfection savor this intellectual contemplation. Those who in their lifetime do not develop the requisite intellectual powers for such perception are not denied a share in the world-to-come as a stern punishment; they are simply incapable of its enjoyment.

This intellectualization of Judaism does not, however, serve to restrict immortality to a select few. There are certain simple and basic theological truths which in their simple formulation are not at all esoteric in nature. These truths can be recognized and comprehended by all, and, when affirmed, provide a degree of intellectual achievement sufficient to guarantee immortality.[8] The Thirteen Principles, then, constitute the minimum degree of knowledge sufficient to assure a portion in the world-to-come. The profession, or better, the awareness without which profession is impossible, of these Thirteen Principles thus serves, so to speak, as the minimum entrance requirements for admission to the Heavenly Academy.

---

6. Translated by David W. Silverman (Garden City, N. Y., 1966), pp. 202-203.
7. Undated typescript in the possession of this writer, p. 61, cited in *Haggadah shel Pesaḥ mi-Bet Levi [Brisk]*, ed. Menachem M. Gerlitz (Jerusalem, 5743) p. 190.
8. See Maimonides, *Mishneh Torah, Hilkhot Yesodei ha-Torah* 4:13.

Moreover, although the quality of bliss enjoyed in the world-to-come is commensurate with the degree to which the individual has perfected his intellectual perception of the nature of God, this is by no means the sole criterion of reward. In addition to compensation for fulfillment of the commandments and performance of meritorious deeds, man is rewarded in the hereafter for yet another type of intellectual pursuit, namely, Torah study, which is not at all theological or philosophical in nature. Thus, in *Hilkhot Yesodei ha-Torah* 4:13, Maimonides cautions the uninitiated against delving into divine mysteries and points out that even among the great scholars of the Mishnah there were those who could not properly comprehend such matters. He points out that "bread and meat" to the extent of satiation are necessary prerequisites for engaging in these esoteric studies. Maimonides defines "bread and meat" as the talmudic discussions of Abbaye and Rava, i.e., Torah study dealing with ritual obligations and the like. These studies must be given priority, declares Maimonides, not only because they are intellectual prerequisites for the study of theology but because these studies are, in themselves, the greatest beneficence bestowed upon man, for it is such study which enables man to inherit the world-to-come. Perfection of the intellect achieved through study of Torah is within the reach of all, "young and old, men and women, those gifted with great intellectual capacity as well as those whose intelligence is limited."

The *Brisker Rav* acknowledges that Albo is correct in pointing to the essential redundancy inherent in Maimonides' list of principles. Albo, indeed with great acumen, formulates the philosophical arguments necessary for deriving additional propositions from the basic postulates. But not everyone has the intellectual prowess to examine these basic truths and to construct for himself the arguments, proofs, and conclusions which they entail. In order to guarantee that even those lacking contemplative power, as well as the intellectually lazy, may remain eligible for a portion in the world-to-come, an enumeration of the Thirteen Principles must be provided so that they may be affirmed by all. Once these principles have been formulated and presented in the form of a creed, it is no longer necessary for every individual to undertake an arduous and intellectually taxing process of derivation in order to arrive at truths which serve as a guarantee of immortality. The *Brisker*

Rav points to Maimonides' use of the verbs "to know" (*leida*) and "to believe" (*le-ha'amin*) rather than "to understand" (*le-havin*) as indicating that what is required is only simple knowledge or awareness rather than comprehensive understanding. The requirement as set forth by Maimonides is awareness rather than formal demonstration, affirmation of the conclusion rather than reconstruction of the argument form, acknowledgment rather than erudite analysis. In acquiring knowledge of the Principles of Faith, the individual attains a threshold of intellectual development sufficient to make the contemplative existence of the world-to-come meaningful and blissful. Although S. Urbach, *The Philosophical Teachings of Crescas,*[9] dismisses this analysis as formulated by Guttmann as an exercise in "philosophical homiletics," it is an exposition which is thoroughly congruous with Maimonides' philosophical system.

This analysis also serves to illuminate an otherwise puzzling statement contained in the *Mishneh Torah, Hilkhot Melakhim* 8:11. Maimonides codifies the talmudic statement which declares that the righteous of all nations possess a share in the world-to-come. He defines righteousness as scrupulous adherence to the seven Noahide commandments but then proceeds to add the stipulation that fulfillment of these precepts guarantees a share in the world-to-come only if they are accepted and carried out because "God commanded them in the Torah and made them known to us through our teacher, Moses, that the children of Noah had already been commanded with regard to them." He excludes from this category those who observe these commandments on the basis of their own subjective decision. Commentators on the *Mishneh Torah* were puzzled by this qualification appended by Maimonides since no explicit talmudic sources exist requiring Noachides to accept the obligations of the Noachide code on the basis of revelation. However, it appears that Maimonides is simply extending his thesis to its logical conclusion.[10] Participation in the delights of the world-to-come is not

---

9. Jerusalem, 1961, p. 26, note 29.

10. See *Kesef Mishneh, ad loc.*, who states that Maimonides posited this qualification on the basis of his own reasoning but without a talmudic source. R. Jacob Emden, however, points to a statement of the Gemara, *Sanhedrin* 105a, elucidating the verse "The wicked shall return to the nether-world, even all the nations that forget God" (Psalms 9:18). R. Joshua interprets the verse with the comment: "'The wicked shall

essentially a reward but is the culmination of an intellectual process. If non-Jews as well are to share in the world-to-come, it can also be only on the basis of the confession of certain basic principles of faith which in their acceptance create at least a minimal level of intellectual attainment. Hence, observance of the Noachide laws alone cannot be sufficient to guarantee a share in the world-to-come.[11] Immortality is assured only on the basis of an intellectual affirmation which must accompany observance of the Noachide commandments.[12] It is this ideological commitment which Maimonides spells out: affirmation of revelation and the divinity of Torah which, of course, entails belief in the existence of God.

It appears that in compiling divergent lists of principles Maimonides, Crescas, and Albo are not so much in disagreement with regard to substantive teachings or the need to accept these teachings as divinely revealed truths (although there do exist disagreements with regard to the nature and status of some of these principles), as they are with regard to what it is that they are endeavoring to formulate. Albo is intent upon formulating a system of axioms consisting of the *sine qua non* of any system of religious belief. Every theological system must, by definition, posit the existence of a Deity. Any such system must embody the concept of revelation, else religion can make no demands upon man. And the concept of reward and punishment must be established in order to provide a basis for compliance with the demands of revelation. Crescas, on the other hand, is not concerned with the premises of religious belief in general but with the unique claims of faith set forth by Judaism. Crescas presents the distinctive demands which Judaism makes upon faith and formulates the beliefs which are unique to Judaism. Finally, Maimonides, depending upon which explanation is accepted, either presents the particular beliefs which require bolstering and reinforce-

---

return to the nether-world' – who are they? 'All the nations that forget God.'" R. Jacob Emden's comments were addressed to Moses Mendelssohn and published in the latter's *Gesammelte Schriften Jubiläumsausgabe* (Berlin, 1929), XVI, 179-153. Cf., the analysis of Maimonides offered by R. Malkiel Zevi Tennenbaum, "Mekhirat Karka'ot be-Shevi'it le-Nokhri," *Torah she-be-al Peh*, XV (5733), 164-165.

11. For a discussion of non-Jews and the world-to-come see R. Aaron Walkin, *Teshuvot Zekan Aharon* (Pinsk, 5638), II, no. 87.

12. Cf., however, R. Raphael Y. T. Heilprin, *Teshuvot Oneg Yom Tov* (Vilna, 5640), no. 19.

ment or enumerates the minimum content of the theological knowledge necessary for development of the "acquired intellect" which, in turn, makes possible the reality of immortality.

3

Divine Unity in Maimonides, the Tosafists and Me'iri

T he writings of medieval rabbinic authorities reflect two, or possibly three, distinct theological positions with regard to Christianity. These positions are not merely theoretical or attitudinal in nature. Rather, they yield disparate halakhic rulings governing the conduct of Jews with regard to interpersonal relationships between members of the different faith-communities as reflected in many aspects of commercial and social conduct.

An entirely negative theological view of Christianity is expressed by Maimonides (1135-1204) both in his *Commentary on the Mishnah* and in his *Mishneh Torah*. The Mishnah, in the opening statement of Tractate *Avodah Zarah*, prohibits various forms of commercial intercourse with idolaters during the three days preceding their days of religious observance. The concern is that an idolater, pleased by the success of a commercial enterprise, may, in the course of the impending religious celebration, give thanks to his pagan deity for his good fortune. Jews are admonished not to be involved even vicariously in acts of idolatry and may not even indirectly cause an idolatrous act to be performed. The Mishnah, *Avodah Zarah* 1:3, goes on to enumerate a number of such days of religious observance. Maimonides declares the references to be to days of Christian observance, although the days named are not readily identifiable as known holy days of the early Christian calendar:[1]

> These feast-days herein mentioned were well-known at that time among the Christians[2] and those who cleave to them…. And know that all the various sects of this Christian people who profess the claim of the Messiah, all of them are idolaters… and one must conduct oneself with respect to them with regard to all [the laws of] the Torah in the manner in which one conducts oneself *vis-à-vis* idolaters.

Maimonides proceeds to declare that Sunday is to be regarded as a day on which commercial traffic with "believers in the Messiah" is forbidden. This principle is codified in his *Mishneh Torah, Hilkhot Avodat Kokhavim* 9:4:

> Edomites are idolaters, and Sunday is their day of religious observance. Therefore, in the Land of Israel, it is forbidden to do business with them on Thursday and Friday of each week. It need not be stated that on Sunday it is forbidden in every locale.[3]

---

1. The names seem to be those of celebrations associated with the pagan cults of Roman deities. See *Tiferet Yisra'el, ad loc.* Moreover, manuscript versions include "Saturnalia" rather than an alternative reading found in the published editions of the Mishnah. Curiously, R. Joseph Kafih incorporates the "Saturnalia" reading in his edition of Maimonides' *Commentary on the Mishnah* (Jerusalem, 1963) without remarking on its incongruity with Maimonides' comments.
2. The Arabic term used in Maimonides' original version is correctly rendered as "*ha-notzrim*" in the Kafih translation of the *Commentary on the Mishnah.* Published versions of the Ibn Tibbon translation, reflecting the handiwork of the censor, render the term "*ha-akum.*"
3. This distinction between the Land of Israel and the Diaspora is formulated by the Gemara, *Avodah Zarah* 11b. Rashi, *ad loc.*, explains that in the Diaspora these

In some censored editions of the *Mishneh Torah* the term "Canaanites" is substituted for "Edomites"; in others the entire section, including the numeral introducing the section, is omitted, so that the published version proceeds from section 3 to section 5, with the total elimination of section 4. Maimonides' position is substantiated by manuscript readings of *Avodah Zarah* 6a and 7b, as cited by Rabbi R. N. Rabbinovicz, *Dikdukkei Sofrim*, X, 15. As will be noted, the texts of *Avodah Zarah* eliminated by the censor pose a formidable problem for those authorities who differ with the Maimonidean categorization of Christianity.

Maimonides reiterates his view in the *Mishneh Torah* in a second context. He rules that it is forbidden to derive any benefit whatever from wine that has been handled by an idolater. But the rule about wine handled by a non-Jew who is not an idolater is somewhat different. Such wine may not be consumed by a Jew but there is no prohibition against

---

restrictions are relaxed during the three-day preparatory period (1) because in the Diaspora the burden of desisting from commercial intercourse for an extended period would be onerous, since Jews in the Diaspora are entirely dependent on commercial relations with non-Jews for their livelihoods and (2) because of "fear." *Leḥem Mishneh, Hilkhot Avodat Kokhavim* 9:1, avers that the distinction is not geographic but socio-economic; hence, in an age when Jews residing in the Land of Israel lack political and economic independence, these restrictions are relaxed in the Land of Israel as well. However, Maimonides' codification does not accommodate such a conclusion. *Leḥem Mishneh* asserts that, according to Maimonides, the distinction lies in the fact that gentiles "in the Diaspora are not idolaters and therefore only the feast day is forbidden." *Leḥem Mishneh* presumably means to suggest that non-Jews in the Diaspora are not staunch in their convictions and observances: lacking the zeal of their counterparts in the Land of Israel, they are unlikely to perform acts of devotion to their deities for beneficences other than those immediately experienced. *Leḥem Mishneh's* distinction undoubtedly relies on the dictum recorded in *Ḥullin* 13b, "Gentiles in the Diaspora are not idol worshippers; rather they adhere to the practice of their forebears." In context, this statement refers only to diminished dedication and zeal on the part of idolaters in the Diaspora. But *Leḥem Mishneh's* use of this dictum to explain Maimonides' codification is problematic. For, regardless of the nature of idolatrous zeal during the talmudic period, there is no reason to assume that twelfth-century Palestinian Christians were more zealous than their co-religionists in other countries. Thus, just as the distinction between residents of the Land of Israel and the Diaspora is not hard and fast according to Rashi, it should not be absolute according to the thesis advanced by *Leḥem Mishneh*.

deriving other benefits from it, e.g., it may be sold to a non-Jew.[4] In *Hilk-hot Ma'akhalot Assurot* 11:7, Maimonides declares that "the Ishmaelites," i.e., Muslims, are non-idolatrous gentiles, but that Christians are idolaters, and hence no benefit may be derived from any wine touched by them. In censored editions of the *Mishneh Torah* the word *"notzrim"* is deleted and replaced with the phrase *"otan ha-ovdim akum."*

A somewhat different view of Christianity is ascribed to the Tosafists (12th-13th centuries) in their comments on *Sanhedrin* 63b and *Bekhorot* 2b.[5] A literal reading indicates that they hold that acceptance of a doctrine of *shittuf* (association) is permitted to non-Jews. The doctrine involves a belief in the "Creator of the heavens," but links a belief in the Creator with a belief in some other being or entity. The term *shittuf* is not uncommon in medieval philosophical literature and connotes plurality in the Godhead.[6] *Tosafot* refer explicitly to the gentiles of their day, and the most obvious example of *shittuf*, clearly the doctrine which *Tosafot* seek to legitimize for non-Jews, is Trinitarianism.

However, this interpretation of *Tosafot* is by no means universally accepted. *Tosafot* state only that one may administer an oath to a Christian even though he swears in the name of the Trinity. This ruling is justified by *Tosafot* with the declaration that nowhere is there recorded a prohibition against causing gentiles to "associate" or to "incorporate" another deity in an oath invoking the Divine Name. R. Ezekiel Landau[7] understands *Tosafot* as carefully distinguishing between *shittuf* or Trinitarianism as a professed doctrine and the swearing of an oath in the name of the Trinity. *Noda bi-Yehudah* declares the former to be idolatry and, as such, forbidden to Jew and gentile alike, since idolatry is forbidden by the Noahide Code. Swearing an oath in the name of a pagan god does not

---

4. Wine handled by an idolatrous gentile is forbidden lest the idolater had intended to perform an idolatrous libation. All benefit is forbidden from any item used in conjunction with idolatrous worship. The wine of non-idolatrous gentiles is forbidden by virtue of a later rabbinic decree *"mishum benoteihem,"* literally, "because of their daughters": intimacy born of drinking wine with gentiles may lead to intermarriage.

5. Parallel statements also appear in *Rosh, Sanhedrin* 7:3; Rabbenu Yeruḥam, *Sefer Adam ve-Ḥavvah* 17:5.

6. See David Kaufmann, *Geschichte der Attributenlehre* (Gotha, 1877), p. 460, n. 148.

7. *Teshuvot Noda bi-Yehudah, Mahadurah Tinyana, Yoreh De'ah,* no. 148.

constitute an act of worship or adoration but is forbidden in the commandment "and in His Name shall you swear" (Deuteronomy 10:20). That commandment, however, is addressed only to Jews. Although this reading of *Tosafot* does not at all strain the plain meaning of the text and is followed by a number of later authorities,[8] it is probably correct to say that the majority of latter-day authorities interpret *Tosafot* more broadly as declaring that *shittuf* does not constitute idolatry for Noahides.[9]

The conventional analysis of *Tosafot* must be understood as distinguishing between the denial of polytheism and the upholding of Divine Unity. In proscribing the worship of foreign gods, the Noahide Code binds gentiles to the acceptance of a monotheistic belief. That concept, however, entails only the rejection of *shetei reshuyot*, i.e., a multiplicity of powers each capable of independent action. The full doctrine of Divine Unity requires much more than abjuration of such a primitive notion. Indeed, Maimonides, in formulating the second of his Thirteen Principles, affirms that God's unity is unique:

1. Mankind, for example, is a single species, a unity composed of all individual men. God, however, is not such a collective unity; He is not to be construed as a genus composed of distinct beings or powers. The unity of God is not the unity of a collectivity.

2. The unity of God is not the unity of an aggregate. God is not a

8. *Sha'ar Efrayim*, no. 24; *Me'il Tzedakah*, no. 22; *Teshuvot ve-Shev ha-Kohen*, no. 38; *Teshuvot Ḥadashot le-Rabbeinu Akiva Eger* (Jerusalem, 5738), pp. 164-66; *Pri Megadim, Yoreh De'ah, Siftei Da'at* 65:11; *idem, Oraḥ Ḥayyim, Eshel Avraham* 156:2; and *Maḥatzit ha-Shekel, Oraḥ Ḥayyim* 156:2.

9. See Rema, *Oraḥ Ḥayyim*, 156:1; *Darkei Mosheh* 151; *Shakh, Yoreh De'ah* 151:1 and 151:7; *Derishah and Baḥ, Ḥoshen Mishpat* 182; *Teshuvot Ḥavvot Ya'ir*, nos. 1 and 185; *Ha-Makneh, Kiddushin* 31b, s.v. *ve-eino yode'a*; R. Ya'akov Emden, *Mor u-Ketzi'ah* 224; *Mishnat Ḥakhamim, Hilkhot Yesodei ha-Torah*; Rabbi Zev Boskowitz, *Seder Mishnah, Hilkhot Yesodei ha-Torah* 1:7 and *Shoshan Edut* (commentary on *Eduyyot*), 188; *Teshuvot ve-Shev ha-Kohen*, no. 38; Rabbi A. Vermeiz, *Me'orei Or* IV, 8a, 13a, V, 111b; *Ravid ha-Zahav, Parashat Yitro; Yad Sha'ul, Yoreh De'ah* 151; *Teshuvot Sho'el u-Meshiv, Mahadurah Tinyana* I nos. 26, 51; R. Zevi Hirsch Chajes, *Kol Sifrei Maharatz Ḥayes*, I 489-90; *Ha-Ketav ve-ha-Kabbalah*, Deuteronomy 4:19; and *Pithei Teshuvah, Yoreh De'ah* 147:2.

compound. His unity is not the unity of a composite divisible into its component parts.

3. Merely to say that God's unity is not the unity of a compound does not exclude the possibility of a nature analogous to that of even the smallest corporeal substance, which, at least in principle or conceptually, may be further divided or broken down. God's unity, however, is not the unity of magnitude. It cannot admit of any division whatsoever. A "simple substance," not composed of parts, cannot be broken down. Since destruction involves the division of an entity into component parts, it follows that God, who is a perfect unity, is not susceptible to destruction.

For Maimonides, renunciation of polytheism is not a separate principle or doctrine standing alone. It flows rationally and necessarily from the notion of Divine Unity and is part and parcel of a sophisticated conception of the unity unique to God. Since rejection of polytheism and acceptance of Divine Unity are but two sides of the same coin, it follows that Noahides, who are commanded to renounce idolatry, are *ipso facto* commanded to accept the doctrine of Divine Unity.[10]

According to this analysis, *Tosafot* posit that Noahides are required only to renounce the notion of multiple, independent deities. This is expressed in the statement that contemporary gentiles recognize the "Creator of the heavens," by which *Tosafot* undoubtedly intend to ascribe to Christians a belief in a single Creator who continues to exercise providence over His creatures. The highly sophisticated belief that the Deity is an absolute unity is demanded of Jews but is not a requirement placed upon non-Jews. So worship of a triune God by Christians is not tantamount to idolatry or to polytheism, since they do not ascribe independent powers to the members of the Trinity.

Support for a distinction between rejection of polytheism and

---

10. Maimonides, in his *Mishneh Torah, Hilkhot Yesodei ha-Torah* 1:7, does refer to polytheism as a belief to be abjured. That reference is both appropriate and necessary in its context, a succinct specification of the requirements of the commandment "I am the Lord your God" rather than in a discussion that is primarily philosophical in nature.

acceptance of the doctrine of Divine Unity may, almost paradoxically, be found in a source that formulates this distinction only to reject any difference that might arise therefrom. In describing the obligations of non-Jews, *Hullin* 92a speaks, not simply of the Seven Commandments of the Sons of Noah, but of thirty commandments "accepted" by Noahides:

> "And I said to them, if ye think good, give me my hire; and if not, forebear. So they weighed out for my hire thirty pieces of silver" (Zechariah 11:12). Ulla said, "These are the thirty commandments which the Sons of Noah accepted upon themselves, but they observe only three [of them]: (i) they do not draw up a *ketubah* for males; (ii) they do not weigh flesh of the dead in the market; and (iii) they respect the Torah."

Rashi, in his commentary, indicates that the identification of these thirty commandments is unclear.[11] But Samuel ben Ḥofni (d. 1034), the last Gaon of Sura, does provide a complete enumeration of these commandments and lists belief in the unity of God among them.[12] Although be posits an obligation binding Noahides to accept the doctrine of Divine Unity, Samuel ben Ḥofni clearly recognizes it as an obligation quite distinct from acceptance of the monotheistic principle which prohibits polytheistic worship. For Samuel ben Ḥofni the two beliefs are distinct; but, since both are binding upon Noahides, this is a distinction without a difference. Yet once it is accepted, as against the view of Maimonides, that the two are distinct notions and not mutually entailed, it is much less surprising to find that *Tosafot* recognize acceptance of Divine Unity as a belief incumbent only upon Jews, while for non-Jews renunciation of polytheism is sufficient.

The belief in a single "Creator of the heavens" sharing the divine essence with another being, or with other beings, ascribed by *Tosafot* to the Christians of the day, is an accurate depiction of a conception of relative unity developed by the Apologists to reconcile Christian

---

11. See, however, sources cited by *Maharab Ranshburg, Ḥullin* 92a.
12. See Aaron Greenbaum, *The Biblical Commentary of Rav Samuel ben Ḥofni Gaon* (Jerusalem, 1978), p. 617.

belief in a triune God with the inherited Jewish belief in one God. The Apologists accepted the concept of Divine Unity as an expression of the concept of unity of rule, i.e., the concept of a single absolute ruler of the universe. To them, however, the Deity was not an absolutely simple being but consisted of three beings inseparably united. Thus, for example, Tatian speaks of Christianity as accepting the "rule of one" as opposed to Greek polytheism which acknowledges "the dominion of many,"[13] and Athenagoras describes God, the Logos, and the Holy Spirit as "united in power."[14] This doctrine is also formulated in the writings of Tertullian who declares, "I am sure that monarchy has no other meaning than single individual rule; but, for all that, this monarchy does not, because it is the government of one, preclude him whose government it is, either from having a son ... or from ministering his own government by whatever agent he will."[15] Tertullian describes the members of the Trinity as "three, however, not in status, but in degree; not in substance, but in form; not in power, but in species; yet of one substance, and of one status and of one power."[16] The terms "monarchy" and "united in power" clearly express the notion of rule.[17] Reflected in each of these citations is a clear renunciation both of a multiplicity of powers and of the notion that Divine Unity demands absolute simplicity. Later Church Fathers formulate the concept of trinity in terms of Aristotelian notions of species, genus and substratum. Statements expressing such concepts do not at all negate the fundamental concept of unity of rule.

A far more positive view of Christianity is expressed by R. Menaḥem ha-Me'iri (1249-1306). In a number of statements scattered throughout his commentary on the various tractates of the Talmud, Me'iri unequivocally rules that Christians are not idolaters.[18] His most explicit ruling occurs in his commentary on the opening Mishnah of

---

13. *Oratio ad Graecos*, 14.
14. *Supplication pro Christianis*, 24.
15. *Adversus Praxeam*, 3.
16. *Adversus Praxeam*, 2.
17. For unity of rule as a rejection of polytheism, see Harry A. Wolfson, *The Philosophy of the Church Fathers*, rev. 2nd ed. (Cambridge, Mass., 1964), I, 312-322.
18. See Me'iri, *Bet ha-Beḥirah, Avodah Zarah*, ed., Abraham Schreiber (Jerusalem, 1944) 2a (p. 4), 6b (p. 9), 15b (p. 39), 20a (p. 46) and 22a (p. 53); *Bava Kamma*, ed., Kal-

Avodah Zarah, where he holds that the restrictions on commercial intercourse with idolaters on their feastdays are not applicable "in these times." He takes pains to note that the uncensored text of the Talmud, *Avodah Zarah* 6a and 7b, refers explicitly to the *"Notzri"* as an idolater.[19] But Me'iri dismisses that text by declaring that the reference is to an ancient people mentioned in Jeremiah 4:16, whose appellation is derived from the name Nebuchadnezzar. He depicts that people as sun-worshipers who observe the first day of the week as a day of religious devotion because it is regarded as the day of the sun's dominion.[20]

Theologically, Me'iri's most positive statement concerning Christianity is his unequivocal declaration that "they believe in God's existence, His unity and power, although they misconceive some points according to our belief" (*Bet ha-Beḥirah, Gittin* 62a, p. 258). This citation is far more significant for determining Me'iri's theological assessment of Christianity than are his frequent and oft-quoted references to *"umot hagedurot be-darkei ha-datot* – nations restrained by the ways of religion."[21] Me'iri's employment of such phraseology is invariably in the context of jurisprudential and interpersonal matters. Hence his comments might well be understood as reflecting the thesis that halakhic distinctions between Jews and gentiles regarding such matters are predicated upon the principle that the advantages enjoyed by Jews, e.g., restoration of lost property, depend on reciprocal respect for property rights and

---

man Schlesinger (Jerusalem, 1963) 113a-b (p. 330); *Gittin,* ed., Kalman Schlesinger (Jerusalem, 1964) 62a (p. 258). See also the comments of Me'iri cited by R. Bezalel Ashkenazi, *Shitah Mekubbetzet, Bava Kamma,* 38a and 113a.

19. See also Mei'iri, *Ta'anit,* ed. Abraham Schreiber (Jerusalem, 5718) 27b (p. 97).

20. See Lawrence Zalcman, "Christians, Noserim and Nebuchadnezzar's Daughter," *Jewish Quarterly Review,* LXXXI, nos. 3-4 (January-April 1991), 411-426, who, citing E. S. Drower, *The Mandeans of Iraq and Iran* (Oxford, 1937); reprinted (Leiden, 1964), draws attention to the tale of "Nebuchadnezzar's Daughter" concerning the sect known as the "Nasurai" whose practices parallel those of the *Notzrim* as recorded in *Avodah Zarah.*

21. See *Bet ha-Beḥirah, Pesaḥim,* ed., Joseph ha-Kohen Klein (Jerusalem, 1966) 21b (p. 67); *Ketubot,* ed., Abraham Sofer (Jerusalem, 1947) 15b (pp. 67 f.); *Kiddushin,* ed., Abraham Sofer (Jerusalem 1963) 17b (p. 108); *Bava Kamma* 113a-b (p. 330); *Bava Metzi'a,* ed., Kalman Schlesinger (Jerusalem, 1963) 59a (p. 219); *Avodah Zarah* 13b (p. 29), 20a (p. 46), 22a (p. 53).

the welfare of others. Hence Jews owe such obligations only to fellow Jews who reciprocate in kind, but not to gentiles "not restrained by the ways of religion," who feel no legal or moral obligation to comport themselves in a similar manner. On such an analysis, Me'iri might well be understood as asserting that law-abiding and benevolent adherents of religions which make similar demands of their devotees are entitled to the same benefits, privileges and protection as Jews. But from such a position nothing can be deduced as to the status of the theological beliefs of the members of such religions. Such a distinction is bolstered by Me'iri's ruling that, unlike a heretic, an apostate Jew is to be accorded the rights and privileges of members of his adopted faith in all matters pertaining to jurisprudence.[22]

Jacob Katz' analysis of Me'iri's stance toward Christianity is flawed by insensitivity to the role of the distinction between positive juridical/moral institutions and valid theological doctrines. Katz characterizes Me'iri's theological comments on Christianity as something that "Ha-Me'iri sometimes adds to the characteristics of the contemporary nations."[23] But Me'iri's references to Christian beliefs are neither an afterthought nor mere theological gilding of the lily of morality. They are formulated precisely in those contexts in which the halakhic issues hinge upon belief and are omitted in discussions of halakhic issues predicated upon juridical and moral institutions and comportment. Thus there is no support for Katz' conclusion that "Ha-Me'iri's positive evaluation of Christianity stems in the main from his esteem for the maintenance of legal institutions and moral standards of society." Me'iri's evaluation is, of necessity, twofold: moral and theological; but there is no entailment between these two evaluations.

Me'iri's theological assessment of Christianity is unique in rabbinic literature. Katz' assertion that "independently of him, a similar line of reasoning was followed by certain seventeenth-century scholars, among them Moshe Rikves…"[24] is simply erroneous. R. Moshe Rikves

---

22. See *Bet ha-Beḥirah, Horiyot*, ed., Abraham Schreiber (Jerusalem, 1969), 11a (p. 274) and *Avodah Zarah*, 26b (p. 61).

23. *Exclusiveness and Tolerance* (Oxford, 1961), p. 121.

24. *Exclusiveness and Tolerance*, p. 164.

in his glosses to the *Shulḥan Arukh* bearing the title *Be'er ha-Golah* does indeed posit an obligation to rescue gentiles from danger, and, moreover, to pray for their welfare.[25] And he does express a positive theological attitude toward Christianity, but it is the attitude of *Tosafot*, not of Me'iri. *Be'er ha-Golah* correctly ascribes to Christians a belief in God as Creator of the universe and author of providence, as evidenced by the phenomena of the Exodus, and adds that "their whole aim and intent is toward the Creator of the heaven and earth, as the codifiers have written." The expression "aim and intent" refers to acts of worship and adoration and is equivalent to the formulation used by *Tosafot* with regard to Christianity as *shittuf*. The phrase "as the codifiers have written" is clearly a reference to the treatment of the doctrine of *shittuf* advanced by *Tosafot*, for that is the only positive categorization of Christianity found in the writings of codifiers of Jewish law.

Moreover, it is extremely difficult to determine whether the comments of *Be'er ha-Golah* are to be taken as an expression of normative Halakhah or whether they were penned with an eye to the censor or otherwise intended to dispel anti-Semitic enmity. Phrases such as "the gentiles in whose shadows we live and under whose wings we shelter" and "hence we stand on guard to pray continually for the welfare and success of the kingdom and the ministers" have a ring that is not halakhic, but can be characterized as almost servile in tone. Certainly, the citation of Maimonides' qualification of R. Joshua's dictum (*Sanhedrin* 105a) that the pious of the nations enjoy a portion in the world-to-come is imprecise and indeed may have been appended as a means of divulging to the discerning reader that the entire statement is hyperbole. Maimonides maintains that the pious of the nations of the world are entitled to a portion in the world-to-come only if they obey the Noahide Code because they accept it on the basis of divine revelation. A Christian who believes that the Sinaitic covenant has been abrogated but adheres to the provisions of the Noahide Code because he accepts them on the basis of natural law, on general humanitarian grounds, or for some other reason, is excluded by Maimonides from the category of the "pious of the nations of the world." If *Be'er ha-Golah*

---

25. *Be'er ha-Golah, Ḥoshen Mishpat* 425:5.

did not accept the limitation Maimonides places upon the concept "the pious of the nations of the world," he might simply have cited the dictum of R. Joshua without reference to Maimonides. So it seems likely that *Be'er ha-Golah's* citation of Maimonides was intended as a clue to the nature of the entire statement.

But Me'iri does not merely distinguish Christianity from polytheism. He makes the far more positive statement that Christians accept Divine Unity. The tenor of his comment about the "misconceptions" of Christianity gives the impression that any doctrinal error on the part of the Christians is not tantamount to a denial of Divine Unity. Nowhere in his categorization of the beliefs of contemporary religions does Me'iri suggest a distinction between idolatry as prohibited to Jews and idolatry as subsumed in the Noahide Code.

Me'iri's position has long been a source of puzzlement to rabbinic scholars.[26] Indeed, there is a strong feeling in some rabbinic circles that these comments are either falsely ascribed to Me'iri or were inserted for fear of the censor. *Ḥatam Sofer*, citing the comment of Me'iri quoted by *Shitah Mekubbetzet, Bava Kamma* 113a, declares, "It is a *mitzvah* to erase it for it did not emerge from his holy mouth."[27] I am inclined to believe that statements concerning financial and interpersonal relations were introduced into the text with an eye to the censor[28] but that the statements concerning Christian theology constitute Me'iri's considered opinion. My reasons for accepting the censor thesis in part and rejecting it in part are twofold:

Only the hovering presence of the censor can elucidate the remarks of Me'iri in his commentary on *Yevamot* 98a.[29] The talmudic

---

26. See this writer's "Entering a Non-Jewish House of Worship," *Tradition*, vol. 44, no. 1 (Summer, 2011), pp. 80-82, notes 18-20.

27. See the responsum of *Ḥatam Sofer* published in R. Baruch Frankel-Teumim's *Ateret Ḥakhamim*, no. 14, repr. in *Kovetz She'elot u-Teshuvot Ḥatam Sofer* (Jerusalem, 5733) no. 90. See also R. David Zevi Hillman, "Leshonot ha-Me'iri she-Nikhtevu le-Teshuvot ha-Minim," *Tzefunot*, I (5749), 65-72.

28. Me'iri's statement in *Bet ha-Beḥirah*, ed. Joseph ha-Kohen Klein (Jerusalem, 1975), 84b (p. 212) regarding a provision of Jewish law was almost certainly introduced into the text with an eye to the censor. For a further discussion of the phenomenon of self-censorship see *Tradition*, 44:1, p. 81, note 20.

29. Ed. Samuel Dickman (Jerusalem, 1962), p. 345.

rule is that no paternal relationship exists among gentiles. The principle regarding paternal relationship is thus analogous to that governing determination of animal species, regarding which "there is no concern whatsoever with the seed of the sire." The practical halakhic application of this principle is that no levirate obligations are attendant upon converts. Me'iri qualifies the discussion by inserting a statement that this status includes "every idolater who is not within the pale of the religions." The implication is that levirate obligations do devolve upon Christians who convert to Judaism. There can be no question that the qualifying phrase was introduced by Me'iri as a means of obscuring a statement the censor was bound to find offensive. If, as is obvious, this passage was emended for the sake of the censor, there is reason to assume that similar liberties may have been taken with other potentially offensive passages.

Moreover, discrepancies among the manuscripts of *Bet ha-Beḥirah, Yoma* 84b, discussing rescue of a gentile on *Shabbat*, clearly reflect the handiwork of the censor. The edition published in Jerusalem in 1885 contains the phrase "the idol-worshippers of antiquity... since they have no religion and are also unconcerned with the detriment of human society." This phrase is absent in the Parma manuscript which is the basis of the Jerusalem, 1975 edition edited by Joseph ha-Kohen Klein.[30]

However, Me'iri's remarks regarding Christian theology in his commentary on *Avodah Zarah* cannot be understood in the same light: Relaxation of the rule against commercial intercourse with idolaters on their feastdays was not born of a desire to appease the censor. Certainly, a distorted theological perspective was not required to justify suspension of that rule. *Tosafot* and other early authorities had no difficulty in justifying the departure from previous practices without attempting to flatter the censor. Moreover, Me'iri's elucidation of the term *Notzri*, unless sincerely held, is entirely gratuitous. He could simply have ignored the term in his commentary. To sustain the "censor thesis," it would be necessary to argue that these comments were inserted, not simply as a means of assuring that Me'iri's work would not be suppressed, but were expressly intended to curry favor with Christian authorities for reasons having nothing to do with dissemination of the volumes in which they occur.

---

30. See p. 212, notes 229 and 237.

Even more baffling is Me'iri's assertion that adherents of the Trinity are believers in the doctrine of Divine Unity. Orthodox Christian views of the Trinity are certainly incompatible with the monotheistic beliefs of Judaism. It appears likely that Me'iri, in formulating his views regarding Christianity, assumed that Christians professed a view of the Trinity which, although erroneous, did not do violence to the doctrine of Divine Unity. Such views did exist within the Church, particularly during its infancy, only later to be branded as heretical by various Church councils. A number of possible views that are theologically compatible with Me'iri's characterization should be examined:

1. The original Jewish adherents of Christianity conceived of the founder of that nascent faith as a mere human being. This doctrine, known as Ebionism, viewed Jesus of Nazareth as the promised Messiah upon whom rested "the spirit of the Lord" (Isaiah 11:2). Somewhat later a form of neo-Ebionism evolved which understood the notion of the incarnation of the Logos in the person of Jesus in much the manner that the Divine Presence may be said to rest upon any righteous and exemplary man. 'However, in this instance, that phenomenon was posited as an act of grace and the presence of the Logos was attributed to a miraculous event associated with Jesus' birth or baptism.[31]

2. Docetism represented a diametrically opposing view introduced by pagan converts to Christianity. Adherents regarded Jesus as God, who only appeared in human form. This doctrine could certainly have been understood as affirming a perfectly monotheistic notion of God and as explaining all corporeal references found in the Gospels as reports of phenomena which exist only in the mind of man. Thus the second-century figure Simon the Gnostic, displaying a thorough consistency, spoke not only of the merely human appearance of the son but also of the mere appearance of his suffering, stating "thus he was thought to have suffered in Judea, when he had not suffered."[32]

31. See Wolfson, *Church Fathers*, pp. 602-04.
32. Iranacus, I 23, 3; Hippolytus, VI, 9, 6; *Church Fathers*, pp. 591-92.

Wolfson notes that a literal reading of the Pentateuch provides a source for belief in the phenomenon of God appearing to man in the form of a human being.[33] Genesis 18:1 records that "the Lord appeared" to Abraham and thereupon informs us that Abraham "lifted up his eyes and, lo, three men stood by him" (Genesis 18:2). Maimonides asserts that the entire incident occurred in a dream.[34] He clearly denies that man can perceive the Deity in a waking state.[35] And the *Midrash ha-Gadol*, commenting on the verse, assumes that such an appearance is possible only in a prophetic vision. Nevertheless, a literal reading of the text suggests precisely a waking appearance. Such an understanding of the text may be completely erroneous, but there is no indication even in Maimonides' comments (whose position on this matter is the most extreme in Judaism) that a literal reading of this biblical narrative would be heresy or a fundamental doctrinal error: Belief in even repeated appearances of the incorporeal God to man in the guise of a corporeal being is no more than the belief that God has repeatedly chosen to generate an optical illusion or mirage. Accordingly, Docetism, if understood as ascribing no substantive reality to the persons of the Trinity, is entirely compatible with a pure monotheistic belief.

Various forms of Ebionism and of Docetism were found among the Gnostics, and a number of forms of neo-Ebionism and neo-Docetism were condemned as heresies by Church councils, including those of Nicaea in 325, Constantinople in 381, Ephesus in 431, and Chalcedon in 451. Condemnation of these doctrines was confirmed by the Council of Constantinople in 556. Thus, any form of Ebionism or Docetism that could conceivably be regarded as monotheistic seems to have disappeared by the middle of the sixth century.

3. The early Christian Apologists made various attempts to present a monotheistic formulation of the notion of the Trinity by

---

33. *Church Fathers*, p. 518.
34. *Guide*, Part II, chap. 42; cf., II, chap. 45.
35. *Guide*, Part II, chap. 45.

describing the members of the Godhead as names, predicates or attributes, rather than discrete entities. Jewish philosophy was later to struggle with the notion of divine attributes precisely because of its belief that multiplicity of attributes, as conventionally understood, is at variance with the doctrine of God as a simple unity. But attributes are ascribed to the Deity by Scripture, and such ascription could well abide explanation. The notion of divine attributes required careful elucidation, a task that commanded the attention of all medieval Jewish philosophers. But what Judaism was to regard as a problem, for some early Christian theologians, became the solution. The "heresies" of Praxeas, Noetus and Sabellius involved a categorization of the distinction among the members of the Trinity as nominal rather than real. If the terms Father, Son and Holy Spirit are regarded as mere names or attributes, devoid of reality, the unity of God is preserved. This view is closely related to Modalism as described by Origen. Modalism regards the Logos as having no reality as a being distinct from God, but as a power of God, a mode of His manifestation to man. This conceptualization of the Trinity was condemned by Justin Martyr and does not appear to have been accepted by any later source.[36]

4. At roughly the same time, other Christian theologians seeking to reconcile the notion of the Logos as endowed with reality with strict Divine Unity formulated a position known as Creationism. They conceived of the Logos as created by God either *ex essentia Dei* or *ex nihilo*. As a created being, the Logos could not be regarded as a Deity in any real sense. This view proved attractive to some and preferable to Modalism in that it permitted acceptance of the Logos, not simply as a power in God, but as a real being outside of God. According to both Philo and Justin Martyr, the Logos originally existed only as a power in God but became a real being outside of God.[37]

The Apologists maintained that the Logos, in its second stage,

---

36. See *Church Fathers*, p. 580.
37. *Church Fathers*, pp. 192-93 and 582.

was generated by God out of His own essence before the creation of the world.[38] Later, Arius adopted a view similar to that of Philo, asserting that the Logos was created by God "out of things nonexistent."[39] Such a Logos cannot be regarded as God. Naturally, the Arian Logos is intimately associated with Jesus of Nazareth. The role of the Logos in that context is, for Arius, roughly equivalent to that of the divine spirit in Philo's description of prophetic experience. Philo speaks of the mind being evicted and replaced by the divine spirit during prophecy and of the return of the mind at the conclusion of the prophetic experience.[40] The Arian Logos, in effect, performs the same function that Philo ascribes to the divine spirit. According to Arius, however, Jesus had no other rational soul; hence, the Logos became immanent in him in a manner analogous, in Philonic terms, to a person continually endowed with a prophetic state, by virtue of the constant immanence of the divine spirit.[41]

Although Arianism was repeatedly condemned by Church councils during the fourth century and ceased to be a power inside the Roman Empire subsequent to the Council of Constantinople in 381, it remained the faith of the barbarian invaders. Despite the fact that Arianism was suppressed by a series of civil decrees, Roman law was binding upon Romans only; no attempt was made by the Roman emperors to interfere with the beliefs of their Gothic soldiers, who remained "privileged heretics in the midst of the orthodox Empire." With the Teutonic conquest of the West in the fifth century, Arianism became dominant in Italy and Spain.[42]

5. Although Arianism declined rapidly in the ensuing period, a related theological tenet gained currency towards the end of the eighth century in the form of Adoptionism. The adherents of this idea held the relationship between the Deity and the founder

---

38. *Church Fathers*, pp. 292-94.
39. *Church Fathers*, p. 586.
40. Philo, *Quis Rerum Divinarum Heres*, 53, 265.
41. *Church Fathers*, pp. 593-94.
42. See Henry M. Gwatkin, *The Arian Controversy* (New York, 1891), p. 165 and his *Studies of Arianism* (Cambridge, 1900), pp. 271-72.

of Christianity to have resulted from God's adoption of a son rather than as flowing from a natural, existential state. Among the Adoptionists, the Cerinthians taught that Jesus became the adopted son of God by virtue of wisdom, virtue and purity; the Basilidians held that Jesus was arbitrarily selected and purified through his baptism to serve as the medium of revelation. The primary focus of the various forms of Adoptionism was insistence upon the humanity of Jesus. Indeed, some historians point to concepts apparently expressed in a letter written in 783 by one of the leaders of this movement, Felix, Bishop of Urgel, to Elipandus, Archbishop of Toledo, as designed to pave the way for a union between Christians and Muslims. The Muslims, of course, would have rejected out of hand any theology in which monotheistic principles were compromised. The doctrines expressed by Felix received wide currency in Spain and France but were repeatedly condemned by Church Councils in the last decades of the ninth century. With the death of Felix in 818 Adoptionism was eclipsed, but similar views are ascribed to Ecumenius in the tenth century and to Euthymius Zigabenus and others in the twelfth. References to, and rejections of, these views appear in the writings of the Schoolmen, including Peter Lombard, Thomas Aquinas and Duns Scotus, suggesting that the positions continued to enjoy a certain currency, even though they were not widely held. Particularly interesting is the fact that Duns Scotus, although he rejected the theory of adoption, was prepared to allow the use of the term with certain modifications and explanations.

Given the fact that neo-Arianism and various forms of Adoptionism did not become entirely extinct during the medieval period, it is not farfetched to hypothesize that the Christianity about which Me'iri made positive comments was not an orthodox Trinitarianism but a Christianity that espoused a theology branded heretical by the Church. Of course, if this is the case, Me'iri must have been misled in assuming that these were the beliefs accepted by the Church as a whole. How this occurred, one can only conjecture. It may be that he lived in the midst of one of the lingering pockets of neo-Arianism or Adoptionism or had conversations with Christian clerics who, in their desire to influence a prominent Jewish scholar, purposely presented Christian theology in a manner most likely to evoke a sympathetic response.[43] Or perhaps Me'iri's information came from a manuscript or manuscripts which, unknown to him, emanated from these "heretical" circles and did not represent mainstream Christian teaching.[44] Since little is known of the circumstances of Me'iri's life and since details of Church history during that period are also obscure, there is little likelihood of finding a "smoking gun" to confirm this thesis.

---

43. The late R. Joseph Messas, formerly chief rabbi of Haifa, *Teshuvot Mayim Ḥayyim*, 11, *Yoreh De'ah* 108, sec. 2, reports that while yet serving as a rabbi in Tlemcen, Algeria he met with a priest in a church who informed him that Christian belief is pure monotheism; prayer is directed to God who is one and that the term "son of God" connotes an angel, as is the meaning of "the sons of God" in Job 1:6, 2:1 and 38:7.

      Rabbi Messas also reports that, upon making inquiries in Algiers, he was sent a copy of a letter addressed to R. Chaim Joseph David Azulai by R. Saadia Amav, chief rabbi of Algeria at the time, in which the latter writes that early-day authorities erred in ascribing a Trinitarian dogma to Christians "for all of them served the one God and Him they always worship; all representations of their messiah and his mother, together with representation of the cross, are mere reminders to avenge his blood and crucifixion.

44. This analysis of Me'iri may well be strained but it certainly does not fail on that account. "Strained" explanations of statements of early-day authorities are so prevalent that R. Moshe Sofer, *Teshuvot Ḥatam Sofer: Kovetz Teshuvot* (Jerusalem, 5742), no. 82, was prompted to observe that "the majority of strained explanations are correct." See also R. Ezekiel Landau, *Teshuvot Noda bi-Yehudah, Mahadura Tinyana, Even ha-Ezer*, no. 79 and R. Moshe Feinstein, *Iggerot Mosheh, Yoreh De'ah*, 111, nos. 114 and 115. Cf., David Berger, "Jews, Gentiles and the Modern Egalitarian Ethos: Some Tentative Thoughts," *Formulating Responses in an Egalitarian Age*, ed. by Marc D. Stern (Lanham, Md., 2005), p. 95 and Yaakov Elman, "Meiri and the Non-Jew: A Comparative Investigation," *New Perspectives on Jewish-Christian Relations*, ed. by Elisheva Carlebach and Jacob J. Schacter (Leiden and Boston, 2012), p. 269.

An Afterword

Since no other medieval authority subscribed to Me'iri's assessment of Christianity,[45] the authenticity of the view ascribed to him is of scant import. Many statements of Mei'ri, particularly those found in manuscripts of unknown provenance, have long been regarded with skepticism by rabbinic scholars.[46] The late R. Joseph B. Soloveitchik peremptorily dismissed views expressed in the newly-published works of Me'iri based upon manuscripts found in the Cairo *genizah* as "a mere curiosity of no normative import" and hence without relevance to the halakhic process.[47] Me'iri's assessment of Christian theology is of equal irrelevance.

---

45. See Berger, "Jews, Gentiles and the Modern Egalitarian Ethos," p. 94.

46. See this writer's "Entering a Non-Jewish House of Worship," pp. 80-83.

47. See R. Hershel Reichman, the Yeshiva University student newspaper, *The Commentator*, November 5, 2006, p. 21. Those comments and any "disdain of ha-Me'iri as a halakhic authority" apply only to statements found in *genizah* manuscripts because of issues regarding the reliability of texts whose provenance is uncertain and possibly with regard to other texts beclouded by suspicion of fear of the censor. Me'iri himself was always regarded with the highest respect and positions ascribed to him by rabbinic decisors of previous generations are indeed part of the *mesorah* of Halakhah. Cf., Berger, "Jews, Gentiles and the Modern Egalitarian Ethos," p. 100.

4

Was Spinoza a Jewish Philosopher?[1]

"Friends, Romans, countrymen, lend me your ears. I come to bury Caesar, not to praise him."

Friends – and I hope we shall remain friends – Cardozans, fellow men and women, lend me your ears, I come to bury Spinoza, not to praise him. I would have used a less harsh phrase and more diplomatic nomenclature but this is the hand that I was dealt by Shakespeare. Let me hasten to add: Not to worry. Even if by some miracle – or by some generous stretch of your imagination – I manage to succeed in the task that I have set for myself, I assure you that the other speakers will disinter Spinoza.

Let me turn to the question that I have been asked to address: "Was Spinoza a Jewish philosopher?" That is a question which is readily trifurcated or, if you prefer, a question that can be formulated in a trinitarian manner. And, by no leap of faith, can the three questions be

---

1. This material was originally presented as the Keynote Address at a symposium on "Spinoza's Law" sponsored by the Benjamin N. Cardozo School of Law of Yeshiva University on October 6, 2002.

conflated into a single query. The question can be formulated in three separate and distinct ways:

First, the question "Was Spinoza a Jewish philosopher?" can be understood as querying: Was Spinoza the philosopher endowed either with Jewish ethnic identity or with halakhic identity as a Jew? That question, if asked, is trivial in nature and has an obvious answer. That Spinoza was raised and educated as a Jew is a matter of historical record. That, halakhically speaking, Spinoza was a Jew goes without saying. After all, Spinoza had a Jewish mother. Spinoza may have been an excommunicated Jew, but he was a Jew. Of course, as formulated, the query represents a compound question. To ask whether Spinoza was a Jewish philosopher antecedently assumes that he was a philosopher. Was Spinoza a philosopher? I am certain that no one really wishes me to define the term "philosopher." Let us simply take judicial notice of the fact that for a period of more than 300 years Spinoza has been deemed to be a philosopher and therefore we can justifiably and safely refer to him as a Jewish philosopher. Thus, we can answer the first, but trivial, formulation of our question in the affirmative.

In a work titled *The Philosopher and Theology*, Etienne Gilson, a professor at the Sorbonne and a historian of medieval philosophy, wrote that there were three remarkable things about the Sorbonne in the early part of the twentieth century: 1) There were a remarkably large number of Jewish philosophers at the Sorbonne; 2) Even more remarkable was the fact that they were, in fact, not Jewish philosophers at all; 3) But most remarkable was the fact that each one of those Jewish philosophers, who was not in fact a Jewish philosopher, espoused two separate and distinct philosophies, one was Spinozism and the second was his own idiosyncratic philosophy.

So let us move to the second of the three formulations of the question "Was Spinoza a Jewish philosopher?" Was Spinoza a Jewish philosopher in the sense that his philosophy was reflective of, or at least compatible with, Jewish thought and ideology? Gilson certainly knew the answer to that question. The many philosophers at the Sorbonne who were of Jewish extraction and who espoused Spinozism were depicted by Gilson as not having been Jewish philosophers at all. However, that assessment, I believe, requires at least a modicum of analysis.

Judaism, as everyone knows, is first and foremost a religion of law; but that is not to imply that Judaism does not have its own philosophy and its own ideology. All that one has to do is to open the very first volume of Maimonides' *Mishneh Torah*, his legal magnum opus, and read the title headings which include a section entitled "Hilkhot De'ot," or "Laws of Belief," or to examine Bahya ibn Pakuda's philosophical work which bears the title *Ḥovot ha-Levavot, The Duties of the Heart,* or, more accurately, *"The Duties of the Intellect,"* and one very quickly comes to the realization that "laws of belief," i.e., philosophy, theology, ideology etc., are all very much integral parts of Jewish law. And of course, as any rabbinic student knows, neither Judaism nor Jewish law is monolithic. But that does not mean that the Dogma of Dogmalessness, as I have referred to it elsewhere, reflects a valid prism through which to contemplate Jewish thought and Jewish philosophy.

There are limits to controversy and diversity within every system of law. There are parameters that serve to limit controversy with regard to more conventional areas of Jewish law and there are also limits to legitimate diversity with regard to matters of ideology and belief. A story is told of an American rabbinic scholar, the late Rabbi Jacob Ruderman, who was the head of the Ner Israel rabbinical seminary. Rabbi Ruderman once made an extremely caustic remark to a visitor whom he held in rather low regard. He said to him, "If you knew as many rabbinic responsa as I, you would be a gentile. If you were acquainted with as many precedents for leniencies as I can cite, your lifestyle would not be the lifestyle of an observant Jew." Why? Because that individual would have eclectically selected each one of those leniencies and have conducted himself accordingly. And, at some point, a person comporting himself in such a manner would have placed himself beyond the pale of the halakhic community. The same is true, *a fortiori*, with regard to matters of dogma. I can envision Benedictus de Spinoza waking up one morning, staring at his reflection in the mirror and saying, "Baruch Spinoza, if you knew as much philosophy as I, you would be a Spinozist!"

There is, however, a third formulation of the question "Was Spinoza a Jewish philosopher?" The third formulation of the question – the formulation which really requires thoughtful analysis – is: Was Spinoza's philosophical system spawned, either legitimately or illegitimately, by

Jewish thought and Jewish ideology? In order to arrive at any meaningful answer to that question, I believe that it is necessary to recognize that Spinoza struggled with a number of classic problems in Jewish philosophy and was profoundly influenced in one way or another by classical Jewish sources.

From its earliest days, Jewish philosophy has repeatedly come to grips with the problem of divine omniscience versus freedom of the will. If God knows everything in advance then human actions are predestined. If so, how can man be free? And if man is truly free, it would apparently follow that the Deity cannot have foreknowledge of human acts. Infallible knowledge of future events is possible only with regard to that which is necessary, as opposed to that which is merely contingent. Infallible knowledge, if it is indeed infallible, entails the necessity of that which is known. That vexing philosophical problem was addressed by Saadia Ga'on, by Judah ha-Levi, by Ibn Daud, by Maimonides and by virtually every one of Maimonides' successors.

For Spinoza, the dilemma was resolved by his acceptance of a form of determinism. But Spinoza was hardly the first person of Jewish birth, let alone of Jewish faith, to uphold determinism at the expense of freedom of the will. For that position Spinoza had a formidable precedent in the philosophical system of Hasdai Crescas.

However, for Spinoza the problem was even deeper than the clash between freedom of the will and omniscience. For Spinoza, there existed an even more troubling problem in the tension between the notion of omnipotence and the notion of freedom. That problem also was both well-known and much debated in both Jewish and Kalam philosophy. If God is all-powerful, and if that notion is understood literally, it means that God is not only potentially all-powerful but He is all-powerful in actuality, i.e., all power not only flows from God but is reserved to God and to God alone. But if God is all-powerful in actuality, it follows that man and man's will are bereft of any independent power and hence human freedom must be a chimera. Thus, Spinoza found yet another reason to reject the notion of an autonomous will.

Spinoza, moreover, rejects not only the reality of human freedom but extends his rejection to a rejection of freedom in any conventional philosophical sense, including freedom as attributed to the Deity. This again represents another area in which Spinoza struggles with problems that were integral to the Jewish philosophical tradition. And here again Spinoza was not struggling in a vacuum.

Ostensibly, there is a logical contradiction between positing a Deity who is a necessary being and at the same time ascribing freedom to that necessary being. "*Netzaḥ Yisra'el lo yeshaker ve-lo yinaḥem* – The Eternal of Israel will not lie nor will He change his mind" (I Samuel 15:29). If God is a necessary being how could He possibly change his mind? But if God cannot change His mind, then how can He intervene in the laws of nature? If the laws of nature are a manifestation of divine wisdom and if they are part and parcel of the divine blueprint for the government of the created universe, then a miracle, which represents a deviation from, and hence a violation of, natural law constitutes nothing less than a renunciation of eternal norms which emanate from the divine intellect. The Deity is a necessary, and hence unchanging, being. How, then, is God free to contravene His own laws of nature by working miracles? On the other hand, a Deity who is powerless to intervene in the natural order can hardly be said to be omnipotent.

Spinoza was certainly not the first to address that dilemma. The problem of miracles was recognized in Jewish sources long before a systematic Jewish philosophy was formulated by any Jewish thinker. The Midrash declares that a miracle originates in "a condition that The Holy One, blessed be He, stipulated with the artifacts of Creation" (*Bereishit Rabbah* 5:4). Indeed, what we are presented with in that classical text is a recognition of precisely this problem: How can there be both natural law and miracles at one and the same time? Or, to express the same problem in different words, how can God change His mind?

This rabbinic dictum might well be interpreted as declaring that the determination that a miracle will occur at a certain time was always inherent in the eternal intellect of the Deity. Since the divine will wills miracles in precisely the same manner as it willed the act of creation, miracles may be spoken of as willed by God from the moment of creation. Accordingly, the actual occurrence of a miraculous phenomenon does not represent a change either in His essence or in His will.

However, the rabbinic reference to a "condition" that was "stipulated" by the Deity is not a mere literary flourish; the nomenclature reflects a profound thesis. In resolving the dilemma posed by the apparently contradictory notions of divine freedom versus the necessary nature of God and of miracles versus divinely willed immutable laws of nature, the Midrash is actually advancing the thesis that all miracles are inherent in the natural order. Although to the perceiver, who is accustomed to regularity in nature, the miraculous events may seem to be incompatible with the laws of nature and hence rationally inexplicable, in actuality, the exceptional occurrences as well as the usual and regular phenomena are subsumed under a more general law of nature that is not immediately grasped by the human intellect. A clock may be programmed to skip a tick every sixty minutes. A clock-gazer who observes that phenomenon for the first time will regard the event as an aberration. Only with the passage of a significant number of hours and multiple observations of that peculiar phenomenon will he be able accurately and precisely to reconstruct the law of clockology in accordance with which the clockmaker has regulated his clocks.

However, in Spinoza's *Tractatus* we find a rejection of the notion of a divine will that is co-eternal with the divine essence. And if divine will does not coexist with the divine essence a freely undertaken act of creation could not occur and, by the same token, there cannot be any form of contingency with regard to natural events.

Thus we encounter in Spinoza a recognition and acceptance of serious problems coupled with rejection of the manifold theses that have been advanced in resolution of those problems throughout the course of the history of Jewish philosophy. Most significant is Spinoza's rejection of the notion of the divine will as co-eternal with the divine essence. That rejection is a direct outgrowth of other aspects of Spinoza's philosophical system. As did the classical Jewish philosophers, Spinoza came to grips with the problem of divine attributes. If God is a unitary being, if He is One in the sense that He is not composed of parts, if He is One in the sense that He is *ousia* par excellence, i.e., that He is pure and simple being and hence there cannot conceivably be any multiplicity in His essence or nature, how is it possible to ascribe attributes to God? The problem of divine attributes was resolved in a variety of ways by medieval Jewish philosophers.

For Spinoza, the problem is not really a problem because Spinoza rejects the conventional theological view regarding the nature of the Deity. According to Spinoza, the entire universe consists of but a single substance. That substance, however, exists in conjunction with an infinite number of attributes. For Spinoza, the Deity and the universe are one and the same. In effect, Spinoza is willing to accept a kind of Monist position with regard to the essence of the Deity and, at one and the same time, to ascribe a multiplicity of attributes to that substance. In effect, Spinoza dismisses the problem of attributes to that substance. In effect, Spinoza dismisses the problem of divine attributes with a wave of his philosophical wand.

A related problem with which Spinoza also grapples stems from the age-old recognition that there is an apparent contradiction between the infinite nature of the Deity and the finite nature of the material universe. As Crescas formulated the problem, one thing cannot be the cause of another thing unless that which is caused is part of the essence of that which is its cause. The effect must be related in some manner to the essence of the cause. However, since the finite is so drastically different from the infinite, how can the infinite possibly be the source of the finite? Or, to pose the problem in the terminology of Gersonides, form cannot be the source of matter because form is totally different from matter and hence matter cannot emanate from form. That problem led Gersonides to acceptance of the existence of a *homer hiyulei* that is eternal. Gersonides posited the existence of a hylic substance that is material in nature but which is eternal just as the Deity is eternal. For having espoused such a radical position, his philosophical work, *Milḥamot ha-Shem*, was derisively referred to as *Milḥamot Neged ha-Shem*, i.e., *Wars Against God* rather than *Wars on Behalf of God*.

It was this problem that led the Kabbalists to formulate the doctrine of *creatio ex essentia Dei* in place of the less complex notion of *creatio ex nihilo*. The kabbalistic doctrine, which regards the created universe as the product of emanations from the essence of the Deity, was designed to explain how a finite entity can proceed from an infinite being. This concept is expressed in kabbalistic literature in the doctrine of *tzimtzum*, i.e., the notion of "contraction" or self-limitation on the part of the Deity.

In focusing upon a different aspect of the problem, the Kabbalists argued that, if God is infinite, there is then no room in the universe for the existence of anything else. "*Hu mekomo shel olam* – God is the locus of the world" (*Bereishit Rabbah* 68:10), or, in other words, the whole world is suffused by the Deity. And if God fills the entire universe then there cannot possibly be room for anything else. And conversely, if a finite universe does exist, there can be no place in that finite universe for an infinite Deity. The Kabbalists resolved the problem by appealing to the doctrine of *tzimtzum* based in part upon the rabbinic aphorism "*Hu mekomo shel olam ve-ein ha-olam mekomo* – God is the locus in which the world exists but the world is not the locus of God's existence."

For pantheists, God and nature are one and the same; for pantheists, God and the universe are one and the same. Hence, *voilà*, there is no longer any problem with regard to how the finite could possibly emanate from the infinite because, although everything is encompassed within the infinite, the infinite is nothing more than an aggregate of finitudes.

In his *Epistola*, Spinoza refers to a certain well-known kabbalistic work, *Pardes Rimmonim*, in which the author, Rabbi Moses Cordovero, develops what some contemporary writers depict as a form of pantheism. Some writers have attempted to identify the pantheism of Spinoza with the doctrine earlier espoused by R. Moses Cordovero and with the doctrine that they see reflected later, after Spinoza, in the writings of the kabbalistic thinker, Rabbi Chaim Vital. In point of fact, the defenders of the kabbalistic tradition vigorously argue that the theory that was expounded in those kabbalistic sources is not pantheism but something that can best be termed panentheism. They reject the notion that the universe and the Deity are one and the same; rather, they assert that the universe and the Deity coexist in the same place at the same time in a manner that may well defy human understanding. On occasion, I have used a little parable to explain this metaphysical phenomenon. Imagine for a moment that a fire breaks out in an apartment. The fire produces a vast amount of smoke and that smoke permeates a clothes closet. If a person were to open the closet he would find the closet to be permeated by smoke but the clothes would nevertheless continue to appear to fill the closet in its entirety. The smoke infiltrates the garments in the closet and ensconces itself within the various strands of fabric. The smoke penetrates the space between the molecules of the fabric. Yet the smoke has certainly not fused with the material to which it adheres and become an integral part of the material of which those clothes are woven. The smoke continues to constitute a separate and distinct substance.

Spinoza, however, rejects panentheism in favor of pantheism in formulating a facile solution to the problem of the generation of the finite from the infinite. For Spinoza there is no problem at all. God and nature are identified as a single entity; the infinite is identified with the finite and the two become one and the same.

I believe it is accurate to describe the philosophy of Spinoza as a system that grapples with hard questions. But there are two ways of dealing with a hard question. The first is to discover or formulate an answer to the question. If I want to determine whether or not Socrates is mortal I start with the major premise "All men are mortal," then proceed to the minor premise "Socrates is a man" and thus arrive at the conclusion that "Socrates is mortal." I may then explain that this conclusion is necessitated by Aristotlean logic and follows from the very nature of the form of the syllogism rather than from its empirical content. I may also use Boolean diagrams to demonstrate exactly the same point.

But there is another way of responding to the question "Is Socrates mortal?" And that is by recognizing that Socrates may not be a man at all; rather "Socrates" may be a cat endowed with nine lives or "Socrates" may be the devil incarnate. If either is the case, an attempt to construct an Aristotelian syllogism will not prove to be a fruitful avenue for finding an answer to the question. The second method of dealing with the problem involves nothing other than rejection of one or more of the premises. Indeed, if the premises are erroneous there is really no need to seek answers. Problems often present themselves in the guise of premises that appear to be antithetical to one another. Hence, if one fails to accept one or the other of those premises the problem simply evaporates. When there is no problem, no solution is required.

Despite the fact that contemporary scholars such as Edwin Curley and Richard Mason have striven valiantly to defend Spinoza from the charge of pantheism, it seems to me that the doctrine of *Deus sive Natura* was designed precisely as a means of denying a cardinal theological premise, a premise that gave rise to many of the classical problems of philosophy in general and of Jewish philosophy in particular. The doctrine of *Deus sive Natura* was basic to Spinoza's philosophical system because it was a way of enabling him to avoid any further grappling with those problems.

In effect, Spinoza has redefined God out of existence. The effect of that redefinition upon philosophical discourse is entirely parallel to the effect that defining Socrates as a cat would have upon the paradigmatic Aristotlean syllogism. If there is no Deity as the theologians understood the term, the problems that philosophers and theologians have struggled with for millennia turn out to be chimeras.

I would venture to add that, if we are talking about whether or not Spinoza was a Jewish philosopher, this is yet another un-Jewish aspect of his philosophy. Traditional Jewish thought engages in head-on confrontation rather than in avoidance of ideological debate. What challenge is there in not having to grapple with philosophical problems? Denial of premises may be convenient but it is hardly satisfying.

"Friends, Romans, countrymen, lend me your ears. I come to bury Caesar, not to praise him. The evil that men do lives after them. The good is oft interred with their bones. So let it be with Caesar." Since I subscribe to the notion of free will, I must leave it to you to decide whether the same can and should be said of Spinoza. For me, and for all exponents of classical Jewish teaching, Spinoza's philosophical system is, at best, the illegitimate issue of authentic precursors. As such, it is beyond the pale of Jewish philosophy.

5

"Lo Ba-Shamayim Hi":
A Philosophical *Pilpul*

I.

One of the most remarkable and unique aspects of Jewish belief, according to Maimonides, lies in the circumscribed nature of the authority of revelation. Torah is divine but *"lo ba-shamayim hi* – it is not in the heavens" (Deuteronomy 30:12). The revelation at Sinai was exhaustive in nature and the Torah was given to man in its entirety. No aspect of Torah was withheld as subject to ongoing jurisdiction.

From this doctrine flow two basic principles. First, since there is no longer a residue of unrevealed Torah in the heavens there cannot be a second substantive revelation. Such a revelation, were it to occur, would be devoid of content. Hence any claim with regard to supplementary revelation must be dismissed peremptorily even if it were in no way to conflict with Sinaitic revelation. Secondly, this doctrine excludes not merely further innovative revelation but, according to Maimonides, it excludes clarificatory revelation as well. Not only can new commandments not be added to the Torah by means of revelation but, moreover, matters of question, doubt, interpretation and application with regard to the content of existing revelation cannot be resolved on the basis of even revelation which is entirely clarificatory in nature.[1]

This doctrine together with these attendant principles could well be understood simply as a corollary to Maimonides' Ninth Principle which affirms the immutability of Torah. As Maimonides himself writes, "This implies that this Law of Moses will not be abrogated and that no other law will come from before God. Nothing is to be added to it nor taken away from it, neither in the written nor in the oral law, as it is said, Thou shalt not add to it nor diminish from it'" (Deuteronomy 13:1).

An addition constitutes a change; a new law superimposed upon an existing corpus of law effects and entirely new system of law. Similarly, explanation, elucidation and commentary are, in a fundamental sense, forms of "addition," since they produce an understanding previously lacking and provide the basis for novel application. Not infrequently, a fresh insight into a timeless text yields a radically changed perspective. Revelatory change, even of such nature, is not possible. Indeed in the *Mishneh Torah, Hilkhot Yesodei ha-Torah* 9:1, Maimonides cites the verse, "It is not in the heavens" and the principle derived therefrom as simply a reiteration of the biblical injunction, "Thou shalt not add to it nor diminish from it." It is in the same context that Maimonides continues in *Hilkhot Yesodei ha-Torah* 9:4 with the statement, "Similarly, ...if, with regard to one of the laws of the Torah, [the prophet] declares that God commanded him that the law is thus and so or that the ruling is in accordance with the words of so-and-so, he is a false prophet and is to be executed by strangling."[2]

One eminent authority, the *Brisker Rav*, R. Isaac Ze'ev Soloveitchik, finds yet a third principle inherent in the doctrine "It is not in the heavens." The Gemara, *Temurah* 16a, reports:

1. This doctrine should not be understood as excluding divine assistance in such matters in a manner which is not prophetic in nature. Maimonides himself, *Teshuvot ha-Rambam* (Jerusalem, 5694), no. 371, writes, "I will reply in accordance with what I have been taught by Heaven."
2. Nahmanides, *Commentary on the Bible*, Deuteronomy 13:4, affirms that a prophet who attempts to promulgate a new commandment allegedly at the divine behest is not to be heeded, but expresses doubt with regard to whether or not the individual is to be executed as a false prophet.

R. Judah stated in the name of Samuel: Three thousand *halakhot* were forgotten during the period of mourning for Moses. [The people] said to Joshua, "Ask!" [Joshua] said to them, "It is not in the heavens." [The people] said to Samuel, "Ask!" [Samuel] said to them, "'These are the commandments' (Leviticus 27:34) – for the prophet has no dispensation to innovate with regard to any matter."

The text contains an apparent redundancy. The request addressed to Samuel is identical with the request earlier dismissed by Joshua. Yet, although Joshua rejected the plea brought to him simply by applying the dictum *"lo ba-shamayim hi,"* Samuel left constrained to invoke the doctrine expounded in *Shabbat* 104a (as well as in *Yoma* 80a and *Megillah* 2b), viz., "These are the *mitzvot*," from which it is inferred that these are the *mitzvot* and there can be no others, i.e., a prophet dare not promulgate new *mitzvot*.

The *Brisker Rav*[3] suggests that the request addressed to Samuel was significantly different from that which was addressed to Joshua. A void was created through failure to remember the laws in question. Samuel was asked to remedy the situation by means of his own prophetic prowess. He was asked, in effect, to request divine re-enactment of legislation to fill the lacunae. To this demand Samuel's reply was, *"These* are the *mitzvot,"* i.e., prophets subsequent to Moses do not function as lawgivers. Hence Samuel could not serve as the channel for renewed promulgation of even the selfsame laws. The demand earlier addressed to Joshua was, in a sense, much more modest in scope. It was not a demand for new legislation but simply a plea that Joshua use his powers of prophecy in order to discover the law which had already been revealed to Moses. Those laws would then have been binding, not by virtue of Joshua's authority, but simply because Joshua's prophecy would have enabled him to "remember" that which had already been revealed to Moses. His function would have been that of a reporter, not of a lawgiver. To this demand Joshua answered, "It is not in the heavens."

---

3. Ḥiddushei ha-Griz (Jerusalem, 5726), *Temurah* 16a.

The implication of this interpretation of the talmudic text is that not only does the prophet lack authority to change the law or to clarify points of obscurity – all of which contain elements of change – but he dare not even use his prophetic power simply for purposes of recall even though the product would be entirely identical with that which was already explicitly expounded by Moses. The implication of *"lo ba-shamayim hi"* is that, not only is there no residual Torah in heaven, but that no duplicate even of the already revealed Torah will be forthcoming upon application to the Heavenly Academy. Accordingly, not only are resolution of doubt and interpretation of ambiguity left to human reason, but even reconstruction of seventeen hundred of the forgotten points of law could be undertaken by Othniel ben Kenaz only on the basis of halakhic dialectic.[4]

The principle *"lo ba-shamayim hi"* as the expression of a doctrine which establishes the impossibility of a subsequent revelation superseding the Sinaitic revelation is certainly a cornerstone of Jewish teaching and presents no philosophical difficulty. The broadening of this doctrine into a dogma precluding prophetic resolution of ambiguity or doubt is somewhat problematic and, as will be shown, was not universally accepted. Interpretation of the doctrine as excluding prophetic intuition of the already revealed Torah presents a major philosophical difficulty with regard to a proper understanding of Maimonides' view of the nature of prophecy. If, as Maimonides believes, the essence of prophetic experience is a state of communion between the human intellect and the Active Intellect enabling the human mind to share in cognition characteristic of the Active Intellect, how is it that the prophet cannot in this manner achieve prophetic intuition of the subject matter of Torah?

II.

The major difficulty which must be resolved in any analysis of Maimonides' view of prophecy is an understanding of the role played by God in the prophetic experience. There are two possibilities. First, that prophetic insight is no different from a perception experienced through any of the five senses in that prophetic experience results from natural

---

4. See *Temurah* 16a.

development of the human faculties. This "sixth sense" differs from the other senses only in that it can be actualized solely by a person possessing an appropriate physical and mental constitution, who leads a moral life, and who has been properly educated and trained. The *shefa* (inspirational overflow) of prophecy lies outside of man waiting to be grasped by the combined action of the rational and imaginative faculties much in the same manner as material objects are grasped by the physical forces inherent in the body. To be sure, divine will can prevent man from achieving prophetic powers, but it requires no specific action on the part of God to grant those powers. In denying prophecy to the prepared and qualified person, God is actually performing a miracle just as it would require a miracle to induce a state of paralysis in a body that is totally lacking physical or chemical defects. The second possibility is that while indeed it is impossible to achieve prophetic powers without first attaining intellectual and moral perfection, final consummation in the state of prophecy is impossible without a specific act on the part of the divine will. God not only denies prophecy by an act of will but also grants it only upon a specific act of His will.

The terminology used by Maimonides, *Guide*, Part II, chapter 32, in presenting his theory of prophecy would seem to bear out this second interpretation. After stating the necessary prerequisites for attaining prophecy, Maimonides states, "and God can cause whosoever He desires to prophesy, whensoever He desires." This statement seems to support the presumption that the will of God is an essential condition of prophecy and thus the selection of the person to whom the prophetic experience will occur and the time of its occurrence are contingent upon the will of God. Again in the same chapter Maimonides states, "This is our thesis: It [prophecy] is impossible without training and perfection, then it depends on the edict of God [whether] the possibility inherent in him [is to be turned into reality]." Here again Maimonides does not seem to be referring to a denial of prophetic power, but rather to the conferring of such power. If so, achievement of the prophetic state is dependent upon an act of the divine will. Further support for this interpretation may be found in Maimonides' discussion of the distinctions between the prophecy of Moses and that of other prophets. In his *Commentary on the Mishnah*, introduction to Ḥelek, Maimonides states:

> For with regard to all prophets, the spirit of prophecy does not rest upon them at their will but upon the will of God, blessed be He, for a prophet may remain days or years without receiving prophecy and he may request of the Creator that he make known to him a certain matter by means of prophecy.

The action of a prophet in pleading that a specific thing be made known to him through a prophetic vision would seem to imply that a specific act of the divine will is a requisite of each individual prophetic experience. This view of Maimonides' doctrine of prophecy is upheld by Shem Tob in his comments on the opening section of Part II, chapter 36, of the *Guide* as well as by *Leḥem Mishneh* in his commentary on *Hilkhot Yesodei ha-Torah* 7:1. Abarbanel, in his commentary on Part II, chapter 32, of the *Guide*, while rejecting this interpretation of Maimonides' doctrine, quotes earlier commentators, including Crescas and Albo, who were of a like opinion.

Although the above cited textual statement would seem to confirm this view, there is also ample evidence pointing in the opposite direction, namely, to the conclusion that a specific act on the part of God is not necessary to induce the prophetic state and that divine will functions with regard to prophecy only when it intervenes in order to deny attainment of the prophetic experience. This is the view espoused by Abarbanel in his analysis of Maimonides' doctrine in his commentary on chapter 32.

Perhaps the most striking evidence substantiating this view is that, while in the summary of the nature of prophecy presented in chapter 7 of *Hilkhot Yesodei ha-Torah* Maimonides enumerates all of the qualifications necessary for attainment of prophecy and describes the prophetic experience in detail, he makes no mention whatsoever of a role reserved to divine will. Nor does Maimonides mention this aspect of the prophetic experience in his discussion of belief in prophecy as one of the thirteen Principles of Faith in his *Commentary on the Mishnah*. If the will of God is significant solely in a negative way, i.e., only in the denial of prophecy, it is not at all astonishing that Maimonides fails to mention this phenomenon in these two discussions. For Maimonides, belief in the actual existence of prophecy is a cardinal principal of faith.

This, for Maimonides, is not a matter of abstract theory, but of practical halakhah. In both instances he is engaged in a careful delineation of the essence of prophecy and how it may be recognized. He may well have considered the phenomenon of the denial of prophetic power to a fully qualified and capable individual as having no halakhic implication and therefore have deemed it sufficient to discuss its philosophical implications in the *Guide*. Much more devastating to the opposing view is Maimonides' explicit statement in *Hilkhot Yesodei ha-Torah* 7:1 that when a person has perfected himself intellectually and morally, "immediately the holy spirit rests upon him." Here Maimonides clearly states that prophecy is the culmination of man's goal in striving for intellectual and moral perfection and the resultant prophetic state is not dependent upon a particular act of the divine will. Again in *Hilkhot Yesodei ha-Torah* 7:4, in listing the impediments to achieving prophecy, Maimonides enumerates melancholy and laziness and speaks of happiness as the only additional qualification required by a person otherwise prepared for prophecy. Furthermore, in *Hilkhot Yesodei ha-Torah* 7:6, in speaking of Moses' prophetic powers, Maimonides states that Moses would achieve the prophetic state at will because he was always emotionally prepared for prophecy. If a specific act of the divine will is necessary for each separate prophetic experience, the mere achievement of "happiness" and the absence of melancholy and laziness would not guarantee entry into the prophetic state. Similarly, the ability of Moses to prophesy at will would not be contingent solely upon his emotional preparedness but also upon the consent of God to communicate with Moses at the latter's desire.

III.

In order to resolve the difficulty to which this maze of conflicting textual evidence gives rise it should be noted that in the early chapters of his discussion of prophecy in the *Guide*, Maimonides fails to distinguish between prophecy as a state of intellectual contemplation or a beatific experience of God, and prophecy as a vehicle through which future events are foretold to man. For this reason, Maimonides, in chapter 32, is able to speak of the prophecy of Moses as being of the highest degree, in this case using the term "prophecy" as meaning that

Moses' comprehension of the Deity was of the highest order since Moses experienced the clearest and most complete revelation of the essence of God of which a mortal is capable, without at the same time finding it incongruous to cite Joel 3:1 which refers to prophecy as the medium through which future events are made known to man. Maimonides' concern in these chapters is primarily with an explication of the metaphysical nature of the prophetic experience. Maimonides' statement in chapter 37 declaring that a person may receive prophecy which enables him not only to perfect himself but also to influence others, does not imply influence over mundane affairs by virtue of prescient knowledge of future events, but refers to influence in the sense of assistance to others in acquiring metaphysical knowledge. Maimonides thus implies only that it may be possible for the prophet to communicate his own mystical experience to others. It is not until chapter 38 that Maimonides explicitly takes note of the second and perhaps more popular aspect of prophecy – that of foretelling future events. The reason for this is obvious. Prophecy as a means of acquiring information concerning events which lie in the future is impossible without attaining a prophetic state of intellectual contemplation. Once this state has been attained the power to foretell future events does not require a separate faculty in itself, but merely the application of this already acquired intellectual faculty:

> This same faculty enables some persons to foretell important coming events. The prophets must have had these two forces, courage and intuition, highly developed, and these were still more strengthened when they were under the influence of the Active Intellect.

With the recognition that at times Maimonides refers to one aspect of prophecy and at times to the other all apparent contradictions may be resolved. While this distinction is far from explicit in Maimonides' writings it would seem that we may interpret Maimonides' description of the prophetic experience as it encompasses the knowledge of future events beyond the capacity of faculties of "courage and imagination" of the ordinary man is contingent upon an act of the divine will.

It seems rather odd that while at times the prophet is able to make use of his faculties of "courage and imagination" to draw inferences whereby he is able to predict future events with extreme clarity and detail at other times the prophet is completely ignorant of matters not directly observable. Moses was astonished when he beheld the golden calf and broke the tablets in a fit of sudden anger; Jonah had no intimation whatsoever that the people of Nineveh would repent. Abarbanel, citing various instances of prophetic prediction, objects that the description of such future events is much too detailed and specific to be the product of the imaginative faculty. It may be surmised that Maimonides would reply that it is ultimately an act on the part of God working upon the faculties of "courage and imagination" which leads the mind to prophetic induction. Note Maimonides' words in chapter 38: "Under the influence of the Active Intellect these two powers [courage and imagination] become strengthened." In this passage Maimonides seems to be referring to an act outside and beyond the activity of man alone. Since in his previous discussion Maimonides speaks first of one and then of the other of the dual aspects of prophecy without clarifying to which of the two he makes reference we may rightfully assume that when he states in chapter 32 "and God can cause whosoever He desires to prophesy, whensoever He desires," Maimonides is referring to the aspect of prophecy which enables the prophet to foretell future events. Maimonides can therefore state that one who has the necessary prerequisites for prophecy, and hence has reached the state of prophetic enlightenment, may be delegated by God, whenever He so desires, to announce future happenings. The further statement in chapter 32, "then [actualization of] the possibility inherent in him is an edict of God, blessed be He," may be readily understood as indicating that actual employment of these faculties for prophesying with regard to the future depends upon the edict of God.

It is clear for yet another reason that in his statement in the *Commentary on the Mishnah*, "And he may request of the Creator that he make known to him a certain matter by means of prophecy," Maimonides can be speaking only of the knowledge of future events. Here, in discussing the difference between the prophetic powers of Moses and those of other prophets, Maimonides states that Moses was at all times capable of communication with God but that there is no way in which other prophets could assure themselves of this accessibility. However, in *Hilkhot Yesodei ha-Torah* 7:6, in a repetition of the identical statement concerning Moses, Maimonides implies that, barring a state of melancholy or laziness described in *Hilkhot Yesodei ha-Torah* 7:4, God is accessible to other prophets just as He was to Moses, the only difference being that Moses was always in a state of preparedness. However, this contradiction is readily resolved if we understand Maimonides' words in the *Commentary on the Mishnah* as having reference to information concerning terrestrial matters not readily available to man save through prophetic means. In that context he quotes the verse in which the prophet tells Jehoshaphat that he will be successful in war against Moab. In *Hilkhot Yesodei ha-Torah* Maimonides is referring to the prophetic experience as a clear understanding of metaphysical matters which does not require a specific act of the divine will. With regard to this aspect of the prophetic experience Moses differed from other prophets in that he was in a constant state of readiness, not in that God chose to communicate with him at all times and did not so choose with regard to other prophets.[5]

---

5. This analysis of Maimonides' position negates a possible resolution of minor difficulty with regard to the proper understanding of *Hilkhot Teshuvah* 3:8. Maimonides classifies heretics variously as *minim*, *apikorsim*, deniers of the Torah and *mumrim*. In *Hilkhot Teshuvah* 3:8 Maimonides states:

> These [categories of people] are called *apikorsim*: he who declares that there is no prophecy at all and that there is no knowledge which reaches from the Creator to the intellect of human beings; he who denies the prophecy of Moses, our teacher; and he who declares that the Creator does not know the deeds of human beings.

Denial of the "prophecy of Moses" might well be understood as synonymous with denial of the divine nature of the Torah. Yet this interpretation does not seem to be correct since in the very same section, *Hilkhot Teshuvah* 3:8, Maimonides posits three categories of individuals who are called "deniers of the Torah" whose status is identical to that of the *apikores*. The first to be enumerated under that classification is "he who says that the Torah is not from God." Hence "he who denies the prophecy of Moses" should presumably be understood in an entirely different sense, *viz.*, as one who denies the unique nature of Moses' prophecy.

According to this understanding, denial of prophecy and denial of the prophecy of Moses are closely related heresies. Yet, the relationship between these heresies and denial of God's knowledge of man is not at all clear. However, if it is posited that

This distinction between the two aspects of prophecy also serves to refute a number of Abarbanel's objections to Maimonides' doctrine of prophecy. Abarbanel's first objection is to Maimonides' statement that "when this influence reaches both faculties together, i.e., the logical and the imaginative, in their most perfect created condition – this is the power of prophets." Abarbanel argues that if Maimonides is correct then all prophecy must occur in parables and riddles. Thereupon Abarbanel cites numerous examples of clear and explicit prophecies resorting to neither parables nor riddles. It would seem that Maimonides' position in this matter is quite clear. Man finds it impossible truly to comprehend metaphysical concepts with his rational faculty alone. Man's mind is so constructed that even the prophetic inspiration cannot make these concepts known to man through his rational faculty alone. For this reason such information is made known to prophets in an allegorical manner through the medium of the imaginative faculty. This is only insofar as the first aspect of prophecy, that of intellectual contemplation, is concerned. Maimonides would say that once the prophetic state has been attained through the combined action of the rational faculty and the imaginative faculty, the logical faculty may make use of its perfection through prophecy in order to foretell future events. This second aspect of prophecy, since in itself it is not metaphysical in nature, is capable of being grasped by the logical or rational faculty without concomitant employment of the imaginative faculty and hence there is no need for the prophet to resort to parables and riddles when he is not discussing metaphysical concepts. Although the prophetic state cannot be achieved without employment of the imaginative faculty, Maimonides would say that knowledge of future events is, in itself, *not* dependent upon the imaginative faculty and the imaginative faculty need play no part in this aspect of prophecy. The logical faculty merely makes use (with or without an act of the divine will) of the intellectual and metaphysical knowledge gleaned

---

prophecy requires an overt divine act, the relationship is quite obvious: God cannot cause an individual to receive a prophetic experience unless He has knowledge both of the person and of the fact that he is deserving of prophecy. Accordingly, the various *apikorsim* are persons who deny some aspect of divine knowledge. However, if as has here been argued, the prophetic experience is not contingent upon a divine act, the relationship between denial of prophecy and denial of divine knowledge is obscure.

through both faculties in order to deduce and infer events which lie in the future. Obviously this contradicts Abarbanel's inference in chapter 36, to the effect that, according to Maimonides, future events are known by the prophet by means of the imaginative faculty. Moses, it should be remembered, was able to achieve even metaphysical knowledge solely through the use of the logical faculty without recourse to imagination. Lesser prophets were able to achieve only precognition without direct employment of the imaginative faculty.

This analysis of Maimonides' doctrine of prophecy, since it basically affirms the naturalistic notion of prophecy, leaves our original problem unresolved: How is it that the prophet, even when in a state of communion with the Active Intellect, cannot become aware of the contents of the Sinaitic revelation?

IV.

Were Maimonides' position to be understood as interpreted by some of his twentieth century rabbinic commentators the problem would cease to exist. Rabbi Menachem Krakovsky, *Avodat ha-Melekh* (Vilna, 5691), *Hilkhot Yesodei ha-Torah* 9:4, asserts that Maimonides does not at all deny the phenomenon of prophetic insight in matters of Torah knowledge. The terminology employed by Maimonides is "Or if [the prophet] declares that God commanded him that the law is thus and so or the ruling is in accordance with the opinion of so-and-so he is a false prophet." *Avodat ha-Melekh* draws a distinction between use of the prophetic faculty as a basis for theoretical understanding of Torah and establishment of normative halakhah on the basis of a prophetic claim. *"Lo ba-shamayim hi,"* according to this interpretation, precludes only the establishment of normative halakhah. All human faculties, including the prophetic, may be harnessed and employed in the understanding of Torah. All insights, including those based upon the prophetic faculty, must be examined in the crucible of human reason and measured against the canons of halakhic dialectic. The prophet's opinions and arguments must be given careful consideration but are not to be regarded as infallible. Only when the prophet claims that "God commanded him" and sought to convey a definitive halakhic ruling through the medium of prophecy does he stand condemned by his own mouth as a false prophet.[6]

Were this interpretation of Maimonides' position to be accepted as correct our problem would be resolved. The prophet is not denied intellectual perspective. He is denied only knowledge of normative halakhic determination when such determination is otherwise not achievable by human intellect. It may perhaps be bold to say so, but such normative determination is not *denied* the prophet. The prophet is branded a "false prophet" not because he claims knowledge which God has denied him, but because he claims knowledge which does not exist. The concept "These and those are the words of the living God"[7] implies that from the transcendental vantage point of the divine lawgiver all conflicting opinions and all ambiguities are intentionally inherent in the halakhic corpus itself. Man must make the necessary legal determinations on the basis of human reason utilizing the appropriate canon of interpretation and halakhic decision-making. That is a human activity and hence cannot be the subject matter of independent divine insight. Absent the human determination, there is nothing for God to know, just as, in a parallel manner, there can be no divine knowledge of the determination of a free will unless at some point a choice is actually made by man.

Appealing as this resolution may seem, it appears to be contradicted by the words of Maimonides himself. The selfsame doctrine which is presented in the *Mishneh Torah* is also formulated by Maimonides in the introduction to his *Commentary on the Mishnah* – but in different words:

> Similarly, if the prophet shall testify that the Holy One, blessed be He, said to him that the law with regard to a certain *mitzvah*

---

6. Essentially the same thesis is advanced by R. Aaron Marcus in his preface to *She'elot u-Teshuvot min ha-Shamayim* (Jerusalem, 5717), p. 10. This author states that Maimonides speaks only of a prophet who claimed that "God told him that the halakhah is thus and that those who disagree must accept his opinion and are not permitted to persist in their determination."

7. *Gittin* 6b.

is thus and so or that a certain explanation is true, that prophet should be put to death for he is a false prophet....

The syntax of the statement in the *Commentary on the Mishnah* is strikingly parallel to Maimonides' ruling in the *Mishneh Torah* but contains two significant variations. Although in the *Mishneh Torah* Maimonides employs the phrase "God *commanded* him," in the *Commentary* his terminology is, "God *said* to him." First, the verb "said" certainly does not have the connotation "commanded." Even if one were to translate the verb as "declare," rendering its meaning closer to that of "commanded" and hence as connoting the declaration of a definitive ruling, the second phrase "that the halakhah is in accordance with the words of so-and-so," certainly does not have a like connotation. The term *"sevarah"* meaning "explanation" or "theory," does not at all appear to be limited to a definitive halakhic ruling.[8] Moreover, in his *Commentary on the Mishnah*, Maimonides declares, "God did not permit us to learn [Torah] from the prophets but only from the wise men." Since prophets are not forbidden to share their insights with others the clear implication is that *qua* prophets they are not privy to such insights.

R. Meir Simchah ha-Kohen of Dvinsk asserts that, for Maimonides, revelation may be a source of halakhic determination in one restricted sense. In his commentary on the *Mishneh Torah, Or Sameaḥ, ad locum,* this authority points to the report found in *Eruvin* 13b regarding a *bat kol*[9] which proclaimed the halakhah to be in accordance with

---

8. This comment is based upon the Ibn Tibbon translation of the text and, regardless of its accuracy as a translation, reflects a definite interpretation of Maimonides' position by one of his own contemporaries. The Kafih translation reads:

    וכן אם אמר הנביא שה' אמר לו כי הפסק במצוה פלונית כך, ושדינו של פלוני הוא הנכון הרי אותו הנביא נהרג לפי שהוא נביא שקר.

    Moreover, Rabbenu Nissim Ga'on, *Berakhot* 19b, unequivocally states:

    לא בשמים היא, כלומר כי תורת ה' תמימה וכבר נתנה לנו בסיני והודיענו כי אינו מחליף ממנה דיבור אחד ואין בתורתנו חסרון ולא ספק כדי שנצטרך אל ראיה מן השמים.

9. The nature of a *bat kol* is discussed by Maimonides in the *Guide of the Perplexed,* II, chap. 42. The *bat kol,* although a form of divine communication, is not prophetic in nature and may be perceived by persons who have not attained the state of perfection which is requisite for prophecy. See *Kuzari,* III, 41 and 73; Nahmanides, *Commentary on the Bible,* Exodus 38:30; and R. Zevi Hirsch Chajes, *Imrei Binah,* chap.

Bet Hillel in their various disputes with Bet Shammai. The phenomenon of a heavenly voice proclaiming halakhic norms quite apparently violated Maimonides' understanding of *"lo ba-shamayim hi."* Or Sameaḥ postulates that the subject matter of that *bat kol* is substantively different from that which Maimonides excludes from the purview of prophetic revelation. Torah cannot be the subject of a new revelation and hence cannot be revealed to a prophet. Even a decision adjudicating between two conflicting views in a particular dispute cannot be the subject of prophetic revelation because establishment of a halakhic norm is part of the halakhic process and hence an aspect of Torah. The *bat kol* of *Eruvin,* insists Or Sameaḥ, must be understood as "meta-halakhic" rather than halakhic; it did not serve to establish any particular halakhah but rather the relative credentials of the contending halakhists. The latter, while having important and obvious ramifications in the establishment of halakhah is in essence a matter of *persona,* not of halakhah *per se.* By way of parallel, one can point to the discussion of Rabbi Zevi Hirsch Chajes, *Torat Nevi'im,* chapter 2 and addendum 9, in which he demonstrates that matters of a factual nature may properly be determined on the basis of prophecy even though such facts have an immediate bearing upon halakhic determinations.[10] Similarly, knowledge of the qualifications and authority of halakhic decisors is not excluded from the prophetic experience since it is not halakhah *per se.*

The major difficulty attendant upon Or Sameaḥ's thesis is that in the *Mishneh Torah* Maimonides lists as an example of a matter beyond the pale of prophecy a declaration to the effect that "the halakhah is in accordance with the words of so-and-so."

---

6. Friedlander's comment that a *bat kol* is "something uncommon or supernatural but no real revelation" is inaccurate and should be amended to read "but no real *prophetic* revelation." It is precisely because the *bat kol* is a form of revelation that it appears to contradict the principle *"lo ba-shamayim hi."*

10. This distinction was earlier formulated by R. Chaim Joseph David Azulai, in his *Birkei Yosef, Oraḥ Ḥayyim* 32:4; *Pnei David, Parshat Beshalaḥ;* and in *Shem ha-Gedolim, Maʾarekhet Gedolim, yud,* no. 224, and is also espoused by Marcus, *op. cit.,* pp. 11 and 13. This distinction was, however, expressly rejected by an earlier authority, Maharam ibn Ḥabib, *Tosefot Yom ha-Kippurim,* p. 3af.

According to *Or Sameah*'s analysis, the text must be read as accommodating only the restricted meaning "or the halakhah is in accordance with so-and-so in a *specific instance*" as distinct from a general endorsement of the pre-eminent halakhic prowess of the same authority. In light of Maimonides' theory of prophecy, the inability of the prophet to utilize his unique powers in understanding matters pertaining to the study of Torah can probably best be understood as a partial denial of prophetic power. Maimonides asserts that although an individual possesses the requisite perfections and preparations for prophecy he may yet be denied the prophetic experience. If this experience may be withheld *in toto* from some individuals it is only logical to assume that it may be denied in part to all. The dictum *"lo ba-shamayim hi"* may then be understood not simply as a statement concerning revelation but as the establishment of a curb upon the prophetic experience. The net effect is, of course, a vast enhancement of the role of reason in the application of halakhah.

V.

Quite apart from the inherent philosophical problem, Maimonides' position seems to be contradicted by a number of talmudic statements. Although there are numerous talmudic references to the phenomenon of a *bat kol* proclaiming matters of halakhah it may be assumed that Maimonides rules in accordance with the opinion of R. Joshua recorded in *Bava Metzi'a* 59b who declares that such heavenly voices are to be disregarded. However, as noted earlier, *Eruvin* 13b relates that for a period of three years Bet Hillel and Bet Shammai quarreled over whether the opinions of Bet Hillel, who constituted the majority, were to be accepted as normative, or whether the opinions of Bet Shammai were to be followed. Bet Shammai, although fewer in number, were conceded to be possessed of greater intellectual acumen than their antagonists. The controversy was settled by a *bat kol* proclaiming that the decisions of Bet Hillel are to be adopted. Needless to say, Maimonides consistently rules in accordance with the opinion of Bet Hillel. Rabbi Chaim Joseph David Azulai[11] cites *Pri Ḥadash*, who, in his commentary on the Mishneh *Torah*,

---

11. *Shem ha-Gedolim, Ma'arekhet Gedolim, yud,* no. 224. However, R. Chaim Joseph

asserts that Maimonides accepted the principle of majority determination as having been established as a canon of halakhic determination on grounds quite independent of the heavenly voice.

However, *Tosafot, Yevamot* 14a and *Ḥullin* 44a, affirms the authoritative nature of the *bat kol* which proclaimed the halakhah to be in accordance with the opinions of Bet Hillel. *Tosafot* is however perplexed by the fact that the *bat kol* supporting the position of Bet Hillel is regarded as authoritative while a similar *bat kol* affirming a ruling of R. Eliezer, as reported in *Bava Metzi'a* 59a, is not deemed authoritative. Nevertheless, the *bat kol* need not be heeded when it is not entirely certain that it expresses a serious, substantive pronouncement of halakhah. A *bat kol* to which an ancillary purpose may be ascribed is not authoritative. The *bat kol* recorded in *Bava Metzi'a* was not a spontaneous heavenly declaration. Its support was invoked by R. Eliezer. Hence it may be categorized, not as a divine pronouncement endowed with binding authority, but *"le-kevodo"* of R. Eliezer, as a token of honor and esteem for R. Eliezer, which is to say that the withholding of a *bat kol* when such endorsement was explicitly solicited would have been an embarrassment for R. Eliezer. Hence, in context, the audience recognized that the *bat kol* was not intended as an authoritative divine resolution of the controversy.[12]

Tosafot presents an alternative resolution to this difficulty. It is clearly established that no prophet can contradict or controvert any aspect of Torah as transmitted by Moses. The same limitation, quite logically, is ascribed by *Tosafot* to the reliability of a *bat kol*. It is an established principle of halakhic decision-making that normative rulings are in accordance with the view of the majority. In the matter under discussion in *Bava Metzi'a*, R. Eliezer's position was the expression of a solitary dissent from the majority view. A *bat kol* upholding the dissenting opinion of an individual is in blatant contradiction to the norms of halakhah and

---

David Azulai, *loc. cit., idem, Ein Zokher, Ya'ir Ozen, ma'arekhet alef,* sec. 15, and *idem, Dvash le-Pi, ma'arekhet nun,* sec. 12, himself states that, even according to Maimonides, divine guidance may be sought and may be forthcoming when a determination between authorities is otherwise not possible. See also R. Reuben Margulies, *She'elot u-Teshuvot min ha-Shamayim* (Jerusalem, 5717), p. 5.

12. Cf. also Rabbenu Nissim Ga'on, *Berakhot* 19b.

hence must go unheeded. In contradistinction, the *bat kol* in support of Bet Hillel contravened no accepted canon of halakhic decision-making.[13]

Neither resolution presented by *Tosafot* is completely satisfactory. While striving to sustain the authority of a *bat kol* in conformity with the apparent implication of the talmudic narrative, *Tosafot* fail to explain the meaning of the earlier-cited discussion presented in *Temurah* 16a.[14] In *Temurah* the Gemara clearly implies that no possibility exists for re-establishment of the three thousand forgotten halakhot by means of divine revelation. Yet, if *"lo ba-shamayim hi"* does not preclude a *bat kol* from pronouncing the halakhah in accordance with Bet Hillel, why does it preclude the re-establishment of the original halakhah on the basis of prophecy? And, if for some reason, there can be no prophecy with regard to such matters, why could the selfsame halakhot not have been the subject of a *bat kol*?

There is indeed one body of commentary which places a restrictive interpretation upon the position of *Tosafot*. *Shem ha-Gedolim*,[15] and apparently Rabbi Israel Salanter as well,[16] understand *Tosafot* as stating that the authority of a *bat kol* is restricted solely to the rendering of a decision between conflicting but clearly delineated opinions, but not to the resolution of matters of doubt or perplexity. Presumably, the premise underlying this analysis is that a choice between two conflicting views is not part of the intellectual corpus of Torah since "these and those are the words of the living God."[17] The halakhic determination is indeed of great significance in ordering the affairs of man but does not add to

---

13. Of course, if *Or Sameah*'s analysis of Maimonides' position is accepted, it is not at all certain that there is any disagreement between *Tosafot* and Maimonides. The examples of *bat kol* cited by *Tosafot* are limited to instances in which the heavenly voice establishes the authority of halakhic decisions. This is obviously the case with regard to the *bat kol* in support of Bet Hillel. Similarly, the *bat kol* recorded in *Bava Mezi'a* proclaimed, "the halakhah is in accordance with [R. Eliezer] in every place."

14. Cf., Margulies, *She'elot u-Teshuvot min ha-Shamayim*, p. 5, no. 11.

15. *Loc. cit.*

16. See note appended to *Or Yisra'el*, chapter 30.

17. Cf., Rema, *Orah Hayyim* 47:4, who rules that the Torah blessings need not be recited prior to pronouncing a halakhic decision unless the decision pronounced includes the reasoning upon which it is based. The simple declaration "permitted," "forbidden," "kosher" or "non-kosher" involves no intellectual endeavor and hence is not a form

an *understanding* of Torah and hence formulation of the halakhic ruling as a pragmatic directive does not violate the principle *"lo ba-shamayim hi."* Understood in this manner, *Temurah* 16a presents no obstacles to the position of *Tosafot.*

However, *Tosafot* was certainly not universally understood in this way. Rabbi Abraham I. Kook, *Mishpat Kohen*, no. 92, for example, clearly ascribes a much broader view to *Tosafot* and sees *Tosafot* as being entirely opposed to the position of Maimonides.[18] If so, the difficulty posed by the discussion in *Temurah* 16a is formidable.

---

of Torah study. Of course, the actual decision must be based upon application of halakhic theory to a specific case, but it is only vocal study, as distinct from thought processes, which require a blessing.

18. This would also seen evident from the comments of *Tosafot, Eruvin* 60b.

There may well be other early authorities who also disagree with Maimonides. Ra'avad, *Hilkhot Bet ha-Beḥirah* 6:14, rules that the sanctity of the Temple site lapsed with its destruction and indicates that this is his position because כך נגלה לי מסוד ה' ליראיו. Similarly, with reference to the ruling regarding a myrtle whose tip has been severed, Ra'avad, *Hilkhot Lulav* 8:5, writes:

כבר הופיע רוח הקודש בבית מדרשנו מכמה שנים.

The various other statements in Ra'avad's writings acknowledging heavenly illumination and participation in divine "secrets" enumerated by Margulies, p. 27, and Isadore Twersky, *Rabad of Posquieres* (Cambridge, 1962), p. 291, are not particularly remarkable; see *supra*, note 1. Mahari ben Lev, in his responsa, 111, no 115, understands these statements as contradicting Maimonides' view that halakhic rulings cannot be the subject of divine revelation. If this is correct, it is difficult to understand why Ra'avad did not append a gloss to *Hilkhot Yesodei ha-Torah* 9:4 expressing his disagreement with Maimonides, particularly since, according to Maimonides, Ra'avad was guilty of a capital transgression. [Marcus, *op. cit.*, p. 11, suggests that the question of the sanctity of the Temple Mount is a controversy concerning a matter of historical fact, since it hinges upon the nature and intent of Ezra's act of sanctification, and hence is not excluded from divine revelation. However, I fail to understand how this explains Ra'avad's statement in *Hilkhot Lulav.*]

Rabbi Aaron Soloveichik, in an oral presentation delivered in New York City at the 1982 *Torah she-be-al Peh* convocation, has suggested that the text of Ra'avad's comments in *Hilkhot Bet ha-Beḥirah* 6:14 is corrupt and should correctly read כך נגלה לי מסוד ה' ליראיו. The incorrect reading, then, arose from a scribal error in transcribing the *vav* of לו as a *yod*. Ra'avad, in the immediately preceding portion of these comments, explains that, although Ezra's act of sanctification was of a nature which served to endow the Land of Israel with permanent sanctity, he did not sanctify Jerusalem or the Temple site in a similar manner "for Ezra knew that the Temple and Jerusalem

A resolution based upon our earlier discussion of Maimonides' doctrine of prophecy does present itself. It was earlier argued that, even upon adoption of a naturalistic notion of prophecy, at least one form of prophecy requires an overt divine act, *viz.*, prescient knowledge of future events.

A position may be ascribed to *Tosafot* with regard to Torah insights which is intermediate between what might be assumed *prima facie* on the basis of the nature of the prophetic experience as a natural phenomenon and that actually espoused by Maimonides. *Tosafot* may maintain, as does Maimonides, that Torah insights are not immediately and universally available as part of the prophetic experience. Although Maimonides asserts that such insights are never available through the medium of prophecy, *Tosafot* parts company with Maimonides with regard to this point. While, for *Tosafot*, such information is not immediately available, it is, nevertheless, not absolutely excluded. God determines whether or not He will make such knowledge available to the prophet, just as He determines whether or not He will make knowledge of future events available to the prophet. Hence it is entirely possible that, at least on some occasions, such information is conveyed by means of a *bat kol* or through the medium of prophecy.

---

would undergo change and be sanctified with a different, eternal sanctity with the glory of God forever." According to this reading, Ra'avad concludes this comment with the phrase כך נגלה לו מסוד ה' ליראיו meaning "So it was revealed to him [Ezra] by means of סוד ה' ליראיו," i.e., Ezra failed to endow the Temple site and Jerusalem with permanent sanctity because he was aware – on the basis of סוד ה' ליראיו – of the enhanced sanctity for which those sites were divinely destined.

It should be noted that Maharam ibn Ḥabib, *Kapot Temarim*, p. 12, dismisses these statements of Ra'avad as mere hyperbole. Indeed, the expression סוד ה' ליראיו occurs in *Sotah* 4b and may have been employed by Raavad as a literary flourish (מליצה). See *Torat Nevi'im*, chapter 1. The identical phrase occurs in *Ḥaggigah* 3b with regard to a ruling concerning the sanctity of the Land of Israel.

Rashi, *Sukkah* 44a, *Ta'anit* 4a, and as cited by *Tosafot*, *Bekhorot* 58a, appears to accept the possibility of prophetic revelation of halakhah, although this possibility is explicitly rejected by Rashi himself in his commentary on *Shabbat* 108a. See *Torat Nevi'im*, chapter 1. R. Jacob ha-Levi's *She'elot u-Teshuvot min ha-Shamayim* and R. Joseph Karo's *Maggid Mesharim* clearly bespeak those authors' acceptance of such phenomena.

If so, the discussion in *Temurah* is readily understandable. New laws cannot be promulgated by the prophet. The demand made of Samuel, as explained by the *Brisker Rav*, was for a new legislative revelation. To this came the reply, "A prophet cannot innovate with regard to any matter." Prophecy which is legislative in nature is an avenue which is totally closed off. The earlier plea to Joshua was for reconstruction of the law on the basis of prophetic communication with the Active Intellect by means of which the prophet would be able to become aware of, and share in, information inherent in the Active Intelligence, *viz.*, halakhot already revealed to Moses. To this came the reply, *"Lo ba-shamayim hi* – It is not in the heavens," i.e., the information requested is not made available to the prophet by heaven upon demand as is the case with regard to other aspects of the prophetic experience.[19] Therefore, there is no reason to assume that a prophet may acquire the information simply by "asking" as was the demand of the populace.[20]

---

19. Cf. *Mishpat Kohen*, no. 92. The suggestion here advanced differs from that of Rabbi Kook in that, cast in this philosophical framework, it is consistent with the statements of *Tosafot*.

20. One problem remains. *Temurah* 16a continues with another narrative which adds that Joshua forgot certain halakhot and became uncertain with regard to others because, with pride, he compared his own erudition to that of Moses. The narrative concluded with a report that the people of Israel became enraged and sought to kill Joshua. Thereupon God sought to preserve Joshua but declared, "To tell you [the forgotten halakhot and the resolution of the uncertainties] is impossible! Go and occupy them with war." Rabbenu Gershom explains that it was "impossible" for God to transmit the desired information to Joshua because *"lo ba-shamayim hi."* This explanation is quite consistent with Maimonides' position which denies that halakhic matters can ever again be the subject of prophetic revelation. It does, however, conflict with the view herein ascribed to *Tosafot* which maintains that God may either make such insight available or withhold it. Hence, if God had chosen to do so, He could have saved Joshua's life by revealing this information to him. However, an entirely different explanation of God's "inability" to reveal the information is possible. Rashi explains that Joshua was made to forget what he had been taught by Moses, not simply as a punishment for his haughty attitude in comparing himself to Moses, but because Moses was pained by the realization that Joshua was as proficient as he. Upon forgetting the halakhot, Joshua was no longer Moses' equal. The Gemara may then be understood as declaring that God found it "impossible" simply to reveal the information to Joshua because, were He to do so, Moses' grievance would not have been redressed.

6

Judaism and Natural Law

I.

During the seventeenth and eighteenth centuries a number of Christian scholars, including the prominent Dutch scholar Hugo Grotius, sought to demonstrate that a concept of natural law might be traced to the Pentateuch. If so, the doctrine of natural law might be regarded as part of the Jewish contribution to Western thought. The Cambridge Hebraist, John Selden, developed a much more elaborate and sophisticated argument in a work entitled *De Jure Naturalis et Gentium Juxta Disciplinam Ebraeorum,* in which he advances the thesis that the Seven Noahide Commandments constitute, in effect, a highly developed doctrine of natural law. The Noahide Code, he argued, is regarded by Judaism both as predating the Sinaitic revelation and as binding upon gentile nations which did not participate in the Sinaitic experience. Accordingly, he maintained, the content of the Noahide Code must be regarded as universally binding on the basis of reason alone.[1]

---

1. This position is also espoused by R. Chaim Hirschensohn, "Sevarah," *Otzar Yisra'el,* ed. J.D. Eisenstein (New York: Hebrew Publishing Co., 1906), VII, 136; *idem, Malki ba-Kodesh* (St. Louis, 5679), I, 21; and *idem, Eleh Divrei ha-Brit* (Jerusalem, 5686), I, 5f. Cf., however, R. Eleazar Meir Preil, *Ha-Ma'or* (Jerusalem, 5689), no. 80.

On the surface, this thesis presents many features auguring in favor of acceptance. The basic proscriptions of the Noahide Code, homicide, theft, sexual licentiousness, etc., involve acts universally viewed with opprobrium.[2] Judaism teaches that all gentiles are bound by the provisions of the Noahide Code and are to be punished for infractions thereof. Since the nations of the world were denied the benefit of direct divine revelation, the binding nature of these commandments can only be rooted in reason.

This thesis is, however, difficult to substantiate in terms of the legal traditions of Judaism. Nowhere in the vast corpus of rabbinic, legal or philosophical literature is there to be found a fully-developed doctrine of natural law; nor, as Marvin Fox has pointed out,[3] is the term natural law used by any Jewish philosopher or legal scholar prior to Joseph Albo in the fifteenth century. Of course, as Norman Lamm and Aaron Kirschenbaum have argued, "Ideas may be implicit in a text or body of literature, and receive their formulation in sophisticated terminology much later"[4] and undoubtedly "concepts, like people, have an existence independent of their names."[5] Nevertheless, it is remarkable that a philosophical doctrine which may be traced back as far as Cicero and which played a major role in the Latin tradition should not receive explicit reference, not to speak of detailed analysis, in Jewish philosophical or legal writings. Any *argumentum ad silencium* is weak at best, yet in the present instance silence[6] with regard to so significant a doctrine does constitute

---

2. The Roman legal system similarly contained a corpus of law, the *ius gentium*, which governed cases in which one of the litigants was not a Roman citizen or in which both litigants were resident aliens. Gaius apparently took the *ius gentium* as the model of a law practiced by all mankind and dictated to all men by natural reason as distinct from the *ius civile* or system of law which each nation gives itself. Selden apparently perceived a similar division in Jewish law.

3. M. Fox, "Maimonides and Aquinas on Natural Law," *Diné Israel* V (1972), xi. The term is also used by a later fifteenth-century scholar, R. Shem Tob ben Shem Tob, *Derashot ha-Torah* (Venice: 5307), 25a, as a synonym for *mitzvot sikhliyot*; see below, note 36.

4. N. Lamm and A. Kirschenbaum, "Freedom and Constraint in the Jewish Judicial Process," *Cardozo Law Review* I/1 (Spring, 1979), 110, note 40.

5. *Ibid.*, p. 112.

6. There are revered latter-day rabbinic scholars who recognize other normatively binding halakhic prescriptions based upon considerations other than revelation,

prima facie evidence that the notion of natural law was not taken seriously by Judaism. It was ignored because it played no significant role in the development of Jewish philosophy or legal theory.

More devastating to Selden's contention that the Noahide code is a reflection of a natural law position are the comments of Maimonides in his *Mishneh Torah, Hilkhot Melakhim* 8:11:

> Any person [i.e., gentile] who accepts the Seven Commandments and is meticulous in observing them is one of the pious of the

---

Mishneh le-Melekh, Hilkhot Melakhim 10:7, s.v. *shuv ra'iti,* questions the purpose of the covenants entered into by Abraham and Isaac with Avimelech, the oath of Esau to Jacob and of Eliezer to Abraham in light of the fact that fulfillment of an oath is not included in the Seven Noahide Commandments. *Avnei Nezer, Yoreh De'ah,* 11, no. 306, further questions the purpose and validity of the oath sworn by Jews at Mount Sinai to uphold the commandments since that oath preceded acceptance of the Torah and of the commandments contained therein prohibiting violation of an oath. *Avnei Nezer* responds that an oath binding oneself to another person is valid on the basis of reason alone. A commandment, he asserts, is necessary only to assure performance of an oath that is entirely personal in its effect. Since the obligation to abide by an oath affecting others is the product of reason it was binding even before Sinai. That concept is quite similar to the contention of Thomas Hobbes, *Leviathan,* Part I, chap. 15, "That men performe their Covenants made."

R. Moses Samuel Glazner, in his commentary on *Ḥullin, Dor Revi'i* (Jerusalem, 5738), *Petiḥah Kelalit,* and in his comments on *Ḥullin* 89b, regards, for example, public nudity, despite the absence of a direct biblical prohibition, as constituting a transgression even more severe in nature than violation of a negative commandment. Consumption of human flesh and of rancid carrion are categorized by this scholar in a similar manner. The concept invoked by *Dor Revi'i* is not, strictly speaking, that of a natural law theory but of *a priori* moral repugnance. He does, however, posit a notion closely akin to that of *obligations naturals* of Roman law in affirming an obligation to support one's infant children that is not predicated upon biblical command or rabbinic legislation.

R. Samuel ha-Levi Woszner, *Teshuvot Shevet ha-Levi,* V, *Kuntres ha-Mitzvot,* no. 23, asserts that the obligation to provide a wife with sustenance and conjugal gratification is based upon *sevarah* whereas the obligation to provide her with clothing is not rooted simply in reason. *Shevet ha-Levi* acknowledges that Ramban, *Commentary on the Bible,* Exodus 21:10, does not accept that view.

Yosef Da'at, Bava Kamma (Jerusalem, 5761), ed. Joseph Ben Arza, p. 9, suggests that no formal prohibition against committing a tort is necessary because the prohibition can be derived on the basis of reason. See also *infra,* note 11.

nations of the world and he possesses a share in the world-to-come. But this is [only] if he accepts them and performs them because God commanded them in the Torah and made known to us through Moses, our teacher, that the children of Noah were previously commanded with regard to them.[7] However, if he performs them because of the determination of reason [*hakhra ha-da'at*] this [person] is not a *ger toshav* [resident-alien] and he is not of the pious of the nations nor of their wise men.[8]

This passage clearly expresses Maimonides' opinion[9] that non-Jews are required to accept the Noahide Code on the basis of revelation, not on the basis of reason.[10] Revelation – and not reason – is endowed with binding force.[11] Furthermore, the perfectly moral Noahide can claim no special merit in the world-to-come save on the basis of prior acceptance of the Noahide Code as the revealed mandate of the Deity.[12] Moreover, when this statement is read in conjunction with Maimonides' statement in *Hilkhot Issurei Bi'ah* 14:7, in which Maimonides equates and identifies *hasidei umot ha-olam* with those who acquire the state of a *ger toshav*, it is evident that yet another condition must be satisfied in order for a gentile to achieve the status of "one of the pious of the nations." In *Hilkhot Avodah Zarah* 10:6 Maimonides declares that status as a *ger toshav*

---

7. See extended endnote A.
8. See extended endnote B.
9. Although, as discussed in endnote B, Maimonides' source is obscure, the only authority who explicitly postulates an opposing view is *Tosafot Re'em*, commentary *Sefer Yer'eim* 233:2.
10. Cf., Maimonides, *Hilkhot Avodat Kokhavim* 10:6 and Ra'avad, *ad loc.*, cf., also *Minhat Hinnukh*, no. 94, and *Hazon Ish*, *Hilkhot Avodat Kokhavim* 65:3 and *Shevi'it* 24:3.
11. Cf., the rather cryptic comment of R. Isaac ben Sheshet, *Teshuvot Rivash*, no. 399, in which he justifies the authority of a community to promulgate binding ordinances "as at Sinai and at the time of the *Megillah* and the fast days." Rivash apparently maintains that the binding authority of the Sinaitic corpus is rooted in its acceptance as a sort of social contract – the binding nature of which can only be explained as a natural law concept.
12. A similar assertion is made by Maimonides with regard to the reward of Noahides for the fulfillment of other commandments whose performance is not obligatory for non-Jews. See *Teshuvot ha-Rambam*, ed. Afred Freimann (Jerusalem, 1934), no. 124 and *Teshuvot ha-Rambam*, ed. Yehoshua Blau (Jerusalem, 1957), I, no. 148.

is conferred only upon formal acceptance before a *Bet Din*. Indeed, this condition is recorded in *Hilkhot Melakhim* 8:11 through incorporation of the phrase "who accepts" (*shekibel alav*).[13] It is therefore evident that not only is observance of the Noahide Code on the basis of revelation a necessary condition for achieving a share in the world-to-come, but that such observance must be preceded by formal acknowledgment in the presence of a qualified *Bet Din* of the obligations inherent in the Seven Commandments.[14]

The demand that in order to merit eternal reward non-Jews accept the Noahide Code on the basis of revelation does not, of course, preclude acceptance of a natural law doctrine. This possibility is, however, barred by Maimonides' apparently gratuitous concluding phrase *"ve-lo me-ḥakhamehem*, nor of their wise men." Numerous scholars have argued that our reading is the result of a scribal or printing error and that the correct version of the passage is *"ela me-ḥakhamehem* – but of their scholars," which, of course, has exactly the reverse import. The discrepancy involves the change of a single Hebrew letter and could have occurred quite readily. The principal support for this emendation is the reading found in the Bodleian manuscript of the *Mishneh Torah*.[15] However, most manuscripts and virtually all printed editions including the *editio*

---

13. See Steven S. Schwarzschild, "Do Noachites Have to Believe in Revelation?" *Jewish Quarterly Review* 53/1 (1962), 36 n. 35, who questions whether the term *ger toshav* in *Hilkhot Melakhim* is used in precisely the same way as in *Hilkhot Issurei Bi'ah*. See, however, *Ḥiddushei Maran Riz ha-Levi*, p. 164, who states explicitly that formal *kabbalah* or acceptance of the Seven Commandments in the presence of a *Bet Din* is required and that in the absence of formal *kabbalah* the Noahide is not deemed to be in the category of "the pious of the nations of the world." The identical point was earlier made by R. Raphael ha-Kohen of Hamburg, *Teshuvot Ve-Shev ha-Kohen*, no. 38. The latter authority also endeavors to identify the talmudic source from which Maimonides' statement is derived.

14. The novel interpretation of Maimonides' statement offered somewhat tentatively by R. Abraham I. Kook, *Iggerot Re'iyah* (Jerusalem, 5722), I, no. 89, yields a diametrically opposite position but is contra the plain meaning of the text and the manner in which Maimonides has been understood by all previous rabbinic and philosophic scholars.

15. For early citations of the *"ela"* reading see *Encyclopedia Talmudit*, VI (Jerusalem, 1954), 290 note 11.

princeps published in Rome in 1480 contain the reading *"ve-lo – nor"*[16] It should be noted that acceptance of the *"ela"* reading does not at all signify that in calling such persons wise men Maimonides necessarily accepted a theory of natural law. A person may be termed wise not solely because of his knowledge of transcendental truth but also, for example, by virtue of his acceptance of pragmatic[17] principles. Aristotle, after all, wrote extensively concerning *praktikos* or practical wisdom yet is not generally regarded as a natural law theorist. Although the *"ela"* reading does not conclusively establish Maimonides' position as an advocate of natural law, the *"ve-lo"* reading does indicate rejection of a doctrine of natural law. Regardless of which version is accepted as being correct, I do not believe that Maimonides did, in fact, accept a theory of natural

---

16. For a discussion of the textual problem see Jacob Katz, *Exclusiveness and Tolerance* (New York: Schocken Books, 1962), 175ff; Steven S. Schwarzschild, "Do Noachites Have to Believe in Revelation?" *Jewish Quarterly Review* 52/4 (1962), 301-303; Fox, *Diné Israel*, p. xiv; and J. Faur, *Iyunim be-Mishneh Torah: Sefer ha-Madda* (Jerusalem, 1978), p. 151 note 43. Among rabbinic scholars the reading *ela* is found twice in the citation of this passage in the response of the 16th-century authority R. Moses al-Ashkar, *Teshuvot Maharam Alashkar*, no. 117 (on pp. 302 and 320 of the Jerusalem, 5719 edition), and more recently by R. Abraham I. Kook, *Iggerot Re'iyah*, I, 89. The text cited in R. Yosef ben Shem Tov, *Kevod Elokim* (Fürth, 1556), 29a, reads *aval* which is a synonym for *ela*. Textual considerations aside, there is one cogent reason for assuming the published text to be accurate and the Bodleian manuscript to be corrupt. It is virtually an axiom of halakhic hermeneutics that early authorities in general, and Maimonides in particular, did not employ unnecessary verbiage. The phrase *ve-lo me-ḥakhamehem* serves to negate natural law doctrines and hence Maimonides would have had reason for its inclusion. The phrase *ela me-ḥakhamehem* has neither halakhic nor philosophical import and would constitute an irrelevant interpolation.

17. Cf., Lamm and Kirschenbaum, *Cardozo Law Review*, p. 117, who write, "it is reasonable to assume, if this reading is correct, that this indicates a natural law theory by Maimonides. The single letter in Maimonides Code is thus of the greatest moment in deciding the question of whether Jewry's greatest jurist and most eminent philosopher advocated or rejected natural law." Quite to the contrary, Maimonides' dismissal of "some of our later sages" who speak of rational laws as suffering from the disease of the Mutakallimun (see *Eight Chapters*, VI, and *Guide*, III, 17) would appear to constitute a denial of natural law. See Munk's note to his translation of this passage in the *Guide*, III, 127, note 1; L. Strauss, *Persecution and the Art of Writing* (Westport, 1977), 97; and R. Lerner, "Moses Maimonides," *History of Political Philosophy*, 2nd edition, eds. L. Strauss and J. Cropsey (Chicago, 1972), pp. 218-219.

law in the usual sense of the notion.[18] This conclusion is based upon a statement found in his *Treatise on Logic*, as will be shown later.

Despite Maimonides' apparent rejection of any possible natural law theory in the phrase *"ve-lo me-ḥakhamehem"* (assuming for the purposes of our discussion that this is the correct version) some talmudic evidence may be adduced for the existence of at least a germinal theory of natural law in rabbinic thought. It is evident that the Talmud recognized the binding legal authority not only of revelation but of *sevarah* or reason as well. A sharp distinction must be made between *sevarah* in the sense of a direct and independent source of law.[19] The former can hardly be assimilated to a notion of natural law; its operation is effected by application of the formal rules of logic or of common sense while ultimate authority for incorporation into law of the resultant conclusions rests upon prior acceptance, on completely different grounds, of the corpus of law upon which intellect is allowed to operate. On the other hand, *sevarah* as an autonomous source of law is *sui generis* in the sense that reason need not look beyond itself for authoritative validation.

Although the Talmud abounds in examples of the former applications of *sevarah*, at times explicitly employing the term,[20] but more often implicitly accepting the methodology of *sevarah* without explicitly applying the label,[21] examples of the latter are rare. Instances of the latter type of *sevarah* appear to be, in total, no more than three in number,[22] of which two do not really bear upon a doctrine of natural law.

---

18. In this I concur with Marvin Fox, *Diné Israel*, p. 6, but on entirely different grounds.

19. Cf., Menachem Elon, *Ha-Mishpat ha-Ivri* (Jerusalem, 1973), II, 805-828 and "Sevarah," *Encyclopedia Judaica* (Jerusalem, 1971), XIV, 195-198. Cf., also, R. Eleazar Meir Preil, *Ha-Ma'or*, no. 80, who does not recognize the latter category of *sevarah* and fails to discuss, or even mention, the example found in *Sanhedrin* 74a.

20. E.g., *Gittin* 6b; *Shabbat* 63a; *Sukkah* 29a. See also examples cited by R. Reuben Margulies, *Margaliyot ha-Yam* (Jerusalem, 5718), *Sanhedrin* 15a, sec.4.

21. See Rabbi Zevi Hirsch Chajes, *The Student's Guide Through the Talmud*, trans. by Jacob Shachter (New York, 1960), pp. 29-31.

22. *Berakhot* 35a also posits *sevarah* as the source of the obligation to recite a blessing prior to partaking of food. However, the *sevarah* cited in that instance cannot be understood as compelling in an absolute sense since the obligation is rabbinic rather than biblical. For a discussion of *sevarah* as establishing a rabbinic obligation see R. Ḥayyim Medini, *Sedei Ḥemed, Kuntres ha-Kelalim, ma'arekhet ha-samakh*, sec. 63.

The Gemara, *Bava Kamma* 46b establishes as a principle of law the rule that the burden of proof is on the claimant. Citation of a biblical verse (Exodus 24:14) to substantiate this principle is dismissed as superfluous and the verse in question in interpreted as establishing an entirely different rule, *viz.*, that the plaintiff must be heard first. In declaring scriptural support to be unnecessary, the Gemara exclaims, "What need have I for a verse? – *Sevarah hu!* A person who is in pain goes to the house of a doctor," i.e., it is the patient who seeks the ministrations of the physician and not the physician who pursues potential patients to determine who is ill. Similarly, the person who has a claim against another must bring proof to substantiate his claim and the defendant need not first prove that he is not liable. The appeal to *sevarah* in this instance does not establish the authority of reason as a source of law for several reasons. First, the matter is one of judicial procedure rather than of substantive law; no normative obligation is born of this application of *sevarah*. Secondly, given a dogmatic system of jurisprudence and statutory provisions for judicial adjudication, a procedural rule for the burden of proof must be established. Failure to do so would result in a legal impasse and effectively eliminate any possible judicial remedy. This would reduce the system of jurisprudence set forth in Scripture to a mere theoretical construct. Hence common sense, as reflected in the therapeutic model adduced by the Gemara, dictates that the burden of proof be upon the plaintiff. Reason is here brought to bear in developing a detail of law; it hardly functions as a forum of original jurisdiction.

The second example is somewhat less clear but upon analysis appears to be of the same genre as well. The Mishnah, *Ketubot* 22a, discusses the credence to be given certain types of self-serving statements. The issue in point is the liberty of a woman whose marital status is unknown to contract a marriage. In the absence of knowledge of prior marriage a woman is presumed to be free to marry. If the existence of a prior marriage has been established, the woman's own statement that the marriage has been terminated by divorce is not acceptable in the absence of corroborating evidence. However, if knowledge of prior marriage is established only on the basis of the woman's own statement, her testimony with regard to subsequent divorce is acceptable. Thus, in the absence of witnesses as to the existence of a prior marriage, the woman's statement that she was married and became divorced is accepted. The rule which is formulated is "The mouth which has rendered prohibited is the mouth which has rendered permissible." In this instance as well, the Gemara seeks scriptural justification only to reject the cited verse (Deuteronomy 22:16) with the statement "What need have I for verse? *Sevarah hu!*" The selfsame testimony which is the source of any possible restriction simultaneously establishes permission to remarry. Here we are confronted not with a rule of procedure, but with a rule of evidence which effectively determines whether or not marriage shall be permitted. Nevertheless, here too, we are not confronted with a matter involving a substantive normative halakhah but with a question of juridical determination. *Sevarah* is here not employed to determine an actual law of marriage or adultery but merely to establish the basis of juridical determination that a state of marriage does or does not exist. Here, again, reason does not operate *sui generis* as the authority to prescribe or to proscribe but enjoys only a certain narrow latitude in determining a question of objective fact – a matter which is a far cry from endowing the intellect with legislative authority.

The third example is a matter of an entirely different nature. In general, a person confronted with a choice between transgression of a biblical prohibition or death should transgress in order to preserve life. Martyrdom is required only in face of coercion with regard to idolatry, certain forms of sexual licentiousness, including incest and adultery, and murder. Insofar as idolatry and sexual licentiousness are concerned, this principle is established on the basis of biblical exegesis. However, with regard to murder the rule is derived by the Gemara, *Sanhedrin* 74a, solely on the basis of reason: "It is a *sevarah*..., How do you know that your blood is sweeter? Perhaps the blood of the other person is sweeter!" Clearly, the matter at hand involves a substantive issue and establishes a prohibition against homicide which is universal in nature and admits of no exception. In effect, then, the prohibition against homicide is legislated by reason and, at least in this area, the prohibition is identical in nature to a natural law prohibition.[23] The effect of the *sevarah* adduced

---

23. It would appear that, as a natural law principle, the obligation to suffer martyrdom rather than commit murder is incumbent upon non-Jews as well. This is explicitly

in this instance has the full force and authority of law and stands on par with dogmatic scriptural prohibitions. This becomes dramatically apparent upon examining the exegesis which yields the same rule with regard to sexual licentiousness. That exegesis is based upon the juxtaposition of homicide and adultery in the same verse (Deuteronomy 22:26). The hermeneutical principle involved is that of *hekesh*, i.e., the juxtaposition of two words or phrases. In this case Scripture explicitly compares murder and adultery: "...for as when a man rises against his neighbor and slays him, even so is this matter." As a result of the *hekesh* between murder and adultery the already established rule with regard to murder is transposed and applied to adultery, with regard to which there exists no otherwise delineated rule. In this case the rule with regard to murder, which is derived on the basis of *sevarah* alone, is transposed as if it were explicit in Scripture and, accordingly, is transposed and applied to adultery. Here we find a legal prohibition derived from *sevarah* which is clearly regarded as having the selfsame binding authority as a divinely revealed biblical law.

The sole Jewish philosopher who explicitly assigns any role to natural law is Joseph Albo. In a short, almost cryptic passage in his *Sefer ha-Ikkarim*, Book I, chapter 7, Albo states, "The purpose of natural law is to repress wrong and to promote right in order that people be kept away from theft, robbery and murder, that society may be able to exist among men and everyone be safe from the wrongdoer and oppressor." Albo cites theft, robbery and murder as the sole instances in which natural law is operative. The infractions enumerated are not merely examples taken from a larger body of natural law; they are the sole areas in which Albo deemed natural law to be operative. We may presume that Albo

---

stated by R. Judah Rosanes, *Mishneh le-Melekh, Hilkhot Melakhim* 10:2 and *idem, Perashat Derakhim, Derush* 2, as well as by R. Joseph Babad, *Minḥat Ḥinnukh*, no. 296, and in a note appended by the grandson of R. Isaac Schorr to the latter's *Teshuvot Koaḥ Shor*, no. 20, p. 35a. See also *Tevat Gome*, cited by *Pithei Teshuvah, Yoreh De'ah* 154:4. An opposing view is adopted by R. Shmuel Jaffe-Ashkenazi, in his commentary on *Bereshit Rabbah, Yefeh To'ar*, (Fürth, 5452), p. 15b; *Shenot Ḥayyim*, p. 36b; R. Barzilai Baruch Ya'avets, *Leshon Arumim* (Izmir, 5516), 7; and R. Abraham Samuel Meyuchas, *Sedei ha-Aretz* I, 55. See also Faur, p. 161.

found talmudic evidence for the authority of natural law in these areas of proscribed conduct but not in others.

The talmudic locus of a natural law prohibition against murder has been cited. A source for theft and robbery as infractions of an authoritative natural law prohibition is much less clear. I believe that Albo's source for a natural law prohibition against theft and robbery may be found in *Bava Metzi'a* 61b. The Gemara questions the need for a prohibition against theft, "You shall not steal" (Leviticus 19:11) and responds with the statement that the prohibition is required in order to ban (1) theft designed for purposes of annoyance and (2) theft designed for the purpose of benefitting the victim by incurring a legal obligation to pay him the fine which is levied upon the thief. Ordinary theft, however, requires no scriptural prohibition. Rashi, undoubtedly troubled by the problem that in the absence of a formal admonition Jewish law would lack a ban against theft, explains that assumed in the Gemara's query is the presumption that a formal prohibition might be derived exegetically on the basis of *meh ha-tzad*, i.e., a derivation predicated upon a factor common to two other proscribed activities and present in theft as well. Since both proscribed activities share a common factor it may be assumed that the presence of that consideration constitutes the essence of the prohibition and hence any activity in which that factor is present must be considered to be banned as well. In this instance Rashi states that a prohibition against theft might be deduced from the fact that usury and fraud are both explicitly forbidden by the Torah. Both usury and fraud involve diminution of the material wealth of another (or what in contemporary legal parlance would be termed "unjust enrichment"). Since theft is the example par excellence of diminution of the material wealth of another (*mehaser mammon*) it would follow that theft is also forbidden by virtue of the fact that it is a form of *mehaser mammon*.

No part of this argumentation is, however, explicit in the words of the Gemara. Albo may well have understood the query of the Gemara in a simple and literal way. Theft requires no scriptural admonition, not because a prohibition may be derived on the basis of hermeneutics, but because theft is known to be forbidden by virtue of natural law. If so, a scriptural admonition is required only in order to encompass within the scope of the prohibition actions which reason alone does not incontrovertibly proscribe.[24] Thus, for Albo, natural law proscribes not only murder but theft and robbery as well.

Other examples of the operation of natural law in the Jewish legal system are more obscure and their talmudic sources uncertain. Albo states that the purpose of natural law is "that society may be able to exist among men and everyone be safe from the wrongdoer and oppressor." This formulation is advanced by Albo simply as a final cause or explanation of why it is that reason legislates against theft, robbery and murder. There is no evidence that preservation of society *per se* is regarded by Albo as directly mandated by natural law[25] or that any other action, whether positive or negative, is commanded or proscribed by natural law as a means of preserving society. Yet other measures designed to preserve the social structure are posited as a matter of law by other early authorities and appear to be rooted solely in natural law concepts.

Maimonides, *Hilkhot Melakhim* 10:11, following his codification of the laws pertaining to non-Jews, declares:

> [The] *Bet Din* of Israel is obligated to establish judges for these resident-aliens to judge them on the basis of these laws so that the world will not become corrupt. If [the] *Bet Din* determines to appoint judges from among them they may [so] appoint; and if they determine to appoint [judges] from among Israel they may [so] appoint.

It is, to be sure, Maimonides' position, *Hilkhot Melakhim* 9:14, that the last of the enumerated Seven Noahide Commandments, *dinin*, constitutes an obligation making it incumbent upon Noahides to sit in judgment and to mete out punishment for infractions of the other six

---

24. The same question may, of course, be raised with regard to the need for a scriptural prohibition against murder, which the Gemara explicitly states can be known on the basis of *sevarah*. It would appear to me that a formal prohibition is required for the one type of homicide in which reason does not unequivocally serve to establish a prohibition, *viz.*, euthanasia. See R. Jacob Zevi Mecklenburg, *Ha-Ketav ve-ha-Kabbalah*, Genesis 9:5. Moreover, absent a scriptural prohibition, capital punishment could not be imposed. See *Sanhedrin* 56b.

25. See extended endnote C.

commandments of the Noahide Code. The *mitzvah* of *dinin* is, however, binding only upon non-Jews.[26] It is also the case that Maimonides, *Hilkhot Melakhim* 8:10, states that Moses was commanded by God to force all inhabitants of the world to accept the *mitzvot* which were commanded to the sons of Noah and put to death any who refuse to accept them.[27] However, that penalty, which is to be imposed by Jews, seems to be mandated only in the event of total rejection as manifest in refusal formally to accept the Seven Commandments. Indeed, mere refusal formally to accept the Seven Commandments even though no actual violation has occurred warrants the penalty described in *Hilkhot Melakhim* 8:10. Punishment for actual infractions subsequent to acceptance of the Seven Commandments does not seem to be encompassed in this provision.[28] Indeed, it is presumably for precisely this reason that Maimonides found it necessary to add the explanatory phrase "lest the world become corrupt" in *Hilkhot Melakhim* 10:11 but does not provide any such explanation in the codification of the earlier regulation in 8:10 which is presented simply as a divine fiat.

Incorporation of the phrase "lest the world become corrupt" would tend to indicate that while the halakhah recorded in 8:10 is a dogmatic obligation based on revelation, the principle reflected in 10:11 is derived by means of reason alone. 8:10 cannot be predicated upon a similar rationale

---

26. It is generally assumed that the Seven Commandments were directed only to non-Jews. See the exposition of Maimonides, *Commentary on the Mishnah, Ḥullin* 7:6 as well as R. Israel Gustman, *Kuntresei Shi'urim, Bava Metzi'a*, no. 29, secs. 4-5. Cf., however, R. Shlomoh ben Shimon Duran, *Teshubot ha-Rashbash*, no. 543, who maintains that the Seven Commandments were reiterated in the wilderness at Marah and thereby became binding upon Jew and gentile alike. See also R. Joseph Engel, *Bet ha-Otzar, ma'arekhet alef, klal* 1, sec. 7, s.v. *od ayen Rambam*, who asserts that this is also the position of Maimonides. See R. Dov Frimer, "Hamatah Mitokh Raḥamim," *Halakhah u-Refu'ah*, ed. R. Moshe Hershler, IV (Jerusalem 1985), 293-295.
27. Formal acceptance is required only by virtue of the Sinaitic revelation but was not part of the Noahide obligation prior to Sinai. This requirement was established at Sinai because observance of the Noahide Code had largely lapsed among non-Jews. See *Ḥiddushei Maran Riz ha-Levi, loc. cit.*
28. Cf., Nahmanides, *Commentary on the Bible*, Deuteronomy 23:18, who declares that Jews bear no responsibility *vis-à-vis* infractions committed by Noahides other than being obliged to prevent Noahides from engaging in idol worship.

since a person who does not violate any of the provisions of the Noahide Code does not endanger the social order and hence there is no readily apparent reason for punishing him simply for refusing to make a formal declaration of acceptance. Punishment of evildoers, however, is mandated, even in the absence of a revealed *mitzvah*, by reason alone; were evildoers not to be punished, the very fabric of society would be destroyed. Thus, this provision is a reflection of a natural law consideration.

Punishment for infractions of the Seven Commandments may be dictated by natural law even though the content of the Noahide Code is not itself the product of natural law, i.e., the provisions of the Noahide Code cannot be viewed as binding obligations on the basis of reason alone. Yet obedience to a law whose authority is established on other grounds is compelled by reason alone: otherwise law would be devoid of meaning. Law can be successful in achieving its legitimate goals only if transgressors are punished; otherwise law would be honored solely in the breach with the result that the world would "become corrupt."

The same concept seems to appear in a different guise in Rashi, *Gittin* 9b. The Mishnah there cited declares that all bills and deeds executed in non-Jewish courts are valid, with the exception of bills of divorce and manumission, even if they bear the signature of gentile witnesses. The exclusion of bills of divorce and manumission is readily explainable. Gentiles are not *bnei kritut*. The institutions of divorce and manumission are constructs of Jewish law from which non-Jews are excluded and therefore gentiles cannot execute efficacious documents of this nature. However, the validity of other documents witnessed by gentiles is problematic. It would appear that all bills and deeds of any nature should be invalid when signed by gentiles because non-Jews are not qualified to serve as witnesses in Jewish courts. Non-Jews are precluded from serving not only as testifying witnesses but also from serving as attesting witnesses.[29] Nevertheless, the rule formulated in the Mishnah states that legal documents witnessed by non-Jews are valid for transactions between Jewish parties. The Gemara, *Gittin* 10b, questions how it is possible for such documents to effect transfer of title. In

---

29. Cf., the quite problematic understanding of Rashi advanced by *Tosafot, Bava Kamma* 88a, s.v. *yehe eved.*

the absence of any other *kinyan*, or formal mode of transfer, title does not pass by deed unless the deed is properly witnessed. This problem is resolved by the Gemara in two alternative ways. The first response is that such documents are deemed valid by virtue of the principle *dina de-malkhuta dina*, i.e. "the law of the land is the law." The second response is that bills which are performative rather than evidentiary are indeed invalid and are subsumed in the Mishnah under the category of bills of divorce which are ruled to be nugatory.

The first resolution is somewhat problematic. Early authorities sought to justify the principle of *dina de-malkhuta dina* on a variety of grounds. Yet, it is not at all clear why the principle of *dina de-malkhuta dina* should apply to jurisprudential matters between Jews in which the government has no active interest. It was obviously this difficulty which prompted Rashi, *Gittin* 9b, to comment, "...but non-Jews were commanded concerning *dinin*." Although he fails to cite explicitly the explanation advanced by the Gemara, *Gittin* 10b, Rashi is obviously advancing his own formulation of the rationale underlying the principle of *dina de-malkhuta* with a view toward providing an explanation for its extension to the rule formulated by the Mishnah.

Quite obviously, Rashi rejects the analysis of *dinin* formulated by Maimonides, *Hilkhot Melakhim* 9:14, viz., that *dinin* constitutes an obligation to enforce the other provisions of the Noahide Code. Instead, he accepts a view closely paralleling that advanced by Nahmanides in his *Commentary on the Bible*, Genesis 34:13, viz., that *dinin* constitutes a commandment to Noahides to establish a comprehensive system of law to govern the manifold facets of commercial and interpersonal relationships. *Dina de-malkhuta* is then no more than the actualization and implementation of such a system of law.[30] Thus the legitimacy of *dina de-malkhuta* is rooted in the *mitzvah* of *dinin*.

---

30. If this is indeed the correct analysis of Rashi's position, Rashi then maintains that non-Jews need not necessarily comport themselves in such matters in accordance with the details of Jewish law but are free to enact any equitable system of law. This is contrary to the manner in which Nahmanides' position is understood by R. Moshe Isserles, *Teshuvot Rema*, no. 10, and R. Moshe Sofer, *Teshuvot Ḥatam Sofer, Likkutim*, no. 14. These authorities interpret Nahmanides as asserting that all of Jewish law pertaining to such matters is incorporated in the Noahide Code via the *mitzvah* of

However, the basic problem remains. The *mitzvah* of *dinin* is ostensibly solely addressed to, and binding upon, non-Jews.[31] By what authority, then, is *dina de-malkhuta* binding upon Jews? The matter is resolved if it is understood that the *mitzvah* of *dinin* is, in essence, a *mitzvah* enjoining preservation of the social order. It can be regarded as binding upon Jews only if its authority may be derived from natural law.[32] For Rashi, as well as for Maimonides, preservation of an ordered society is mandated by reason.[33]

It is evident that, as found in these sources, the scope of natural law is limited to say the least. In a sense it would be easier to understand a total exclusion of natural law from Jewish legal theory. Total exclusion would lead to the conclusion that reason is not legislatively autonomous and that divine sanction accompanies revealed law but not law mandated by reason. Once the authority of reason is accepted in a limited area the problem to be addressed is why Jewish thought does not accept a fully developed system of *lex naturalis*.

A solution to this vexing problem may be found in Maimonides, *Hilkhot Melakhim* 9:1. Chapter eight of *Hilkhot Melakhim* concludes with the statement that the Seven Commandments must be accepted on the basis of Sinaitic revelation and the corollary that acceptance on the basis of determination of reason does not engender the status either of one of the "pious of the nations of the world" or of one of

---

dinin. The analysis of Rashi's position here presented is, however, consistent with R. Naphtali Zevi Yehudah Berlin's understanding of Nahmanides as presented in R. Berlin's *Ha'amek She'elah*, *She'ilta* 2:3; cf., R. Iser Zalman Meltzer, *Even he-Azel, Hilkhot Malveh ve-Loveh* 27:11.

31. See, however, *supra*, note 26.

32. A similar position, albeit not predicated upon the notion of *dinin*, is espoused by R. Shlomo Luria, *Yam shel Shlomoh, Bava Kamma* 6:14. *Yam shel Shlomoh* declares, "It appears that [the king] can promulgate laws and practices in his land and punish one who violates his edict... for, if not, the world would not exist and will be destroyed."

33. Consistent with this position, Rashi, *Niddah*, 61a, s.v. *meiḥash leih miba'i*, may be understood as applying the identical concept in legitimization of penal sanctions for violation of criminal codes promulgated by virtue of *dina de-malkhuta*. See also *Yam shel Shlomoh, supra*, note 30. For a fuller discussion of Rashi's comment in *Niddah*, see this writer's *"Hasgarat Poshe'a Yehudi she-Baraḥ le-Eretz Yisrael," Be-Netivot ha-Halakhah*, I (New York, 5756), 85-105.

"their wise men." The very next chapter, 9:1, begins with the statement, "Adam was commanded with regard to six matters... even though all of them are a tradition in our hands from our teacher Moses and reason inclines toward them it may be seen from the context of the words of the Torah that he was commanded with regard to these." At first glance, Maimonides seems to have contradicted himself. In 8:11 he declares that one who accepts the Noahide Code on the basis of *hekhra ha-da'at* is not a wise man, whereas in 9:1 he states that indeed *hekhra ha-da'at noteh lahen*. The difficulty however, dissipates if the terminology is examined carefully. *"Ha-da'at noteh"* means literally that reason inclines in a certain direction; *hekhra ha-da'at* is a final, conclusive determination of the intellect. Herein lies not only a resolution of the apparent contradiction but also an explanation of why Judaism cannot admit a fully developed system of natural law. Reason is by no means infallible. There are many matters which appear to be true by virtue of reason but which cannot be known with certainty. The propositions of logic are the best examples of *a priori* truths which are known with certainty. Those propositions commend themselves to the intellect with compelling rational force; they cannot be rejected by any rational person. Moral propositions may be commended to the intellect by reason but their binding validity cannot, in most cases[34] be known with compelling certainty. Reason certainly "inclines" toward their acceptance but rational inclination falls short of final determination. Thus the intellect of a wise man will incline strongly toward acceptance, but the same wise man will recognize that, epistemologically, even strong inclination cannot be equated with *hekhra ha-da'at* or absolute certainty of determination. One who mistakenly confuses rational inclination, no matter how strong, with certainty fails to perceive a crucial epistemological distinction. Such confusion reflects ignorance of a fundamental nature; hence such an individual assuredly does not merit the encomium "wise man."

Certainly, not all propositions postulated by various natural law theorists commend themselves with equal moral force. Undoubtedly, the most compelling of such moral propositions is the admonition "thou

---

34. See extended endnote D.

shalt not kill." At the other extreme of the spectrum, the natural law argument against onanism, for example, is so weak that objective moralists would probably be disinclined to view it as a legitimate application of *lex naturalis*. The very fact that natural law theorists frequently dispute whether or not natural law is applicable with regard to a particular act or activity surely demonstrates the absence of rational compulsion of a nature similar to that which is evident in the propositions of logic.[35] Thus in Jewish legal theory the prohibition against murder is accepted by all as interdicted by *sevarah* or *lex naturalis*. This is because in a system of moral judgments the admonition "Thou shalt not kill" is the epistemological equivalent of the propositions of logic. With regard to proscription of theft, the force of reason is less clear, while preservation of the social order as a natural law imperative is perhaps even more debatable. The crucial question is that of determining at which point along the epistemological spectrum "inclination" is so strong that it becomes endowed with legal authority. If homicide alone is to be accepted as a legitimate application of *lex naturalis* then only the certainty which accompanies the moral equivalent of the propositions of logic and mathematics is acceptable. If other propositions are to be admitted as well, then something less than absolute certainty must be accepted as sufficient for purposes of establishing legal prohibitions. Be that as it may, failure to recognize the precise point on the spectrum which establishes legal certainty, or mistaken identification of a less compelling inclination with a more compelling inclination sufficient to establish legal certainty, reflects ignorance which is not the hallmark of a wise man.[36]

This analysis entails the acceptance of at least the prohibition against murder on the basis of natural law and, arguably, a limited number of other moral principles as well. Other moral rules may not be established with certainty but are indeed rational in the sense that it is reason which inclines toward their acceptance.

Marvin Fox argues that Maimonides consistently maintains that moral rules are not capable of demonstration.[37] Moral judgments, like

---

35. Cf., Thomas Aquinas, *Summa Theologica*, 11, 2, 57.
36. See extended endnote E.
37. See Marvin Fox, *Diné Israel*, pp. xv-xviii.

aesthetic perceptions, are not subject to logical demonstration; either they are perceived or they are not. Moreover, he argues, moral rules, for Maimonides, are mere conventions. The most crucial passage in establishing this thesis occurs in Maimonides' well-known discussion of the punishment of Adam and Eve in the *Guide of the Perplexed*, Book I, chapter 2: "Through the intellect one distinguishes between truth and falsehood, and that was found in Adam in its perfection and integrity. Beautiful and ugly, on the other hand, belong to the things generally accepted as known [i.e., conventions] not to those cognized by the intellect."[38] This statement does not, however, serve to establish that moral judgments are devoid of objective validity.

The crucial point which Maimonides is intent upon establishing is a resolution of the problem of how "knowledge" can be described as punishment rather than perfection. To this he responds that when Adam was yet in a state of innocence there was no reason to judge nudity to be unbecoming to man. "After Adam's disobedience ... he began to give way to desires which had their source in the imagination and in the gratification of his bodily appetites ..." With his disobedience Adam became a sensual creature to whom avoidance of nakedness became a meaningful concept. Adam's punishment was metamorphosis into a sensual being. Aversion to nakedness is a meaningful judgment only when made by a sensual creature. This passage does not, therefore, serve to demonstrate that all moral judgments are subjective or matters of convention or even that aversion to nakedness is a matter of convention.

Moreover, the statement that moral rules are not capable of demonstration does not entail the conclusion that all moral judgments are mere conventions and that particular moral decisions are subjective in the sense that there exists not even a theoretical norm against which such decisions can be measured. Such a standard or norm may well exist, yet not be available to the human intellect. Nevertheless, since such norms are not perceived by means of the rational faculty, moral judgments are made on other grounds. Accordingly, Adam cannot be deemed to have been granted greater rational perceptions subsequent to his disobedience.

---

38. *Ibid.*, p. xviii, note 27.

A statement which appears in the opening section of the eighth chapter of Maimonides' *Treatise on Logic* provides much stronger support for Fox's contention. "The propositions which are known[39] and require no proof for their truthfulness are of four kinds... first ideas as when we know that the whole is greater than the part, that two is an even number, and things equal to the very same thing are equal to each other; conventions, as when we know that uncovering the privy parts is ugly, that compensating a benefactor generously is beautiful..." The first example of a convention is identical with Maimonides' later statement in the *Guide* and may be understood in the same way. The second example, namely that compensating a benefactor is beautiful, is another matter entirely. Maimonides here declares that the propriety of compensating a benefactor is a matter of convention and explicitly distinguishes this proposition from those which he categorizes as first ideas, i.e., those ideas immediately perceived by the intellect.

Yet, one should not extrapolate from this example and universalize the statement as applying to all moral judgments. There may well be other moral perceptions which *are* in the category of first ideas, e.g., the prohibition against homicide. Hence, even for Maimonides, there remains room for a limited theory of natural law.

Marvin Fox states:

> One of the marks of a well trained mind, according to Aristotle, is that it knows how to distinguish between various types of subject-matters, and that it never expects more precision than a subject is capable of yielding.[40] Maimonides knew his Aristotle well and had great regard for the Philosopher. As a follower of the Aristotelian teaching, he quite properly would refuse to recognize a man as wise who could be so confused that he would

---

39. Fox is correct in rejecting Efros' insertion of the phrase "to be true" for two reasons: (1) The phrase is absent in the ibn Tibbon text which reads, *ha-mishpatim asher yevade'u velo yitztarekh ra'ayah al amitatam*; (2) Maimonides, in the *Guide*, explicitly rejects the adjective "true" as a categorization of aversion to nakedness. These propositions require "no proof for their truth" because, although they are "known," they are neither true nor false. See Fox, *Diné Israel*, p. xv, note 22.
40. Aristotle, *Nicomachean Ethics*, I, iii, 1094b, 12-28.

treat matters of convention or taste as if they were capable of rational demonstration. There is, in addition, a danger to society in such an error, since it rejects authority for pseudo-reason, an error which cannot long be suppressed. Once it is clear that moral distinctions are not rational, and they are no longer accepted on the authority of sovereign or God, there is no longer any ground whatsoever for restraint in human behavior.[41]

I would recast the statement somewhat by stating that when reason "inclines" toward acceptance of a moral proposition, but is not compelling, the proposition cannot be regarded as a first principle; acceptance is therefore in the category of convention. One who confuses a convention with a first principle is hardly a wise man.

II.

Two talmudic citations are frequently cited as proof-texts demonstrating that Judaism accepts a much broader doctrine of natural law than has been here outlined. *Eruvin* 100b teaches, "If the Torah had not been given we could have learned modesty from the cat, aversion to robbery from the ant, chastity from the dove and sexual mores from the rooster." Assumed in this passage, it has been argued, is the existence of a natural morality which, upon reflection, is apparent to the properly attuned mind. Yet, as one contemporary scholar has queried, "But what does this passage really prove? How many Jews (or gentiles, for that matter) have learned modesty from the cat? And if one could learn modesty from a cat, why not promiscuity from a dog?"[42] The last question is certainly cogent. If nature is the model for a moral conduct why is chastity valued

---

41. *Diné Israel*, p. xix.
42. S. Z. Leiman, "Critique of Louis Jacobs," in *Contemporary Jewish Ethics*, ed. M. Kellner (New York, 1978), p. 59. Similarly, Marvin Fox, *The Philosophical Foundations of Jewish Ethics: Some Initial Reflections* (Cincinnati, 1979), p. 14, queries, "Might we not have decided just as readily to imitate the ferocity of the lion, the murderousness of an aroused pack of wolves, or the sexual behavior of a rabbit?" See also Richard Wollheim, "Natural Law," *Encyclopedia of Philosophy* (New York, 1967), V, p. 451, who, without reference to *Eruvin* 100b, asks, "Are we … to model ourselves upon the peaceful habits of sheep or upon the internecine conflicts of ants? Is the egalitarian-

and promiscuity disparaged? Why should respect for the property of others be emulated and theft eschewed? The latter are certainly much more common than the former. Indeed, in nature, as in the human jungle, the practice of what are regarded as virtues is the exception rather than the rule. Most certainly, we cannot discern a uniform message simply by observing the conduct of members of the animal kingdom.

Properly understood, the passage does not at all establish the binding, prescriptive power of reason.[43] It does, however, eloquently demonstrate a certain "inclination" of reason. Confronted with different, diverse and conflicting models in nature some persons commit themselves to be guided by moral principles and some do not. Were reason totally autonomous it would look solely to itself, not to the cat, the ant, the dove or the rooster. The faculty of moral reason is, however, attracted by certain forms of behavior and repulsed by others. It is precisely because morality is so infrequently encountered in nature that man must seek out models of moral behavior for emulation. In the absence of a revealed corpus of law man could "learn" moral principles from nature in the sense that when confronted by antithetical models man would make choices on the basis of intuitive responses. Man might emulate certain models of behavior found in the animal kingdom and adopt them as the paradigms for his own conduct but could legislate them as binding law on the basis of reason alone. The product of such an endeavor would not be a system of law but an emotivist ethic. Reason could not be so certain of itself as to proclaim a universally binding law. In the absence of epistemological certainty moral decisions are essentially aesthetic judgments. Under such circumstances reason can but exclaim in the manner of C.L. Stevenson, "I do like this; do so as well." The result is a subjective morality which one recommends to others.

---

ism of the beaver or the hierarchical life of the bee the proper exemplar for human society? Should we imitate the widespread polygamy of the animal kingdom, or is there some higher regularity of which this is no more than a misleading instance?"

43. Fox, *Diné Israel*, pp. viii-ix, is quite right in rejecting a natural law interpretation of the passage. However, I do not see a reflection of pragmatism in this statement as does Fox. Cf., R. Aharon Lichtenstein, "Does Jewish Tradition Recognize an Ethic Independent of Halakha?" *Contemporary Jewish Ethics*, p. 104.

Yoma 67b seems at first glance to provide stronger support for a theory of natural law, but upon further examination is even less compelling. "'You shall keep My statutes' (Leviticus 18:5). This refers to those commandments which had they not been written [in Scripture] should properly have been written. These include the prohibitions against idolatry, adultery, bloodshed, robbery and blasphemy." The crucial phrase in *"re'uyim hayu le-kotevan"* meaning "it would have been proper" or "it would have been fitting" for them to be written.[44] "Proper" or "fitting" means simply that such laws serve a necessary function. This statement implies only that in the absence of divine legislation society would find it useful to enact such laws. Indeed such legislation is found in countless societies which deny the authority of divine law. Here, then, we find not an exposition of natural law but a recognition of the need for what Albo refers to as conventional law. In context, the Gemara then proceeds to distinguish such laws from commandments which are entirely ritual in nature and which, therefore, can derive sanction only from divine law.

Saadia's distinction between *mitzvot sikhliyot* and *mitzvot shimiyot* should be understood in precisely the same manner. There are laws which *ha-sekhel meḥayev*, i.e., which reason mandates, not in the sense that reason serves as a sufficient and authoritative source of law, but which reason commends to us for enactment. Those are known as "rational laws" as distinct from laws which are accepted solely on the basis of tradition, i.e., revelation.[45] In dismissing this distinction, and in asserting that all of the divine law is ultimately rational, Maimonides certainly does not imply that reason could endow all such rules with the authority of law; he means simply that were human reason capable of fathoming the purpose and benefit of every divine law it would recommend such modes of behavior in order that man might achieve the desired ends.

III.

There is, however, another sense in which Jewish thought may be said to reflect natural law theory. Various forms of natural law theory have

---

44. The Soncino translation, "they should by right have been written" is stylistically felicitous but conveys a wrong connotation; cf. Fox, *Diné Israel*, p. viii, note 8.
45. See extended endnote F.

been advanced over the centuries by a host of thinkers from Zeno to John Locke. The simplest and oldest developed theory is found in the writings of the Stoics who observed that the entire universe is governed by laws which exhibit rationality. Inanimate objects adhere to such laws because they are inherent in nature itself. The laws of physics and chemistry exhibit rationality in establishing regularity and predictability. The conduct of animals is regulated by a rational pattern of behavior which we call instinct. Since the universe is a unitary whole governed by rational principles it follows that similar rational, natural laws should exist for the ordering of human conduct. Such rules or laws are readily discoverable by application of the rational faculty with which man has been endowed. Thomas Aquinas, in part as an aid in discovering the rational principles which govern the universe and hence which should be adopted by man in ordering his conduct, invoked the Aristotelian concept of nature as a teleological system. The essence of every created entity stipulates an end. Reason, and hence natural law, requires the fulfillment of those ends and militates against any form of behavior which will serve to thwart such fulfillment. Common to all formulations of natural law theory is the notion that man should seek to identify the rational principles inherent in the natural order and seek to guide himself by "the light of reason."

It is the demand that human conduct be modeled upon the rationality of the natural order which poses a formidable problem. Law, as the term is used by jurists and legal scholars, is a rule which is authoritative and binding and which, when violated, may result in imposition of sanctions against the violator. Law, as the term is used by scientists, is merely a manifestation of regularity and rationality in nature. The former is prescriptive; the latter descriptive. Reducing laws prescribed by the intellect to the rational principles manifest in the universe fails to answer the one crucial metaethical question which must be asked of any moral system: Why be moral? Granted that the universe exhibits rationality and that human conduct is part of a unitary rational mosaic of cosmic proportions, the question remains: Why must man endeavor to manifest such patterns of rationality in his moral behavior? Or as the question is put in its classic formulation: how can prescriptive laws be derived from descriptive laws?

This, in turn, is but a variant of the most crucial of all metaethical problems, *viz.*, the bifurcation of "is" and "ought." Granted that we have successfully accomplished the task of defining and identifying the good and the moral, the question remains, "Why be moral?" The religionist who posits a theistic system of morality has a relatively simple solution to this question, *viz.*, divine authority. One must be moral because such is the will and command of God. Any natural law theory is subject to challenge on the following grounds. Granted that the universe exhibits unitary reason, granted that such rationality was instilled in the universe by the Creator, and granted that man can govern himself by the same rationality only if he obeys the injunction "Follow nature," there is as yet no moral imperative which demands of man that he identify with the rationality of the universe and regulate his conduct accordingly.[46]

The question may be resolved only by an appeal to an anteced-ent metaphysical principle, *viz.*, man ought to obey the will of the Deity insofar as he is capable of discerning His will. Since it was created by God, and since it exhibits a ubiquitous rationality, the universe testi-fies to God's desire that all of creation guide itself by the principles of reason. Therefore, in regulating his personal conduct, man is bound to pursue the dictates of natural law as discerned by reason. Recasting this explanation in the Jewish version of the doctrine of *imitatio Dei*, it is as if God were to address His creatures and to say to them, "Even as I am rational (as evidenced by the rationality of the universe which I have created), be you also rational!"[47] Only by invoking a notion such as this

---

46. See *Shabbat* 133b which records Abba Sha'ul's exegetical interpretation of the phrase *"ve-anvehu"* which occurs in Exodus 15:2. Interpreting this phrase as a contraction of the words *"ani ve-hu"* Abba Sha'ul understands this passage as declaring "Be similar to Him. Just as He is merciful and gracious so also you be merciful and gracious." See also *Sotah* 14a and *Midrash Rabbah, Shemot* 26:2. In his codification of this halakhah, Maimonides, *Hilkhot De'ot* 1:6, explicitly incorporates other divine attributes as well.

47. Aristotle, *Nicomachean Ethics*, VII, iii, 1146b24-1147b17, argues that the conclusion of a moral syllogism is as compelling as that of a logical syllogism. No rational person can accept the premises "All men are mortal" and "Socrates is a man" and deny the conclusion "Socrates is mortal." Aristotle argues that the moral syllogism, when the premises are properly perceived, compels conduct in a manner analogous to the manner in which a logical syllogism compels the assent of reason. The natural law moralist goes beyond this position in arguing, not that man is compelled in the

can prescriptive law be made to flow from its descriptive counterpart. It should be remembered that the admonition upon which the principle of *imitatio Dei* is based is regarded as a formal commandment included in the enumeration of the 613 binding precepts. The scriptural authority for regarding the doctrine of *imitatio Dei* as a formal *mitzvah* is the verse "…and you shall walk in His ways" (Deuteronomy 28:9).[48]

Thus, if Judaism does attribute even limited legislative authority to the intellect, this, too, is so only because such authority is vested in reason by virtue of a direct divine command.

Of course, in a certain fundamental sense casting even a limited natural law theory in a "mitzvahitic" guise only pushes the question back one step. The question which then must be pondered is: "Why must man obey the will of God?" Fear of retribution, while it may constitute a compelling motive for many, is not a complete answer. Conceivably, a person may be willing to accept the punishment entailed in disobeying the will of God, yet no religionist would agree that morally man has a right to do so. One may park overtime at a meter and pay the fine because the infraction does not involve moral turpitude, but no legal moralist would sanction a felony on the plea that the perpetrator is quite willing to pay the penalty exacted by society. Moreover, religious teaching demands that the moral agent strive to act out of a sense of love rather than out of a sense of fear.

The question thus formulated is a challenge not only to the acceptance of moral maxims predicated upon a natural law theory but to the entire corpus of *mitzvot*. It should be remembered that *Ba'al Halakhot Gedolot*, the earliest authority to compose a detailed enumeration of the 613 precepts of Judaism, failed to include belief in God as one of the 613 commandments. The problem for *Ba'al Halakhot Gedolot* is not only

---

intuitive sense, but that man is morally bound to act in conformity with the principles of reason. This leaves us with precisely the original question: Granted that the moral is to be identified with the demand of reason, by what authority is man bound to accept rational principles in regulating his conduct?

48. See Maimonides, *Sefer ha-Mitzvot, mitzvot aseh*, no. 8; *Ba'al Halakhot Gedolot, mitzvot aseh; Sefer Yere'im*, no. 4; *Sefer Mitzvot Katzer*, no. 46; *Sefer Mitzvot Gadol, mitzvot aseh*, no. 7, *Sefer ha-Ḥinnukh*, no. 611. See also *Sifre* on Deuteronomy 13:5: "'After the Lord your God shall you walk' – this is a positive commandment."

that belief cannot be commanded but that the notion of a commandment presupposes a commander. As Bertrand Russell stated in formulating his Theory of Types, a statement about a class cannot itself be a member of that class. God, the commander, stands outside the system of commandments and constitutes the authority by which commandments must be accepted. Commandments are binding because they are decreed by God. But logically prior to a system of commandment is the principle that God's decrees must be obeyed. A commandment to that effect is not self-validating. By what authority is the commandment to accept God's authority mandated?

At this point there must perforce be an appeal to some *a priori* concept.[49] Saadia declares, "reason calls for gratitude to God for His kindness."[50] Filial devotion is common to all members of the human species. The child reacts with love and devotion to parents who have bestowed the gift of love upon him and who have showered him with concern and affection. This reaction is instinctive and intuitive; it is an *a priori* response rooted in reason. It follows, *a fortiori*, that man should respond in the same manner to his heavenly Father, the author of life itself, Who continuously exercises providential guardianship over His creatures. Such a reaction need not be commanded; it is demanded by reason. It follows, then, that obedience to the will of God is a dictate of reason and is the *a priori* assumption underlying the binding nature of the entire corpus of divine commandments.

IV.

The crucial notion that reason demands that man obey the will of God – even that he seek to discover the propositions mandated by divine will – is a concept for which explicit talmudic support may be found.[51]

---

49. Cf., the statement of Rivash cited *supra*, note 11. For Rivash the *a priori* concept seems to be the authority vested in a community by virtue of a social contract to accept legislation on behalf of the community.

50. *Book of Beliefs and Opinion*, Treatise III, chap. 3.

51. Of interest with regard to this point is the citation by the Gemara, *Bava Kamma* 85a, of Exodus 21:19 and the declaration, "From here [it is derived] that the physician is granted permission to cure." The obvious implication is that in the absence of scriptural dispensation such activity would be forbidden. Rashi comments that a

Jewish law prescribes that Noahides are to be held accountable even for transgressions committed in ignorance of the law. The Noahide is culpable, declares the Gemara, *Makkot* 9b, "because he should have learned but did not learn." This is probably the earliest formulation of the legal maxim "Ignorance of the law is no excuse," although in Jewish law this principle is restricted to violations of the Noahide Code. This dictum, which is ostensibly merely the formulation of a punitive principle, implies much more than appears on the surface. The Noahide Code applies to all gentiles, whether or not they are or were exposed to information regarding the historical phenomenon of revelation at Sinai and whether or not the Noahide tradition was transmitted to their progenitors. Judaism recognizes no doctrine of invincible ignorance. The problem of theodicy is self-apparent. How can a just God hold disadvantaged creatures who have not been the privileged recipients of revelation accountable for obedience to a law of which they have no knowledge? The answer, "He should have learned," is a cogent answer only if an underlying prior assumption is accepted, namely, that there exists an *obligation* on the part of Noahides to seek such information. By what authority is a person obliged to seek such knowledge? Indeed, in the absence of revelation, how is the uninitiated to be held responsible for (a) the discovery of the existence of God, and (b) an awareness that God has revealed a corpus of law which is binding upon all mankind? Clearly, only if both premises are known and accepted can one address the question of obligation to discover and learn the contents of that corpus of law.

It should, however, be recognized that Judaism posits that the existence of God is readily discernible to the human mind, either on the basis of an immediate *a priori* awareness or on the basis of a simple formulation of one of the classic proofs for the existence of God. Judaism must also

---

biblical verse is required to teach us that we are not to say "How is it that God smites and man heals?" In much the same vein *Tosafot* and R. Solomon ben Abraham Adret state that without such sanction, "he who heals might appear as if he invalidated a divine decree." The implications of the Gemara's statement are: (1) Reason itself perceives that intervention in physiological processes in the absence of specific divine permission to do so is an attempt to thwart the will of God; and (2) man, even in the absence of a formal prohibition, ought not to act in a manner which is contrary to the will of God.

posit that a rational mind necessarily perceives that God may well make certain demands of man and, furthermore, if He does so, God must have made His will known to mankind. Reason demands that man obey the will of God; therefore, reason demands both that man make an effort to discover God's will as expressed in revelation to man and that man obey the revealed will of God.[52] All of this must be accepted by man, not on the basis of divine command, because at this point in his intellectual inquiry man has not become aware of the content of divine commandments, but on the basis of reason alone. In this sense one may indeed speak of the presence of a natural law theory in Jewish thought, albeit the natural law here described is of a very particular and limited kind.

Extended Notes

A. Maimonides requires not merely that non-Jews accept the Noahide Code on the basis of revelation but specifically on the basis of Sinaitic revelation. Maimonides here extends to non-Jews the principle earlier formulated by him with regard to Jews. The Mishnah, *Ḥullin* 7:6, declares that the prohibition concerning the sciatic sinew does not extend to the sciatic sinew of non-kosher animals. R. Judah, in objecting to the ruling, argues that the prohibition was directed to the children of Jacob at a time when all animals were permitted. Responding to the objection, the Sages declare, "[The prohibition] was stated at Sinai but written in its proper place." Rashi, *Ḥullin* 100b, amplifies this statement and interprets it in a literal manner as meaning that the passage prohibiting the sciatic sinew, Genesis 32:33, was transmitted for the first time at Sinai but "until Sinai they were not admonished." The verse in question "was written in its place after it was declared at Sinai; and Moses, [when] he wrote and arranged the Torah recorded this verse in association with the event...." According to Rashi, the prohibition was promulgated at Sinai for the first time but was recorded in the Torah in conjunction with the narrative concerning Jacob's strife with the angel since that incident is the reason underlying the subsequent prohibition.

---

52. See R. Elchanan Wasserman, *"Dugma le-Bi'urei Aggadot al Derekh ha-Peshat,"* no. 1; *Kovetz He'arot* (New York, 5712); reprinted in his "Ma'amar al Emunah," *Kovetz Ma'amarim* (Jerusalem, 5723), pp. 11-16.

Maimonides, in his *Commentary on the Mishnah*, explains the statement of the Mishnah in a quite different manner:

> Give heart to this great principle which is included in the Mishnah, *viz.*, … all that we disdain or perform today we do so solely by virtue of the command of the Holy One, blessed be He, through our teacher Moses, may he rest in peace, not because the Holy One, blessed be He, stated this to the prophets who preceded him. For example, we do not eat a limb torn from a live animal because God forbade [it] to Noah, but because Moses forbade to us a limb torn from a live animal by virtue of what he was commanded at Sinai to the effect that the prohibition against [eating] a limb torn from a living animal remains in effect; similarly, we do not circumcise because our father Abraham, may he rest in peace, circumcised himself and the members of his household but because the Holy One, blessed be He, commanded us through our teacher Moses, may he rest in peace, that we circumcise just as our father Abraham, may he rest in peace, circumcised; and, similarly [with regard to] the sciatic sinew, we do not follow the prohibition of our father Jacob, but the command of our teacher Moses, may he rest in peace. …

[Cf., however, *Tosafot, Sanhedrin* 56b, s.v. *eser mitzvot*; R. Reuben Margulies, *Margaliyot ha-Yam* (Jerusalem, 5718), *ad locum*; and R. Shimon Moshe Diskin, *Ohel Yehoshu'a* (Jerusalem: 5738), 56ff.] Maimonides, thus, accepts the notion of binding prohibitions before Sinai, other than those of the Noahide Code, but maintains that the original command of such prohibitions lacks binding authority subsequent to Sinai. In the cited passage in the *Mishneh Torah*, Maimonides extends this principle to the Noahide Code as well. The original revelation to Adam and Noah was binding only until Sinai; the Noahide Code continues to be binding only because it was renewed at Sinai. Gentiles must accept the Noahide Code, not on the basis of the original revelation, but on the basis of Sinaitic revelation. Thus, in addition to moral conduct, a faith commitment in the form of acceptance of the validity of the Sinaitic revelation is required of all non-Jews and such acceptance is a precondition of eternal heavenly reward. See this writer's discussion in this volume, *supra*, pp. 26-29. Cf., however, R. Yom Tov Lipman Heilprin, *Teshuvot Oneg Yom Tov* (Vilna, 5640), no. 19.]

B. A similar dictum occurs in a letter to R. Hasdai ha-Levi; see *Teshuvot ha-Rambam ve-Iggerotav* (Leipzig, 1859), Part 2, 23b. R. Joseph Karo in his commentary on the *Mishneh Torah, Kesef Mishneh, loc. cit.*, states that this is Maimonides' own opinion and lacks earlier textual support, but is correct nonetheless. A number of later scholars have attempted to demonstrate that Maimonides' statement is based upon earlier authority.

R. Ezekiel Feivel, *Sefer Toldot Adam* (Dyhrenfurth, 1801), chapter 6, 35a, reports that an anonymous scholar from the Orient visited Vilna and, marveling at the encyclopedic knowledge of R. Zalman of Volozhin (a brother of the famed R. Chaim of Volozhin), asked him to elucidate a number of difficult passages in Maimonides' writings. When questioned with regard to the source of Maimonides' statement concerning Noahides and their obligation to accept the Seven Commandments on the basis of Sinaitic revelation, R. Zalman produced an unidentified Midrash which states:

> Rabbi Y. said, "I have heard that the pious of the nations of the world have a share in the world-to-come. We have, however, not been taught this with regard to the wise men of the nations of the world. Who is a pious man from among the nations of the world? He who accepts the Seven Commandments because they are written in the Torah. A wise man from among the nations of the world is one who fulfills them on the basis of the determination of his reason."

It is interesting to note that this Midrash refers to one who accepts the Seven Commandments on the basis of reason as "a wise man" See Steven S. Schwarzschild, "Do Noachites Have to Believe in Revelation?" *Jewish Quarterly Review* 52/4 (1962), 305-306.

One midrashic collection, *The Mishnah of R. Eliezer (The Midrash of Thirty-two Hermeneutic Rules)*, ed. H. G. Enelow (New York, 1933), p. 121 contains a most interesting statement with regard to the definition of "the pious of the nations of the world." Such an appellation may be ascribed, declares the Midrash, "only when they perform [the Seven Commandments] and say 'we perform [them] because our father Noah commanded us [regarding them] by the mouth of God.' ...But if they fulfill the Seven Commandments and say, 'We have heard them from so and so' or [if they perform them] of their own accord for so does reason determine... they receive their reward only in this world." Maimonides' central point, *viz.*, that the Noahide Code must be accepted on the basis of revelation is certainly substantiated by this midrashic passage. Yet this Midrash could not have been Maimonides' source since Maimonides differs from the Midrash with regard to one important point. The Midrash states that Noahides may accept the Seven Commandments because they were revealed to Noah. Maimonides insists (as will be further clarified in the text) that Noahides must accept the Seven Commandments on the basis of revelation at Sinai rather than on the basis of revelation to Adam or Noah. For Maimonides, Noahides may aspire to reward in the world-to-come only upon acceptance of the veracity and validity of the Sinaitic revelation; see R. Abraham I. Karelitz, *Ḥazon Ish, Shevi'it* 24:2 and *Hilkhot Avodat Kokhavim* 65:2. Moreover, while the Mishnah of R. Eliezer speaks of "reward only in this world," *Teshuvot ha-Rambam*, ed. Alfred Freimann (Jerusalem, 1934), no. 124 and *Teshuvot ha-Rambam*, ed. Yehoshua Blau (Jerusalem, 1957), I, no. 148, appears to exclude any type of reward unless observance is predicated upon revelation. Nevertheless, the Midrash, precisely because it could not have been Maimonides' source, constitutes strong corroborative evidence for his contention that the Noahide Code must be accepted by non-Jews on the basis of revelation. Since the Midrash could not have been Maimonides' source it must reflect the existence of a well-established tradition with regard to this point. Cf., Schwarzschild, p. 306. Although Maimonides, in his earlier noted *Teshuvot ha-Rambam* cites a work bearing the title *Beraita shel R. Eli'ezer* as a source for this position, that work, because of the reasons indicated, does not seem to be identical with the extant text of the *Mishnah of R. Eli'ezer*. Cf., however, *Encyclopedia Talmudit*, VI (Jerusalem, 1954), 290, no. 11.

In a letter addressed to Moses Mendelssohn and published in Mendelssohn's *Gesammelte Schriften*, XVI (Berlin, 1929), R. Jacob

Emden states that Maimonides' position is based upon *Sanhedrin* 105a. R. Joshua, who maintains that non-Jews may share in the world-to-come, interprets the verse "The wicked shall return to the nether-world, even all the nations that forget God" (Psalms 9:18) as follows: "The wicked shall return to the nether-world'... Who are they? [They are] 'all the nations who forget God.'" Maimonides, avers R. Emden, understands 'the nations who forget God' as including those who observe the Noahide code but 'forget' that it was commanded by God.

In a posthumously published article, R. Malkiel Zevi Tennenbaum (author of *Teshuvot Divrei Malki'el*), *Torah she-be-al Peh*, XV (5733), 164, suggests that Maimonides' position is deduced from *Bava Kamma* 38a. The Gemara cites the verse "He stands and shakes the earth. He beholds and makes the nations to tremble" (Habakkuk 3:6), and comments, "What did He see? He saw the Seven Commandments which the sons of Noah accepted but did not observe [therefore] 'He arose and He permitted them [to the sons of Noah]." The Gemara, for exegetical purposes, renders the word *"va-yater"* as "permitted" rather than "makes to tremble." The Gemara, in the ensuing discussion, modifies this interpretation by stating that the prohibitions of the Noahide Code were not actually rescinded, but were reduced in status so that a non-Jew who observes them is rewarded "as one who is not commanded but observes," i.e., receives lesser compensation than "one who is commanded and observes." R. Tennenbaum avers that acceptance of the Noahide Code on the basis of Sinaitic revelation carries with it reward as "one who is commanded and observes." Such compensation is only just since gentiles are indeed bound by the Noahide Code as revealed at Sinai. A new revelation of the Noahide Code at Sinai became necessary because of widespread non-adherence to its provisions by gentiles. Accordingly, the original mandate was revoked at Sinai to be replaced by a new obligation. In speaking of one who observes the Noahide Code as being rewarded as "one who is not commanded," the Gemara, declares Rabbi Tennenbaum, refers solely to the non-Jew who does not accept the Seven Commandments on the basis of Sinaitic revelation but accepts them on the basis of an earlier revelation or because of some extraneous consideration. (This analysis of *Bava Kamma* 38a is also independently advanced by R. Meir Simchah ha-Kohen of Dvinsk, *Or Sameaḥ*, *Hilk-*

hot Issurei Bi'ah 14:7 and by R. Yitzchak Ze'ev Soloveitchik, *Ḥiddushei Maran Riz ha-Levi* (Jerusalem, 5723), 164. This position is also explicitly formulated by an early authority, Ritva, in his commentary to *Makkot* 9a.) R. Tennenbaum adds that Maimonides inferred that only the gentile who observes the Noahide code as "one who is commanded and performs" receives a share in the world-to-come. See also R. Yitzchak Ze'ev Soloveitchik, *Ḥiddushei ha-Griz al ha-Torah (mi-pi ha-shemu'ah)* (undated), no. 152, who finds Maimonides' position reflected in the words of 11 Kings 5:8. See also R. Shlomoh ben Shimon Duran, *Teshuvot ha-Rashbash*, no. 543, who finds a source for Rambam's position in *Sanhedrin* 59a and R. Zevi Hirsch Chajes, *Torat ha-Nevi'im*, chap. 11, who finds a source in *Ḥullin* 92a; see also *idem*, in R. Abraham Naphtali Jener, *Zekhuta de-Avraham* (Lemberg, 1868), no. 21.

See also R. Chaim Hirschensohn, *Eleh Divrei ha-Brit*, I, 6, who advances a deductive argument in explanation of Maimonides' position predicated upon his view that prior to the Sinaitic revelation the Noahide commandments were binding solely by virtue of *sevarah*; see *supra* note 1.

The foregoing is merely an attempt to uncover a Talmudic or midrashic source for Maimonides' view regarding Noahides and the world-to-come but does not address the question of why belief in Sinaitic revelation should be a necessary condition for eternal reward; see above, note A.

C. Earlier, in Book One, chapter 5, Albo does state:

> It is because association and aggregation are necessary for the existence and support of the human species that the wise men have said that man is political by nature. They mean by this that it is almost necessary for a man by his nature to live in a city (state) with a large group of men that he may be able to obtain what he needs for his life and support. It is clear therefore that the whole group residing in a city, or a district, or a region, or all the human beings in the world should have some order which they follow in their conduct, maintaining justice in general and suppressing wrong, so as to keep men from quarreling in their

transactions and business relations with one another. Such order would include protection against murder, theft, robbery and the like, and in general all those measures which are calculated to maintain the political group and enable the people to live in welfare. This order the wise men call natural law, meaning by natural that it is necessary for man by his nature, whether the order emanates from a wise man or a prophet.

"Association and aggregation" are "almost necessary" but not absolutely necessary. Society, to exist, requires "some order" and it is this order which "the wise men" call natural law. Such order, which includes "protection against murder, theft, robbery and the like" is necessary for man by his nature. It is because such order is natural to man by virtue of his nature that Albo asserts that men can coexist within a society without difficulty. Albo does not argue that preservation of society is mandated by natural law but, rather, that natural law is logically prior to formation of society, and makes possible the existence of society.

On the other hand, it would be an error to suppose that, for Albo, natural law is manifest only in an organized society. Ralph Lerner has stated, "Albo suggests that this natural law is not absolutely necessary for man because it is not absolutely necessary for man to live in political society; moreover, he suggests that the validity of this natural law depends upon its establishment by some human individual. By pointing to the possibility of life outside the city, Albo casts some doubt on the obligatory character of natural law. By further distinguishing the purpose of this natural law from the perfection that is proper to man, Albo in effect denies that natural law is, strictly speaking, natural." See Lerner, "Moses Maimonides," *History of Political Philosophy*, p. 221. Elsewhere, the same author writes, "We may say more generally, then, that natural law's injunctions are needed for human perfection as such, but only insofar as man is part of a city or of some kind of association." See "Natural Law in Albo's *Book of Roots*," in *Ancients and Moderns*, ed. Joseph Cropsey (New York and London, 1964), p. 141ff. However, in chapter 7, Albo does not at all present natural law as a function of political philosophy and even in chapter 5, as has been stated, natural law is cited as a logically prior concept which has the salutary effect of making society possible. The validity of natural law certainly does not "depend upon its establishment by some human individual." Albo does speak of an order which "emanates from a wise man or a prophet" but the function of such individuals is pedagogic rather than legislative. The order to which reference is made "is necessary for man by his nature" even though society itself is only "almost necessary" in contradistinction to being absolutely necessary.

D. The principle "How do you know that your blood is sweeter than the blood of your fellow" which is postulated by the Gemara on the basis of *sevarah* is one proposition which is declared to be known with certainty on the basis of reason. Nevertheless, Maimonides, *Hilkhot Yesodei ha-Torah* 5:7, speaks of this principle as *"davar she-ha-da'at noteh lo,"* although even stronger terminology would be in order.

It is conceivable that Maimonides used the weaker expression in order to indicate that the obligation to suffer martyrdom rather than commit an act of murder encompasses situations in which this *sevarah* is not applicable. In the same chapter, *Hilkhot Yesodei ha-Torah* 5:5, Maimonides rules that the principle "be killed and do not transgress" applies even in a situation in which a victim is singled out and the entire group warned that, if the specific individual is not delivered, all will perish. The *sevarah* "How do you know that your blood is sweeter" certainly does not apply in this instance. *Kesef Mishneh, ad loc.,* states that the Sages were in possession of a tradition extending this principle even to cases in which this *sevarah* does not apply. R. Chaim Ozer Grodzinski, *Teshuvot Aḥi'ezer,* II no. 16, sec. 5, presents a formal hermeneutic derivation substantiating the extension of the rule to encompass situations in which this *sevarah* is not applicable. Similarly, it may cogently be argued that, according to Maimonides, the principle "be killed but do not transgress" applies even to the taking of fetal life despite the fact that fetal life is "less sweet" as evidenced by the fact that feticide does not constitute a capital crime. See J. David Bleich, "Abortion in Halakhic Literature," *Jewish Bioethics,* ed. Fred Rosner and J. David Bleich (New York, 1979), pp. 141-142 and 173 note 71.

Maimonides' statement, *Hilkhot Yesodei ha-Torah* 5:2, describing as a *mitzvah* the obligation to accept martyrdom rather than commit an act of homicide, should not be misunderstood. Maimonides means thereby only that once established as an obligation on the basis of *sevarah* actual fulfillment constitutes an act of sanctification of the Divine Name; in the absence of the *sevarah* such an obligation would not be subsumed under the *mitzvah* of sanctification of the Divine Name. Faur, *Iyunim*, p. 121, apparently misses this point.

E. This analysis of Maimonides' position is at variance with the position set forth by Strauss, *Persecution*, p. 97, note 4. Strauss declares, "The Noahidic commandments cannot be identified with the natural law, at least not according to Maimonides. For – to say nothing of *ever min ha-ḥai* – the prohibition against incest or unchastity which occupies the central place in his enumeration of the Noahidic commandments … is considered by him to belong to the revealed laws as distinguished from the so-called rational laws (*Eight Chapters*, vi) … This is not contradicted by Maimonides' statement that the *da'at* inclines man toward six of the seven Noahidic commandments … for *da'at* does not necessarily mean 'reason' or 'intelligence.'" [Strauss infers from Maimonides' statement, *Hilkhot Melakhim* 9:1, "Adam was commanded with regard to six matters … and reason inclines toward them … He added to Noah [the prohibition against] the limb of a living animal…" that reason inclines only toward the first six. To be sure, the phrase "and reason inclines toward them" was used by Maimonides in association with the six commandments revealed to Adam, but there is no reason to assume that Maimonides intends to exclude the seventh from this categorization. Certainly, the *ela* reading in 8:11 which refers to all seven Noahide commandments encompasses *ever min ha-ḥai* as well.]

It is my contention that *da'at* does indeed mean "reason" or "intelligence." Reason would indeed be inclined to abjure *ever min ha-ḥai* as involving wanton and needless cruelty to animals.

The problem which Strauss raises with regard to *arayot* (and which was noted earlier by R. Isaiah Pik in a marginal gloss to *Yoma* 67b) does, however, require resolution. This problem may be resolved upon careful analysis of Maimonides' source. *Yoma* 67b declares:

> Our Rabbis taught: "Mine ordinances shall ye do," i.e., such commandments which, if they were not written [in scripture], they

should by right have been written and these are they: [the laws concerning] idolatry, immorality and bloodshed, robbery and blasphemy. "And My statutes shall ye keep," i.e., such commandments to which Satan objects, they are [those relating to] the putting on of *sha'atnez, ḥalitzah* [performed] by a sister-in-law, the purification of the leper, and the he-goat-to-be-sent-away. And perhaps you might think these are vain things, therefore Scripture says: "I am the Lord," i.e., I, the Lord have made it a statute and you have no right to criticize it.

The Gemara clearly lists *giluy arayot* among the *mishpatim* rather than among the *ḥukkim* or "revealed laws." The Gemara then proceeds to enumerate five examples of *ḥukkim*. Maimonides initially gives only three examples in the passage cited but shortly thereafter adds additional ones:

Rather they cite matters all of which are based on tradition; partaking of meat and milk together, wearing clothes made of wool and linen and forbidden sexual relationships (*arayot*). These and similar commandments are what God called "My statutes (*ḥukkotai*)" which as they [the Sages] said, are statutes which I have enacted for you, which you have no permission to question, which the nations of the world attack and which Satan denounces, such as the red heifer, the scapegoat and so forth.

If one compares the five examples listed by Maimonides with the five enumerated by the Gemara it is readily evident that the second and fifth are identical in both listings. The first example of the Gemara, *akhilat ḥazir*, is replaced by *basar be-ḥalav* in Maimonides' enumeration; the fourth, *taharat metzora*, is replaced with *parah adumah*. In both cases the substitute is of a like for a like: one dietary prohibition for another dietary prohibition and one purification ritual for another. The third in the Gemara's series, *ḥalitzat yevamot*, i.e., the rite of removing the shoe which releases the childless widow from the obligation of levirate marriage, is replaced by the term *arayot*. It is, of course, possible that the text of the Eight Chapters is corrupt. This would, however, not really resolve the problem completely for reasons which will be indicated shortly. More likely, Maimonides' reference is not to consanguineous or blood relatives but to a specific type of *ervah*, namely, to the prohibition against marrying a sister-in-law who has borne a child – and perhaps to the prohibition against marriage between the childless widow and any person save her deceased husband's brother. Such marriage is certainly not negated by reason. [See R. Abraham ibn Ezra, *Yesod Mora*, chap. 5, who declares that the prohibition against simultaneous marriage to two sisters could not have been prior to Sinai on the basis of *"shikul ha-da'at"* but that *arayot* are *nit'av be-toladah*.] Indeed, were there a natural abhorrence militating against marrying a brother's wife, the distinction between the childless widow and a widow with children would not be readily discernible. Maimonides' reference to *arayot* is thus a reference to the laws of levirate obligation which is a paraphrase of the Gemara's *halitzat yevamah* and certainly falls within the category of *hukkim*. Reason, however, does incline against conjugal relationship with blood relatives. Prohibitions in the category of *giluy arayot* in the Noahide Code are solely of the latter nature: a widowed sister-in-law is never proscribed to Noahides.

Indeed, this distinction must be made even in the absence of Maimonides' statement classifying *arayot* among the *hukkim*. *Sifra* on Leviticus 20:26 states:

> R. Elazar b. Azariyah said: From whence [is it known] that one should not say "I do not wish to eat the flesh of the swine; I do not wish to cohabit with an *ervah*" rather [he should say] "I wish, but what shall I do for my Father in heaven has decreed upon me thus."

Assuming, as does Maimonides, that a worthy person has no desire for that which is forbidden by the *mishpatim* but that the opposite is true with regard to *hukkim*, *Sifra* appears to contradict *Yoma* 67b. *Arayot* are among the rational laws, declares *Yoma*, yet *Sifra* states that one should eschew an *ervah* only because "My Father in heaven decreed upon me." The contradiction is resolved if it is understood that *Yoma* refers to blood relatives only, whereas *Sifra* refers solely to other types of *ervah*. Cf., D. Rosen, *Die Ethik des Maimonides* (Berslau, 1879), p. 94 note 4. It should be noted that both R. Isaiah Pik, in this gloss to *Yoma* 67b, and R. David

Kafih in annotations to his translation of *Maimonides' Commentary on the Mishnah, Nashim-Nezikin* in (Jerusalem, 5724), p. 268, note 14, suggest that the phrase *giluy arayot* did not appear in Maimonides' text of *Yoma* 67b. See also *Ḥiddushei Maharsha, Yoma* 67b.

F. Fox's analysis of this point, *Diné Israel*, pp. x-xi, is correct, although I believe he overemphasizes the concept of "useful" as the criterion of the rational. I cannot agree with Lamm and Kirschenbaum, *Cardozo Law Review*, I (1979), pp. 111-113, who ascribe a natural law position to Saadia. Saadia's *mitzvot sikhliyot* are quite distinct from the concept of natural law. The former, since they include many laws which are not binding upon Noahides are not at all universal in nature and hence lack the crucial determinant criterion of natural law. Cf. also, Lerner, "Natural Law," *Ancients and Moderns*, pp. 143f. Similarly, Grotius, citing Maimonides, *Guide*, III, 26, identifies *mishpatim* with natural law: see I. Husik, "The Law of Nature, Hugo Grotius, and the Bible," *Hebrew Union College Annual*, II (1925), 399.

Some support for identification of the term *mitzvot sikhliyot* with the concept of natural law may be found in the following passage of R. Shem Tob ben Shem Tob's *Derashot ha-Torah* 25:

> It should be known that of the laws and ordinances some are called natural, some are called conventional, and some are called divine. The rational are those which nature mandates and consist of all the laws and ordinances which are identical in the entire world, such as "Thou shalt not kill" and the like. In sum, all matters which reason (*sekhel*) mandates are called in our Torah rational commandments.

Nevertheless, in context it appears that R. Shem Tob presents no more than the standard definition of *sikhliyot* and merely introduces the term *teva* as a synonym for *sekhel*. It cannot be deduced from this statement that reason constitutes binding authority for natural law.

7

Is There an Ethic Beyond Halakhah?

The question, as formulated, constitutes not one but at least four separate questions. It would seem appropriate to consider those questions in serial order.

I.

Is there a standard of conduct to which persons may be held, and according to which human actions may be judged, other than the standard reflected in normative law? The identical question may be rephrased in another form: Is there a standard of *lifnim mi-shurat ha-din* or is the sole moral standard that of *din* itself? The answer to the question thus formulated is obvious. Rabbinic literature is replete with references to ethical norms described as *lifnim mi-shurat ha-din*. The very juxtaposition of the two categories constitutes an acknowledgement of standards of *lifnim mi-shurat ha-din* which are not coextensive with *din*.

Nevertheless, the question is entirely cogent; it need only be recast in a somewhat different form. The question properly posed is: Is the standard described as *lifnim mi-shurat ha-din*, in actuality, simply another aspect of a multifaceted Halakhah or does the category of *lifnim mi-shurat ha-din*, in some fundamental sense, transcend Halakhah?

Despite the nomenclature employed in describing this norm, *viz.*, "*lifnim mi-shurat ha-din* – *beyond* the boundary of the law," adherence to the standard denoted thereby is prescribed as normative and binding and hence endowed with the essential attributes of Halakhah. This was certainly the position of Rabbi Isaac of Corbeille who, in his *Sefer Mitzvot Katan (Semak)*, enumerates the obligation to act *lifnim mi-shurat ha-din* as one of the 613 divinely ordained commandments. In support of that thesis *Semak* cites the statement of the Gemara: "Rav Yoḥanan said, 'Jerusalem was destroyed because [the inhabitants] judged [in accordance with] Torah law.' Should they rather have followed the law of the Magians? Say, rather, because they based their judgments solely upon Torah law and did not act *lifnim mi-shurat ha-din*."[1]

It must be granted that *Semak's* conclusion reflects an individual opinion rather than a halakhic consensus. Yet, *di minimus*, his proof-text certainly established beyond a reasonable doubt that failure to adhere to a standard of *lifnim mi-shurat ha-din* is a culpable offense – and the punishment meted out at one point in Jewish national history was the destruction of Jerusalem. No less! "*Ain onshin ela im ken mazhirin* – There can be no punishment other than upon admonition"[2] is not only a fundamental principle of Jewish law, but is the expression of an elemental principle of justice. Accordingly, *Semak's* basic point, i.e., that *lifnim mi-shurat ha-din* is mandated as a normative and binding standard of conduct, must be conceded by all. The sole issue which is the subject of contention among early authorities (*Rishonim*) is whether or not this obligation is accorded the status of an explicitly enumerated and self-contained *mitzvah*. The concept of a binding Sinaitic obligation not explicitly enumerated as one of the 613 precepts is not at all foreign to the annals of Halakhah. In all cases, inclusion or exclusion from the formal catalogue of 613 commandments is entirely devoid of substantive import.

To be sure, Rosh, *Bava Metzi'a* 2:7, declares that a human court cannot compel action *lifnim mi-shurat ha-din*. However, *Mordekhai, Bava*

---

1. *Bava Metzi'a* 30b.
2. *Sanhedrin* 56b.

Metzi'a, sec. 257, cites two earlier authorities, Ravan and Ravya, who maintain that such action could indeed be compelled. Ravya is similarly cited by *Hagahot Maimuniyot, Hilkhot Gezelah* 11:3. That controversy, in turn, appears to be predicated upon a disagreement between Rabbah, the son of Rav Huna, and Rav which is recorded in *Bava Metzi'a* 83a:

> Some porters [negligently] broke a barrel of wine belonging to Rabbah, the son of R. Huna. Thereupon he seized their garments; so they went and complained to Rav. "Return them their garments," he ordered. "Is that the law?" he inquired. "Even so," he rejoined: "'That thou mayest walk in the way of good men'" (Proverbs 2:20). Their garments having been returned, they observed, "we are poor men, have worked all day, and are in need. Are we to get nothing?" "Go and pay them," he ordered. "Is that the law?" he asked. "Even so,"[3] was his reply: "'and keep the path of the righteous'" (Proverbs 2:20).

3. *Dikdukei Sofrim* reports that the word *"in"* meaning "even so" does not appear in any of the manuscripts available to him. Relying largely upon the absence of the word *"in,"* Ephraim E. Urbach, *Ḥazal Pirkei Emunot ve-Deot* (Jerusalem, 5736), p. 291, asserts that determination of *lifnim mi-shurat ha-din* is entirely subjective and hence conformity with that standard is a matter of voluntary decision. Assuming, *arguendo*, that the matter rests upon the presence or absence of this single word Urbach's conclusion is overstated. The presence of the word cannot be dismissed as a mere printer's error. The word *"in"* is present in all published texts which, in turn, were based in part upon manuscripts not available to *Dikdukei Sofrim*. More significantly, the authorities cited by *Mordekhai* and *Hagahot Maimuniyot* cannot be ignored or dismissed out of hand. Those authorities clearly understand Rav's response as indicating a normative, binding obligation. Hence, if Urbach's textual analysis is accepted, it must be concluded that the word *"in"* was indeed present in the manuscripts consulted by those authorities. In actuality, the manuscript reading lends itself to the identical interpretation. In response to the query "Is that the law?" Rav replies, "and keep the path of the righteous." Rabbah was clearly reluctant to pay the porters' wages as he was already advised to do so by Rav – hence his query with regard to legal liability. The authorities cited quite cogently understand Rav's reply not as a mere reiteration of his earlier advice, which might have been understood by Rav as merely moral in nature, but as explicitly affirming a normative and binding obligation. In either event, whatever the correct textual reading may be, it is undeniable that Ravan and Ravya regarded the *lifnim mi-shurat ha-din* of *Bava Metzi'a* 83a as reduced to *din* itself.

There is no question that the strict letter of the law holds porters liable for damages resulting from their negligence. Having failed to perform their duties, they certainly had no claim in *din* for compensation. Nevertheless, Rav not only absolves them of all tort liability but also accords them an actionable claim for their hire. The actionability of a claim, which can only be described as a claim *lifnim mi-shurat ha-din*, is assuredly proof positive that the obligation is firmly rooted in Halakhah. Actionability is, after all, the litmus test of a cognizable legal obligation.

It should not be inferred that Rav – or *Mordekhai* – assert that all obligations *lifnim mi-shurat ha-din* are actionable. That is patently not the case. On the contrary, actionability with regard to such matters is the exception rather than the norm. A precise analysis of the circumstances in which such obligations are actionable is beyond the scope of the present discussion. Suffice it to say that, as pointed out by Rabbi Isaac ha-Levi Herzog,[4] examination of the relevant talmudic discussions yields at least eight diverse categories of *lifnim mi-shurat ha-din* which do not ordinarily give rise to actionable claims. These distinct categories of *lifnim mi-shurat ha-din* reflect diverse degrees of ethical obligation and are accompanied by varying degrees of moral censure for failure to comply. Listed in decreasing order or resemblance to normative-law they are as follows:

1. *Dinei shamayim* – obligations with regard to which the individual is culpable in terms of the "Judgments of Heaven" – obligations which are imposed in order to fulfill one's duty *vis-à-vis* Heaven, as distinct from obligations which are recognized by human courts.[5] Chief among obligations of this nature is the obligation to make restitution for tort damages inflicted other than by means of a proximate cause (*gerama be-nezakin*) and an obligation to make whole for losses suffered as a result of failure to give evidence. These talmudic formulae expressly acknowledge both obligation (*ḥayyav*) and legal norms (*dinei shamayim*). Such

---

4. "Moral Right and Duties in Jewish Law," *The Main Institutions of Jewish Law* (London, 1936), I, 383-385.
5. See *Bava Kamma* 55b-56a.

obligations are distinguished from other legal obligations solely by virtue of the fact that they are non-actionable.

2. *Nikra rasha* – acts of commission or of omission which give rise to application to the perpetrator of the epithet "wicked person." Censure of this nature is expressed by means of formal proclamation of the individual's wickedness in the form of public denunciation in the synagogue. Although less ominous than excommunication by means of "bell, book and candle," the very prospect of public censure and humiliation undoubtedly sufficed, at least in the vast majority of instances, to guarantee adherence to otherwise unenforceable standards of conduct. Thus, if the details of a contemplated sale, including the purchase price, have been negotiated and agreed upon, third parties are enjoined from interfering with consummation of the transaction by tendering a more enticing offer to the seller.[6] Insofar as *din* is concerned, since the conveyance has not yet been finalized, there is nothing which prevents a third party from interposing himself and consummating the sale on his own behalf. One who does so, in violation of the norms of *lifnim mi-shurat ha-din*, certainly acquires valid title.

3. *Mi she-para* – a formal curse invoking divine retribution pronounced upon a vendor who actually accepts the purchase price but takes advantage of the technicality of law under which he may withdraw from the bargain because of failure formally to transfer title by means of executing one of the statutory modes of conveyance (*kinyan*).[7]

4. *Latzet yedei shamayim* – a duty that must be performed in order to satisfy an obligation imposed at the "hands of Heaven." Example: A person commits an act of theft but the victim cannot be identified with certainty. In the absence of positive identification of the victim, no claim can be pressed against the thief. The nature of his obligation *vis-à-vis* any one of the possible victims is in the nature of an "obligation doubtful" rather than of an "obligation

---

6. See *Kiddushin* 59a.
7. See *Bava Metzi'a* 44a.

positive." Although the thief can avoid the claim of any plaintiff, the onus of guilt, nevertheless, remains upon him. He has, after all, committed an act of theft and remains in possession of the stolen property. He may only purge himself of guilt in the eyes of Heaven by restoring the stolen property to its rightful owner. The only certain method by which this can be accomplished is by making restitution to each of the persons he may have victimized.[8]

5. *Meḥusar amanah* – a person lacking in trustworthiness. An oral promise to buy or to sell is not binding, but one who fails to honor his word exposes himself to censure and to the social and societal sanctions attendant upon a determination of dishonesty.[9] Both censure and sanctions are regarded as entirely appropriate despite the absence of a culpable offense.

6. *Ein ruaḥ ḥakhamim noḥeh heimenu* – "The spirit of the Sages is not pleased by him." A primary example is that of an individual who totally disinherits his children in favor of others.[10] The children certainly have no rights which may be asserted against the testator or his property and the latter owes his children no pecuniary duty. The concern, as evident from the comments of Rashi, *Bava Batra* 133b, is to avoid arousing feelings of animosity, to prevent alienation of filial affection and to preserve familial harmony and tranquility. Quite evidently, promotion of such goals generates obligations, which devolve upon the individual.

As stated, this category of *lifnim mi-shurat ha-din* serves to enjoin conduct which produces an undesirable effect. A corollary principle stated in the positive serves to command certain affirmative actions: *Ruaḥ ḥakhamin noḥeh heimenu* – "The spirit of the Sages is pleased by him." Moral approbation is bestowed upon an individual who behaves in a manner which serves to advance certain *desiderata*, e.g., a debtor who repays a loan cancelled by

---

8. See *Bava Metzi'a* 37a.
9. See *Bava Metzi'a* 49a.
10. See *Bava Batra* 133b.

the advent of the Sabbatical year despite the absence of any formal obligation to do so.[11]

7. *Ein lo alav ela ta'arumot* – "He has only a grievance against him." An agreement for the performance of labor or personal service may be cancelled by either party prior to actual commencement of performance. Nevertheless, the person relying upon the agreement is justifiably aggrieved and the person breeching the agreement is deemed to have violated a moral norm.[12]

8. *Midat ḥasidut* – a trait of the pious. A prime example of conduct categorized in this manner is the case of an individual of substantial means who, as a wayfarer, legitimately accepts tithes which, ordinarily, only the poor are entitled to collect. Since he has no access to his own funds this individual is technically a "poor man" and is entitled to benefit from such tithes. Such a person is under no obligation subsequently to restore the tithes which he has accepted when he was in need. His obligation is no greater than that of a pauper who accepts alms but subsequently becomes wealthy. Acceptance of charity does not generate a contingent obligation to return charitable gifts when the recipient is in a financial position to do so. The wayfarer is a "poor man"; the tithes are a gift, not a loan. However, since the net result is that the truly needy are not able to benefit from the resources which have been appropriated by this individual, it is to be hoped that he will act in the manner of the pious and that upon reaching his home, he will set aside a sum equal to the value of the tithes which he has received and make those funds available to the poor.[13] This final category of *lifnim mi-shurat ha-din* is distinguishable from the earlier enumerated categories in that, while conduct in accordance with the "trait of the pious" is commended, failure to comport oneself in this manner does not entail disapprobation.

---

11. See *Shvi'it* 10:9.
12. See *Bava Metzi'a* 75b.
13. See *Ḥullin* 130b. For a further example see *Bava Metzi'a* 52b.

Although these categories do not give rise to actionable claims, they are very much part of the legal system of Judaism. The concept of *lifnim mi-shurat ha-din* assuredly plays a much more prominent role in Jewish jurisprudence than it does in other systems of law. This is not at all surprising in light of the strong emphasis in Jewish jurisprudence upon the concept of duty as distinct from the concept of right. As the late Professor Moshe Silberg has so eloquently pointed out, even in enforcing matters of justiciable law, the *Bet Din* is concerned primarily with assuring fulfillment of duties rather than in enforcing rights.[14]

Yet these categories are not without parallel in other legal systems. The prominent Roman law scholar, J. W. Salmond, distinguished between "perfect rights" and "imperfect rights." Perfect rights are actionable in a court of law while imperfect rights are rights which are recognized by law but which do not generate correlative duties enforceable in a court of law.[15] Imperfect rights, although they are accorded a measure of recognition, are not actionable. The claim is recognized but not enforced although the claim may entail certain legal ramifications. The best example is a statute of limitations for monetary claims. After the statute of limitations has expired, no action for recovery of a debt can be instituted. Nevertheless, the debt does not become extinct with the result that if the debt is honored, by reason of ignorance of the law or otherwise, there can be no recovery on the part of the debtor. In other words, the obligation exists, but is not enforceable. The right is recognized with the result that it is a "ground of defense though not of action," i.e., if the debt is repaid the debtor cannot sue to recover on the grounds that the debt has been extinguished by operation of the statute of limitations.

---

14. "Law and Morals in Jewish Jurisprudence," *Harvard Law Review*, LXXV (1961-62), 306-331.
15. It should be noted that Kant formulates a distinction between "perfect duties" and "imperfect duties." See *The Philosophy of Law*, trans. by W. Hastie (Edinburgh, 1887), p. 26 and *Fundamental Principles of the Metaphysics of Morals*, trans. by Thomas K. Abbott (New York, 1949), p. 39. Although Kant uses the terms in an entirely different sense, a note to the discussion in the *Metaphysics of Morals* indicates that in "the use of the word adopted by the schools ... [*Perfect* duties are usually understood to be those which can be enforced by external law; *imperfect*, those which cannot be enforced]."

The concept of an obligation solely *latzet yedei shamayim* is closely analogous. Although an obligation solely "at the hands of Heaven" is not enforceable by a human court, nevertheless, an individual who, through ignorance of the legal nature of such a claim or otherwise does satisfy such an obligation, has no claim for recovery. Moreover, according to many authorities, obligations encompassed in this category are such that, although the court will not enforce the obligation, if the claimant exercises self-help in seizing property for the purpose of satisfying such a claim, the party against whom such a right is asserted has no claim for recovery.

The various categories of *lifnim mi-shurat ha-din* are carefully delineated in rabbinic sources and assigned appropriate gradations of approbation or opprobrium. Definition of the varying concepts is primarily by example. Application of these categories to other unspecified forms of conduct can be accomplished only by means of extrapolation of the underlying principles or by analogy. Yet it is clear that (1) the principles are deemed to be objective rather than subjective and (2) the categories are themselves encompassed within the corpus of Halakhah.

I suspect that these comments are substantively in agreement with the position adopted by Rabbi Aharon Lichtenstein in his classic essay on this topic.[16] Yet, I do not believe that the question is ultimately one of definition of terms, as Rabbi Lichtenstein asserts, with the result that it is possible to define the concept of an ethic beyond Halakhah in a manner which allows for an affirmative answer to the question as heretofore formulated.

II.

Having assimilated the concept of *lifnim mi-shurat ha-din* to *din* itself, we are now in a position to pose the second question: "Does Judaism recognize an ethical standard beyond the eight categories herein enumerated?" Having, in effect, stated that the Jewish legal system may be reduced to a dichotomy consisting of duties which can be compelled

---

16. "Does Jewish Tradition Recognize an Ethic Independent of Halakha?" *Modern Jewish Ethics: Theory and Practice,* ed. Marvin Fox (Columbus, 1975), pp. 62-88; reprinted in *Contemporary Jewish Ethics,* ed. Menachem Marc Kellner (New York, 1978), pp. 102-123.

and duties which cannot be compelled, the next question which must be asked is whether there exist principles of ethical conduct which are not encompassed within any of the delineated classes but which enjoy recognized standing. There can be little question that rabbinic writings reflect a certain tension with regard to this issue. At times such writings appear to recognize the existence of standards of this nature; and at other times they appear to deny the contention that there can be any legitimacy to a claim of ethical standing on behalf of any standard or value not explicitly posited within the corpus of Halakhah.

Ostensibly, one example of this tension is to be found in the exchange of letters between Rabbi Mordechai Jacob Breisch and Rabbi Moses Feinstein regarding the permissibility of artificial insemination utilizing the semen of a gentile donor.[17] Rabbi Feinstein's responsa addressing this question are a model of formal legalism.[18] He marshals the objections which have been set forth with regard to artificial insemination and demonstrates that they are not applicable to situations in which the donor is a non-Jew. Thus, he finds a permissive conclusion to be inescapable. Rabbi Breisch, on the other hand, quite apart from the legalistic caveats which he advances, dwells repeatedly and at length upon what he perceives to be the morally reprehensible nature of the procedure. Certainly, the causal reader could well be left with the impression that Rabbi Feinstein is concerned only with technical formulation of the law and rejects the notion of an ethical standard which transcends Halakhah, while Rabbi Breisch, unwilling to assume that his legal prowess will enable him to make his point convincingly within the confines of Halakhah itself, appeals to a standard of moral behavior which is not rooted in narrow technicalities of the law. But, in point of fact, such a reading of that exchange would be a complete misreading of their debate. In actuality, each of the arguments advanced, including an appeal to concepts of abomination (*to'evah*) and sanctity, is an argument

---

17. *She'elot u-Teshuvot Ḥelkat Ya'akov*, III (Bnei Brak, 5726), nos. 45-52.
18. *Iggerot Mosheh, Even ha-Ezer*, I (New York, 5721), nos. 10 and 71. Rabbi Feinstein's reply to Rabbi Breisch which originally appeared in *Ḥelkat Ya'akov*, III, nos. 45-52, has been included with brief additions in Rabbi Feinstein's *Dibberot Mosheh* on *Ketubot* (Bnei Brak, 5744), responsa, no. 1. Additional replies to opposing views appear in the same volume, responsa nos. 2 and 3.

based upon technical, formal provisions of Halakhah and supported by proof-texts designed to show that the ethical standard which is posited is, in reality, a halakhic standard.

The question of whether or not there exist ethical standards in addition to the eight earlier enumerated categories of *lifnim mi-shurat ha-din* can itself be formulated in two distinct ways:

1. Does Judaism recognize a subjective morality? Is there room in Judaism for accommodation of the moral demands advanced by individual conscience? To that question the answer must be an emphatic no. Indeed, the question is unequivocally answered in the negative by R. Ovadia Bartenura in the opening section of his commentary on *Ethics of the Fathers.*

> I declare that because this tractate is not predicated upon explication of any particular commandment of the Torah, as are other tractates of the Mishnah, rather [it consists] in its entirety of moral maxims and ethical qualities. And [since] the wise men of the nations of the world also composed works according to the fancies of their hearts dealing with ethical conduct... therefore the Tanna began this tractate [with the words] "Moses received the Torah from Sinai" indicating that the ethical qualities and moral maxims which are [contained] in this tractate were not the fancies of the Sages of the Mishnah, but that even they were revealed at Sinai.

It clearly follows from these comments of Bartenura that any valid system of ethics must be Sinaitic in origin. The very possibility of a subjective morality is dismissed out of hand. The contents of Tractate *Avot* are clearly regarded as being in the nature of *halakhah le-Mosheh me-Sinai*. As such, the content of a system of ethics of this nature is not only objective, rather than subjective, but is, accurately speaking, merely a sub-category of Halakhah.

2. However, precisely the same question can be reformulated in a second manner: Is there a natural morality which is discoverable by reason? The content of such a moral system might well be

coextensive with the content of dogmatic ethics but might yet be endowed with independent validity. That such a concept exists is manifest in biblical verses such as "Shall the Judge of all the earth not do justice?" (Genesis 18:25). Nevertheless, an affirmative answer to this question does not dispose of the issue. The concept of natural morality must be distinguished from the concept of natural law. To say that a proposition is endowed with moral meaning and validity on the basis of reason alone does not *ipso facto* endow it with the status of a legal norm binding upon all upon pain of punishment. Moreover, if raised to the status of law by virtue of revelation, the metaethical issue recedes into insignificance. The crucial question is whether the claims of natural morality are to be affirmed only in a trivial sense or whether they are to be regarded as valid in any sense which carries with it ethical significance. If the content of a putative natural morality has been confirmed and endowed with binding force by revelation, it is then no longer terribly significant to determine whether natural morality does indeed exist independently of revelation. The question which then must be resolved is whether there is a content of natural morality which is not encompassed within the subject matter of Halakhah.

The proof-text usually cited in support of such a position is the statement recorded in *Eruvin* 100b, "If the Torah had not been given, we could have learned modesty from the cat, not to rob from the ant, chastity from the dove, proper conjugal behavior from the rooster." Yet, the very formulation of the conditional phrase "if the Torah had not been given" indicates that the content of these maxims of natural morality is identical with the moral precepts of revealed Sinaitic law. Moreover, as Marvin Fox has pointed out, if we lived in a pure state of nature what would have prompted us to emulate these particular animals and these particular modes of behavior? We might just as readily have decided to imitate the ferocity of the lion, the murderousness of an aroused pack of wolves and the sexual behavior of the rabbit.[19] Or, as Richard Wollheim,

---

19. *The Philosophical Foundation of Jewish Ethics: Some Initial Reflections* (Cincinnati,

who did not have the text of *Eruvin* before him, asks, "Are we ... to model ourselves upon the peaceful habits of sheep or upon the internecine conflicts of ants? Is the egalitarianism of the beaver or the hierarchical life of the bee the proper exemplar for human society? Should we imitate the widespread polygamy of the animal kingdom, or is there some higher regularity of which this is no more than a misleading instance?"[20] Moreover, any attempt to assert a natural morality leads to several problems:

(i) Natural morality can be apprehended only by the light of reason. How can conflicts between individuals involving contradictory claims asserted in the name of natural morality be resolved? Acceptance of a concept of natural morality can very readily lead to a state of affairs that can perhaps best be described as ethical solipsism, i.e., a person may well find himself the sole inhabitant of a private ethical realm in which he recognizes moral principles which are shared with no other person. Elsewhere[21] I have argued that it is for this reason that Maimonides rejects the notion of a natural law of any really meaningful scope.

(ii) Granted that reason can apprehend certain moral principles, the problem which then presents itself is: What compels an individual to accept such a morality as binding? What are its sanctions? Or put somewhat differently: Why be moral if such morality is predicated simply upon the dictate of reason?

Recognition of the inherent difficulties associated with a concept of natural morality leads to a position which can best be described as halakhic formalism or halakhic positivism. Such a position recognizes the norms of Halakhah as constituting the sole constraints upon human conduct. In turn, a system of this nature makes possible improvisation of devices such as *prozbul, hetter iska*, carefully drafted testaments to avoid statutory principles of inheritance, etc. This is not necessarily to condemn such legal constructs as being tainted with any degree of immorality. But, such a position does lead to a moral stance, which permits an individual to take advantage of any loophole in the law which

---

1979), p. 14.
20. "Natural Law," *The Encyclopedia of Philosophy* (New York, 1967), v, 451.
21. "Judaism and Natural Law," chapter six of this volume.

may present itself and to do so without feeling any degree of culpability based upon an ultimate moral concern.

Nevertheless, there does appear to be at least one significant area of morality which is at one and the same time both natural in essence and Sinaitic in normative form. The morality thus described establishes broad categories of conduct but does not provide details governing specific action. This morality is grounded upon the commandment *"Ve-halakhta be-derakhav –* You shall walk in His ways" (Deuteronomy 28:9) and reflects the principle of *imitatio Dei.* A morality based upon this principle has as its first premise the notion that "God is good" is an analytic proposition. Man, then, is commanded to emulate the essence of the Deity. In doing so, man aspires to a standard of conduct which, of necessity, is not spelled out in formal, legalistic codes. Establishment of this standard of conduct is predicated upon a prior ontological commitment. The Midrash, *Va-Yikra Rabbah* 24:9, states: "'Be thou holy.' Perhaps even as I? Therefore it is stated, 'for I am holy.' My sanctity transcends your sanctity." That remarkable statement is primarily an ontological proposition and only derivatively a statement regarding human actions. It constitutes an invitation to partake of the divine essence but qualifies the invitation with the caveat that the goal can be achieved only imperfectly. The command is normative, but at the same time it establishes a relative norm commensurate with each individual's apprehension of the divine essence.

The relative nature of this concept is perhaps best reflected in the anecdote concerning Rabbi Judah the Prince related by the Gemara, *Bava Metzi'a* 85a. R. Judah suffered excruciating pain for many years until the pain subsided suddenly. In the following narrative, the Gemara explains both why R. Judah experienced suffering and why the suffering was ultimately alleviated:

> A calf, when it was being taken to slaughter, went and hung its head under Rabbi [Judah's] cloak and cried. He said to it, "Go, for this wast thou created." [In heaven] they said, "Since he has no mercy, let suffering come upon him."... One day Rabbi [Judah]'s maidservant was sweeping the house; some young weasels were lying there and she was sweeping them away. Rabbi [Judah] said

to her, "Let them be; it is written 'And His tender mercies are over all His works' (Psalms 135:9)." [In heaven] they said, "Since he is compassionate, let us be compassionate to him."

Reflected in this account, and in the moral principle derived therefrom, is the distinction between normative law and ethical conduct above and beyond the requirements of law. In its normative law, Judaism codifies standards applicable to everyone and makes no demands that are beyond the capacity of the common man; but, at the same time, Jewish teaching recognizes that, ideally, man must aspire to a higher level of conduct. That higher standard is posited as a moral desideratum, albeit a norm which is not enforceable by human courts. As stated by Rabbi Moshe Chaim Luzzatto in a different context, "The majority of the community cannot be *ḥasidim* [pietists], rather, it is sufficient for them that they be *tzaddikim* [righteous]."[22]

To be sure, not every person succeeds in reaching a degree of intellectual and moral excellence such that he perceives the need and the obligation to conduct himself in accordance with a higher standard of conduct of such a nature. Nevertheless, those who do attain such a level of moral perfection are obliged, at least in the eyes of Heaven, to conduct themselves in accordance with that higher standard. No human court can inquire into the degree of moral perfection attained by a particular individual and hence, such a court cannot apply varying standards to different persons. The heavenly court, however, *is* in a position to do so and, accordingly, will punish a person who does not comport himself in accordance with the degree of moral perfection which he has attained. In this vein, the Gemara, *Bava Kamma* 50a, cites the verse "And it shall be very tempestuous about Him" (Psalms 50:3) and, in a play on the Hebrew word "*sa'arah*" which connotes both "tempestuous" and "hair," declares, "The Holy one, blessed be He, is particular with those around Him even with regard to matters as light as a single hair."

Rabbi Judah's conduct, for lesser mortals, would be beyond reproach. Indeed, we have difficulty understanding why even Rabbi Judah should have been found to have been ethically remiss. Certainly,

---

22. *Mesillat Yesharim*, chapter 13.

the slaughter of the animal did not constitute a moral lapse. Yet, Rabbi Judah's reaction betrays a certain insensitivity. That insensitivity is morally anomalous in a man of Rabbi Judah's intellectual stature. Heightened moral sensitivity is born of intellectual perfection and hence standards of behavior to which a person is held are commensurate with the individual's awareness and apprehension of the divine essence. Such obligations are clearly relative, just as awareness of the divine essence is relative. The standard of conduct to which the individual is to be held is relative and, in a sense, is indeed solipsistic in nature, since no two individuals can have the same apprehension of the divine.

Yet, although the standard is relative and varies from person to person, the standard to be applied to each individual is, at least in the eyes of the Deity, objective and mandatory. Hence, even ethical obligations of this nature can well be termed a facet of Halakhah or normative law. That, too, is reflected in the story concerning Rabbi Judah and the calf.

There is, to be sure, a certain tension in the emphasis placed upon a relative standard as distinct from emphasis upon an objective standard applicable to all. This is reflected in the fear expressed in some rabbinic circles concerning concentration upon "ethical" obligations as distinct from normative Halakhah. The "disdain" of the ethical is born of two considerations. The dictum, "Would that they would forsake Me but observe My Torah" (Palestinian Talmud, *Ḥaggigah* 1:7) means nothing other than "Would that they were concerned with normative law rather than with ethical conduct." Reflected in this concern is the fear that undue concentration upon an attempt to capture the essence of the divine and attendant obligations which transcend normative law may degenerate into antinomianism.[23] The second concern is that ethical reflection can, after all, add but little to what may be discovered by an examination of normative law.[24] Hence, the opposition in some circles to the study of *mussar* literature.[25] Ultimately, as illustrated by

---

23. Cf., *Ḥazon Ish al Inyanei Emunah Bitaḥon ve-Od*, ed. S. Greineman (Jerusalem, 5714), chap. 3.
24. Cf., R. Chaim of Volozhin, *Nefesh ha-Ḥayyim, sha'ar* 4, chap. 1.
25. See the comments of R. Chaim ha-Levi Soloveitchik cited in R. Joseph B. Soloveitchik, "*Ish ha-Halakhah*," *Talpiyot*, I (April-September, 1944) no. 3-4, p. 698.

the above-cited dictum, God's essence can be discovered, not from the study of ethics, but from the pages of the Talmud.

III.

This then leads us to a final reformulation of the original question. Is there an ethic beyond the recorded Halakhah? To this the answer is: Of course! To the extent that the much misused term *da'at Torah* denotes a cognitive discipline that is precisely what it endeavors to explicate and it is precisely for this reason that Halakhah is an art rather than a science.

The crucial problem with regard to the content of this ethic, which is beyond the recorded Halakhah, is that, by virtue of its very nature, it cannot be captured in precise, unequivocal formulae. This is so, at least in part, because it is so highly relative and because it is both commensurate with, as well as derivable from, an individual's metaphysical comprehension of the nature of the Deity. To the extent that it is recorded, it is recorded in the Aggadah rather than in the Halakhah. It is precisely because the content of this ethic is not amenable to a precise formulation that it is expressed in figurative, metaphorical language and often couched in hyperbole.

8

Duran's View of the Nature of Providence

Simon ben Zemah Duran (1361-1444) is perhaps best known for his formulation of the dogmas of Judaism which was adopted and popularized by a younger contemporary, Joseph Albo, and became the structural theme of the latter's *Sefer ha-Ikkarim*. Finding no basis for Maimonides' selection of thirteen principles of faith, Duran substituted his own list of three dogmas: the existence of God, revelation, and retribution. The existence of God and retribution are both entailed by the doctrine of revelation. Revelation would be impossible without a God who has revealed Himself, and acceptance of the law revealed by God is fostered by the anticipation of retribution. Retribution would, of course, be impossible if not for the reality of Providence. To Duran, these three dogmas are the basic principles which are necessarily shared by all revealed religions. Duran believed that Maimonides' thirteen principles could be reduced to these three dogmas from which the other principles could be deduced.

Like Crescas, Duran takes issue with the excessive intellectualism of Maimonides. Immortality in Duran's view depends not upon perfection of the intellect but upon ethical conduct and obedience to the divine commandments. Similarly, Divine Providence is not limited to persons who are in communion with God by virtue of their superior intelligence but affects all men irrespective of their intellectuality. His theory of Providence is developed at length in the introduction to his commentary on the Book of Job, *Ohev Mishpat* (Venice, 1589) and is summarized briefly in Book III, chapter 2, of his philosophical work, *Magen Avot* (Leghorn, 1745).

Duran recognizes that the question of whether Providence is commensurate with the degree to which the individual has succeeded in perfecting his intellect (as was the view of Maimonides), is actually dependent upon the correct analysis of the nature of the soul. Maimonides, says Duran, believed that the rational soul at its inception is no different from the nutritive soul or the sensitive soul in that it is a faculty or power capable of receiving intelligibles, whose perfection is commensurate with the degree to which this potential is actualized. Since it is the rational soul which is immortal, development of the intellect is the preliminary condition for its immortality. Maimonides thus accepts the doctrine of acquired immortality, according to which only the actualization of man's intellectual power conveys immortality. If the requisite knowledge and understanding is not acquired, the soul cannot achieve immortality. This, according to Maimonides, is the correct interpretation of the biblical punishment of *karet* or "cutting off."

Duran finds this analysis of the soul and its immortality difficult to accept on several counts. According to Maimonides, the soul is deprived of immortality simply because it has not acquired knowledge of intelligibles, for it is only through such knowledge that the soul is immortal. It would then follow that the evildoer who has been exceedingly wicked and has not developed his intellect, and the lazy person who has not developed his intellect because of idleness, are equal with regard to a share in the world-to-come. Duran deems such a situation to be unjust. Furthermore, if immortality is the result of intellectual perfection, it should follow that the souls of children do not possess immortality. Yet the Talmud clearly states that children have a share in

the world-to-come from the time that they are able to respond "Amen."[1]
Also, according to Maimonides' analysis of the nature of the soul, it
is difficult to explain the reunification of body and soul at the time of
resurrection. Moreover, both Scripture and rabbinic tradition indicate
that Providence is contingent upon performance of the divine commandments, without in any way hinting that intellectual perfection
is a corequisite. Thus the Torah promises that "neither shall any man
covet thy land, when thou goest up to appear before the Lord thy God
three times in the year" (Exodus 34:24). Similarly, the Sages declare
that "those traveling for the purpose of a good deed suffer no harm."[2]
In neither case is reflection or meditation upon intelligibles required.
Providence is thus seen to be contingent entirely upon performance
of good deeds rather than upon intellectual activity. Furthermore, the
Kabbalists teach that *shedim*[3] remove themselves from one who recites

---

1. *Sanhedrin* 110b.
2. *Pesaḥim* 8a.
3. Kabbalistic literature is, of course, replete with references to evil spirits, demons,
   etc. Although within the philosophical tradition the existence of *shedim* was denied
   by Maimonides (*Guide of the Perplexed*, III, 37, and *Mishneh Torah*, "Laws Concerning Idolatry," 11:16), and according to Menasseh ben Israel, by Ibn Ezra as well, the
   existence of demonic spirits was accepted by Judah ha-Levi (*Kuzari*, V, 14), but in
   a context which makes no mention of the question of diverse sources of good and
   evil. Among later medieval writers the reality of such spirits was accepted by Shem
   Tob ibn Shem Tob (*Sefer ha-Emunot*, Ferrara, 1556, V, 1), Crescas (*Or ha-Shem*, IV,
   6), Moses Tachau (*Ketav Tamim*, published in *Otzar Neḥmad*, ed. Ignatz Blumenfeld,
   Vienna, 1860, III, 97); Isaac Abravanel (in his commentary on Deuteronomy 18:9),
   and by so late an authority as Elijah Gaon of Vilna (cf. his oft cited stricture on
   Maimonides in which he claims that Maimonides was misled by "philosophy" and
   hence interpreted talmudic references to spirits and demons in an overly rational
   spirit, *Shulḥan Arukh, Yoreh Deʾah* 179, *Biʾur ha-Gra*, note 13). For a discussion of the
   sources and justification of the conflicting views see Menasseh ben Israel, *Mishnat
   Ḥayyim* (Warsaw, 1876), III, 12-14. Averroes also alludes to a belief in the existence of
   such beings as intermediaries between the Intelligences of the spheres and sublunary
   creatures (*Die Hauptlehren des Averroes*, trans. M. M. Horton [Bonn, 1913], p. 277).
   Gersonides (*Milḥamot ha-Shem*, IV, 3), in attributing such a belief to the "multitude

the *Shema* before retiring,[4] even though he cannot possibly be engaged in intellectual activity while asleep.

Duran, citing the kabbalistic tradition as his source, declares that the soul is "of the soul of God and of the breath of His nostrils."[5] In addition to those parts of the soul which are bound to the human body man is endowed with another immaterial soul, the *neshamah*. This immaterial soul was created by God at the time of the original creation and was designed to be immortal. The soul is joined with the body so that it may acquire even greater perfection through the performance of the commandments, just as the soul of the sphere achieves enhanced perfection each day even though it was already in a state of wondrous perfection at the time of creation. Hence man's immortality depends not upon development and perfection of the intellect but upon his ethical conduct and his obedience to the divine commandments.

It may be assumed that since qualitatively speaking all souls are intrinsically equal, they should all participate equally in Divine Providence. Nevertheless, Duran agrees that the degree of Providence varies from individual to individual. The quality of Providence is, however, not commensurate with intellectual perfection but rather with the individual's righteousness or piety. Again disagreeing with Maimonides, Duran states that punishment does not consist simply of the removal of Providence and the subjection of the wicked to the vicissitudes of chance, but is the result of a direct act of Providence. For this reason the righteous are more likely to be punished for even minor infractions, since they are the recipients of a more intense form of Providence. Evil which occurs by way of punishment is not evil at all but a form of good, because when people see that transgressions are punished, they are admonished and take heed to mend their ways.

Duran adopts a somewhat equivocal attitude with regard to the power of astral influences. Citing Ibn Ezra, "who is knowledgeable in

---

of our coreligionists" in contrast to his earlier reference to the "philosophers," probably had no specific figure in mind, but was referring to Kabbalistic views which the masses tended to accept in an unsophisticated manner.

4. See *Zohar*, Introduction, p. 11.
5. *Ohev Mishpat*, chap. 19, p. 26b.

this science,"[6] Duran declares that even astrologers do not claim that human affairs are regulated by the stars in a deterministic manner. The constellations merely "indicate a situation which may change for good or evil."[7] Man may negate any decree of the stars through the exercise of his free will. The Talmud records a difference of opinion among the Sages as to whether Israel is governed by the stars. According to Duran, neither opinion denies the reality of Providence. God, exercising Providence through the intermediacy of the angels, may annul the decree of the stars. When astral influences indicate benefits for the righteous, God will not intervene and the heavenly reward of the righteous will in no way be diminished because of the temporal benefits received in this manner, since such benefits are the result of the celestial order and are not in the nature of Providence. Similarly, when misfortune is indicated by the stars, God does not interfere so long as those misfortunes do not hinder the righteous person in achieving spiritual perfection. God does not intervene since such intervention on His part would necessarily result in diminished reward in the world-to-come.

Gersonides cites the talmudic dictum "Even though he does not perceive, his *mazal* does perceive"[8] as proof of his contention that human events are determined by astral influences,[9] to which Duran retorts that the term *mazal* in this context refers not to a configuration of heavenly bodies but to an angel. Every person, declares Duran, has a guardian angel,[10] sometimes termed *mazal*, who preserves him from misfortune. Providence manifests itself with regard to each individual through the intermediacy of his guardian angel.

The reality of individual Providence, states Duran, is mandated by reason but apparently negated by experience.[11] Nevertheless, the Pentateuch, not being a polemical work, simply postulates the reality of Providence and makes no attempt to advance demonstrative proof. But since the reality of Providence, more so than that of any other principle

---

6. *Ibid.*, chap. 21, p. 32a.
7. *Loc. cit.*
8. *Megillah* 3a.
9. *Milḥamot ha-Shem* IV, 5.
10. Cf. Rashi, *Megillah* 3a, s.v. *mazlaihu*.
11. *Ohev Mishpat*, chap. 1, p. 7a.

of faith, is subject to doubt on the part of both the masses and wise men, an entire book of Scripture is devoted to an exhaustive analysis of this question. Duran accepts the talmudic opinion which ascribes authorship of the book of Job to Moses,[12] as did Gersonides before him,[13] and adds the comment that "its composition properly belongs to the person to whom the Torah was given, so that his gift may endure forever and no fool or wicked person may seek to throw off responsibility, cast aspersions on his gift and bring evidence from common sensory experience."[14]

Duran believes that the basic reason underlying Aristotle's denial of individual Providence was empirical rather than philosophical. In his *Magen Avot*[15] Duran says that Aristotle was prompted to deny Providence not on the basis of philosophical arguments but because of the age-old problem of the adversity of the righteous and the prosperity of the wicked. In denying a speculative basis for the Aristotelian position Duran does not give credence to the argument found in *De Mundo*,[16] according to which God could not exercise Providence over terrestrial matters because it is unworthy of His dignity that He should concern himself with the affairs of creatures as insignificant as human beings. Even though Duran himself cites this argument in his *Ohev Mishpat*,[17] he not only believes it to be erroneous but also feels that it is so patently specious that Aristotle could not possibly have been misled thereby. As will be shown later, Duran accepts Saadia's notion of a homocentric universe and in apparent consistency with this position refuses to ascribe a conflicting view to Aristotle. Nevertheless, it is difficult to understand how Duran can deny that philosophical considerations were the cause of Aristotle's denial of individual Providence since, as Duran himself notes,[18] Providence presupposes divine knowledge of particulars. This principle was, of course, denied by Aristotle and is mentioned by Duran

---

12. See *Bava Batra* 14b.

13. *Commentary on the Bible* (New York, 1958), Introduction to the Book of Job, p. 2.

14. *Ohev Mishpat*, chap. 1, p. 7b.

15. Book III, chap. 2, p. 32b.

16. *The Works of Aristotle*, III, ed. W. D. Ross (Oxford, 1931), p. 298a.

17. Chap. 12, p. 17a.

18. *Ibid.*, chap. 5, p. 10a.

as an argument contradicting the reality of Providence.[19] Furthermore, the notion of individual Providence is somewhat incompatible with Aristotle's view of God as a passive Unmoved Mover, whose sole activity is thought and who has only Himself as the object of His thought. Most revealing with regard to Duran's attitude is a passage in *Ohev Mishpat*, in which he states that his words are addressed only to those who accept the teachings of the Torah in their entirety and are, like Job, perplexed only with regard to the question of Providence.[20] Accordingly, Duran takes no cognizance of other philosophical views which render the doctrine of individual Providence untenable.

Duran believes that proofs demonstrating the reality of Providence in a positive manner are not really necessary. Once the Aristotelian arguments negating the reality of Providence are refuted, acceptance of the reality of individual Providence becomes self-evident to a rational mind as an *a priori* postulate. Duran asserts that Providence follows necessarily from the concept of God as a Perfect Being, and conversely, the absence of Providence would constitute a defect.[21] Nevertheless, the Book of Job was composed in order to provide demonstrative proofs for the truth of this principle. These proofs are divided into two groups: the first is based upon the theological consideration of divine perfection, while the second contains arguments drawn from manifestations of God's activities in the world. The second group is further broken down into three groups: 1) proofs based upon existence in general; 2) proofs drawn from certain categories of existent beings, such as animals or vegetation; and 3) proofs based upon phenomena of human life.

Duran's principal theological proof is predicated upon the concept of divine perfection. The perfect master will not be oblivious of the deeds of those governed by him, and will not fail to accord to each his due in accordance with his actions. Conversely, a lack of order on the part of human beings in their guidance of those under their jurisdiction would be accounted a defect. Since no imperfection can be ascribed to God, it follows that He exercises Providence with regard to His creatures. This

---

19. *Ibid.*, chap. 12, p. 13a.
20. Chap. 14, p. 14b.
21. *Ibid.*, chap. 12, p. 13a.

argument cannot, however, be employed in order to demonstrate that Providence extends to individual members of lower species as well as to individual human beings, because among mortal beings man alone is deserving of reward and punishment by virtue of the fact that he is a rational creature.

This argument as formulated by Duran is an almost literal quotation of the first argument advanced by Gersonides in support of his view that Divine Providence extends to all members of the human species.[22] Duran ascribes this argument to Eliphaz who exclaims, "Shall mortal man be just before God? Shall a man be pure before his Maker?" (Job 4:17), thereby affirming the absolute perfection of God. Job, even while accusing God of injustice, was forced to accept this argument as evidenced by his admission, "I know that it is so; and how can man be just with God?" (Job 9:2).

Duran advances two proofs based upon divine activity *vis-à-vis* the world in general. It is obvious, he claims, that if a person makes something which has not previously existed, and if that thing is as perfect as it can possibly be, he will wish it to continue to exist in as perfect a state as possible. If he desired the opposite, we would deem it foolishness and lunacy on his part and not inability or deficiency; we assume that he is capable of preserving that which he created, since creation from nonexistence is more difficult than the preservation of that which already exists. It is clear that anything which constitutes a defect in man cannot be ascribed to God. Hence, since God created all of existence, it is fitting that He should desire its preservation in as perfect a state as possible. Since God was capable of creating the world *ex nihilo*, He is certainly capable of exercising Providence, and since man possesses reason, it is proper that God should exercise Providence with regard to man and mete out reward and punishment on the basis of man's actions. This argument is attributed by Duran to Elihu in the Book of Job. The verse "Who gave Him a charge over the earth? Or who hath disposed the whole worlds?" (Job 34:13) is interpreted by Duran as implying that God did not act under coercion in creating the universe; rather, He created it by reason of His will and would certainly not harm His creatures. In this vein God

---

22. *Milḥamot ha-Shem*, IV, 2.

says to Job, "Where wast thou when I laid the foundations of the earth?" (Job 38:4), which Duran interprets as meaning that since God created the world, He certainly will not abandon His creatures.[23]

Aristotelians would offer two objections to this argument. First, it is predicated upon the notion of a created universe, whereas Aristotle maintains that the universe is eternal. Secondly, there is nothing in this argument which would serve to demonstrate the reality of individual Providence. God's concern for, and guardianship of, His creatures may well be expressed in a form of Providence which is limited to guardianship of the species as a whole. Even those who affirm the reality of individual Providence with regard to human beings concede that only general Providence exists with regard to lower animals. The argument that God preserves that which He has created does not seem to demonstrate more than the existence of a general Providence limited to preservation of the species.

In answer to the first objection Duran argues that Aristotle, even though affirming the eternity of the universe, believes that God is the First Cause of it. The argument can then be simply reformulated by stating that God is thus the Cause of the universe, instead of saying that God has created the world *ex nihilo*. In arguing that this proof is compatible with Aristotelian cosmology, Duran seems to be ascribing a position to Aristotle which the latter has never held. The notion of an Unmoved Mover is quite different from that of an efficient cause. For Aristotle God's role as the cause of the universe is limited to His being the unmoved source of motion.[24] Furthermore, even if it can be demonstrated that God is the First Cause, according to Aristotle's concept of

---

23. Albo interprets this verse in a completely different manner. Cf., *Ikkarim*, IV, 8, and Isaac Husik, "Joseph Albo, the Last of the Medieval Jewish Philosophers," *Philosophical Essays*, ed. Milton Nahm and Leo Strauss (Oxford, 1952), pp. 263 ff.

24. Duran, of course, does not mean to speak of a first cause as being first in the temporal order but rather as being supreme or first in the ontological order. Since he is referring not to a series stretching back into the past but to a hierarchy of causes in which a subordinate member is dependent upon the causal activity of a higher member, Duran may have felt that this concept is identical with that of an Unmoved Mover. F. C. Copleston offers a similar interpretation of Aquinas' first proof for the existence of God; see F. C. Copleston, *Aquinas* (Baltimore, 1955), pp. 117-19.

God He would presumably be entirely passive in the process of creation and hence the argument that the Creator should logically be concerned about the existence and perfection of that which He has created simply does not apply.

The objection that the argument is compatible with the existence of general Providence with regard to the human species and does not demonstrate the reality of individual Providence, is not really refuted by Duran. Instead he argues that if general Providence exists with regard to other species, it necessarily follows that individual Providence is a reality *vis-à-vis* human beings. He accepts as "self-evident" the fact that general Providence with regard to species is a reality by virtue of the eternity of the species; Providence, for some unspecified reason, is a concomitant of eternity. Therefore, since individual human beings are eternal insofar as their rational souls are immortal, it follows that Providence must extend to such individuals' eternal souls. In *Magen Avot*[25] Duran presents a somewhat fuller, albeit highly abstruse, formulation of this contention, and it appears from his discussion that the argument is predicated upon three antecedent premises: 1) Providence can attach itself only to that which has permanence; 2) Providence is not exercised by God directly vis-à-vis the species which inhabit the sublunar world – they are provided for indirectly through the heavenly spheres which are subject directly to divine guardianship; 3) man's existence is not predicated upon the existence of the spheres or their Intelligences. Since Providence can attach itself only to that which has permanence, Providence can exist only *vis-à-vis* species; the Philosopher, however, recognized that species do not exist, i.e., there are no objective existents corresponding to the terms designating the various species. Thus Duran attributes to Aristotle a nominalist position and regards him as believing that universals are mere vocal utterances and refer to nothing other than mental constructs.[26] Since species are nonexistent, there can be no Providence with regard to

---

25. III, 2, p. 33a.

26. Maimonides, *Guide*, III, 18, also declares that "species have no existence except in our own minds" and uses this assertion to demonstrate the reality of individual Providence, but in a manner compatible only with his own view of the nature of Providence. According to Maimonides, Providence is exercised through the medium of the intellect. Since species have no objective existences, Providence must operate

them. If so, how are the species preserved? They can be preserved only indirectly through the Separate Intelligences and the spheres which are inhabited by these Intelligences; only through their influence is the existence of terrestrial species assured. Thus Providence is the concomitant not of permanence but of the immortality of the Intelligences. Man's existence, declares Duran, is not contingent upon the existence of the Separate Intelligences and the Intelligences of the spheres. Thus man, by virtue of his immortality, is on a par with the Intelligences. Accordingly, Providence extends directly to each individual human being. Moreover, Duran accepts the notion of a homocentric universe – the idea that man is central in creation and that everything else was created for his sake and is in some way designed to be of benefit to mankind.[27] Therefore the Providence which extends to species within the animal kingdom is derived from the Providence which extends to individual human beings, so that through the preservation of the animal species the continued existence of man may be guaranteed. In this argument Duran agrees that general Providence which preserves the species is indirect in nature, but asserts that instead of proceeding from the Providence which provides for the spheres it proceeds from the Providence which is manifest *vis-à-vis* individual human beings.

The second proof advanced by Duran, which is based upon divine activity with regard to the world in general, focuses upon the phenomenon of rain.[28] The world could not exist without rain, yet the phenomenon of rain cannot be explained on the basis of laws of nature, since it is not constant,[29] like the motion of the spheres or the alternation of fixed

---

through the medium of the individual intellect. Hence, concludes Maimonides, not only is individual Providence a reality, but Providence is also proportional to the endowment of the intellect.

27. In maintaining this view Duran accepts the position of Saadia, *Emunot ve-De'ot*, IV, Introduction. Maimonides, *Guide*, III, 13, disagrees and asserts that the universe has no purpose other than its own existence.

28. This argument was cited later almost verbatim and enlarged upon by Albo in his *Ikkarim*, IV, 8.

29. I presume that Duran really means that the phenomenon of regularity, rather than the phenomenon of constancy, is absent. Although the phrase employed in the text is *she-eno inyan matmid* it is regularity, not constancy, which is the hallmark of law inherent in nature. This is borne out by Duran's subsequent statement, "for chance oc-

periods of day and night; on the contrary, rain is sporadic and intermittent. Secondly, the vapors out of which rain is formed are present in populated areas in concentrations insufficient to account for the amount of rain which falls there. The vapors must therefore be brought by winds and clouds from other places. This cannot be attributed to chance, for chance occurrences do not take place constantly. Since rain does not follow the patterns of natural law and is not the result of chance, it must be the result of Divine Providence. The Book of Job is replete with references to rain as a manifestation of Providence. Duran believes that this phenomenon is the most convincing proof of the reality of individual Providence, a proof which he says "should tear the heart of those who set aside Providence."[30]

Further proof for the reality of Providence is found in God's activity with regard to the various species within the plant and animal kingdoms. Duran offers a number of examples designed to show that each species is endowed with organs, faculties and instincts uniquely designed to guarantee its well-being.[31] Among the more interesting examples given by him are the claws with which carnivorous animals have been provided and the "poison" which they inject into their prey in order to "cook" their food, for "the power of the poison and its heat stand them in place of the power of fire which cooks meat."[32] Horned animals that eat grass have no teeth in the upper jaw because the material otherwise used for the teeth is utilized in the formation of the horns. As a result they cannot masticate their food properly, and therefore nature

---

currences do not take place constantly – *ki ha-devarim ha-mikriyim enam temidiyim.*" Constancy negates the possibility of chance occurrence, while regularity indicates the operation of natural law. Since both natural law and chance are excluded, the phenomenon of rain must be attributed to Providence.

30. *Ohev Mishpat*, chap. 13, p. 19b.

31. A similar argument is advanced by Gersonides, *Milḥamot ha-Shem*, IV, 5. While the examples offered by Duran are different from those cited by Gersonides, the argument is the same.

32. *Ohev Mishpat*, chap. 15, p. 19b. The Talmud (*Ketubot* 30b, *Sanhedrin* 37b and *Sotah* 8b) declares that although the Sanhedrin no longer exists and consequently the four modes of execution cannot be imposed, the guilty nevertheless receive a similar punishment at the hands of Heaven. Thus "a person incurring [the punishment] of burning either falls into a fire or is bitten by a snake."

gave them the power to chew the cud.[33] The neck of the camel is as long as his legs, in order to facilitate the finding of food. Fish and fowl find their food readily and therefore digest what they eat quickly, whereas the dog cannot find food in sufficiency and therefore its food remains in its intestines for a period of three days.[34] The ant is a fragile creature and therefore hides itself in holes in the earth throughout the rainy season. It instinctively collects food in the summer and before storing it cleverly divides the kernels of wheat into two parts, so that should rain fall on the kernel it will not sprout. The embryo within the egg has no air to breathe and no means of foraging for food, yet is provided with sustenance and instinctively pecks itself out of the shell when its food supply is exhausted. A single kernel of wheat can produce three hundred ears, and in each ear are more than 30 kernels; thus a single kernel can readily be the source of 10,000 kernels. We can consequently conclude that but for man's disobedience Providence would have provided for him also in such a wondrous manner. Duran quotes the talmudic statement recorded in the name of R. Simeon ben Eleazar: "In all my days I have not seen a deer engaged in gathering fruit, or a lion carrying loads, or a fox engaged as a shopkeeper, yet they receive sustenance without pain, though they were created only to serve me, whereas I was created only to serve my Creator. If they, who were created only to serve me, receive sustenance without pain, I, who was created to serve my Creator, should *a fortiori* receive sustenance without pain! But I have corrupted my actions and have cut off my sustenance."[35]

Duran recognizes that the proximate cause of the various phenomena he has described is Nature or the Active Intellect, but he nevertheless maintains that the First Cause of each of these phenomena is Divine Providence. Of course, each of these examples serves only to demonstrate the reality of general Providence, which extends to a spe-

---

33. Cf. Aristotle, *De Historia Animalium*, tr. A. L. Peck (Cambridge, 1965), II, 17, p. 507a34, and *Parts of Animals*, tr. A. L. Peck (London, 1937), III, 14, p. 674b67. Aristotle, however, does not explain the association of rumination with the possession of teeth. See Joseph Albo, *Sefer ha-Ikkarim*, ed. Isaac Husik (Philadelphia, 1946), IV, 91, note I.

34. *Shabbat* 155b.

35. *Kiddushin* 82b.

cies as a whole and cannot prove the reality of individual Providence with regard to human beings. Duran has, however, equated Providence *vis-à-vis* individual human beings with Providence *vis-à-vis* the species; hence anything which proves the reality of general Providence with regard to animal species *ipso facto* confirms the reality of Providence with regard to individual human beings.[36]

Further proofs demonstrating the reality of individual Providence are drawn directly from evidence of God's activity with regard to man. Duran has previously shown that the various species of animals are each endowed with organs and faculties, each in accordance with its needs. He refers the reader to the second book of Bahya's *Ḥovot ha-Levavot* and quotes briefly from Maimonides' *Guide* to show that physiologically man is constructed in a manner which affords him optimum protection.[37] While Crescas speaks of the divine commandments and prophecy[38] as being modes of Providence, Duran goes beyond him and, accepting the reality of both revelation and prophecy, points to these phenomena not as modes of Providence but as phenomena which serve to verify the reality of Providence. This argument would contain an element of circularity were it not for the fact that, as noted earlier, Duran has stated that his arguments are addressed only to those who accept the truth of the teachings of the Torah in their entirety, and are perplexed only with regard to the reality of Providence because they believe it to be negated by common sensory experience.

Duran's third proof under this subgroup is identical with the second of the proofs advanced by Gersonides in support of the opinion of

36. Albo, *Ikkarim*, IV, 11, takes Duran's line of argument and employs it to demonstrate the reality of individual Providence in a completely different manner. This proof was, however, originally advanced by Duran, as first noted by Heinrich Jaulus, "R. Simeon ben Zemach Duran: Ein Zeit- und Lebensbild," *Monatsschrift für Geschichte und Wissenschaft des Judentums*, XXIII (1874), 462-463.

37. Much later the same point was made with great eloquence by William Paley in a book devoted to this theme, *Evidence of the Existence and Attributes of the Deity* (London, 1802).

38. Gersonides, *Milḥamot ha-Shem*, IV, 3, cites the phenomenon of "foreknowledge which is received through magic, dreams, and prophecy" in refutation of Aristotle's denial of Providence. Duran cites prognostication by means of dreams as a separate proof.

those who maintain that Providence extends to all individuals.[39] There are many wicked individuals whose sole purpose is to kill, to pillage and to plunder. Yet despite their great perseverance, the misfortunes which actually occur to human beings as a result of their action are few in number. This argument is ascribed by Duran to Eliphaz who said, "He frustrateth the devices of the crafty, so that the hands can perform nothing substantial" (Job 5:12).

Duran's fourth proof for the reality of individual Providence, based upon empirical evidence of God's influence upon the life of man, is the phenomenon of the punishment of the wicked. Gersonides had advanced a similar proof but qualified his argument by predicating it upon the phenomenon of punishment in kind in the many instances in which the wicked are punished measure for measure.[40] Duran does not find it necessary to base his proof upon punishments which are uniquely measure for measure; the phenomenon of punishment is, to his mind, in itself sufficient proof of the reality of individual Providence. The phenomenon of punishment in kind constitutes yet a further proof, and is advanced as such as the last of this series of proofs.

The penultimate proof advanced by Duran for the reality of individual Providence is similar to the argument advanced by Gersonides[41] in refutation of the Aristotelian premise that Providence extends to mankind only as to a species. The phenomenon of foreknowledge of future events received through dreams, which enables the recipient to avoid misfortune and to seek benefits, confirms the existence of Divine Providence with regard to individuals. Gersonides, in keeping with his own view that not all individuals are recipients of Divine Providence, more accurately noted that this phenomenon serves to confirm the existence of individual Providence with regard to *some* individuals. Duran notes that Gersonides was troubled by the fact that this type of foreknowledge may at times be acquired also by the wicked.[42] Duran himself remarks that he, in accordance with his resolution of the problems of the

---

39. *Ibid.*, IV, 2.
40. *Loc. cit.*
41. *Ibid.*, chap. 3.
42. *Ibid.*, chap. 6.

prosperity of the wicked, sees no anomaly in the providential safeguarding of the wicked.

Duran's final proof is identical with the third and final proof advanced by Gersonides in support of those who maintain that Divine Providence extends to all individuals.[43] Evildoers are often punished measure for measure, i.e., one who murders is killed, one who cuts off another's hand has his own hand cut off, etc. Recording his own personal observation, Duran reports, "We have seen one who had killed another person and a few days later was devoured by a lion"[44] and argues that such phenomena occur quite frequently and cannot be ascribed to chance, "because things which occur by chance are few in number."[45]

For many, the crucial problem with regard to the concept of individual Providence is an empirical one, namely, the adversity of the righteous and the prosperity of the wicked. As noted earlier, Duran believes that it was this problem which caused Aristotle to reject the doctrine of individual Providence.[46] Resolution of this problem requires a demonstration that neither the adversity of the righteous nor the prosperity of the wicked is inconsistent with providential guardianship. Duran's discussion of the various factors which may cause Providence to ordain adversity for the righteous or prosperity for the wicked is significant and merits careful study. Analysis of Duran's treatment of that problem is, however, beyond the bounds of the present discussion.

---

43. *Ibid.*, chap. 2. Gersonides, in defending his own position, refutes this argument.
44. *Ohev Mishpat*, chap. 16, p. 23a.
45. *Loc. cit.*
46. *Magen Avot*, III, 2, p. 32b.

9

Providence in the Philosophy of Hasdai Crescas and Joseph Albo

I.

Hasdai ben Abraham Crescas has been described as the most interesting Jewish philosopher to emerge in the period spanning the death of Maimonides in 1204 and the abrupt termination of the Golden Age of Jewish scholarship in Spain as a result of the expulsion of the Jews from that country in 1492.[1] Crescas was indeed the first post-Maimonidean philosopher to challenge the Aristotelianism that began to influence Jewish thought as early as Saadia and which became dominant in Jewish philosophy as a result of the influence of Maimonides and later of Gersonides.

Maimonides accepted the crucial elements of Aristotle's philosophy, but in upholding the purposeful and providential activity of

---

1. Shlomo Pines, "Scholasticism after Thomas Aquinas and the Teachings of Hasdai Crescas and his Predecessors," *Proceedings of the Israel Academy of Sciences and Humanities* (Jerusalem, 1966), vol. I, no. 11, p. 10.

God he rejected the Aristotelian notion that all natural phenomena are ruled by necessity. Gersonides went further and, carrying the Aristotelian principles to their inevitable conclusions, accepted the principle of necessity, which he attributed to celestial influences, while at the same time limiting God's knowledge to universals. As a result of the growing prevalence of intellectualism, the authority of Aristotle came to be regarded as supreme, and even biblical exegesis acquired an Aristotelian flavor. As Judah ha-Levi had sought to do even before the advent of Maimonides, Crescas endeavored to challenge the dominant intellectualistic attitude and to expound a system of thought free of Aristotelian rationalism but characterized by a strong emphasis upon the spiritual and emotional aspects of human nature.

Crescas' most significant contribution is his philosophical work, *Or ha-Shem*, written in Hebrew and completed in 1410, the year of his death, as a polemic against Aristotelianism in general and directed against the overpowering influence of Maimonides in particular.[2] As such, it is directed primarily against Maimonides' *Guide of the Perplexed.* Whereas Maimonides and Gersonides sought to harmonize revelation and faith with philosophy, Crescas endeavors to show that philosophy and belief occupy separate realms. Crescas has been aptly compared to the Islamic philosopher al-Ghazali, who composed the *Tehafut al-Falasifah* (Destruction of the Philosopher) as a defense of orthodox religious beliefs against the doctrines of the philosophers.[3] Yet Crescas recognizes the validity

---

2. For a discussion of the reasons underlying Crescas' limited influence upon his contemporaries and immediate successors, with the exception of his disciple R. Joseph Albo, see E. Schweid's introduction to the Jerusalem, 1970 facsimile of the *edition princeps* of Or ha-Shem (Ferrara, 1555), pp. 1-6.

3. Solomon Munk, *Mèlanges de philophie juive et arabe* (Paris, 1859), pp. 273 ff.; cf. Julius Guttmann, *Philosophies of Judaism*, trans. David W. Silverman (New York, 1964), p. 56. Many scholars maintain that Crescas' criticism of Aristotle was inspired by al-Ghazali's *Tehafut al-Falasifah*. See M. Joel, *Don Chasdai Crescas' religionsphilosophische Lehren, Beiträge zur Geschichte der Philosophie* (Breslau, 1876), p. 3; David Kaufmann, *Geschichte der Attributenlehre in der jüdischen Religionshilosophie des Mittelalters von Saadia bis Maimuni* (Gotha, 1879), p. 134; I. Broyde, "Ghazali," *Jewish Encyclopedia*, V, 649; Isaac Husik, *A History of Medieval Jewish Philosophy* (New York, 1966), p. 392; cf., also, Julius Wolfsohn, *Der Einfluss Gazali's auf Chasdai Crescas* (Frankfurt a.M., 1905).

of philosophical investigation and seeks to employ the methods and arguments of Aristotelian philosophy in order to justify his own conclusions. Indeed, he often finds it necessary to present and elucidate the case for the Aristotelians before attempting to disprove it. He does not condemn reason but, on the contrary, makes use of it to expose its very limitations. His style is consistently free from rhetoric and is characterized by brevity and precision.[4]

Or ha-Shem deals with the principal doctrines of Judaism in the order of their dogmatic importance rather than in terms of their systematic connection. The work is divided into four treatises: the first deals with the existence of God; the second, with the fundamental doctrines of faith; the third, with other doctrines which, although not fundamental in nature, are binding upon all adherents of Judaism; the fourth, with doctrines that are not obligatory in nature. The latter, although open to philosophical speculation, are accepted traditions in Judaism. Providence is discussed in the second treatise. The second section of this treatise, composed of six chapters, is devoted to an analysis of our topic.

Crescas' theory of Providence stands in sharp contrast to the rationalistic theory propounded by both Maimonides[5] and Gersonides.[6] In his exposition of the nature of Providence, Crescas engages in a detailed refutation of the views of his predecessors and presents a precise formulation of his own views. Although ostensibly directing himself against Maimonides, Crescas takes full cognizance of the arguments for, and the ramifications of, Maimonides' basic position as subsequently developed by Gersonides.

Whereas Maimonides and Gersonides advanced naturalistic theories of Providence, Crescas views Providence, at least in its highest

---

4. Crescas' penchant for brevity often makes his meaning obscure. Cf., Harry A. Wolfson, *Crescas' Critique of Aristotle* (Cambridge, 1929), pp. 29f., who believes that the *Or ha-Shem* had its origin in classroom lectures and discussions, and that this fact determined the style of the book. Accordingly, Wolfson asserts, "It was while thus addressing himself to a group of initiated students, expecting to be interrupted with questions whenever he failed to make himself clear… that his style assumed that allusive and elliptical form by which it is characterized."

5. *Guide*, Part III, chaps. 17, 23, and 51.

6. *Milḥamot ha-Shem*, Fourth Treatise.

form, as proceeding directly from God. Misfortune occurs, not as a result of "hiding of the face," or severance of the bond that exists between the human intellect and the Active Intellect, but as a result of an act of God. Providence is exercised with regard to individuals *qua* individuals. God created and conserves the world for reasons of beneficence. God's love for His creatures assures that He continuously watches over and guides the destiny of mankind. Divine love, and hence Providence, is in no way commensurate with intellectual achievement; Providence is not exercised through the medium of the intellect and hence does not depend upon intellectual perfection. Rather, Divine Providence is manifested in direct correlation to the degree of love manifested by man for God as evidenced by man's obedience to the will of God and his performance of the Divine commandments. Not infrequently, a simple, pious individual may manifest a greater love for God than does the accomplished intellectual. In rejection of the intellectualism of his predecessors, Crescas asserts that communion with God is predicated upon love of God rather than upon intellectual apprehension. Providence is born of the reciprocal love of man for God and of God for man.

For Aristotle, God's perfection consists of self-contemplation. Since He is νόεσις νοεσεως or Thought of Thought, God's bliss lies in the self-enjoyment of His thinking. In opposition to this view, Crescas asserts that the essence of God is goodness, and, moreover, he perceives God's expressions of goodness as being entirely voluntaristic.[7] God's essence is the ultimate goodness; He allows this goodness to overflow in the act of creation and in continually maintaining the universe in existence. In answer to the question of the ultimate purpose of the world, Crescas replies that since the essence of God is ultimate goodness, the doing of

---

7. *Or ha-Shem*, Third Treatise, *kelal* 1, chap. 5. This view stands in contradistinction to the position of Avicenna, for example, who actually maintains that thinking is God's perfection. In speaking of the love of God, Avicenna refers to God's love of Himself as ultimate perfection, adding that it befits such perfection that its goodness should overflow. Avicenna, however, rejects the idea that this occurs as a result of God's benevolence toward the world. For Avicenna, goodness proceeds from God because it is grounded in His essence rather than because He wills it. See *Die Metaphysik Avicennas*, trans. M. Horton (Halle a.S. and New York, 1907), pp. 595 ff., and Guttmann, *Philosophies of Judaism*, p. 266.

good deeds is the ultimate purpose of all of existence. Unlike the Aristotelians, who considered love for His creatures as being unworthy of God's dignity, Crescas views this love as being grounded in God's essence and as being infinitely greater than the love of created beings for God.

The highest form of Providence, declares Crescas, assumes the form of direct and overt activity on the part of God.[8] Scriptural evidence attesting to the possibility of this type of Providence is found in the description of the nature of God's communication with Moses, "And the Lord spoke with Moses face to face, as a man speaketh unto his friend" (Exodus 33:11). This passage demonstrates that God is not a transcendental being, aloof and unconcerned with terrestrial affairs. It also shows that Divine Providence may assume the form of a direct act on the part of the Deity without the interposition of intermediaries. Furthermore, it serves as a prime example of Providence in that "face to face" communication constitutes the highest possible quality of Providence. Although this is the only instance in which Scripture explicitly ascribes Providence directly to God, to the exclusion of intermediary forces or beings, Crescas notes that, according to rabbinic exegesis, the last of the ten plagues was visited upon the Egyptians by God Himself, whereas the earlier punishments were administered through intermediaries. Stressing the use of the first-person pronoun in the verse "And I will go through the land of Egypt in that night, and I will smite all the first-born of the land of Egypt" (Exodus 12:12), the Sages interpreted this passage as meaning: " 'I will go through the land of Egypt' – 'I,' and not an angel; 'I will smite every first-born' – 'I,' and not a seraph."[9] This verse, according to accepted rabbinic interpretation, establishes the possibility of direct Providence without intermediate agency, not only in the nature of Divine revelation or communication with men, but also for purposes of protection[10] and, of equal if not greater significance, for purposes of punishment and retribution.

---

8. *Or ha-Shem*, Second Treatise, *kelal* 2, chap. 1.

9. The quotation is from the Passover *Haggadah*, which in turn is presumably based upon the *Mekhilta* 7:45 and/or the Palestinian Talmud, *Sanhedrin* 2:1, where the same concept is expressed in somewhat different form.

10. "I will smite every first-born" spells out the punishment of the Egyptians, rendering the phrase "I will go through" somewhat redundant. Crescas, therefore, interprets this

Crescas, however, recognizes that Providence more often than not is indirect rather than direct, i.e., Providence becomes manifest through the intermediacy of various forces or beings. The most obvious form of indirect Providence is the form in which natural objects or natural forces are employed as the conduits of Providence. All evidence of design in nature, all powers in plants and animals which guide their growth, reproduction, and conservation, are manifestations of this type of Providence.[11] In such manifestations of Providence, natural bodies or forces are used simply as implements or "utensils" (כלים) that remain entirely nonvolitional. Miracles, which by definition involve the contravention or suspension of natural processes, are of this nature. In the performance of a miracle, physical bodies or forces are manipulated by Providence in order to bring about a desired effect.

Providence may also become manifest through the intermediacy of various beings which play an active, rather than passive, role in bringing about Providential effects. Scripture is replete with reference to angels[12] charged with specific missions. Prophets and wise men are also employed in the channelling of Providential guidance and guardianship. Angels, prophets, and wise men differ from inanimate objects and natural forces in that they are endowed with volition. Accordingly, they play an active role in the operation of Providence by virtue of the fact that they will to perform acts directed by Providence and serve as intermediate voluntary agents.

Crescas does not at all doubt that angels, prophets, and wise men are used as vehicles of Providence. Since they are endowed with volition, the form of Providence that finds expression through them is classified as being of a separate category. He does ponder, and leave unresolved,

---

passage as indicating that protection was accorded to the children of Israel directly by God. That such protection was necessary is indicated by the verse, "...and there shall be no plague upon you to destroy you" (Exodus 12:13).

11. Crescas' description of the laws of nature as implanted in the created universe by God is not at all novel. Earlier philosophers, however, did not characterize such phenomena as the product of Providence. See Schweid, *Or ha-Shem*, introduction, p. 52.

12. Described by Crescas as שכליים נפרדים, "Separate Intelligences"; cf., Maimonides, *Guide*, Part II, chap. 6.

the question of whether or not there exists a fourth class of voluntary agents, the members of which are intermediaries for the manifestation of Providence, namely, "celestial influences," or, as Maimonides termed them, the "Intelligences."[13] Gersonides had earlier declared that Providence presents itself solely through astrological influences.[14] However, for Gersonides, the heavenly spheres are governed by natural law and act in a thoroughly deterministic manner. For Gersonides, the recipient of Providence is privileged to discern what has been destined by the stars so that he may govern himself accordingly. Such knowledge is conveyed to recipients by means of dreams, divination, prophecy, intuition, or in some other unconscious manner. Crescas agrees that terrestrial events are ordained by the heavenly bodies. As such, one would assume that they are to be categorized as inanimate objects or natural forces. Crescas, however, cites the opinion of Maimonides and "some wise men" who maintained that the spheres were governed by souls or Intelligences, and then proceeds to ascribe to those Intelligences the ability to act in accordance with volition and free choice[15] much in the manner of a prophet or seer. If so, the Intelligences must be numbered together with angels, prophets and wise men as belonging to the category of beings who by exercise of will actively participate in the operation of Providence.

Maimonides accepted the Aristotelian position that maintained that the spheres were governed by Intelligences. He argued that the existence of Separate Intelligences can be proven on the basis of the motions of the celestial spheres. These motions, argued Maimonides, cannot be purely unconscious and involuntary, as are the motions of the elements (fire, air, water, and earth), because if that were the case they would cease at some point, just as elements in motion cease when they reach their natural places. It must therefore be concluded that they are endowed with souls, and that their motions are conscious and voluntary. The only

---

13. See *Guide*, Part II, chaps. 10-12.
14. *Milḥamot ha-Shem*, Fourth Treatise, chap. 6. For a discussion of Gersonides' view regarding Providence, see this writer's *Providence in the Philosophy of Gersonides* (New York, 1973), pp. 30-44.
15. "ויהיה בכאן לפ' זה מין רביעי מהאמצעיים הפועלים בחירה ורצון והם הגרמים השמימיים שיפעלו ויציירו מה שיפעלו בסדור אשר וירצו נפשם בו."
    Or ha-Shem, Second Treatise, *kelal* 2, chap. 1.

way to account for the continuous circular motion of the spheres is by assuming that the sphere is endowed with reason or intellect, and that its motion is due to a desire on its part to achieve a certain conception. The sphere yearns to achieve similarity to God, and it is the love of God which is the cause of the sphere's motion. The sphere seeks to achieve conception of God by means of circular motion because this is the only continuous act possible for a body and is the simplest of bodily motions.[16]

It is indeed true that Maimonides describes the Intelligences as rational souls endowed with wills. However, it must be remembered that Maimonides was an opponent of astrology. For him the Intelligences were limited in the exercise of reason in that their intelligence and volition was directed solely toward attaining a conception of God. Maimonides specifically denies that the Intelligences influence the destiny of mankind.[17] Crescas, in equating volition on the part of the Intelligences with that of angels, prophets, and wise men, goes far beyond Maimonides in ascribing intellectual and volitional functions to the

---

16. Cf. *Guide*, Part III, chaps. 2-9.

17. *Ibid.*, chap. 12; *Epistle to Yemen* and *Letter on Astrology*, ed. A. Marx, "The Correspondence between the Rabbis of Southern France and Maimonides about Astrology," *Hebrew Union College Annual*, III (1926), 311-358.

Within medieval Jewish philosophy there exist two distinct trends with regard to astrology. Ibn Ezra, in his *Commentary on the Bible* (Exodus 23:26), emphatically accepts the powers of astrological forces. Maimonides, on the other hand, vehemently denies their potency. Interestingly, the post-Maimonidean Aristotelians, despite the overpowering influence of Maimonides, accepted astrology as a legitimate scientific pursuit. Gersonides, for example, not only accepts astrology but uses it to explain various religious-philosophical concepts, such as prophecy. Acceptance of astrology is a logical outgrowth of Aristotelianism, since Aristotle believed the spheres to be living, intelligent creatures. Given the additional fact that Aristotle's God is a transcendental being far removed from terrestrial reality, it is easy to see why Aristotelians ascribed regulation of earthly affairs to these celestial bodies. The influence of astrological causes upon the elements and their combinations is not seriously questioned by the Aristotelians. The question to which they addressed themselves is the efficacy of astrological influences over man and over his fortunes. Crescas accepts the reality of astrological influences over the affairs of men and avoids fatalism by asserting that individuals who are privileged to be recipients of personal Divine Providence are able to transcend astrological influences by becoming subject to the direct providential guardianship of God. Crescas' view in this respect is similar to that of Ibn Ezra and Nahmanides, who both quote Samuel Ibn Nagrela's

Separate Intelligences. This follows, of course, from the fact that Crescas had already parted company from Maimonides in accepting the reality of astral influences. Yet should it turn out that the spheres are in turn governed by Intelligences, it would logically follow that terrestrial events are governed by rational, volitional acts of these Intelligences.[18] Thus, Crescas expresses reservation not with regard to the influence of the Intelligences over the affairs of man but with regard to whether or not Separate Intelligences actually exist. But, in accepting their hypothetical existence, he ascribes to the Intelligences powers that his predecessors would have most vehemently denied they possess.

Crescas maintains that the mode through which Providence is manifest is directly dependent upon the spiritual perfection of the recipient. Moses had no need for any intermediary and communicated with God "face to face." Communication with lesser prophets, since they had not attained the perfection of Moses, was through an intermediary.[19] Communication with the community of Israel, who were less perfect than the prophets and hence were not themselves endowed with prophecy, was through the prophets. In later generations, when the spiritual state of the community of Israel became even more inferior, communication was through the Judges and wise men.

Providence may be individual or general in nature, or both. The spiritual attainments of a nation or society as a whole may merit certain benefits which are then enjoyed by even the less deserving members of that society. General Providence of this nature is nevertheless manifest in a measure commensurate with the spiritual perfection of the society as a whole. Individual Providence exists side by side with general Providence

---

interpretation of the Divine name, *Shaddai*, which they felt connoted God's power to withdraw man from the influence of the stars. See Salo W. Baron, *A Social and Religious History of the Jews* (New York, 1958), VIII, 179.

18. Small wonder then that, in his *Letter on Astrology*, Maimonides, using sharp language, equates astrology with idolatry. Having himself demonstrated that the spheres are governed by Intelligences, he viewed the ascription of domination over the affairs of men to such independent stellar forces as being tantamount to idolatry.

19. It would appear that yet another form of intermediacy should have been added by Crescas to his list of four conduits of Providence, *viz.*, the mode by which the prophets received their communication.

and is predicated upon the spiritual perfection of the individual. Indeed, individual Providence may be completely absent in persons deficient in spiritual perfection. Regarding such persons Scripture declares, "I shall surely hide my face" (Deuteronomy 31:18).

Providence with regard to the gentile nations is, however, significantly different. Such Providence exists only through the intermediary of celestial causes. It is general in nature rather than individual. Moreover, it is not contingent upon the degree of spiritual perfection of the recipient nation. In drawing this distinction Crescas follows the basic position adopted by Judah ha-Levi, who also, albeit on the basis of entirely different assumptions, drew a similar distinction.[20] Providential care resulting from natural causes, says Crescas, is experienced by all nations, since the laws of nature apply equally to all. This is, of course, the lowest form of Providence, and it is perhaps stretching the term a bit to subsume general laws of nature under the category of Providence. Crescas does so because the embodiment in the natural order of regular and universal laws is itself an expression of Divine love and beneficence. Higher forms of Providence requiring Divine intervention are enjoyed only by the community of Israel by virtue of the special relationship which exists between Israel and God and, therefore, are contingent upon the spiritual perfection of the recipients.

As previously noted, Providence assumes many guises. This is true of general Providence no less than of individual Providence. The more general forms of Providence are entirely natural and are in no way contingent upon ethical conduct or spiritual perfection. This type of Providence extends not only to man, but to all living creatures, as evidenced by the fact that all species are endowed with organs, faculties, and instincts that are utilized for self-preservation and thereby guarantee the continuity of the species. Providence of this type is essentially egalitarian in nature. While the mode or modes through which the goal is achieved vary from species to species, the purpose, *viz.*, preservation of the species, remains the same, and, of course, within any given species all members of the species participate equally in such manifestations of Providence.

---

20. See *Kuzari*, Part I, sec. 109; Part II, sec. 32; and Part IV, sec. 3.

With regard to human beings, Crescas discerns a form of Providence which he regards as general in one sense yet particular in another, but on the whole more general than particular. Man alone is endowed with reason, and by virtue of his reason man is superior to other species. He possesses both practical reason,[21] which makes it possible for him to engage in tasks necessary for his self-preservation, and speculative reason through which he is enabled to achieve intellectual perfection. This form of Providence is general and natural in that it is rooted in the natural processes of physiology and biology,[22] and is present in all human beings by virtue of the natural propensities of the human species.

Crescas is, however, well aware that there exist gradations between individual human beings with regard to natural intelligence, and it is in accounting for the variations between individuals that he parts company with Maimonides and other Aristotelians. Maimonides maintains that human perfection is to be equated with intellectual achievement; hence, the greater the intellectual perfection of the person, the greater the Providence he deserves. Crescas denies that human perfection is a correlate of intellectual perfection. On the contrary, there are individuals who have achieved a high degree of spiritual excellence but are endowed by nature with an intellectual capacity far inferior to that of others of much lower spiritual perfection. Intelligence, for Crescas, is fundamentally a faculty determined by natural causes, such as the composition of the humors or astrological influences, rather than by effort put forth on the part of the individual himself. Although individuals may be unique in that these natural causes result in the presence of varying degrees of intelligence, the possession of the rational faculty is common to all members of the human species and hence a manifestation of a general form of Providence.[23]

---

21. Really *techne*, or technical reason. *Praktikos*, or practical reason, is the term used by Aristotle for the faculty utilized in interpersonal relationships, the faculty which makes ethics and political science possible.

22. See *supra*, note 11.

23. One is reminded of the statement by Hobbes in Book I, chapter 13, of the *Leviathan* in which he says: "And as to the faculties of the mind … I find yet a greater equality amongst men, than that of strength. … That which may perhaps make such equality incredible is but a vain conceit of one's owne wisdome, which almost all men think

Another manifestation of Providence, less general in nature, was bestowed upon the Jewish people who constitute a unique faith community, "the community of believers." The giving of the Torah is a manifestation of Providence, which serves as a primary medium for the acquisition of perfection. This form of Providence is general in that it extends to an entire people, but not so general as to extend to the entire human race. It is a "non-natural" form of Providence in that it is the product of a specific and nonrecurring act of Divine will, i.e., the choice by the Deity of a specific people at a specific point in time. The Torah is classified by Crescas as a manifestation of general Providence, since it is given to all Jews equally and is not contingent upon the religious or moral conduct of the individual. Although some subgroups received more commandments than others, i.e., males more than females, and priests more than Israelites, the disparity is not a function of individual Providence but of the intrinsic value and potentiality for perfection which, according to Crescas, males naturally possess to a higher degree than females, and members of the priestly tribe to a higher degree than other Israelites. Nevertheless, all members of the given class are equal.

The Torah and the performance of its commandments does, however, lead to a form of Providence which is personal in nature and which completely transcends natural phenomena. Reward and punishment commensurate with individual actions are not built into the structure of the world-order but occur by virtue of individual Providence. Providence in terms of reward and punishment assumes two forms. The first is in the nature of physical or material reward and punishment, and may be influenced by factors other than the actions of the individual, as will be shown subsequently. The second is reward and punishment, which is meted out to the soul as ordained by Divine wisdom and is directly and undeviatingly commensurate with individual merit.

---

they have in a greater degree than the Vulgar.… For such is the nature of men … they will hardly believe there be so many wise as themselves: for they set their own wit at hand, and other men's at a distance. But this proveth rather that men are in that point equall, than unequall. For there is not ordinarily a greater signe of the equall distribution of anything, than that every man is contented with his share."

Difficulties arise with regard to all theories of Providence when examined in the light of the principle of theodicy. How can a just, beneficent, and compassionate Deity, who exercises providential guardianship over His creatures, permit the wicked to prosper while the righteous are afflicted by severe misfortune? Maimonides,[24] followed by Gersonides,[25] addressed this question, and asserted that the prosperity of the wicked and the misfortune of the righteous are not at all to be attributed to Providence. Gersonides explains these phenomena by postulating that the righteous person may fail to take advantage of the opportunities presented to him which would assure his happiness and success; the wicked person may seize upon opportunities which present themselves, but were not providentially designed for his benefit. Furthermore, upon careful examination it may well turn out to be the case that the paradox rests upon an erroneous assumption. The person who appears to be righteous may not be righteous at all. Despite the performance of good deeds, he may be seriously remiss in not performing righteous deeds in a measure commensurate with his talents and capabilities. Similarly, the wicked person, by virtue of his character and genetic makeup, may in reality have a natural propensity for far greater evil which he endeavours to overcome with all his might. Such a person is therefore deserving of reward by virtue of the moral struggle and the torment he suffers in suppressing or sublimating his passions. In addition, what appears to mortal eyes as misfortune may be a vehicle or means toward ultimate benefit, and, conversely, the apparent prosperity of the wicked may ultimately lead to misfortune and adversity.

Crescas finds Gersonides' resolution of this problem to be refuted by experience and hence unsatisfactory.[26] One can point to righteous individuals who toil tirelessly and leave no stone unturned but who nevertheless remain unsuccessful. The question raised with regard to whether or not the righteous person has fulfilled his potential and has measured up to what is to be expected of him Crescas finds specious. A person may perform good deeds all his life and experience naught but

---

24. *Guide*, Part III, chaps. 23 and 51.
25. *Milḥamot ha-Shem*, Fourth Treatise, chap. 2, and *Commentary on the Bible*, Job 5:26.
26. *Or ha-Shem*, Second Treatise, *kelal* 2, chap. 2.

adversity, yet precisely when he embarks upon the path of evildoing his fortunes begin to take a turn for the better.[27] Similarly, experience shows that misfortunes befall the righteous that in no way lead to ultimate benefits, and *vice versa*, benefits accrue to the wicked that in no way lead to misfortune or adversity.

Crescas[28] next examines an alternative Aristotelian solution to the problem of the adversity of the righteous. Aristotle, in his *Metaphysics*, followed by Maimonides,[29] argues that God cannot be the source of evil.[30] Acceptance of this premise leads the Aristotelians to the formulation of a hypothetical syllogism negating the logical possibility of Providence: If God exercises Providence in rewarding the righteous and punishing the wicked, then, of necessity, God is the author of the evil meted out to the wicked. Since it has been established that God is not the source of evil, it follows that Providence does not exist. This argument is a classic instance of *modens tollens*, the argument form which employs the principle that if the consequence is known to be false, it then follows that the antecedent cannot be true. Maimonides, having accepted the basic principle that God is not the author of evil but rather that evils are either caused by man's own actions or proceed inevitably but accidentally from the negative or privative aspect of matter which makes it the cause of defect and evil, was forced to redefine the nature of Providence. In doing so, Maimonides denies individual Providence in the sense of reward and punishment directed toward individuals by the Deity. Misfortune, according to Maimonides, occurs not as a result of Divine intervention but as a result of "hiding the face" and allowing the individual to be buffeted by the vicissitudes of nature and left to

---

27. This possibility was noted by Saadia Ga'on, *Emunot ve-De'ot*, Fifth Treatise, chap. 2. For an English translation, see Saadia Ga'on, *The Book of Beliefs and Opinions*, trans. Samuel Rosenblatt, Yale Judaica Series (New Haven, 1958), p. 212.

28. *Or ha-Shem*, Second Treatise, *kelal* 2, chap. 2.

29. *Guide*, Part III, chap. 10. Cf. also, Saadia Ga'on, *Emunot ve-De'ot*, First Treatise, chap. 3; *Book of Beliefs and Opinions*, p. 66.

30. Crescas cites the rabbinic dictum ״אין דבר רע יוצא מן השמים״, "no evil descends from Heaven," *Bereishit Rabbah* 51:3, which serves to establish the validity of this position. The identical dictum had previously been cited in a similar context by Gersonides, *Milḥamot ha-Shem*, Fourth Treatise, chap. 3.

the governance of chance.[31] The essence of the theory of Providence espoused by both Maimonides and Gersonides is that Providence becomes operational through the medium of the intellect. Providence depends directly upon communication between the human intellect and the Active Intellect. As enunciated by Gersonides, Providence consists solely of the receiving of information regarding potential benefits and misfortunes, the quality of this information varying in a degree commensurate with the individual's intellectual achievement. According to this analysis, Providence is not the result of Divine grace but the natural product of man's own endeavors. According to this theory, the problem of the prosperity of the wicked is resolved in the recognition that there is nothing that intervenes in order to prevent beneficial occurrences from befalling the wicked as ordained by natural law or astrological influences.

Crescas raises two serious objections with regard to this position. Since Providence is a function of intellectual development, it would follow, argues Crescas, that an evildoer who has cultivated his intellect would achieve a high degree of communion with the Active Intellect and thereby become the recipient of Providence, with the result that he is enabled to avoid adversity. Secondly, Scripture foretells the grievous punishments that will befall the wicked, punishments which are apparently directed against evildoers by design and are not simply the result of "hiding the face" and the denial of providential guardianship.

Crescas answers his first objection by arguing that the evildoer cannot conceivably be in communion with the Active Intellect. His predilection for evil and the wicked acts themselves cause him to become matter-oriented. Concern for the sensual is the antithesis of what is required for maintaining a bond with the Active Intellect. Turning toward the material involves a turning away from the intellectual, and hence Providence is denied to that person.[32] The second objection is

---

31. *Guide*, Part III, chap. 51.
32. This notion quite possibly has its antecedent in Aristotle's doctrine of eudaimonia. Eudaimonia is defined as an "activity of the soul in accordance with virtue." Perfect happiness, for Aristotle lies in the exercise of the contemplative faculty, i.e., the faculty of intellectual or philosophical activity. Although moral action is a necessary concomitant to contemplation in achieving eudaimonia, Aristotle does not spell out the precise relationship between them. Although he is obscure on this point,

countered by Crescas with the assertion that the misfortunes referred to by Scripture are not essentially punishments but are rather admonitions. When misfortunes are present in this guise, they are either visited upon individuals who have hitherto been righteous but have begun to backslide and are designed as a corrective measure or they are directed against the wicked but not so much to punish them as to serve as a warning to the righteous so that they do not fall into evil practice. It should be noted that Gersonides listed admonition as one of the four causes of the adversity of the righteous. Gersonides states that if a person has committed minor infractions, misfortune may cause the afflicted individual to take heed and correct his conduct. He may thereby be preserved from ultimate punishment, which, for Gersonides, is intellectual or spiritual in nature.[33]

Subsequently,[34] however, Crescas asserts that this does not really solve the problem. He argues that not all biblical narratives can be explained in this manner. The story of Noah and the flood is particularly problematic. On the assumption that punishment of the wicked is designed as a form of admonition to the righteous, it would follow that had Noah – the only righteous individual in his generation – been an evildoer, the flood would not have occurred! Furthermore, *karet* ("cutting off"), which may assume the form of either death at the hands of Heaven or destruction of the soul, is prescribed by the Bible as punishment for no less than thirty-six different sins. Understood as a physical punishment involving death at the hands of Heaven, it would follow from this thesis that *karet* serves only as a warning to the righteous. Accordingly, it would stand to reason that this punishment should be meted out only if the transgression is committed publicly and hence known to

---

Aristotle apparently thought that moral action is required because the passions must be kept in subjection in order to make intellectual activity possible. Cf. W. D. Ross, *Aristotle* (Cleveland, 1963), pp. 226-227 and Frederick Copleston, *A History of Philosophy* (Westminster, 1960), 1, 348. The parallel in the thesis here advanced by Crescas is obvious. Providence is rooted in the intellectual faculty. Evildoing results in the dominance of corporeality and the sensual in man which in turn impedes intellectual activity.

33. *Milḥamot ha-Shem*, Fourth Treatise, chap. 6.
34. *Or ha-Shem*, Second Treatise, *kelal* 2, chap. 3.

others – a conclusion which is clearly not borne out in the rabbinic tradition. If *karet* is understood as the destruction of the soul, it certainly cannot serve as a form of admonition, since it cannot be witnessed by the righteous in this world, while in the world-to-come such admonition serves no purpose. Nor can *karet* in the form of destruction of the soul be understood as the natural result of certain specified misdeeds, since according to the rationalist philosophers whose theory of Providence is under discussion, immortality of the soul is the natural result of communion with the Active Intellect, while immortality is denied to those who fail to develop their intellectual faculty. Destruction of the soul by way of punishment can be understood only as a direct act of God serving as retribution in the punishment of misdeeds.

Another difficulty raised by Crescas[35] is the very notion of the destruction of the soul. Gersonides accepted the Artistotelian principle that matter can neither be created *ex nihilo* nor be destroyed, and was therefore led to accept the eternity of primordial matter.[36] It is then difficult to understand how a soul which is naturally immortal can be destroyed. It is conceivable that its form may change, but its "matter" cannot perish. The soul thus remains an immortal substance, which regardless of whatever form it might conceivably be forced to assume by way of punishment, nevertheless remains immortal.

At a later point in his discussion,[37] Crescas points out that the notion of retribution directed against the wicked in order that it may serve as a warning to the righteous cannot be accommodated by a naturalistic theory of Providence. Since the evildoer has no communication with the Active Intellect, there is simply no vehicle by virtue of which he may be directed to adversity. The inability to explain the punishment of the wicked is, for Crescas, the crucial and paradoxical philosophical flaw in the position espoused by Maimonides and Gersonides.[38]

---

35. *Or ha-Shem*, Second Treatise, *kelal* 2, chap. 3.
36. *Milḥamot ha-Shem*, Sixth Treatise, part 1, chap. 17.
37. *Or ha-Shem*, Second Treatise, *kelal* 2, chap. 4.
38. It is noteworthy that, in speaking of adversity as a form of admonition, Gersonides does so only in the context of the adversity of the righteous. He significantly fails to state that the wicked are punished so that the righteous may take heed. In addition to the problem raised by Crescas with regard to heavenly punishment of the

Crescas next raises what is conceptually virtually the same objection but in a different form. Scripture foretells not only punishment for the wicked but also reward for the righteous. Among the rewards and benefits thus prognosticated are many which cannot be ascribed to natural causes or astrological influences. Among the examples cited by Crescas are the promise of victory in battle, "And five of you shall chase a hundred, and a hundred of you shall chase ten thousand..." (Leviticus 26:8), the guarantee that the produce of the sixth year will be sufficient to enable the seventh to be observed as a Sabbatical year (Leviticus 25:20-23), and the examination and exoneration of the wrongly suspected adulteress by means of the bitter water (Numbers 5:11-31), none of which can be explained simply as fortuitous natural occurrences. These phenomena can be explained only by postulating a form of Providence that is both personal and transcends the natural order; they cannot be explained on the basis of a Providence that simply enables man to become knowledgeable regarding future natural occurrences.

In order to understand why Gersonides propounds his particular theory of Providence, it is necessary to look beyond the theory itself. Crescas points out that conventional theories of Providence entail a knowledge of particulars. Certainly Gersonides, who denies Divine knowledge of particulars,[39] could not have accepted a form of personal Providence other than of a type in which God is completely passive. This problem is ingeniously overcome by Gersonides in the enunciation of a theory of Providence in which Providence becomes operative as a result of apprehension of the Active Intellect by human reason. Crescas,[40] on the other hand, argues that the Bible is replete with references to Divine

wicked, it is difficult to account for Gersonides' explanation that adversity of the righteous is intended as a means of sparing them from more severe adversity or as an admonition to take heed and make amends for minor infractions. If Providence consists solely of the ability to acquire information concerning future occurrences, what is it which prompts such individuals to seek rather than to shun adversity? Presentation of information in an obscure or incomplete manner designed to promote misconstrual would imply, at the very minimum, some form of positive intervention by the Active Intellect.

39. *Milḥamot ha-Shem*, Third Treatise, chaps. 4-6.
40. *Or ha-Shem*, Second Treatise, *kelal* 1, chap 1.

knowledge of particulars. With the acceptance of Divine knowledge of particulars, one of the chief considerations which entered into Gersonides' formulation of his theory of Providence disappears.

There is yet another assumption upon which this theory is based that Crescas dismisses as erroneous. Aristotle had advanced one very cogent argument in support of his denial of Providence, *viz.*, that there is no reason to assume that the Deity would concern Himself with the affairs of creatures so lowly and insignificant as man. This problem Maimonides and Gersonides sought to avoid by assigning a passive role to the Active Intellect. Crescas, however, argues that if this argument is to be given credence, it would follow that the very gulf which exists between God and man, and which precludes God's direct concern, also eliminates the possibility of any union between the human intellect and the Active Intellect, since they are alike only in terms of accident, i.e., intelligence, but different in essence. According to Maimonides they are not even alike in accident; the very term "intellect," Maimonides argues, is a homonym and has a completely different meaning when applied to the Deity.[41]

In developing his own views regarding Providence, Crescas seizes upon one aspect of the theory of his predecessor and makes it the cornerstone of his own theory. Gersonides had already made the point that true reward and punishment are spiritual rather than physical and are accordingly meted out to the soul rather than to the body.[42] Crescas develops this notion further and makes it the focal point of his own theory of Providence. For Gersonides, ultimate reward necessarily has to be of a nature which the soul may enjoy; for Crescas, the welfare of the soul is the *only* criterion against which all other phenomena are to be measured. Viewed transcendentally, temporal pleasures and misfortunes are insignificant in value; of genuine concern are only matters which affect the immortal soul.[43]

From this vantage point Crescas perceives no injustice in temporal evils which may befall the righteous. A true accounting can be taken

---

41. *Guide*, Part III, chap. 2.
42. *Milḥamot ha-Shem*, Fourth Treatise, chap. 6.
43. *Or ha-Shem, kelal* 2, chap. 2.

only in the realm of spiritual good and evil, against which the good and evil which exists in the physical realm is insignificant and inconsequential. Furthermore, and of even greater significance, great advantage may be derived from physical misfortune: it may serve the righteous as a means of attaining perfection of the soul and lead to spiritual benefit. Thus, in effect, temporal well-being is exchanged for eternal life.[44] Conversely, material benefits accorded to the wicked may lead to ultimate adversity, not to sentient or material misfortune but to spiritual misfortune in that they serve to impede spiritual advancement. Crescas thus follows an argument cited by Gersonides in resolving the problem of the adversity of the righteous and the prosperity of the wicked by postulating that such adversity or prosperity may be the vehicle toward the opposite result. Crescas' theory is quite similar to the resolution of this problem ascribed to Bildad by Gersonides in chapter 2 of the Fourth Treatise of the *Milḥamot* and in chapter 8 of his commentary on Job. However, in one point, Crescas' hypothesis differs radically from the view attributed by Gersonides to Bildad. For Bildad (according to Gersonides), the ultimate goal which Providence seeks to achieve is temporal good or evil, and this, Crescas believes, is negated by experience. Indeed, Gersonides presents the same refutation of Bildad's defense of Job in chapter 3 of the Fourth Treatise and in chapter 10 of his commentary on Job. For Crescas it is *spiritual* advantage that is promoted by physical adversity, and *spiritual* benefit that is precluded by temporal advantage. Quite obviously, this view is not susceptible to refutation on the basis of empirical evidence.

In developing this theory, Crescas does not at all rule out other possible causes for the misfortune of the righteous. He recognizes that such adversity may be attributed to various causes. Adopting one of

---

44. Crescas, in presenting his theory, is well aware that placing real reward and punishment in the next world does not in itself justify why reward and punishment in this world are not completely controlled by conduct. He is fully aware that the righteous man does not deserve to suffer for his righteousness even though his good deeds will not go unrewarded in the next world. It is for this reason that Crescas stresses the point that temporal adversity should be welcomed because of the spiritual benefit it brings in its wake. Husik's stricture on this point is unfounded; cf., Husik, *History of Medieval Jewish Philosophy*, p. 394.

Gersonides' explanations, Crescas notes that a righteous person may find himself in abject circumstances as a result of punishment earlier meted out to his forebears, while his own merit is insufficient to warrant intervention by Providence in order to effect a change in his situation. The sole difference between Gersonides and Crescas with regard to this point is that for Gersonides the hereditary and environmental disadvantages are originally brought about by the natural order, while for Crescas they may be the result of direct Divine intervention.

Misfortune may also occur as the result of a temporary severance of the bond of attachment between the individual and God, as a result of which personal Providence is withdrawn and the individual reverts to the governance of the constellations. Severance of the bond between the human and the Divine leading to a withdrawal of Providence is, of course, a concept advanced by both Maimonides[45] and Gersonides.[46] For Crescas,[47] however, it is the severance of an attachment born of a spiritual bond created by the love of God rather than severance of an intellectual bond resulting from the perfection of the intellect.

Crescas regards any misfortune which cannot be explained in one of these three ways as accidental in nature and the result of astrological causes. Since the positions and movements of the constellations were ordained in a manner designed to preserve the universe and to provide maximum perfection, occasional or accidental evil cannot be viewed as an injustice or imperfection on the part of God. In formulating this point, Crescas adapted Maimonides' explanation of evil and made it conform to his own view concerning the world-order. Whereas for Maimonides evil results from the defects of matter, defects which are inevitable and inseparable from matter,[48] for Crescas they result from the position of the stars. Although the celestial bodies are designed to produce optimal conditions, certain benefits necessarily lead to certain misfortunes that result from the selfsame arrangements of the stars which bring about more advantageous benefits. The extent of this problem is

---

45. *Guide*, Part III, chap. 51.
46. *Milḥamot ha-Shem*, Fourth Treatise chap 5.
47. *Or ha-Shem*, Second Treatise, *kelal* 2, chap. 4.
48. *Guide*, Part III, chaps. 10 and 12.

mitigated for Crescas, much as it was for Gersonides, by the assertion that true reward and punishment are not temporal but are reserved for the world-to-come. For Gersonides true reward and punishment must of necessity be "human," i.e., intellectual in nature, and hence pertain to the soul; for Crescas the emphasis is on the otherworldly aspect of ultimate reward and punishment.

But for Crescas the most significant explanation is the one given earlier, namely, that misfortune may prevent the righteous person from following his evil inclinations; suffering may develop his character, make him more compassionate, and enhance his spiritual perfection. Employing this concept, Crescas engages in a bit of biblical exegesis which serves to provide a scriptural basis for his theory. The notion of a *nisayon* as it occurs in the Bible is understood by most commentators as a "test" or a "trial" through which the Deity seeks to establish a certain fact with regard to the character of the person being put to the test. The test serves no purpose in and of itself other than to demonstrate the presence of an already existing spiritual quality, just as, academically, an examination is usually administered not as a pedagogical tool but as a device designed to measure knowledge which has already been acquired. Not so for Crescas. For Crescas, the misfortune and adversity visited upon the righteous bring enhanced perfection to such individuals. Having withstood the trial and remaining steadfast in his faith, the righteous man becomes a new person, an individual more noble than his original self. Crescas believes that such occurrences can create a metamorphosis in the individual's character traits and propensities. Applying this thesis, Crescas resolves a difficulty which had earlier perplexed Maimonides. The verse "...for the Lord your God putteth you to test, to know whether you do love the Lord your God with all your heart and with all your soul" (Deuteronomy 13:6) contains an obvious anthropomorphism. On the basis of a literal reading of this passage, it would appear that the test is required by God as a means of acquiring knowledge concerning the individual – an obvious absurdity and a conclusion that is incompatible with the notion of Divine omniscience. Crescas explains that the test is not needed to apprise God of already existing facts, but is designed rather to effect a change in reality.[49] It is reality which is changed by means of the trial, because through the trial there emerges a wholly changed person, one whose existence was heretofore unknown. To know this new reality requires a new state of awareness, an awareness which could not have existed earlier since it would not have had correspondence in reality.[50] Similarly, following the binding of Isaac by Abraham, God exclaims, "...for now I know that thou art a God-fearing man..." (Genesis 22:12), not because He suddenly became aware of the fact that Abraham was a God-fearing man, but because the act of binding Isaac upon the altar created a quality of God-fearingness which Abraham had not previously possessed.

Talmudic and midrashic discussions dwelling upon the concept of "afflictions of love"[51] constitute a vexing problem for Crescas. The references, according to Crescas,[52] are clearly to the types of afflictions just discussed, the type of adversity which effects heightened spiritual awareness in the recipient. Care should be taken not to confuse Crescas' position with the opinion of the Mu'atazila which is recorded by Maimonides[53] and adopted by Saadia.[54] According to the Mu'atazila doctrine, suffering is meted out, not as retribution for prior sin, but in order to provide enhanced reward in the afterlife for trials endured without

---

49. Maimonides attempts to resolve the problem by advancing a novel interpretation of the term "to know." Maimonides understands the word in question, לדעת, as meaning "to make known," in the sense of "to make known to the world at large your love of God."

50. In advancing this interpretation, Crescas also finds it necessary to reinterpret the Hebrew word הישכם, which biblical exegetes translate as "whether." The more likely term for "whether you love" would be אם אתם אוהבים, or הישכם. האם נראים אתם אוהבים, argues Crescas, is to be understood in the fundamental sense of יש, as pertaining to existence. The verse thus speaks of the test leading to knowledge of the "existence" or reality of the love of God because such love comes into existence as a direct result of the test.

51. See *Berakhot* 8a and *Bereishit Rabbah* 92:1.

52. *Or ha-Shem*, Second Treatise, *kelal* 2, chap. 4.

53. *Guide*, Part III, chap. 17.

54. *Emunot ve-De'ot*, Fourth Treatise, chap. 3; *Book of Opinions and Beliefs*, p. 214.

complaint. According to this position, the afflictions serve no purpose in and of themselves; their purpose is solely to justify future compensation. For Crescas the purpose of affliction is the intrinsic benefit it brings in terms of developing the soul and character of the person so afflicted; any enhanced reward which may subsequently accrue to the soul in the world-to-come is purely secondary.

The prosperity of the wicked can be explained in a similar manner. Some forms of prosperity are simply the residual effects of benefits accorded to more worthy forebears. In some instances the evildoer has performed some good deeds which stand him in good stead in preventing positive intervention that would remove from him the benefits ordained by celestial influences. Other benefits bring misfortune in their wake. Such misfortune may be temporal or spiritual, as, for example, in a case in which, due to his enjoyment of certain benefits, the evildoer allows himself to be overpowered by his passions and is led to devote himself to a life of sensuality.

Yet another solution to this problem is advanced by Crescas. Citing the talmudic dictum, "The world is judged according to the majority."[55] Crescas explains that adversity intended for the majority of a given society may affect an individual righteous person, and, conversely, the evildoer may experience prosperity so long as the degree of evildoing or righteousness of the individual so affected does not warrant intervention in the natural order on his behalf. Crescas, however, differs significantly from his predecessors who formulated a similar thesis. Since he has accepted a notion of individual Providence according to which there is a strict correlation between the individual's actions and the workings of Providence, merely explaining the source of unwarranted good or unearned evil is not sufficient; Crescas must show that Providence somehow succeeds in balancing the scales. Crescas does so by drawing upon his previously enunciated position that true reward and punishment are spiritual in nature, whereas temporal benefits and misfortunes are far too insignificant and inconsequential to serve as conduits of Divine justice.

---

55. *Kiddushin* 40b.

This thesis also enables Crescas to resolve the apparent contradiction between the postulate that God cannot be the source of evil and acceptance of the belief that Providence is the author of punishment of the wicked. Crescas finds that acceptance of both assumptions does not constitute a paradox. Punishment, explains Crescas, is merely a relative evil, never absolute. Punishment intended as a form of admonition to the righteous clearly has a goal which is good. Punishment which is intended purely as such is a manifestation of Divine justice and is thus good in essence, since Divine justice is intrinsically good. Accordingly, "evil" which befalls the wicked for either of these purposes is entirely good.

This theory enables Crescas to explain a number of biblical passages and midrashic comments which otherwise appear to be incomprehensible. "And behold it was very good" (Genesis 1:31) is explained in *Bereishit Rabbah* as having reference to death, the phenomenon of death being described as "very good." Similarly, the verse "For a moment of His wrath is life according to His will" (Psalms 30:6) is interpreted by Crescas as follows: The Psalmist, says Crescas, intends to convey the notion that the relationship between evil and good is analogous, quantitatively speaking, to the relationship between a single moment and the entire continuum of time. The term "wrath" is employed by the Psalmist as a cognomen for evil because God's wrath leads to misfortune. Qualitatively, this evil is designed to promote life and the good, i.e., "life according to His will." The *telos*, or end result, of this evil or wrath is life.

The most fundamental of the Aristotelian arguments against Providence rests upon the concept of the inferiority and insignificance of man *vis-à-vis* the Deity and the assumption that it is unseemly for God to concern Himself with the affairs of man. This argument is completely rejected by Crescas. God not only created all things, but He continuously recreates man by virtue of His will or desire. Desire for a certain thing cannot be understood other than as love for that thing. Thus God's love extends to His creatures. It is inconceivable, declares Crescas, that God should know and love His creatures and not exercise Providence over them. Accordingly, God's concern and attention with regard to His creatures who are beloved by Him is no cause for amazement regardless of the great gap which exists between them and the Deity. It is also perfectly reasonable that His Providence should extend in enhanced and greater measure to those most beloved by Him. Most beloved are those which are noblest. Therefore, the highest form of Providence is that which extends to man, who is the noblest of creatures and hence the most beloved by God.

In disagreement with Maimonides, who maintained that individual Providence extends solely to members of the human species,[56] Crescas maintains that Divine Providence extends to all created beings. Yet, at the same time, Crescas declares that the form of Providence that transcends the natural order is extended only to members of the community of Israel. Other peoples are governed by a form of Providence that is manifest only through the operation of the laws of nature.

Crescas' theory of Providence follows logically from his views concerning the nature of creation. Since Crescas accepts the notion of continuous creation,[57] it follows that there is constant and uninterrupted desire or love on the part of the Creator with regard to His creatures. Crescas' emphasis is upon God engaged in an act of love rather than upon the notion of God as pure intellect as portrayed in the philosophy of Maimonides. Since Maimonides sees God as essentially a pure intellect, it is only through man's intellectual faculty that he can, albeit with great difficulty, relate to God. Gersonides adopts a more radical view and regards God solely as the creator of forms, not as the creator of individuals who are corporeal substances.[58] Hence, for Gersonides, since individuals are completely removed from the realm of the Divine, there can be no room for direct individual Providence. Since, according to Crescas, God's relationship with man is a product of Divine love, it follows that, for Crescas, Providence is in no way contingent upon the quality or perfection of the human intellect but is, rather, predicated entirely upon God's love for man. This, in turn, enables Crescas to resolve the vexing problems of how the soul of a wicked person can be destroyed even though it may have achieved a high degree of intellectual perfection. If, as believed by Maimonides, for example, development of the

---

56. *Guide*, Part III, chap. 17.
57. *Or ha-Shem*, Third Treatise, *kelal* 1, chap. 5.
58. *Milḥamot ha-Shem*, Sixth Treatise, chap. 17.

intellect naturally guarantees immortality of the soul,[59] destruction of the intellect would require an overt act on the part of God, an act which would contravene the natural order. But according to Crescas, it is not intellectual development but rather the individual's spiritual and moral attainment that determines the degree of Providence he is to be accorded. Accordingly, destruction of the soul of the wicked can be explained as a natural phenomenon, i.e., since the soul is spiritually deficient, the soul is annihilated and destroyed through natural processes.

In concluding his discussion of Providence, Crescas undertakes an investigation of the underlying reasons for the unique form of Providence that is manifested by God with regard to the community of Israel. He broadens the discussion to include an analysis of the concept of a "chosen people."

Crescas maintains that the unique relationship between the people of Israel and God has its source principally in the rite of circumcision. The circumcision ritual itself, according to Crescas, endows the infant who thereby enters into the covenant of Abraham with a particular form of Providence and conveys upon him immortality of the soul. As proof, Crescas cites the formula of the benediction pronounced upon completion of the circumcision ritual: "Therefore as recompense for this [circumcision], O living God, our portion and our rock, commence that the dearly beloved holy seed[60] of our flesh be delivered from destruction for the sake of His covenant which He has set in our flesh. ..." Crescas understands the term "destruction" in this prayer as having reference to destruction of the soul. Thus the rite of circumcision preserves the Jew from annihilation and assures eternal life through the immortality of the soul. For Crescas immortality of the soul is itself a manifestation of Providence and constitutes a form of eternal reward.

Crescas is troubled by the cause-effect relationship that apparently exists between circumcision and the immortality of the soul. He is also disturbed by a technical liturgical point. The text of the benediction

---

59. *Guide*, Part I, chap. 70, and Part III, chap. 27.

60. The phrase זרע קדש, "holy seed," is not part of the accepted liturgical form. Crescas himself, at a later point in the discussion, again quotes the formula of the benediction minus the phrase.

is couched in negative terms as a prayer for preservation from destruction rather than in positive language as a supplication for eternal life. In resolving these questions, Crescas propounds a Jewish version of the doctrine of original sin. Contrary to popular opinion, the doctrine of original sin is rooted in Jewish sources and is not entirely Christological in origin, although, to be sure, it is presented in a completely different guise in Jewish sources. Although talmudic in origin, this doctrine is certainly not central to Judaism and indeed is ignored completely by all of Crescas' philosophical predecessors. It assumes real significance in Jewish thought only within the kabbalistic tradition. According to the talmudic account (*Shabbat* 146a, *Yevamot* 103b, and *Avodah Zarah* 22b), when the serpent approached Eve and tempted her to eat of the forbidden fruit of the Tree of Knowledge, the serpent also engaged in sexual relations with her[61] and infected her with "decay" which was subsequently transmitted to her progeny. The Talmud declares: "When the serpent had sexual relations with Eve he deposited in her 'decay.' Israel, who stood on Mount Sinai, lost their decay; the nations of the world, who did not stand on Mount Sinai, did not lose their decay." Crescas explains this statement in a thoroughly rationalistic manner.[62] Adam and Eve were the progenitors of the human race. The disobedience of Adam and Eve had important physiological consequences for all their descendants. Their actions instilled in them a marked propensity for all things sensual, and this trait was passed on to their progeny. The serpent infected Eve and through her the entire human race with lasciviousness and sensual desire; this, in turn, had the effect of causing man to become a creature of the flesh and hence mortal. With the receiving of the Torah at Sinai through an act of Divine grace, the sensual passions of Israel ceased, i.e., they were checked and held in rein by means of the influence of religion. The Law received at Mount Sinai had the effect of inculcating a set of moral values and transformed Israel from a community of sensuous individuals into a community of moral people. Thus, for Crescas, it is the development of ethical sensitivity and the casting

---

61. הנחש השיאני, "The serpent enticed me" (Genesis 3:13), is understood as a *double entendre* having the added connotation of נישואין, "marital relations."

62. *Or ha-Shem*, Second Treatise, *kelal* 2, chap. 6.

off of excessive sensuality which frees man from the stigma of original sin. According to Crescas, the Divine commandments serve primarily as a means of acquiring a sense of morality and ethics. This position is markedly different from the view of Judah ha-Levi, for example, who regarded the commandments as being endowed with mystical powers.[63]

A second source of the unique form of Providence which exists with regard to Israel is found in the historical incident of the *akeidah* – the binding of Isaac upon the altar as a sacrifice. Abraham is seen by Crescas as the moral antithesis of Adam. Adam was created directly by God, provided with all his needs, and given optimal conditions for achieving spiritual perfection, but nevertheless Adam disobeyed and rebelled. Abraham, on the contrary, was raised among idolaters but nevertheless excelled in the love of God and was found worthy by virtue of his own action of becoming the progenitor of a people devoted to the service of God. To this end he was given the commandment concerning circumcision, the performance of which represents both a sacrificial act and a negation of sensuality in general. Sensuality is represented by the male organ, since sexual desire is the strongest of the passions. Crescas apparently agrees with Maimonides in viewing circumcision as being designed as a means of diminishing sexual gratification. Maimonides certainly believed that the presence of the foreskin enhances sexual pleasure and that its removal effectively diminishes sexual gratification. Maimonides viewed this effect as the desideratum that serves as the rationale underlying the commandment concerning circumcision.[64] Accordingly, declares Crescas, this commandment is indeed specifically intended to "save the beloved of our flesh" from the otherwise imminent destruction that follows as a result of original sin.

With the selection of Abraham as the founder of the Chosen People, some method had to be found to gain the release of this people from the influence of astrological forces and to effect a transfer to the jurisdiction of Providence emanating directly from the Deity. This was effected through the binding of Isaac, in the course of which Isaac, together with all his offspring, was given as a sacrificial offering to God.

---

63. Cf., *Kuzari*, Part II, sec. 48.
64. *Guide*, Part III, chap. 49.

Through this offering they were all freed from the domination of the celestial spheres and became the recipients of a unique form of Divine Providence. In arguing that astrological influences can somehow be obviated and immunity to their causal efficacy secured, Crescas draws upon the writings of Ptolemy, who postulated that astrological influences could be circumvented through specific action.[65] It was the binding of Isaac, concludes Crescas, which had the effect of negating naturalistic Providence in favour of direct Divine Providence. His analysis of this phenomenon specifically negates a eugenic or biological theory in explanation of the selection of Israel, such as occurs in the writings of Judah ha-Levi,[66] and instead ascribes this phenomenon to specific historical events.

Having clarified the reasons for, and the nature of, the diverse forms of Providence which are operative with regard to different individuals, Crescas finds it necessary to account for the fact that Scripture and rabbinic tradition associate more intense forms of Providence with

---

65. The unvocalized Hebrew text of *Or ha-Shem* refers to a work entitled פרי, which one would be inclined to read as *P'ri*, "The Fruit" or "The Fruit of..." Since among the known works of Ptolemy there is no book bearing this title, I assume that the word should be vocalized as *Peri* and understood as the translation of the Greek word περί. The reference would then appear to be to Ptolemy's περε αναλίμματος, usually known by its Latin title, *De Analemmate*. However, I have been unable to find any relevant passage in the available versions of that work. The view here ascribed to Ptolemy by Crescas is rather puzzling, since in the *Tetrabiblos*, which has been described by one authority as having "enjoyed almost the authority of the Bible among astrological writers for a thousand years or more" (see *Tetrabiblos*, ed. and trans. by F. E. Robbins [Cambridge, 1940], p. x), Ptolemy expresses a completely contradictory view, In discussing the practical value of the study of astrology, Ptolemy writes: "...if future happenings to men are not known, or if they are known and the remedies are not applied, they will by all means follow the course of primary nature; but if they are recognized ahead of time and remedies are provided, *again quite in accord with nature and fate* [emphasis added], they either do not occur at all or are rendered less severe. [*Tetrabiblos*, Book I, chap. 3, pp. 28-29]... and since the force of nature takes its course without hindrance... all future events are inevitable and unescapable [*ibid.*, p. 31]."

It is of interest that Ibn Ezra, in his *Commentary on the Bible*, Genesis 17:1, indicates that the study of astrology may itself in some way lead to the alteration of the course indicated by the stars.

66. *Kuzari*, Part I, sec. 95.

specific places and specified times. Thus Jacob exclaims, "How full of awe is this place! This is none other than the House of God, and this is the gate of Heaven" (Genesis 28:18). God Himself says to the children of Israel, "And they shall make Me a sanctuary, and I will dwell among them" (Exodus 25:8), and says to Moses, "And there I will make Myself known unto you, and I will speak to you from above the ark cover, from between the two cherubim which are upon the ark" (Exodus 25:22). Crescas asserts that insofar as the Deity Himself is concerned, no distinction exists between one geographical locale and another. From the point of view of God, all places are equally suited for the manifestation of Providence. The difference between one locale and another is significant solely because of its influence upon the recipient of Providence. For astrological and naturalistic reasons which Crescas does not spell out, certain locations provide greater opportunity for an individual to prepare himself for the service of God. It should be emphasized that the service of God is not intrinsically restricted to certain places, but rather certain areas provide proper conditions for embarking upon such service. Since Providence is directly correlated with the degree or quality of the love of God exhibited by individual recipients, it is readily understandable that, as a result, Providence of a higher intensity is manifested in areas which provide optimum conditions for Divine service. Similarly, certain times or seasons enable individuals to achieve a higher state of preparation for the service of God. For example, the rituals associated with the New Year and the Day of Atonement render the individual receptive to the acceptance of the yoke of the kingdom of heaven and hence deserving of an enhanced measure of Providence. But Providence itself is intrinsically unrelated to time or place and is extended in a degree directly commensurate with the individual's love of God as expressed in performance of the Divine commandments and obedience to His law.

II.

Joseph Albo was thoroughly familiar with the works of his predecessors and presented their ideas in his philosophical work, *Sefer ha-Ikkarim*, in a popular and highly readable manner. His style is that of a homilist and he devotes much space to lengthy metaphysical, ethical, psychological, and theological interpretations of biblical and rabbinic passages. The style of the *Sefer ha-Ikkarim* assured that work a wide circulation and a popularity that was denied the *Or ha-Shem* of his teacher Hasdai Crescas, to whom Albo is heavily indebted for the content of the *Sefer ha-Ikkarim*. Despite the polemics of Isaac Abravanel and others against Albo, the *Sefer ha-Ikkarim* has come to be a standard and accepted treatise and has wielded considerable influence upon the religious beliefs of Judaism.

In terms of his general philosophical approach, Albo's stance is somewhere between that of the rationalists and that of philosophers such as ha-Levi and Crescas, who stress the spiritual aspects of man. He agrees with the rationalists that man is the noblest creature in the sublunar world by virtue of having been endowed with reason.[67] Hence man's goal must be the development of his intellect. Nevertheless he agrees with ha-Levi and Crescas in maintaining that the perfection of the soul lies in doing the will of God and in the performance of good deeds.[68]

Together with Crescas, Albo believes that the goal of the pious man is to love God and not merely to fear Him. Such an individual seeks to perform God's commandments out of a sense of love rather than fear. Albo analyzes and defines the concept of love in a discussion which closely parallels Aristotle's discussion of friendship in the last two books of the *Nichomachean Ethics*. There are three kinds of love, asserts Albo, each distinguishable from the other by its goal or motive: namely, love of the agreeable, love of the useful, and love of the good. The love of God is the highest form of love because in God man finds pleasure, utility, and the good.[69]

Most intriguing is Albo's discussion of Divine love for man. Love, apparently, is a human quality. God can certainly find neither pleasure nor utility nor ultimate good in a creature so imperfect as man. Nevertheless, Scripture assumes that God loves Israel. In his analysis of love, Albo declares that the love felt by a superior toward an inferior is inversely proportional to the former's degree of superiority. It would then follow that God's love for lowly human beings is nil, since God's superiority is infinite. Albo concludes that God's love for man is irrational in nature

---

67. *Sefer ha-Ikkarim*, Book III, chap. 1.
68. *Sefer ha-Ikkarim*, Book III, chaps. 35-37, and Book IV, chap. 28.
69. *Sefer ha-Ikkarim*, Book III, chaps. 35-36.

and much akin to that of a lover toward his beloved though he knows that other women are more beautiful and more alluring. In Hebrew, this is not love (*ahavah*) but rather *ḥeshek*, as indicated in Deuteronomy 7:7, where the verb *ḥashak* is used in reference to the election of Israel. Similarly the Song of Songs, which in Jewish tradition has always been recognized as a parable symbolizing God's love for Israel, employs the analogy of the love of a lover for his beloved.[70] It is as a result of this relationship that God exercises Providence over Israel.

In comparing the treatment of Providence by Albo with earlier treatments of this topic in the writings of Maimonides, Gersonides, Crescas, and Duran, one striking point presents itself. Albo devotes himself entirely to a demonstration of the reality of individual Providence and to a resolution of the problems of the adversity of the righteous and the prosperity of the wicked – phenomena which constitute the most serious empirical challenge to this doctrine. With the exception of one brief statement in which Albo asserts that Providence is commensurate with the degree of intellectual perfection attained by the individual,[71] little effort is expended by him in an attempt to present an explication of the nature and essence of Providence and the means by which it becomes manifest. Maimonides, Gersonides, and Crescas were at least as much concerned with the analysis of the nature of Providence as they were in demonstrating its reality and refuting any contradictory evidence which might be advanced against the doctrine of individual Providence. In Duran[72] the discussion of the nature of Providence is less central, but only in Albo is it virtually ignored.

Crescas, as we have seen, did not question whether or not the world is governed by Providence, as did his predecessors, but rather

---

70. *Sefer ha-Ikkarim*, Book III, chap. 37. See also Isaac Husik, "Joseph Albo, the Last of the Medieval Jewish Philosophers," *Philosophical Essays*, ed. Milton Nahm and Leo Strauss (Oxford, 1952), pp. 263 ff.

71. *Sefer ha-Ikkarim*, Book IV, chap. 11; Joseph Albo, *Sefer ha-Ikkarim*, ed. and trans. by Isaac Husik (Philadelphia, 1946), IV, 93.

72. Duran's theory of Providence is developed at length in the introduction to his commentary on the Book of Job, *Ohev Mishpat* (Venice, 1589) and is summarized briefly in Book III, chap. 2, of his philosophical work, *Magen Avot* (Leghorn, 1745). For a discussion of Duran's theory of Providence, see chapter eight of this volume.

embarked upon an inquiry with regard to the nature and manifestations of Providence. However, to a considerable degree, the distinction is merely a matter of semantics, since the ordered patterns of nature and astral influences are subsumed by Crescas under the category of Providence in recognition of the fact that God is the author of natural law and of the patterns of the constellations. The thesis that the world is governed by chance and that human beings are left to the mercy of the vicissitudes of time, which Maimonides saw as the alternative to a doctrine of Providence, is not at all mentioned by Crescas. Crescas apparently thought that this position was not a viable one and hence did not merit examination.

It is then readily understandable that his disciple, Albo, prefaces his own discussion with an analysis of astrology and the causal power of the stars.[73] For Albo the question is whether the world is governed by Providence or by the celestial bodies. As was the case for Crescas, chance is not a third possibility. However, in terms of Albo's nomenclature, a sharp distinction is drawn between astrology and Providence.

Accordingly, for Albo the question of the efficacy of astrological forces is antecedent to a discussion of Providence. That such forces do indeed exist is, for Albo, not open to question; after all, empirical observation demonstrates that "the sun warms the air, and the moon moistens and cools it, and increases the force of water."[74] The question is, what are the parameters of the influence exercised by the celestial bodies? Albo presents the view of the "Philosopher" who, even while denigrating astrology, was nevertheless quite willing to ascribe not only atmospheric and geological phenomena to the celestial bodies but also attributed to them causal power with regard to the combinations of the various elements. The particular combination of elements in a given corporeal substance renders that body capable of becoming imbued with certain forms and renders it incapable of receiving other forms. Hence even the Philosopher admits that the ability to acquire wisdom, for example, is dependent upon astrological configurations.

---

73. *Sefer ha-Ikkarim*, Book IV, chap. 4.
74. *Loc. cit.*; Husik, *Sefer ha-Ikkarim*, IV, 24.

The view of the astrologers and "stargazers" is presented as an antithesis to the thesis of the Philosopher. These individuals believed that everything that occurs to man, including such matters as the number of wives or children he will have, occurs in a deterministic manner as a result of the decree of the stars. In support of this position Albo cites the Talmudic statement, "The constellations make rich, the constellations make wise – Israel is governed by the constellations."[75] Albo's primary objection to this view is that acceptance of astrology eliminates the category of the contingent and thus necessitates the denial of freedom of the will.

Albo's solution to this question is a synthesis of both positions. Albo accepts the basic position of the astrologers regarding the reality of astrological influences, but denies that they are necessary causes in a deterministic sense. Citing both Rashi[76] and Ibn Ezra,[77] Albo avers that the astrological indications can be nullified or circumvented through exercise of free will, by reason of some merit or good deed, and most importantly, by the will of God. According to Albo's view, Divine commandments were bestowed upon man so that through their fulfillment man may be saved from the decrees of the stars. Albo has, in effect, emended the doctrine of the astrologers to the extent of inserting a *ceteris paribus* clause. The positions and motions of the stars produce certain effects, but only if no other concomitant causes are present. Since the latter may negate astral influences, the fatalistic nature of astrology is denied by Albo.

One crucial point is left obscure by Albo, and perhaps this obscurity is purposeful on his part. Crescas, speaking of governance by Providence transcending the stellar order, employs terminology which makes it quite clear that such individuals are removed from the jurisdiction of the stars and placed under the direct governance of Providence. Rashi comments that the effect of prayer or some meritorious deed is that it

75. *Shabbat* 156a. The quoted statement constitutes one of the two opposing views recorded in that discussion.

76. *Shabbat* 156a, s.v. *ein mazal*.

77. Albo cites Ibn Ezra's unpublished *Sefer ha-Moledet (Book on Nativities)*. Husik, *Sefer ha-Ikkarim*, IV, 33, quotes the cited passage on the basis of a manuscript version.

"can *change* the horoscope from evil to good."[78] The implication is not that astrological indications are nullified by some nonastrological factor, but rather that through charity, prayer, or good deeds some new element is introduced into the astrological configuration of forces which results in a new horoscope insofar as the individual is concerned; the result is a modified horoscope, but an astrological horoscope nevertheless. Albo quotes this comment in developing his position, and it would appear that this is his view as well.

A midrashic commentary concerning the binding of Isaac that is cited by Albo with approbation also supports this analysis. According to the Midrash,[79] Isaac was born under the sign of Mars, an indication that he would meet a violent death. God therefore ordered that Isaac be bound on the altar as a burnt-offering and thereupon substituted a lamb as ransom in order that Isaac be delivered from his fate. The implication is that God did not simply remove Isaac from the governance of the stars, but manipulated the existent astral influences by means of the binding of Isaac and the substitution of the lamb.

Furthermore, Albo emphasizes that the operations of the stars are entirely nonvolitional, although they may have different effects upon different individuals. The celestial powers are finite and can act only upon persons or things that have the capacity of receiving their influence. Fire has the power of warming substances that have the capacity of becoming hot, but it cannot possibly have the opposite effect. Thus Mars has the power to destroy, to kill, and to ruin, and Jupiter has the power to make people prosperous and wealthy, but each planet can do so only if the recipient has the capacity of receiving such influences, just as drugs are effective only upon persons susceptible to the effect of such drugs. Similarly, each of these planets is limited with regard to the effect it can bring about, and neither planet can cause the opposite effect.

A person may receive the influence of a star as the result of some act that he has performed which renders him potentially capable of receiving that influence, although the causal relationship between the preparatory act and the development of the potential for receiving the

---

78. *Shabbat* 156a, s.v. *ein mazal*. Emphasis added.
79. *Yalkut Re'uveni* (Jerusalem, 1962), vol. I, *Va-Yeira*, p. 201.

influence of the star is unkown. As a result, people are led to the erroneous belief that this effect is due to the volition of the star and are thus led
to idolatry. But in truth, "just as the influence of the teacher affects the
pupil who is prepared more than the one who is not prepared, though
the teacher is not directing his instruction to the one more than the
other, so the influence of a star reaches the one who is prepared more
than the one who is unprepared, without any intention or will on the
part of the star."[80] The error of the idolaters was compounded by the
fact that certain factors which had the effect of developing the potential
for receiving the influence of the star in a purely natural and causal way
were thought by people who did not perceive the existence of a causal
relationship of this nature to be acts of particular interest to the star and
their performance to be a means of gaining the favor of the star. This, of
course, led to the deification and worship of the stars.

Albo accepts the doctrine of Divine knowledge of particulars.
God's knowledge embraces all existing things and all individual acts,
both of men and of lower animals. God, however, does not reward or
punish individual members of the animal kingdom and provides for
them only as members of the species to which they belong.[81] Albo
accepts the reality of Providence with regard to the preservation of species without advancing proof for this belief. The question he poses is
whether Providence extends to individual human beings or is limited
to the providential guardianship of the species as a whole in the case of
human beings as well.[82]

Albo advances two distinct sets of proofs in demonstrating the
reality of individual Providence. The first group consists of a total of
five empirical proofs;[83] the second set is based entirely upon *a priori*
rational considerations.[84]

The first two proofs advanced by Albo are predicated upon general phenomena which Albo believes cannot be ascribed to natural law

80. *Sefer ha-Ikkarim*, Book IV, chap. 16; Husik, *Sefer ha-Ikkarim*, IV, 148.
81. *Sefer ha-Ikkarim*, Book IV, chaps. 1-3.
82. *Sefer ha-Ikkarim*, Book IV, chap. 7.
83. *Sefer ha-Ikkarim*, Book IV, chaps. 8-9.
84. *Sefer ha-Ikkarim*, Book IV, chaps. 10.

and hence must be an expression of Divine solicitude. The first of these proofs lies in the existence of dry land, for which Albo, having accepted Aristotelian physics, was at a loss to account. Medieval thinkers accepted Aristotle's identification of the four elements: earth, water, air, and fire. But, for Aristotle, earth is the heaviest element and should be located at the center of the universe.[85] Water is the second-heaviest element and should find its natural location directly above the earth, followed by the more rarified elements, air and fire. Thus, by virtue of the laws of nature, earth, the heaviest element, should sink below water. Hence, according to natural law, the earth should be covered with water and terrestrial life would be an impossibility. That this has not occurred is due to the "miraculous" contravention of nature by Providence.[86]

In advancing this argument, Albo contends that it proves not only the phenomenon of Providence but the doctrine of *creatio ex nihilo*: "For if the world were eternal and had always been going on according to the laws of nature observable today, without interference of a voluntary agent, we would necessarily expect that that which nature requires should at some time exist actually."[87] Albo apparently believes that, in obedience to natural law, the earth is in the process of sinking but that the process is not yet completed; therefore in some places the earth is

---

85. Cf., Aristotle, *De Caelo*, trans. W. K. C. Guthrie (Cambridge, 1945), vol. IV, chap. 5, p. 312b; cf., Eduard Zeller, *Aristotle and the Earlier Peripatetics* (London, 1897), I, 479, note 1; Maimonides, *Guide*, Part I, chap. 72; Husik, *History of Medieval Jewish Philosophy*, p. 176 and Husik, *Sefer ha-Ikkarim*, IV, 58, note 1. The argument itself may be traced to Judah ha-Levi, *Kuzari*, Part Five, sec. 19. Duran mentions this phenomenon in *Magen Avot*, I, 9a, as a sign that the world was created for the sake of man, as well as in *Magen Avot*, III, 96a, and in *Ohev Mishpat*, Preface, p. 4b, as proof of the created nature of the universe.

86. Albo interprets Job 38:5-11 in a way which gives expression to this argument. Job denies Providence and accepts the eternity of the universe. God says to him, "Declare if thou hast the understanding, where wast thou when I laid the foundations of the earth?" bidding him to declare how the earth became uncovered if not by means of an act of God. "Wherefore were the foundations thereof fastened," is interpreted as meaning "What natural law made it necessary that earth should stand above the water?" In light of the repeated charge that Albo's arguments are borrowed from Duran, it should be noted that Duran interprets this verse in an entirely different manner. See *Ohev Mishpat*, Introduction, chap. 14, p. 18b.

87. *Sefer ha-Ikkarim*, Book IV, chap. 8; Husik, *Sefer ha-Ikkarim*, IV, 58.

covered by water and in other places not. However, given the hypothesis of an eternal universe, this process should already have been completed. The covering of the entire surface of the earth by water should already have occurred. Given an infinite amount of time, anything which is possible will become actual. Certainly, in the infinite period of time which, if the universe is eternal, has already elapsed, a phenomenon that, according to the laws of nature, is not only possible but necessary, should have been actualized.[88] If this is Albo's proof, it does not really prove the reality of Providence, but only serves to demonstrate the inconsistency inherent in denying the reality of Providence while at the same time affirming the eternity of the universe. Since Albo at the very outset declares that those who deny Providence accept the eternity of the universe, the argument as presented by him is insufficient to show that denial of Providence leads to a logical inconsistency.

The second proof advanced by Albo is based upon the phenomenon of rain. Albo himself notes that the Book of Job is replete with references to rain as a sign of God's concern for the proper governance of the universe. The importance of rain and the impossibility of terrestrial life without this phenomenon need not be belaboured. Thus the continued recurrence of rain constitutes a demonstration of Divine Providence.

As first noted by Heinrich Jaulus,[89] this proof of Providence was originally advanced by Duran.[90] Albo also points out a crucial weakness in the argument as presented thus far and proceeds to show that the argument is nevertheless demonstrative.[91] If rain can be ascribed to nature, and can be shown to follow a pattern of natural law, the phenomenon of rain cannot be invoked as a demonstration of individual Providence. This, says Albo, was the import of Job's comment "When He

---

88. This idea is quite similar to the concept employed by Aquinas in the formulation of his third proof for the existence of God.

89. Heinrich Jaulus, "R. Simeon ben Zemach Duran: Ein Zeit- und Lebensbild," *Monatsschrift für Geschichte und Wissenschaft des Judentums*, XXIII (1874), 462-463.

90. *Ohev Mishpat*, Introduction, chap. 14, p. 19a.

91. Indeed, in introducing this argument, Albo states, "The second argument... does not seem to be a real argument..." (*Sefer ha-Ikkarim*, Book IV, chap. 8; Husik, *Sefer ha-Ikkarim*, IV, 63). His language gives the impression that he is quoting a known argument for the purpose of defending it against possible objection.

made a decree for the rain..." (Job 28:26), i.e., that rain does not prove the reality of Providence, as Eliphaz and Elihu had argued, because rain may occur by virtue of the decree of natural law. To this objection God replies, "Hath the rain a father? Or who hath begotten the drops of dew?" (Job 38:28), thereby denying that rain has a "father," i.e., that it is begotten by natural law. Albo argues that rain cannot be ascribed to nature because it does not follow a set pattern as do other natural phenomena. Regularity, the hallmark of natural law, is absent in the distribution of rainfall. Accordingly, rain must be either a manifestation of Providence or a chance occurrence. Rain cannot be ascribed to chance because rain occurs repeatedly in a manner designed to preserve the existence of the world in a perfect manner.[92] Since it cannot be ascribed to chance, it must be a manifestation of Providence.

The argument thus far, with the exception of Albo's excursus into biblical exegesis, is identical with the argument based upon the phenomenon of rain advanced earlier by Duran, as has been pointed out by Jaulus. Jaulus, however, fails to note that while a second objection to this proof is advanced by both writers, it is resolved by Albo in a manner quite different from that of Duran.

The objection which remains to be resolved is that the phenomenon of rain serves to demonstrate only the existence of Providence as manifested with regard to species; it does not provide evidence for individual Providence. Duran attempted to resolve this difficulty by showing that each individual human being is to be equated with a complete species insofar as Providence is concerned.[93] Albo argues that although the phenomenon of rain cannot demonstrate the reality of individual Providence, the fact that individuals such as Elijah and Ḥoni ha-Maʿagel

---

92. The clause שהדברים המקריים אינם תמידיים באופן שיושלם בהם קיום המציאות should be translated: "For chance phenomena do not repeatedly [occur] in such a manner that through them the preservation of the existence of the world is perfected...." The word תמידיים in this context means "repeatedly" or "constantly" it cannot connote regularity because, as Albo has argued, it is precisely the lack of regularity in rainfall which demonstrates that it is not governed by natural law. Husik's translation of this passage is faulty. See Husik, *Sefer ha-Ikkarim*, IV, 66.

93. *Ohev Mishpat*, Introduction, chap. 14, p. 19a, and *Magen Avot*, Book III, chap. 2, p. 33a.

were able to cause rain to fall in answer to their prayers,[94] and the fact that rainfall is often forthcoming in answer to communal prayer do confirm the reality of individual Providence. Albo's answer is somewhat puzzling because it appears that the proof is actually based upon the notion of the efficacy of prayer, in regard to which rain is only one of many examples which might be advanced.

Albo's third proof is identical with the second proof advanced by Gersonides in support of the notion of individual Providence in chapter 2 of his treatise on Providence, *viz.*, that there are innumerable malevolent individuals intent upon doing harm to others. Their lack of success demonstrates the reality of Providence. To this Albo adds one point not mentioned by Gersonides, a point that serves to make the argument even stronger. Quite often the very means employed with intent to do harm may be the cause of unanticipated benefit, as seen, for example, in the narrative of Joseph and his brothers and in Saul's design against David, which resulted in his own downfall and David's ascension to the throne. Such phenomena point to the reality of Providence.

Albo's fourth proof corresponds to Gersonides' third proof in the previously cited chapter and is also advanced by Duran,[95] namely, that the punishment that comes upon the wicked corresponds to their offenses. It has been repeatedly observed that the wicked are punished measure for measure, i.e., if a person injures another financially, he is himself injured financially; if he cuts off the hand of another, his own hand is cut off; if he blinds another person, his own eye is blinded; if he kills another, he himself is killed. The Egyptians cast every male child of Israel into the sea; as punishment, they were drowned in the Red Sea. Scripture is replete with similar instances of punishments designed to fit the crime. Albo regards this as the most convincing proof of the reality of Providence, a proof which should "tear the heart of those of little faith."[96]

---

94. See *Ta'anit* 23a.

95. *Ohev Mishpat*, Introduction, chap. 16, p. 23a.

96. *Sefer ha-Ikkarim*, IV, chap. 9; Husik, *Sefer ha-Ikkarim*, IV, 74, Duran uses a similar expression with regard to the proof based upon the phenomenon of rain.

Albo's final proof based upon experience is predicated upon the divination of future occurrences by means of dreams. Following Duran,[97] Albo accepts that phenomenon as conclusive proof for the reality of individual Providence. For both Duran and Albo, all dreams concerning future occurrences are instances of individual Providence. Albo argues that such dreams cannot be the product of general Providence exercised with regard to the human species, since (1) no comparable form of Providence exists with regard to other species, and (2) the contents of such dreams are specific and individual in nature.

Gersonides, in the third chapter of his treatise on Providence, cites the phenomenon of dreams together with magic and prophecy in refutation of the Philosopher's premise that Providence extends to man only by virtue of general Providence with regard to the species. Subsequently, in chapter 6 of that treatise, after developing his own thesis asserting that some persons enjoy individual Providence while others do not, Gersonides attributes divination of future events by those who do not enjoy the privilege of being the recipients of individual Providence to general Providence exercised with regard to the entire species.

Gersonides would undoubtedly counter the first argument employed by Albo to show that this phenomenon is not the product of general Providence by pointing out that the nature of general Providence varies from species to species. Not all species have identical organs and limbs. Man alone possesses reason, and reason in itself, as both Gersonides and Crescas have noted, is a manifestation of general Providence that is limited to the human species.[98] Prognostication by means of dreams would then fall within the same category.

If Gersonides' analysis of the notion of divination by means of dreams is accepted, Albo's second objection based upon the fact that the contents of dreams are specific and individual in nature is not really a telling objection. The knowledge acquired through dreams is present

---

97. *Ohev Mishpat*, Introduction, chap. 16, p. 22b.
98. Albo himself, as shall be shown later, believes that reason is not merely a manifestation of general Providence but also entails individual Providence. This point is made by Albo in Book IV, chap. 10. Accordingly, it would appear that Albo's argument based upon the phenomenon of dreams, presented in Book IV, chap. 9, is predicated upon a claim that he does not make until later.

in the Active Intellect and is available to man through the medium of the imperfect communication that is operative in the dream state. This medium of communication is a function of the human intellect that is general in nature and extends to all members of the species.

The first of the nonempirical arguments formulated by Albo is predicated upon the existence of a rational faculty. It appears that reason is not required for the preservation of the species, since animal species are successfully preserved without being endowed with a rational faculty. Man is superior to other members of the animal kingdom by virtue of his intellect. The gift of reason indicates that God takes greater notice of man than of other species. It follows that Providence would be exercised with regard to individual human beings in accordance with the superiority of the individual's intellect, as was asserted by Maimonides.[99] Individuals who do not develop their intellectual faculties are reduced to the level of the lower animal species and are not privileged to be recipients of Divine Providence.

Another proof advanced by Albo focuses on the concept of Divine perfection. It is a sign of perfection in man if he watches over his handiwork so that it may realize its purpose; it is a sign of perfection in man if he takes care to govern those under his jurisdiction with righteousness and justice. Failure to do so is a defect and imperfection. Since God is both omniscient and omnipotent and is supremely perfect, is follows that He exercises Providence over His creatures. Albo follows Duran[100] in ascribing this argument to Elihu in the Book of Job.

In a second formulation of the same proof, Albo states that the strongest argument against the reality of Providence is based upon man's inferiority *vis-à-vis* the Deity. Job thought that because man is despicable and contemptible in the sight of God, He does not deign to take cognizance of man's actions. To this Elihu answered that it is impossible that God should ignore human beings by reason of their inferiority. It is not the nature of a wise worker to abandon his handiwork because of its

---

99. *Guide*, Part III, chap. 18.

100. *Ohev Mishpat*, Introduction, chap. 14, p. 18b. A briefer form of the same argument is advanced by Gersonides in the second chapter of his treatise on Providence in support of his view that all individuals are recipients of individual Providence.

inferiority if he is capable of improving it. Since man has great intellectual potentiality, it stands to reason that God will aid him in actualizing this potentiality and will assist him in the attainment of the perfection which he is capable of attaining. Not to do so would be a defect in God.

This proof bears only a superficial resemblance to the argument based upon the concept of Divine perfection advanced by Duran. For Duran, Providence is necessary in order to guarantee reward and punishment as mandated in a proper master-servant or ruler-subject relationship.[101] For Albo, it is development of potentiality which is mandated by the concept of Divine perfection, and this can be accomplished only through the exercise of Providence. Duran's point is merely mentioned by Albo in passing and is not developed by Albo as an independent proof.

Albo further develops this line of argument in order to show that general Providence with regard to the human species is insufficient to assure that each individual will attain his intellectual potential.[102] As had already been stated by Albo's predecessors, it is evident that each of the animal species is endowed with organs and faculties uniquely designed to meet its needs and to guarantee the continuity of the species. Nevertheless, the precise nature of such organs and faculties varies in accordance with what each species requires in order to attain its perfection. Individual human beings differ from one another with respect to the perfection of their rational faculties even more widely than one animal species differs from another. The disparity is so great that some persons appear to be on a level with irrational animals while the intellectual capacity of others approaches the degree of angels. It therefore follows that Providence should vary with regard to individual human beings just as it varies with regard to the different species in the animal kingdom.[103]

---

101. *Ohev Mishpat*, Introduction, chap. 13, p. 13a.

102. *Sefer ha-Ikkarim*, Book IV, chap. 11.

103. Husik, *Sefer ha-Ikkarim*, IV, 90, note 3 and IV, 93, note 3, implies that this argument is taken from chapters 14 and 15 of Duran's *Ohev Mishpat*. This is not so. Duran does argue that with regard to God's providential concern, individual human beings must be on a par with entire species within the animal kingdom. His argument, however, is quite different and most ingenious. Duran assumes that Providence is a function of immortality. Providence extends to animal species and not to individual animals

The highest form of Providence assumes the form of prophetic revelation. Divine communication comes to other individuals through the intermediacy of a prophet. A lesser form of Providence, asserts Albo, assumes the guise of an instinct or Divine impulse. As examples he cites Judah's assignation with his daughter-in-law, Tamar, which was providentially designed to bring about the birth of Perez and Zerah, as well as Abigail's impulse which prompted her to go out to meet David. Such providential instincts may at times be designed to cause punishment for past sins, as, for example, Ahab's impulse to do battle which led to his death as punishment for the killing of Naboth.

Having established the reality of Providence, Albo turns to the vexing problem of the prosperity of the wicked and the adversity of the righteous. Following Duran, who did not believe that even the Aristotelians accepted the philosophical arguments negating Providence as decisive, Albo states that it is the seemingly unjust distribution of benefits and misfortunes that led thinkers who accept Divine knowledge of particulars to deny individual Providence. Albo regards the prosperity of the wicked to be far more serious a problem than the adversity of the righteous. Punishment of the righteous does not occasion surprise because wrongdoing is not visible to everybody, and indeed "There is not a righteous man upon the earth, that doeth good and sinneth not" (Ecclesiastes 7:20). Furthermore, says Albo, punishment may be meted out for the mere intention to sin, even if the intent is never actualized.[104] Hence one can never know who is a truly righteous person.

Albo offers four explanations for the prosperity of the wicked.[105]

---

because the species is eternal while the individual animal is not. Therefore, argues Duran, Providence must extend to individual human beings, since each individual is endowed with a rational soul that is immortal.

104. Cf., however, *Kiddushin* 39b, which declares that intention to sin, other than intention to commit idolatry, does not warrant punishment.

105. *Sefer ha-Ikkarim*, Book IV, chap. 12.

1. In common with Gersonides,[106] Crescas,[107] and Duran,[108] Albo asserts that certain benefits may accrue to the wicked as a result of general Providence. God does not change the order of the constellations or alter a decree concerning a nation in order to prevent a wicked person from receiving benefits such as peace and tranquillity. Similarly, astral influences may decree a certain benefit for an individual whose wickedness is not so great that intervention by Providence is warranted in order to countermand the dictates of the stars.

2. The evildoer may even receive benefits as a result of individual Providence as a reward for some good deed. The wicked man is rewarded for his good deeds in this world in order to exclude him from heavenly reward and happiness. This point was also made by Albo's philosophical predecessors.[109] Albo follows Duran in citing as a source the much earlier Aramaic translation of the Bible by Onkelos. "And repays them that hate Him to their face to destroy them" (Deuteronomy 7:10) is rendered by Onkelos "And repays his enemies for those good deeds which they performed before Him in their lifetime, in order to destroy them [in the future life]."

3. Again following Duran, Albo asserts that benefits may accrue to the wicked by virtue of providential guardianship of others. For example, Laban prospered on account of Jacob, and the inhabitants of Zoar were spared for the sake of Lot, who in turn was saved for the sake of Abraham.[110] Crescas had earlier explained that undeserving sons may inherit the wealth of righteous progenitors.[111] To this Albo adds that fathers may prosper for the sake of their children. A wicked man may enjoy longevity in order that he may beget a righteous son. The Talmud indicates that God prolonged the life of Ahaz in order that Hezekiah might

---

106. *Milḥamot ha-Shem*, Fourth Treatise, chap. 6.

107. *Or ha-Shem*, Second Treatise, *kelal* 2, chap. 2.

108. *Ohev Mishpat*, Introduction, chap. 22, p. 32b, and chap. 23, p. 33b.

109. Gersonides, *Milḥamot ha-Shem*, Fourth Treatise, chap. 6 and Duran, *Ohev Mishpat*, Introduction, chap. 23, p. 33b.

110. *Ohev Mishpat*, Introduction, chap. 23 p. 33b.

111. *Or ha-Shem*, Second Treatise, *kelal* 2, chap. 4.

be descended from him.[112] A wicked person may also receive benefits in order effectively to bring about the punishment of other evildoers. For example, God bestowed prosperity upon Nebuchadnezzar, Sennacherib, and Titus in order that they might be instrumental in punishing the wicked of Israel and other nations. This latter point was enumerated by Duran as a separate explanation of the prosperity of the wicked.[113]

4. The wicked may prosper in order that they harden their hearts and not repent.

5. Furthermore, if the wicked were to be punished immediately upon committing a sin, one might suspect that the righteous serve God not out of love but out of a fear of receiving the selfsame punishment which they see coming upon the wicked. These last two explanations are quite evidently also borrowed from Duran.[114]

In addition to these explanations, Albo also argues, as did his predecessors, that a person we regard as wicked may in reality be a righteous person, and similarly, what appears to us to be good and beneficial may not be good at all.

Albo explains the adversity of the righteous in a similar manner.[115] As did his predecessors, Albo notes that many who are deemed to be righteous have, in fact, committed misdeeds for which they are punished. At times the individual is not punished for transgressions he has committed until a long period of time has elapsed, and he feels an injustice has been done to him because he has forgotten his own misdeeds. Also, as noted earlier, punishment may be for a mere intention that never became actualized. Again, what appears to be a misfortune may, in fact, be a means of warding off an even greater calamity.

But granted that the individual is really righteous and that the misfortune that befalls him is a real evil, the adversity of the righteous

---

112. *Sanhedrin* 104a.

113. *Ohev Mishpat*, Introduction, chap. 23, p. 34a.

114. *Ibid.*, pp. 33b and 34b respectively.

115. *Sefer ha-Ikkarim*, Book IV, chap. 13.

may be accounted for in four ways paralleling the explanations earlier advocated in accounting for the prosperity of the wicked:

1. The laws of nature do not discriminate between the righteous and the wicked. Unless he merits a high degree of direct individual Providence, the individual is subject to that which is decreed by nature or the stars. This point is made by Albo's predecessors. Similarly, as noted by both Crescas[116] and Duran,[117] an innocent individual may suffer because of an adverse decree designed to punish a nation, e.g., Daniel and his companions and Jeremiah did not themselves deserve to be exiled but were subject to the general decree concerning Jerusalem and Israel.

   Although he does not cite it as a separate explanation, Albo adds that a righteous person may be afflicted with misfortune as a punishment for not having prayed for mercy on behalf of his fellow man.[118] Moreover, declares Albo, the righteous may experience suffering in order to atone for their nation as a whole, thereby preventing a calamity that was destined to come upon the entire nation.

2. In agreement with his predecessors, Albo indicated that no man is completely free of sin. The righteous man may be punished in this world for his few transgressions so that he may enjoy unmitigated reward in the world-to-come.

   In agreement with Duran,[119] Albo asserts that Providence may decree suffering in order to protect the righteous person from a sin which he is about to commit. Comfort and prosperity lead to self-satisfaction and sin, as indicated by Scripture, "Jeshurun waxed fat and kicked" (Deuteronomy 32:15). Hence, misfortune may be administered by Providence as a prophylactic measure in order to prevent the righteous from falling into temptation.

116. *Or ha-Shem*, Second Treatise, *kelal* 2, chap. 4.
117. *Ohev Mishpat*, Introduction, chap. 24, p. 36a.
118. This point is not made by Duran. Husik's citation, *Sefer ha-Ikkarim*, IV, 112, note 1, is erroneous. Duran's point is that the righteous are punished if they remain silent when, by their protest, they could have prevented transgression.
119. *Ohev Mishpat*, Introduction, chap. 24, p. 35b.

3. As had already been noted by Duran,[120] some forms of suffering are inherited in the sense that they were decreed as punishment for evildoers but are of a nature that affects their descendants as well, e.g., the mortality of man, which arose as the result of a change in the nature of Adam in punishment of his sin. Thus a father may lose his wealth by reason of his sins with the result that the children are born into a poor family. In such instances misfortune befalls the children *per accidens*.

4. Albo's final explanation involves the talmudic notion of "sufferings of love." This concept has been defined in a variety of ways by Albo's predecessors. Albo accepts virtually all of these various explanations simultaneously[121] as being subsumed by the Talmud under a single general category. Thus Albo states that sufferings of love may be of three kinds. Following the explanation advanced by Nahmanides in his *Sha'ar ha-Gemul* (Gate of Recompense)[122] which had also been accepted by Duran,[123] Albo explains that even minor infractions require punishment for purposes of expiation in order that the soul be purged of the impurity with which it has become tainted so that its status will not be diminished in the future world. Eradication of such impurities is a manifestation of Divine love.

A second mode of sufferings of love involves no prior sin whatsoever. Sufferings of love may be administered in the form of a trial or test in order to determine whether the individual serves God with pure love or whether he serves God for love of reward and fear of punishment. Some people serve God out of love in times of tranquillity and prosperity, but lack the will or strength of character to endure hardship and suffering and to serve God in poverty and affliction without complaining and finding fault with God. Such afflictions are termed sufferings of love because they denote that the person so afflicted does indeed serve

120. *Ohev Mishpat*, Introduction, chap. 24, p. 36a.

121. Crescas' definition of sufferings of love is conspicuous in its absence.

122. *Kol Kitvei Ramban*, ed. Bernard Chavel (Jerusalem, 1964), II, 270-271.

123. *Ohev Mishpat*, Introduction, chap. 24, p. 35b.

God by virtue of perfect love and not out of love of reward and fear of punishment. Thus, Job was "wholehearted and upright, and one that feared God and shunned evil" (Job 1:1) in times of prosperity and success, but when suffering came upon him he found fault with God. Job's sin was that, lacking true love of God, he grumbled against God and accused Him of wrong. Only those who are motivated by pure love of God accept suffering gracefully. If a person accepts suffering with good grace, his reward is enhanced because his example inspires others to serve God from pure love.

The category of sufferings of love, declares Albo, also encompasses afflictions designed solely to increase reward. This was the doctrine of the Mu'atazila and was accepted by the *Ge'onim*. One cannot argue that, since God knows whether or not the individual will withstand the test, such trials are superfluous because the reward of a person who has actually endured pain and suffering because of his love for God cannot be the same as the reward of one who has not endured such afflictions, just as the reward for a good deed is given for performance of the good deed and not merely for the thought or intention of performing it. To this Albo adds that withstanding such trials in actuality habituates a person to, and strengthens his heart in, the love of God.

10

Tikkun Olam: Jewish Obligations to Non-Jewish Society

> *Every person is created for his telos and that is his "service." Likewise, Israel was created to be an illumination unto the nations and to cause them to achieve knowledge of the Lord of the universe.*
>
> Ha'amek Davar, Exodus 12:51.

The phrase "Therefore do we place our hope in You... to perfect the universe through the sovereignty of the Almighty" serves as a focal point of the latter portion of the *Aleinu* prayer uttered by Jews thrice daily. This is an expression of yearning, not simply for the perfection of Israel but, as reflected in the very next phrase, "and all mortals will call upon Your name," a yearning for the perfection of all mankind. Thus, perfection of mankind in the service of God is the acknowledged *telos* of human existence. Less obvious but, nevertheless, as will be shown, widely accepted among rabbinic scholars, is the recognition that the nation of Israel is charged with facilitating the perfection of mankind as a whole. However, the nature and parameters of that obligation on the part of Israel vis-à-vis the nations of the world require careful elucidation.

Any examination of the obligations of Jewry with regard to *tikkun ha-olam* in the sense of perfection of society must perforce proceed from an understanding of the nature of that *tikkun* – i.e., what it is that the Creator expects of mankind at large. That understanding, in turn, must begin with a thorough awareness of the ramifications and applications of the Seven Commandments of the Sons of Noah.

I.

Judaism is at once both universalistic and particularistic. The very existence of two religio-legal codes of widely disparate content side by side, i.e., the Sinaitic Covenant and the Noahide Code, is itself reflective, at the very minimum, of differing standards of moral and devotional responsibility. Any thinking person will perceive that the establishment of differing standards of religio-legal responsibility is either the product of capricious whim on the part of the divine lawgiver or is a correlative of disparate capacities, talents or potentials with which different peoples have been endowed or of disparate missions with which they have been charged. Any attempt to explicate the nature of Jewish responsibility vis-à-vis the nations of the world must proceed from a clear perspective of the differing roles played by Jews and the community of nations in the divine scheme of creation. From this perspective is born an assessment of the nature of the human *telos*, that, in turn, leads to explication of the concept of *tikkun ha-olam*.

The concept of the election of Israel may indeed serve as a thesis unifying manifold provisions of Halakhah. Nevertheless, it is hardly central to the philosophy of Halakhah. Theologically, it is probably most significant as a means of understanding divine intervention in shaping history. It is only in Christianity that the concept assumes supreme doctrinal significance only to be redefined in order to allow for the supplanting of the children of Israel by members of another faith community as the subjects of this election. Nevertheless, for good and sufficient reason, the concept of the election of Israel is indeed a focal point in Jewish liturgy and a dominant factor in popular thought, attitudes, actions and reactions of the Jewish populace throughout the course of millennia.

The election of Israel is certainly manifest in the covenantal relationship established by God with the people of Israel, a covenantal relationship inaugurated with the *berit bein ha-betarim* (covenant between the parts) entered into with Abraham and reaffirmed in subsequent covenants. Israel is twice described in the Pentateuch as the "chosen" people: "...the Lord your God has chosen you to be His treasure ... out of all the peoples that are upon the face of the earth" (Deuteronomy 7:6); and "...the Lord has chosen you to be a treasure to Him out of all the people that are upon the face of the earth" (Deuteronomy 14:2). Similar descriptions occur in Psalms 33:12, Psalms 135:4 and elsewhere. Scriptural passages repeatedly refer to Israel as an *"am segulah."* In addition to the earlier citation of biblical references to "chosenness," the term *"segulah"* occurs in the verse "and you shall be a treasure to me from all the nations" (Exodus 19:5) and in the verse "And the Lord has avouched you this day to be unto Him a treasured nation" (Deuteronomy 26:18), while in Psalms 33:12 there occurs a reference to the choice of Israel as a divine *naḥalah*. The rendering of *"segulah"* as "treasure" and *"naḥalah"* as "inheritance" in standard English translation, although not inaccurate, is nevertheless less than totally faithful to the concepts connoted by the Hebrew terms employed. In biblical Hebrew the terms overlap as nouns describing a *res* that is the subject of a property interest. Thus, in each of these passages, Israel is described as chosen by God for the purpose of being made the subject of some type of proprietary interest vested in Him as is otherwise expressed in the verse "...for unto Me are the children of Israel slaves" (Leviticus 25:55). The latter verse serves to make explicit the notion of a proprietary interest in the sense of a personal servitude requiring the rendering of particular services, i.e., performance of divine commandments.[1]

---

1. See the comments of R. Samson Raphael Hirsch in his *The Nineteen Letters of Ben Uziel*, Fifteenth Letter: "The Bible terms Israel *segulah*, a peculiar treasure, but this designation does not imply, as some have falsely interpreted, that Israel has a monopoly of the Divine love and favor, but on the contrary, that God has the sole and

Asserting the existence of such a relationship between Israel and the Deity is straightforward and unambiguous. Less clear is why Israel, rather than some other nation, is chosen for this servitude. The biblical references as well as the liturgical formulae "You have chosen us out of all the peoples," "who has chosen us from [among] every people," "who has chosen us from [among] all the peoples and given us His Torah," and "for us have You chosen" seemingly connote a unilateral choice on the part of the Deity. The concept of choice connotes, in turn, the existence of alternative possibilities. The choice of x over y by an intelligent being will, of course, be predicated upon carefully weighed rational and/or pragmatic considerations but nevertheless implies the existence of an alternative option that, albeit not optimal, is nevertheless viable.

Rambam, in *Guide of the Perplexed*, Book II, chapter 25, apparently agrees that the election of Israel represents a choice of that nature. In a very brief comment he asserts that it is impossible for us to understand why God should have revealed His will to one particular nation; in the words of Rambam, man can say only "[God] willed it so; or His wisdom decided so." From the human perspective, the question is totally unanswerable. In answering the same question from the divine perspective, Rambam is equivocal. The election of Israel is the product either of divine wisdom or of divine will – of which, we cannot tell. If the choice is born of divine wisdom, the reasons are of a nature that we cannot discern on the basis of human intelligence. But unlike his position in rejecting Saadia's view that *mitzvot* may be based upon the arbitrary will of God and need not proceed from divine wisdom, Rambam is perfectly willing to accept the possibility that the election of Israel is an arbitrary determination of divine will. Perhaps he regards determination of the particular recipients of revelation to be analogous to other matters with regard to which there is no reasoned basis for choosing between available alternatives, with the result that it is logically necessary to choose between making an arbitrary determination or suffering the paralysis of inaction. An example of such a choice is the determination of the

---

exclusive claim to Israel's devotion and service; that Israel may not render Divine homage to any other being." *The Nineteen Letters of Ben Uziel*, trans. Bernard Drachman (New York, 1942), p. 142.

species of animal or the specific number of animals to be sacrificed. In
the latter case, argues Rambam, the quest for a rationale is pointless.[2]
Some determinate number must be selected; there need not be a reason
for choosing one rather than another. Assuming, as Rambam certainly
does, that God has good and sufficient reason for revealing the Torah,
Rambam may find it pointless to ask why it was revealed to one people
rather than to another. One nation must be chosen – perhaps to serve
as the vehicle for transmission to all of mankind. There need be no particular reason, then, for the choice of one people over another.

A sharply contrasting picture emerges from the comments of
Sifri 20:2 upon the verse, "The Lord came from Sinai, and shined forth
from Seir unto them: He radiated splendor from Mount Paran" (Deuteronomy 33:2). The verse itself cries out for clarification. Moses begins
his valedictory blessing with a reference to the giving of the Law at Sinai.
There is no biblical reference to any divine activity at either Seir or Paran
prior to that event, nor is there any perceivable nexus between any event
that took place in those locales and the giving of the Torah at Sinai. In
identifying the events to which allusion is made, *Sifri* comments:

> When God revealed [Himself] to give the Torah to Israel, He did
> not reveal Himself only to Israel but to all the nations. First He
> went to the children of Esau and said to them, "Do you accept
> the Torah?" They said to Him, "What is written therein?" He
> said to them, "Thou shalt not kill." They said to Him, "The very
> essence of that ancestor was that of a murderer as it is said 'but
> the hands are the hands of Esau' [Genesis 27:22] and such was
> the promise of [Esau's] father 'And by your sword shall you live'
> [Genesis 28:40]."

> He went to the children of Ammon and Moab and said to them,
> "Do you accept the Torah?" They said to Him, "What is written
> therein?" He said to them, "Thou shalt not commit adultery."
> They said to Him, "Sovereign of the universe, [ours] is the very

---

2. See Rambam, *Guide of the Perplexed*, Part III, chap. 26.

essence of sexual relations as it is said, 'And the two daughters of Lot were with child of their father' [Genesis 10:36]."

He went and found the children of Ishmael. He said to them, "Do you accept the Torah?" They said to Him, "What is written therein?" He said to them, "Thou shalt not steal." They said to Him, "Sovereign of the universe, the very essence of our father was armed robbery as it is said, 'and he shall be a wild man' [Genesis 16:12]."

There was no nation among the nations to which He did not go and speak and knock on the door to [see] if it could agree to accept the Torah... even the Seven Commandments that the Sons of Noah accepted they could not sustain with the result that [the Seven Commandments] were removed [from them] and given to Israel....[3]

The comments of *Sifri* are paraphrased in a parallel comment recorded in the Gemara, *Avodah Zarah* 2b: "What did [God] seek in Seir and what did He seek in Paran? Said R. Yoḥanan, 'This teaches [us] that the Holy One, blessed be He, offered the Torah to every nation and every tongue but they did not accept it until He came to Israel and they accepted it.'"[4]

---

3. See *Bava Kamma* 38a and *Avodah Zarah* 2b. The Gemara renders Habakkuk 3:6, "*ra'ah va'yatter goyim*," as "He saw and He released the nations" and interprets the passage as declaring that God saw that gentiles did not observe the Noahide Code and "released" them from it. The Gemara then proceeds to explain that the nature of the "release" is such that they do not receive the reward for observance of those commandments that is vouchsafed to the commanded. Cf., *Or Sameaḥ, Hilkhot Isurei Bi'ah* 14:7.

The opinion of *Teshuvot P'nei Yehoshu'a*, I, *Yoreh De'ah*, no. 3 and 11, *Even ha-Ezer* no. 43, to the effect that the prohibitions of the Seven Commandments have been rescinded "but they will be judged for not having fulfilled them" is rejected by *Teshuvot Ḥatam Sofer, Ḥoshen Mishpat*, no. 185; *Bet Yehudah, Yoreh De'ah*, no 17; and *Sedei Ḥemed, Ma'arekhet ha-Vav, klal* 26, sec. 22. That view is also contradicted by *Teshuvot ha-Rema*, no. 10.

4. This is also the theme of yet another midrashic statement, cited by R. Jacob Ettlinger, *Minḥat Ani, Parashat be-Midbar*. The *midrash* states: "Why was the Torah given in

Read literally, the scenario depicted by the *Sifri* does not reflect a free choice on the part of the Deity from among a number of potential recipients. Quite to the contrary, "There was no nation among the nations to which He did not go and speak and knock on the door." God did not choose to make Israel the recipient of the Torah; He chose each and every other nation in turn only to be treated as a rejected suitor. It appears that, as it were, God is reduced to peddling His wares and can find no nation willing to give Him entrée – save Israel. Language describing the "chosenness" of Israel seems highly inappropriate. It would seem that it would be far more accurate to speak of Israel choosing to accept the Torah than to speak of God as choosing Israel as its recipient.

But, of course, such aggadic statements are not to be taken literally. Moreover, acceptance of any of the classical philosophical analyses of the nature of the prophetic experience makes it difficult to accept the phenomenon of a dialogue between God and each and every nation – in effect, all of humanity – in a literal sense. Undoubtedly, the description of the proffered offer of the Torah to each of the nations of the world *seriatim* must be understood not as an actual offer, but as a constructive offer. As such, it follows that the refusal of the offer was constructive as well.[5]

Edom could not accept the Torah because it was constitutionally incapable of renouncing bloodshed; Ammon and Moab could not possibly purge themselves of a proclivity for sexual licentiousness; and Ishmael could not sustain itself other than by preying upon other innocent peoples. Collectively, the nations of the world could not find it within themselves even to abjure activities proscribed by the provisions of the Noahide Code. It is both pointless and unjust to bind a people to

---

the month of twins? So that the nations of the world would not have grounds to complain, 'If He had given us the Torah we would have observed it.' The Holy One, blessed be He, said to them, 'Behold I give you the Torah in the third month which is the month of twins, of Jacob and of Esau. If you wish to accept [the Torah] come and accept [it].'"

The heavens are divided into the twelve signs of the zodiac. Each of the twelve *mazalot*, or constellations of the zodiac, bears a distinctive name and representation in the form of a sign. The sign of the third month, the month in which the Torah was revealed at Sinai, is Gemini, i.e., *te'omim*, or "twins," representing Esau and Jacob.

5. Cf., Maharal of Prague, *Tiferet Yisra'el*, chap. 1.

acceptance of additional commandments that they will undoubtedly be incapable of observing. By the process of elimination, Israel was the only candidate for meaningful acceptance of the Sinaitic Code.

Since this was known to God, any actual offer to other nations would have been superfluous. But this is known to God not simply because He is omniscient; it is known to Him because, as the Creator of all flesh, He knows the nature of His creatures. God is assuredly aware of the capacities and limitations of His creatures precisely because He imbued them with those capabilities and limitations. Thus, from the moment of creation, Jews – and only Jews – were destined to become the beneficiaries of revelation at Sinai. Hence, Jews are indeed "chosen" not arbitrarily or capriciously, but in the sense of having been purposefully endowed with the qualities necessary for obedience to divine law.

The comments of *Sifri* constitute eloquent support for the doctrine of the election of Israel set forth by R. Judah ha-Levi in his *Kuzari*.[6] As explained by R. Judah ha-Levi, Adam was endowed with particular and superior physical and intellectual traits and represented a supreme state of human perfection. Adam was possessed of a diminished sensual and corporeal nature by virtue of the fact that he was directly created by the hand of God. Moreover, since he was not the offspring of human parents he was not heir to the deficiencies of their constitution, nor did he suffer the adverse effects of food and climate to which other mortals are subjected during the period of their growth and maturation. Those distinctive qualities, asserts R. Judah ha-Levi, were not shared equally by all of his progeny. They were transmitted first to Abel, then to Seth, and then passed on to but a single individual in each generation. The chain of transmission included Noah, Shem, Ever and, finally, Abraham. The heir of Abraham was Isaac and the heir of Isaac was Jacob. Only with the birth of the sons of Jacob do multiple heirs appear. These qualities are then transmitted to the entire seed of Jacob and become the inheritance, albeit in varying degrees, of the entire people of Israel.[7]

---

6. Part I, secs. 27-43, 95, and 101-103.
7. See also the comments of R. Israel Lipschutz, *Tiferet Yisra'el, Avot, Bo'az* 3:1. For a kabbalistic exposition of the unique nature of the Jewish soul see *Tanya*, chaps. 1-2.

The spiritual and psychological qualities described by R. Judah ha-Levi serve a teleological purpose. Creation of a people endowed with such a nature constitutes a necessary aspect of the creation of a universe in conformity with the divine blueprint. Centuries later, R. Joseph Ber Soloveitchik[8] in his *Bet ha-Levi*, similarly commented that the rabbinic teaching regarding the existence of the Torah prior to creation of the world reflects a teleological view of the universe. This concept is similarly reflected in the dictum "The Holy One, blessed be He, scrutinized the Torah and created the world."[9] The Sages sought to emphasize that God did not first create a universe and then devise a legal and religious code tailored to the needs of the universe that He created. Quite to the contrary, first God composed a Torah and only then did He proceed to create a universe in which fulfillment of the provisions of the Torah would be possible as well as advantageous.

The practical effect of this perspective is to engender a Copernican revolution in perception of the relationship of the Torah to the conditions of human life. In effect, the Sages tell us: Do not ask whether the Torah is relevant to the world in which you live, but whether the world in which you live is relevant to the Torah. If the world in which you live is not relevant to the Torah, it is not the Torah that requires modification; rather it is human mores, values, economic policies, political structure and/or social institutions that require modification so that they become meaningful and relevant in implementation of biblical laws, norms and values. According to R. Judah ha-Levi, it was in order to provide for the empirical possibility of implementation of the provisions of the corpus of law contained in the Torah that God found it necessary to create a people imbued with the requisite psychological and spiritual qualities.

R. Samson Raphael Hirsch's depiction of the "*Yisroel-Mensch*"[10] is effectively an expansion of the categories posited by medieval philosophers in describing the constituents of the created world and serves to provide appropriate nomenclature for expression of what is, in actuality, the seminal thesis propounded by R. Judah ha-Levi. Medieval

---

8. *Bet Ha-Levi, Parashat Bo*, s.v. *"ve-higadata."*
9. *Zohar, Parashat Terumah*, p. 161b.
10. See *Nineteen Letters*, Twelfth Letter.

philosophers divided the world into four categories: inanimate objects (*domem*), vegetable life (*tzome'ah*), animal life (*hai*) and rational creatures, i.e., man (*medabber*). To these R. Hirsch, in effect, adds a fifth category, viz., *Yisroel-Mensch*. R. Hirsch underscores the fact that both the role and the function of Jews in the scheme of Creation are fundamentally different from those of other rational beings. Diverse categories of created entities are assigned differing roles and functions and are designed to achieve distinct purposes. Animate life is a necessary but not sufficient condition of the human state; reason is required in order for man to function in the role assigned to human beings. Similarly, reason and intelligence are unique to mankind, but these are necessary rather than sufficient conditions for fulfillment of the unique mission assigned to Israel. The *Yisroel-Mensch*, unlike the rest of mankind, is imbued with the metaphysical qualities necessary for fulfilling his designated purpose.

It is the idiosyncratic spiritual quality described by R. Judah ha-Levi or, as some would categorize it, their religious disposition that renders Israel capable of obedience to the will of God. God's election of Israel is then nothing more, and nothing less, than the shaping of that spiritual disposition. Once created, this spiritual quality must be nurtured and preserved. This unique disposition is delicate in nature and must be protected as is so clearly evident from the comments of *Midrash Tanhuma, Parashat Shemini* on the verse "He saw and made the nations tremble" (Habakkuk 3:6). There are a number of diverse rabbinic interpretations of the phrase *"ra'ah va-yatter goyim"* based upon translation of *"va-yatter goyim"* as "and He released the nations" or "and he permitted to the nations" rather than "and he made the nations tremble."[11] *Tanhuma* comments:

> R. Tanhuma ben Haglia'i said: He permitted to them the forbidden, detestable creatures and swarming creatures. To what is the matter to be compared? To a physician who goes to visit two patients. He perceives that one of them is in grave danger and tells the members of his family, "Give him any food that he requests."

---

11. For a differing rabbinic interpretation based on the translation "and he released the nations" see *Bava Kamma* 38a and *Avodah Zarah* 2b. See *supra*, note 3.

He perceives that the other will survive [and] tells [the members of his family], "Such and such food he may eat; such and such he may not eat." They said to the physician, "What is the meaning of this? To this one you say he may eat any food that he requests and to the other you said he may eat such and such." The physician said to them, "To the one that will live I said 'This you may eat and this you may not eat' but [regarding] the one which will die I said to them, 'Give him anything that he requests.'" Similarly the Holy One, blessed be He, permitted detestable creatures and swarming creatures to gentiles. But to Israel who are destined for life He said, "And you shall be holy for I am holy; do not defile yourselves" [Leviticus 11:44]; "This you shall eat" [Leviticus 11:21], "and this you shall not eat" [Leviticus 11:4]; "do not make yourselves unclean with them that you become impure through them" [Leviticus 11:43]. Why? Because they are destined to life as it is said "But you who cleave unto the Lord your God are alive every one of you this day" [Deuteronomy 4:4].[12]

Thus, the relationship between the propensity for observance of divine commandments and actual observance of those commandments is seen as reciprocal in nature. Taken as a unitary corpus of law, divine edicts can be observed only by a people endowed with the requisite nature for doing so; by the same token, at least some of these commandments are designed to preserve and secure that nature.

The "chosenness" of Israel as their election for instrumental purposes rather than as an intrinsically elect nation is reflected in *Avot* 3:14 in the declaration: "Beloved is man for he was created in the image [of God]. It is indicative of greater love that it was made known to him that he was created in the image [of God], as is said: 'For in the image of God did He make man' [Genesis 9:6]." The term "man" is used as a reference to all of humanity as evidenced by the very next statement "Beloved are Israel who are called children of God." As noted by the author of *Tiferet Yisra'el*, in his commentary *ad locum*, the juxtaposition of the terms "man" and "Israel" makes it abundantly clear that the two terms are not

---

12. Cf., *Shemot Rabbah* 30:18.

employed synonymously but that "man" is used in a generic sense as a reference to all human beings.

This does not at all imply that the Creator chose to deny gentile nations a role in His service by making obedience to His law constitutionally impossible for them. Quite to the contrary, as understood by a number of the classic commentators, the statement of the Mishnah in *Avot* establishes a similar, albeit more limited, role for gentile nations as well. *Tosefet Yom Tov* astutely questions why the Mishnah cites Genesis 9:6 in establishing that man is created in the image of God, since man is earlier described in precisely the same terms in Genesis 1:26-29. Citing Rashi's comment to *Avot* 3:14, "Man is beloved because he was created in the image [of God]; therefore, it is incumbent upon him to perform the will of his Master," *Tosefet Yom Tov* points out that the reference in Genesis 9:6 occurs in the context of God's issuance of a command to Noah. The love bestowed upon man is expressed in endowing man with the divine image – that is, God-like qualities making it possible for him to obey the divine commandments. Thus, creation in the "image of God" does not represent status or privilege but is a description of human capacity to obey the divine will. The obligations of gentiles are, of course, limited to observance of the Noahide Code while Jews are bound by 613 commandments. Although both Jews and gentiles share in participation in the "image of God," additional proclivity is required for acceptance of the yoke of the 613 commandments, a responsibility for which Israel alone was chosen.

II.

Noteworthy is an *obiter dictum* introduced by the author of *Tosefet Yom Tov* in his elucidation of the words of the Mishnah (in *Avot* 3:14) that goes beyond explication of the text to formulate an implied behavioral principle. Since gentiles are described as "beloved" by virtue of the fact that they have the capacity to obey the divine will "…we are commanded (*nitztavinu*) to coerce them by means of words to draw their heart to the will of their Master and the desire of their Rock, may they be remembered for good." Were the provisions of the Noahide Code designed simply for the benefit of mankind, i.e., to regulate human conduct and to prevent anarchy, non-observance on the part of gentiles might be of no concern to Jews unless, of course, they were directly affected by negative forms of social conduct. But since the *raison d'être* of gentile nations lies in the fulfillment of a divine mission, Jews also have an obligation to assure that God is served by all of His creatures.

The obligation incumbent upon Jews to assure the moral perfection of non-Jews is greatest in the Land of Israel. That is not at all surprising. The Land of Israel was designated as the homeland of the people of Israel, i.e., as the soil upon which the divine plan for realization and perfection of the purpose of creation might be maximally effected.[13] Observance of Torah was designed to be maximized in the Land of Israel both in the sheer number of applicable commandments and in the quality of observance. Reciprocally, or at least concomitantly, divine providence is manifest most intensely within the boundaries of the Land of Israel.[14] Consequently, even for gentiles, the possibility of adherence to higher standards is greater in the Land of Israel. Hence, demands upon the spirit may be pressed more adamantly in that land. Moreover, the deleterious effects of immoral conduct, were such conduct to be tolerated, would inevitably mar the near-utopian moral climate to which the inhabitants of the land of Israel must aspire. Thus, Rambam, in *Hilkhot Melakhim* 8:10, records that Moses was commanded to compel all the nations of the world to accept the Noahide Code, while in *Hilkhot Melakhim* 8:9, he rules that a peace treaty cannot be concluded with any gentile city within the Land of Israel unless the inhabitants "subject to our jurisdiction (*taḥat yadeinu*)" renounce idolatry and accept the Noahide Code. Again, in *Hilkhot Melakhim* 10:11, Rambam rules that the *bet din* is obliged to establish a judiciary for the purpose of administering and enforcing the Noahide Code.

The obligation to compel non-Jews to accept the Noahide Code is limited to places and epochs in which non-Jews are subject to the absolute authority of a Jewish commonwealth. As a practical matter, such authority does not exist in our age even in the modern-day State of Israel. Upon promulgation of the Balfour Declaration, R. Me'ir Simchah of Dvinsk, author of *Or Sameaḥ* did indeed write, "The fear of the oaths

---

13. See *Kuzari*, Part II, secs. 8-16.
14. See, for example, Deuteronomy 11:12 and Rashi, *ad loc*.

has departed."[15] However, in light of the attendant exigencies of *Real-politik*, the prayerful anticipation of untrammeled sovereignty has not yet been realized. Indeed, a political climate in which imposition of the Noahide obligations upon non-Jewish nationals will become possible is not likely to arise prior to the advent of the messianic era. Rambam, in *Hilkhot Melakhim* 10:4, enumerates the conditions that must be fulfilled by a putative messiah in order to substantiate a claim of messiahship with certainty. Among them are that he must "wage the wars of God" and "perfect the entire world (*ve-yetaken et ha-olam kulo*) to serve God together." It is in that context – and in that context only – that Rambam refers to the concept of *tikkun ha-olam*.

Nevertheless, as reflected in the previously cited comments of *Tosefet Yom Tov*, absence of an obligation to compel acceptance of Noahide obligations does not imply abnegation of less drastic means of achieving the same effect. To be sure, the nature of that obligation is far different from similar obligations vis-à-vis fellow Jews. The obligation of *arevut*, or "surety," renders a Jew culpable for preventable transgressions of a fellow Jew. That obligation flows from a reciprocal covenant entered into by all Jews prior to entry into the Promised Land and consequently is limited to members of the Jewish faith-community. Responsibility of Jews for one another's conduct is rooted in the unique covenantal relationship described in Deuteronomy 9:9-14 and is accordingly limited to those who have entered into that covenant.

Rambam's formulation of Jewish responsibility vis-à-vis non-Jews serves to define the obligation as limited to achievement of a general acceptance of Noahide commandments (*le-kabel mitzvot she-nitztavu bnei Noah*) by non-Jews rather than as an obligation to prevent particular infractions of the Noahide Code.[16] For most authorities, the obligation

---

15. The reference is to the oaths cited in *Ketubot* 111a which include an undertaking not to rebel against the nations of the world. For the text of R. Meir Simchah's statement see Z. A. Rabiner, *Toledot R. Me'ir Simḥah* (Tel Aviv, 5727), p. 164.

16. See *Teshuvot ve-Shev ha-Kohen*, no. 38; R. Yitzchak Ze'ev ha-Levi Soloveitchik, *Ḥiddushei Maran Riz ha-Levi* (Jerusalem, 5723), p. 164; R. Yosef Shlomoh Kahaneman, *Shem Olam* (Wickliff, 5745), pp. 382-384; R. Moshe Sternbuch, *Edut*, no 7 (11 Adar 5749), pp. 27-31; and R. Shmu'el Tuvya Stern, *Teshuvot ha-Shavit*, viii, *Ḥoshen Mishpat*, no. 3. Cf., however, R. Menachem Mendel Schneerson, *Ha-Pardes* (Iyar 5745)

to prevent a particular infraction (*le-afrushei me-issura*)[17] on the part of a fellow Jew[18] is born of the responsibility of *arevut*;[19] for others, the obligation is subsumed in the commandment "You shall surely rebuke your fellow" (Leviticus 19:17).[20] Neither of those considerations applies to conduct vis-à-vis a non-Jew.[21] Accordingly, *Shakh, Yoreh De'ah* 151:6,

pp. 7-11. The view cited by Rema, *Yoreh De'ah* 151:1, permitting sale to a non-Jew of items to be used in conjunction with idolatrous practices when such sale involves no technical violation of *lifnei ivver* appears to be incompatible with an obligation to prevent infractions of the Noahide Code. The suggestion of Rabbi Stern, *Teshuvot ha-Shavit*, VII, *Oraḥ Ḥayyim*, no. 1, note 2, that, assuming such an obligation does exist, it cannot mandate financial expenditures or loss of profit is without support.

Sefer Ḥasidim, sec. 1124, declares: "If one sees a gentile committing a transgression, if he can protest, he should protest for the Holy One, blessed be He, sent Jonah to Nineveh to cause them to repent. Because when the Holy One, blessed be He, is angry it is not a time of favor before Him." The chastisement advocated by *Sefer Ḥasidim* is clearly an act of piety, not a normative obligation, as evidenced by reference to God's concern for non-Jews rather than to a normative halakhic provision. The consideration advanced by *Sefer Ḥasidim* regarding God's anger and the absence of "a time of favor" is clearly extra-halakhic and in the nature of Jewish self-interest. Cf., however, the comment of the editor of the Mosad ha-Rav Kook edition of *Sefer Ḥasidim* (Jerusalem, 5720), *ad locum*, and R. Yitzchak Ya'akov Weisz, *Teshuvot Minḥat Yitzḥak*, IV, no. 79, sec. 4.

17. *Mishnah Berurah, Sha'ar ha-Tziyyun* 347:8, and *Maharatz Ḥayes, Shabbat* 3a, maintain that this obligations is biblical in nature. See also *Sedei Ḥemed, ma'arekhet ha-vav, klal* 26, sec. 3. A host of authorities maintain that this obligation is rabbinic in nature. See *Tosafot*, Rosh and Rashba, *Shabbat* 3a; Ran, *Shabbat* 3a and *Avodah Zarah* 6b; and *Rabbenu Yeruḥam, Netiv* 12, *halakhah* 5.

18. See, however, *Rabbenu Yeruḥam, Netiv* 14, *halakhah* 7, who apparently denies the existence of such an obligation. This is apparently also the view of *Teshuvot Radvaz*, III, no. 535; see R. Yitzchak Teib, *Erekh ha-Shulḥan, Yoreh De'ah* 151:1 Cf., *Turei Even, Ḥagigah, Avnei Milu'im* 13a, who analyzes the apparently similar position of *Tosafot* and Rosh, *Avodah Zarah* 6b. Cf. also, Ritva, *Avodah Zarah* 6b. For possible resolutions of the seemingly contradictory positions of some of these authorities see *Shakh, Yoreh De'ah* 152:6; *Teshuvot Binyan Tziyyon*, no. 15; and *Teshuvot Meshiv Davar*, no. 31.

19. See *Teshuvot Ḥatam Sofer, Yoreh De'ah*, no. 19; *Teshuvot Maharash Engel*, VIII, no. 219; *Teshuvot Bet Yehudah, Yoreh De'ah*, no. 17; and R. Aaron Moses Kisilev, *Mishberei Yam*, no. 10.

20. See *Teshuvot Ketav Sofer, Yoreh De'ah*, no. 83; and *Maharatz Ḥayes, Shabbat* 3a, who imputes this view to Rambam, *Sefer ha-Mitzvot, mitzvot aseh*, no. 205. Cf., Rashi, *Sanhedrin* 75a, s.v. "*ve-im ita*," who states that "your fellow" excludes even a *ger toshav*.

21. See *Teshuvot Meshiv Davar*, II, no. 31, who states, "With regard to a non-Jew, we do

rules that there is no obligation to prevent a non-Jew from committing a transgression.[22] Accordingly, the obligation to secure a general commitment to the binding nature of the Noahide commandments is entirely distinct from any obligation to prevent infractions.[23]

The obligation to secure commitment to acceptance of Noahide law may not, in and of itself, entail an obligation to provide detailed instruction with regard to the minutiae of that code. Nevertheless, the matter is more complex than it may appear. "Ignorance of the law excuses no man" is a legal maxim whose counterpart was first enunciated in Jewish law in the context of Noahide obligations. The Gemara, *Makkot* 9b, declares that a non-Jew is culpable even if he acts in ignorance of Noahide prohibitions because "he should have learned, but did not learn." The conceptual problem is obvious.

Rambam, in his *Commentary on the Mishnah, Ḥullin* 7:7, declares that commandments announced prior to revelation at Sinai that are still binding today do not derive their binding authority from the original command but from reiteration at Sinai. Thus, circumcision is practiced today not because of the divine command addressed to Abraham, but because God commanded us through Moses to practice circumcision as it was practiced by Abraham; we are forbidden to eat the sciatic nerve not because it was forbidden to Jacob but (as was Rambam's reading of the text of the Mishnah) because it was forbidden at Sinai.[24] Similarly,

---

not find that we are obligated to prevent him from transgressing." See also *Mishberei Yam*, no. 10, who maintains that the obligation *le-afrushei me-issura* is rabbinic in nature but nevertheless maintains that no obligation was imposed to prevent non-Jews from transgressing.

22. Cf., however, *Teshuvot Tashbatz*, III, no. 133, who declares that assistance to a non-Jew in committing a transgression that is not in the category of "placing a stumbling block before the blind" is nevertheless forbidden since "there is an obligation to prevent them [from sinning]." That position is apparently contradicted by Rema, *Yoreh De'ah* 151:1 (see *supra*, note 16) and is clearly contradicted by *Shakh, Yoreh De'ah* 151:6; *Teshuvot Meshiv Davar*, II, no. 31; and *Mishberei Yam*, no. 10.

23. Ramban, in his *Commentary on the Bible*, Deuteronomy 23:18, states, "for we are not commanded with regard to the nations other than with regard to idolatry." Ramban seems to imply that there is an obligation *le-afrushei me-issura* with regard to non-Jews in the limited case of idolatry. Cf., *idem*, Numbers 15:26 and Deuteronomy 20:18.

24. The Mishnah records a dispute between the Sages and R. Judah with regard to

Tikkun Olam

declares Rambam, the prohibition concerning eating flesh torn from
living animals is not binding upon us because it was commanded to
Noah, but because it was confirmed through Moses at Sinai. This is
true not only for the contents of the Noahide Code that remain binding upon Jews but is true as well for the Noahide Code as it pertains
to non-Jews. Put somewhat differently, all pre-Sinaitic legislation was
abrogated at Sinai with the result that, to the extent that any such legislation remains binding, whether upon Jews or non-Jews, it is because
of reenactment by divine fiat at Sinai. That this is true also with regard
to the Noahide law as it pertains to non-Jews is clear from Rambam's
statement, *Hilkhot Melakhim* 8:15, in which he declares that, in order to
achieve eternal reward, non-Jews must accept and observe the Noahide
Code as the command of God. Rambam, however, does not content
himself with stating that the commandments must be accepted as the
product of dogmatic revelation rather than on the basis of human conviction, but adds that they must be accepted because it was revealed at
Sinai that they had been commanded to Noahides by God. Noahides,
then, have no independent binding revelation concerning the Noahide
Code. Jews are the bearer of the *mesorah*, not only of the 613 commandments addressed to Jews and recorded in the Sinaitic Code, but of the
Noahide Code as well.[25]

whether the prohibition includes the sciatic nerve of unclean species. R. Judah argues
that the prohibition occasioned by Jacob's encounter with the angel as recorded in
Genesis 32:33 was announced before unclean species were prohibited and hence
encompasses such species as well. The Sages respond that the sciatic nerve was
prohibited at Sinai but recorded in the appropriate place in the historical narrative.
A literal reading of the Mishnah would yield a controversy with regard to whether
there was at all a prohibition in the interim period between Jacob's encounter with
the angel and revelation at Sinai. Rambam seems to indicate that the Sages concede
that the prohibition was indeed announced at the earlier time but that the original
commandment and the circumstances attendant thereupon are irrelevant since, if not
for reiteration at Sinai, the commandment would have been completely abrogated.
Rambam, *Hilkhot Melakhim* 9:1, also states that the *gid ha-nasheh* was forbidden at
the time of Jacob.

25. See R. Yitzchak Ze'ev ha-Levi Soloveitchik, *Ḥiddushei Maran Riz ha-Levi al ha-Torah*
(Jerusalem, 5723), *Parashat va-Etḥanan*, s.v. *"ve-ameru,"* who interprets the verse "for
this is your wisdom and your understanding in the eyes of the peoples who will hear

But if non-Jews are not the recipients of an independent source of revelation and were not present at Sinai to receive the Noahide Code, how can they be responsible for its contents? "A Noahide is executed because he should have learned, but did not learn," declares the Gemara, *Makkot* 9b.[26] However, as Rambam emphatically declares, the Noahide Code is not to be observed on the basis of an *a priori* moral awareness, but as the product of revelation. How can nonparticipants in the phenomenon of revelation become familiar with its contents other than through instruction by a teacher? Assuredly, matters of doubt and ambiguity can be resolved only by application to the bearers of the *mesorah*, i.e., Jews. Logically, then, the Jewish scholar must be under some reciprocal obligation requiring him to impart knowledge to the Noahide. Although there may be no obligation to volunteer information or to seek out Noahides in order to teach them the contents of the Noahide Code, there must be, at the minimum, an obligation to respond to a request for information. "The Holy One, blessed be He, does not deal with His creatures with trickery" (*Avodah Zarah* 3a). "He should have learned" can be a normative legal principle only if such learning is a possibility in reality. It can be a possibility only if there are teachers who are under a concomitant obligation to teach. Accordingly, if information or advice is solicited there must be a definite obligation to respond.

Apparently, one rabbinic authority expressly recognized an independent obligation of that nature at least with regard to Jews. R. Moses Sofer, in *Teshuvot Ḥatam Sofer, Ḥoshen Mishpat,* 164, propounds a remarkable thesis. A former student had accepted a rabbinic position but apparently his community was unwilling or unable to provide compensation at a level sufficient to keep body and soul together. It appears that the student sought Ḥatam Sofer's advice with regard to the propriety of engaging in some form of "work action." Ḥatam Sofer responds

---

all these statutes and say, 'surely this great nation is a wise and understanding people'" (Deuteronomy 4:6) in consonance with the principle that Jews are the bearers of the *mesorah* of the Noahide Code.

26. The problematic comments of *Kometz le-Minḥah* that are apparently contradicted by this source are discussed in this writer's *Contemporary Halakhic Problems*, 11 (New York, 1983), 331, note 38. The resolution there suggested has now also been advanced by R. Isaac Elijah ha-Kohen, *Lifnei Ivver* (Ofakim, 5749), p. 108.

to his interlocutor by stating unequivocally that, if he must indeed seek
some mundane form of securing a livelihood, he is under no obligation
whatsoever to interrupt gainful activities in order to respond to halakhic
queries or to sit in judgment in monetary disputes. Nevertheless, Ḥatam
Sofer admonishes the student that every Jew is obligated to devote the
lion's share of his time to Torah study. And, continues Ḥatam Sofer, "during such time dedicated to Torah and [divine] service, if a person comes
to learn something from him or [requests that he] judge between man
and his fellow or render a decision with regard to a matter of ritual law,
he is obligated to do so without compensation and he is not permitted
to accept any remuneration even though his own study is diminished
thereby for, with regard to this [matter], that of his fellow takes prece-
dence over that of himself."[27]

Ḥatam Sofer carefully and precisely spells out three areas of obligation: 1) to teach a particular matter with regard to which information
is sought; 2) to rule in response to a halakhic inquiry; and 3) to serve as
a judge in a financial or interpersonal dispute. The first obligation is relatively easy to comprehend: "And you shall teach them to your children"
(Deuteronomy 6:7) is understood by Ḥatam Sofer as prioritization of
the obligation to teach others over the obligation of Torah study that
is of benefit only to oneself. But the declaration *"muttar"* ("permitted")
or *"asur"* ("forbidden") and most certainly the adjudication of financial
disputes does not constitute fulfillment of the *mitzvah* of *talmud Torah*
as evidenced by the halakhic provision codified by Rema, *Oraḥ Ḥayyim*
47:4, to the effect that a halakhic ruling unaccompanied by an explanation may be issued prior to recitation of *birkat ha-Torah*.[28] What, then, is
the nature of the obligation to interrupt one's own Torah study in order
to issue a halakhic ruling? The issuance of a ruling, or of a decision in a
monetary dispute, certainly constitutes the transmission of the *mesorah*
and, apparently, Ḥatam Sofer posits an obligation to transmit the *mesorah*

---

27. Cf. the apparently conflicting position of R. Eliyahu David Rabinowitz-Teumim
(Aderet), *Seder Eliyahu* (Jerusalem, 5744), pp. 62 and 65.

28. The contradictory opinion of *Bi'ur ha-Gra, Oraḥ Ḥayyim* 47:4, is predicated upon that
authority's antecedent view that not only oral study, but also mental study, requires
birkat ha-Torah and is based upon recognition that a halakhic determination cannot
be reached other than upon at least silent deliberation.

that is quite independent of the *mitzvah* of *talmud Torah*.[29] If so, it may cogently be argued that Jews, as bearers of the *mesorah* regarding the Noahide Code, are also duty-bound to respond to solicitation of information with regard to elucidation of the provisions of the Noahide Code.[30]

III.

The corpus of the Noahide Code consists of only seven commandments, as opposed to the 613 commandments binding upon Jews. Yet resolution of any particular matter of doubt regarding ramifications of the Seven Commandments, or of any novel or heretofore unaddressed problem of Noahide law, is vastly more difficult than resolution of similar matters pertaining to the 613 commandments. When confronted by a question involving a matter of Jewish law, the rabbinic decisor, if he does not already know the answer, has available to him vast libraries of codes and

---

29. The source of that obligation is elusive. The Gemara, *Shabbat* 23a, questions the appropriateness of the liturgical formula "who has sanctified us through His commandments and has commanded us" with regard to the blessing pronounced prior to performance of a rabbinically commanded *mitzvah*: "Where have we been commanded?" queries the Gemara. The Gemara proceeds to cite two alternative sources: "You shall not turn aside from the matter they shall declare unto you" (Deuteronomy 17:11) and "Ask your father and he will declare unto you, your elders and they will tell you" (Deuteronomy 32:7). Although the latter verse is not cited in this context by Rambam, *Hilkhot Berakhot* 11:3, Ḥatam Sofer may have regarded that verse as being of halakhic import connoting, not an obligation with regard to obedience to rabbinic legislation, but an obligation upon the father and the elders to transmit the *mesorah* by responding to solicitation of information.

30. Ḥatam Sofer himself, in *Teshuvot Ḥatam Sofer, Ḥoshen Mishpat*, no. 185, states: "...it is a *mitzvah* to teach them as recorded by Rambam, chap. 10 of [*Hilkhot*] *Melakhim*." There is, however, no such explicit statement in Rambam. [Cf., R. Menachem Mendel Schneersohn, *Ha-Pardes*, Iyar 5745, p. 8. The statement to which that author refers, even if his interpretation is accepted, does not appear in chapter 10 of *Hilkhot Melakhim*.] Rambam, *Hilkhot Melakhim* 10:12, rules: "Two gentiles who come before you to adjudicate according to the laws of Israel and both wish to adjudicate according to the law of the Torah, we adjudicate." Rambam's term, "we adjudicate" (*danin*), must presumably be understood as meaning "we are *obligated* to adjudicate." That statement, then, reflects the position later enunciated by *Teshuvot Ḥatam Sofer* concerning the obligation to serve as a judge in financial disputes and signifies an obligation to serve in that capacity even when the litigants are gentiles. As has been argued, the "teaching" described is the transmission of the *mesorah*.

compendia, commentaries and supercommentaries, responsa and essays, dealing with every facet of Jewish law. Even if the particular question that he must address has not previously been dealt with explicitly, it is most likely that diligent research will uncover principles and precedents leading to a resolution of the problem. Not so with regard to the Noahide Code. The task of a rabbinic decisor confronting a question of Noahide law is formidable because of the paucity of rabbinic literature dealing with even fundamental problems confronting Noahides on a daily basis.

Every student of the Talmud is aware of recorded controversies between *tanna'im* and *amora'im*. Those controversies were adjudicated by the codifiers of Jewish law, at times with unanimity and at times without. Occasionally, early-day authorities disagree with regard to whether or not ostensibly disparate talmudic discussions represent conflicting views and, if so, which discussion is to be regarded as normative. Thus, to take a well-known example, Rambam, contra the position of the Tosafists, seemingly posits a controversy with regard to the explicitly formulated principle "There is nothing permitted to Jews that is prohibited to gentiles" (*Sanhedrin* 59a; *Ḥullin* 31a). Upon the severing of the trachea and the esophagus, internal organs are deemed to be "as if placed in a basket (*ke-manḥa be-dikula damya*)," torn from the yet living animal and reposing within its skeletal structure. Such organs are rendered permissible to Jews by virtue of ritual slaughter but would be forbidden to non-Jews as organs torn from a living animal save for the principle "There is nothing permitted to Jews that is prohibited to gentiles." Rambam, however, apparently regarded the validity of that principle to be the subject of a talmudic dispute and accordingly, in *Hilkhot Melakhim* 9:11, apparently rules that organ meat of a ritually slaughtered animal is prohibited to non-Jews as meat of an organ torn from a living animal.[31] Whether non-Jews should be counseled on the basis of the tosafists' position or advised to abstain from such meat, as is Rambam's view, is not immediately clear. A further ramification of Rambam's position is that a Jew

---

31. Cf., however, *Mirkevet ha-Mishneh, Hilkhot Melakhim* 9:11, who understands Rambam as forbidding such meat to a non-Jew only as long as the animal is yet alive on precisely the grounds that at such time the animal is prohibited to Jews by virtue of the prohibition "Thou shalt not eat of the blood" (Leviticus 19:26).

may not sell or serve such meat to a non-Jew. The internal organs of an animal defectively slaughtered by a ritual slaughterer, and hence forbidden to Jews, would apparently be prohibited to non-Jews according to all authorities as "organs torn from a living animal." No doubt due to their frequent impact upon Jews engaged in the sale of meat, those questions have received significant attention. Surprisingly, in dealing with actual situations, even the latter question is resolved in a permissive manner by no less a personage than R. Moses Sofer in his *Teshuvot Ḥatam Sofer, Yoreh De'ah*, 19. Yet it is probably fair to assume that, since Ḥatam Sofer's responsum is not widely quoted, most candidates for a rabbinical diploma are unaware of its existence; since it is not cited in later halakhic précis, those who are familiar with its contents may well be perplexed with regard to whether or not Ḥatam Sofer's responsum represents the final word regarding this matter.[32]

Other, far more prevalent, problems pertaining to "*kashrut*" of meat for non-Jews are no less difficult to resolve, and indeed even the

---

32. More perplexing is the fact that R. Joel Schwartz, *Or la-Amim* (Jerusalem, 5743), p. 131, despite his generally wide-ranging citation of sources in a work devoted to Noahide law, ignores Ḥatam Sofer's position entirely.

[*Ḥatam Sofer's* conclusion is indeed debatable. It is based on the empirical contention that all miscarriages of the process of ritual slaughter result in doubtful (*safek*) *neveilah* rather than certain (*vadai*) *neveilah*. For Jews, doubtful *neveilah* is treated as certain *neveilah* because of the animal's prior forbidden status as an unslaughtered animal (*ḥezkat einah zevuḥah*). Noahides are not bound by the commandment concerning ritual slaughter and hence, insofar as Noahide law is concerned, there is no *ḥezkat einah zevuḥah*. Accordingly, argues Ḥatam Sofer, since for Noahides, the animal's prior status was that of a permitted animal, Noahides should be permitted to partake of its flesh unless there is positive evidence that the animal has been rendered impermissible.

An objection may be raised to this line of reasoning on the basis of the fact that the internal organs of an animal slaughtered in the ritual manner would always be forbidden to Noahides as organs "torn from a living animal" if not for the principle that all things permitted to Jews are also permitted to Noahides. The animal in question is clearly not permitted to Jews. The fact that it is forbidden to a Jew for a reason having no bearing upon the Noahide Code should be irrelevant. Since, in the final analysis, the animal is not permitted to a Jew there appears to be no applicable halakhic provision negating the status of the animal's internal organs as organs "torn from a living animal." Cf., *Likkutei He'arot al She'elot u-Teshuvot Ḥatam Sofer*, 111 (Jerusalem, 5736), *Yoreh De'ah*, no 19, sec 5.]

existence of those problems is hardly common knowledge. One who has studied the tractate Ḥullin is probably aware of the view espoused by a number of early-day authorities deeming the meat of an animal that has died of natural causes to be forbidden to Noahides.[33] More problematic is the question of whether an animal killed by hunters by means of a rifle shot is permitted to non-Jews.[34] Nor, for that matter, is it at all certain that a non-Jew is permitted to cause pain to an animal simply for sport.[35]

Oddly enough, a rabbinic scholar might feel far more comfortable and confident in counseling a gentile with regard to certain esoteric matters, such as sacrificing an animal on an altar, than with regard to perfectly common matters, such as whether he may retain lost property even if it came into his possession after *ye'ush*, i.e., after the owner has lamented his loss. The first matter involves an activity permitted to non-Jews but prohibited to Jews. A rabbinic scholar whose advice is sought with regard to incidental questions pertaining to Noahide sacrifices will find such matters addressed in great detail in *Mishneh le-Melekh*, in

---

33. See Rashi, *Ḥullin* 92b, s.v. *"be-mekulin"* (but cf., Rashi, *Sanhedrin* 57a, s.v. *"le-meisheri"*); *Tosafot, Ḥullin* 91a, s.v. *"ke-man de-amar"* and *Tosefot Rabbenu Peretz, Sanhedrin* 56b. See also *Pesikta Zutrata*, cited by Rema of Panu, *Asarah Ma'amarot, Ma'amar Ḥakor Din*, part 3, chap. 21, p. 103. Cf., R. Samuel ben Ḥofni Ga'on, introduction to his commentary on the Pentateuch, and *Naḥal Eshkol, Hilkhot Treifot*, 15:15. Cf., however, R. Ya'akov Kahana-Shapiro, *Teshuvot Ne'ot Ya'akov*, no. 11; R. Meir Dan Plocki, *Ḥemdat Yisra'el*, "Kuntres Ner Mitzvah," no. 28, s.v. *"lakhen,"* who maintain that, even according to those authorities, this prohibition was abrogated at Sinai. An opposing view to that of Rashi and *Tosafot* on *Ḥullin* is held by *Sefer ha-Eshkol, Hilkhot Treifot*, no. 15, and by *Tosafot, Sanhedrin* 56b, s.v. *"akhal."*

34. *Tosafot, Ḥullin* 92a, s.v. *"ke-man,"* seems to require slaughter by means of *neḥirah* to render animals permissible to non-Jews. See commentaries of Reshash, Maharatz Chajes and *Dor Revi'i, ad locum*. Cf., however, *Be'er Sheva, ad locum*. Rashi, *Ḥullin* 28a, s.v. *"le-taharah"* and *Ḥullin* 81b, s.v. *"ve-ha-noḥer,"* depicts *neḥirah* as involving the trachea and esophagus. According to Rashi, severance of those structures in any manner satisfies the requirement of *neḥirah*. Indeed, Rashi, *Ḥullin* 17a, defines *neḥirah* as a vertical perforation of those structures. See *Dor Revi'i*, introduction, nos. 1-2. However, Rashi, *Ḥullin* 85b, s.v. *"noḥaro,"* defines the process as strangulation (*ḥonko*). Cf., however, R. Ovadiah of Bartenura, who, in his commentary on the Mishnah, *Ḥullin* 4:2, defines *neḥirah* as an incision made at the site of the nostrils and *Tosefet Yom Tov, ad locum*, who comments that *neḥirah* does not at all involve the trachea or the esophagus.

35. See R. Ya'akov Ze'ev Kahana, *Toledot Ya'akov* (Vilna, 5667), *Yoreh De'ah*, no. 33.

his commentary on Rambam's *Hilkhot Ma'aseh ha-Korbanot*. Adjudication of the provisions of the Noahide Code regarding ownership of lost property has not received such detailed attention.[36]

Issues that impact upon broader social policies are even more murky. To offer as an example a matter that perhaps is of relatively minor societal significance, there exists a talmudic controversy regarding whether or not Noahides are forbidden to castrate animals. That controversy is mirrored in a dispute among early-day authorities who differ with regard to adjudication of the issue. The impact of that controversy upon the propriety of neutering pets and upon related matters of animal husbandry is obvious. Assuming that surgical sterilization of female animals is prohibited by rabbinic decree, does such rabbinic legislation extend to non-Jews as well? Of course, the much broader issue is the question of whether Noahides are subject to rabbinic legislative authority.[37] Here, again, the implication with regard to the spaying of household pets is obvious.

---

36. See the sources cited by R. Ya'akov Blau, *Pitḥei Ḥoshen, I, Hilkhot Aveidah*, chap. 1, note 55, and his accompanying inconclusive discussion.

37. *Semak*, cited by *Shakh, Yoreh De'ah* 55:11, rules that rabbinically prohibited extensions of *ever min ha-ḥai* are forbidden to non-Jews as well as to Jews. *Pri Ḥadash, Yoreh De'ah* 55:16, challenges this position and asks in astonishment, "Since when did the Sages promulgate edicts for gentiles? And [gentiles] themselves, do they then obey?" See R. Chaim Ozer Grodzinski, *Teshuvot Aḥi'ezer*, III, no. 37, sec. 3, who ascribes a similar position to *Bet Yosef, Yoreh De'ah* 4. *Mishneh le-Melekh, Hilkhot Melakhim* 10:7; *Minḥat Ḥinukh* (Jerusalem, 5748), no. 2, sec. 12, s.v. *akh*; and *Reshash, Sanhedrin* 58b, assert that the Sages did not enact prohibitions binding upon Noahides. [There is some ambiguity with regard to whether *Mishneh le-Melekh* denies rabbinic authority to legislate on behalf of Noahides or whether he states only that we have no indication that they actually did so. See R. Chaim Sofer, *Teshuvot Maḥaneh Ḥayyim*, I, no. 91, sec. 3]. See also R. Jacob of Lissa, *Naḥalat Ya'akov*, 11, Responsa, no. 2; R. Menasheh Klein, *Mishneh Halakhot*, IX, no. 396; and R. Ovadiah Yosef, *Yabi'a Omer*, V, *Oraḥ Ḥayyim*, no. 19, sec. 7. Indeed, it is not clear that there exists authority for enactment of such edicts. Rabbinic authority to promulgate legislation binding upon Jews is derived by the Gemara, *Shabbat* 23a, from biblical sources. Since those sources are not rooted in Noahide commandments the source of rabbinic authority vis-à-vis non-Jews would require further elucidation. Nevertheless, *Sedei Ḥemed, ma'arekhet ha-vav, klal* 26, sec. 20, and *ibid., Pe'at ha-Sadeh, ma'arekhet ha-gimmel, ot vav,* sec. 10, cites authorities who maintain that all rabbinic edicts pertaining to commandments

included in the Noahide Code are also binding upon non-Jews. See also R. Eliezer Silver, *Tzemah Erez, Sanhedrin* 56b and this writer's *Be-Netivot ha-Halakhah*, 11 (New York, 5759), 140-143 and IV (5771), 192-193.

Teshuvot Hatam Sofer, Hoshen Mishpat, no. 79, s.v. *"pesik ha-shem ha-revi'i,"* develops the thesis that competition that interferes with the ability of another person to earn a livelihood constitutes a biblical transgression. See also R. Moshe Sofer, *Hiddushei Hatam Sofer, Bava Batra* 21b. In establishing that point *Teshuvot Hatam Sofer* cites the ruling of *Teshuvot ha-Rema*, no. 10, prohibiting a non-Jew from engaging in such competition. *Hatam Sofer* clearly assumes that such a prohibition could not be made binding upon gentiles by rabbinic decree. If, however, the prohibition against such activity is regarded as rabbinic in nature, as would be assumed upon a literal reading of the comments of *Bet Yosef, Hoshen Mishpat* 157, *Teshuvot ha-Rema* must be regarded as affirming the principle that rabbinic extension of prohibitions included in the Noahide code are binding upon gentiles as well as upon Jews. However, R. Shlomoh Luria, *Teshuvot Maharshal*, no. 36, and R. Mordecai Benet, *Perashat Mordekhai, Hoshen Mishpat*, no. 7, disagree in maintaining that rabbinic forms of theft are not prohibited to Noahides.

It seems to be certain that Noahides enjoy the authority to promulgate binding edicts in order to strengthen adherence to the Noahide code as evidenced by the statement of the Gemara, *Avodah Zarah* 36b, indicating that Tamar was sentenced to death for violation of an enactment of the *bet din* of Shechem prohibiting intercourse with an idolator. *Or ha-Hayyim*, Genesis 38:24, comments, "…and perhaps they possessed a tradition [authorizing] them to promulgate edicts and to execute one who transgresses the edict." There is, however, no evidence of a tradition explicitly granting Jews the power to legislate on behalf of Noahides. An alternative explanation of the source of the authority of the *bet din* of Shechem and of other Noahide judicial bodies to promulgate edicts may be found in Rambam's analysis of the commandment of *dinin*. Rambam, *Hilkhot Melakhim* 9:14, regards the seventh of the Noahide commandments as imposing an obligation upon non-Jews to establish a judiciary, not only for the purpose of punishing transgression of the provisions of the Noahide Code, but also "to admonish the populace." It may be suggested that legislation to provide a "fence" around the law is a legitimate exercise of the mandate requiring judges "to admonish the populace." [Indeed, this thesis, if correct, may serve to resolve a difficulty inherent in Rambam's formulation of a duty "to admonish the populace" as integral to the *mitzvah of dinin, viz.,* the identification of a talmudic source for that statement. On the basis of the foregoing it may be postulated that Rambam deduced that conclusion from the authority ascribed to the enactment of the *bet din* of Shechem. That authority, Rambam may have reasoned, could be derived only from an antecedent premise to the effect that the commandment of *dinin* includes an obligation "to admonish the populace," i.e., to prevent transgression of the Noahide Code. The phrase employed by Rambam, "to admonish the populace" (*le-hazhir et ha-am*), has the connotation of a general ad-

Other such uncertainties have much more profound implications for the development of a Jewish position regarding matters of topical concern. It can be definitively stated that, for Jews, a fetus that, if carried to term, would cause the demise of its mother may, and indeed must, be destroyed. *Tosafot Sanhedrin* 59a, express doubt with regard to whether such a principle exists in the Noahide Code. How is that doubt to be resolved in terms of practical guidance of non-Jews?[38] Assuming that such intervention is generally proscribed, does Jewish law recognize a double-effect theory as a valid principle within the Noahide Code with the result that excision of a cancerous uterus would represent an exception to the general rule?[39]

The talmudic narrative concerning R. Ḥananyah ben Teradion and his executioner, in which R. Ḥananyah assures his executioner of a portion in the world-to-come in return for adding additional fuel to the fire presents a highly perplexing problem precisely because of an absence

monition rather than simply the injunction of an individual. That phraseology may well be understood as including the obligation to issue general admonitions in the form of edicts binding upon all that are designed to prevent transgression. Thus, if Rambam derives his analysis of *dinin* from the talmudic reference to the powers of the *bet din* of Shechem, that precedent reflects exercise of the authority, not simply to restrain individual malfeasors, but also to enact prophylactic legislation binding upon all.] In addition, Rambam, *Hilkhot Melakhim* 10:11, declares that Jews have an obligation to establish a judiciary to administer the Noahide Code on behalf of *gerei toshav* subject to Jewish sovereignty. Rambam further declares that, if the "*bet din* of Israel" chooses to do so, it may appoint Jewish judges to sit on Noahide courts for the purpose of passing judgment upon Noahides. If it is accepted that the duty "to admonish the populace" gives rise to authority to promulgate general legislation for that purpose, that power might no doubt also be exercised by Jews sitting as members of Noahide courts. Accordingly, it might be argued that rabbinic authorities have the right to constitute themselves as a Noahide court and invoke that court's duty "to admonish the populace" as authority to promulgate legislation binding upon Noahides.

38. It would appear to this writer that, particularly in the absence of a conflicting statement by any early authority, overt intervention must be eschewed on the grounds that "doubtful" homicide cannot be countenanced even for the purpose of rescuing a human life. Nevertheless, at least one contemporary rabbinic writer is less than unequivocal with regard to this matter. See *Or la-Amim*, p. 128.

39. For a discussion of this question see this writer's *Contemporary Halakhic Problems*, III (New York, 1989), 7-9.

of elucidation by early-day authorities. Does the narrative stand for the proposition that hastening the death of an already moribund person, i.e., active euthanasia, does not constitute homicide in the Noahide Code, as is the expressed view of several contemporary rabbinic authorities,[40] or does it reflect an entirely different principle?[41]

Formulation of a Jewish policy position with regard to capital punishment similarly presents highly complex questions of Noahide law whose resolution is fraught with difficulty. On the one hand, the Noahide Code provides for capital punishment for a number of crimes. Moreover, according to Rambam, imposition of capital punishment, when prescribed by the Noahide Code, is mandatory rather than discretionary. The crux of the problem is the standard of evidence required for imposition of such punishment by Noahides. In practice, most convictions resulting in the death penalty are obtained, not upon the unimpeached testimony of at least a single eyewitness, but upon circumstantial evidence. It must be remembered that, from the vantage point of Jewish law, fingerprints, forensic evidence and the like must be categorized as forms of circumstantial evidence. Sources from which a resolution of the question of whether or not non-Jewish courts may convict on the basis of circumstantial evidence are far from obvious.[42]

---

40. See R. Samuel Baruch Werner, *Torah she-be-al Peh*, 18 (5736), 42 and R. Schneur Zusha Reiss, *Ha-Ma'or* (Iyar-Sivan 5734), pp. 19-20. R. Moses Feinstein, *Ha-Pardes* (Shevat 5736), p. 12 and *idem, Iggerot Mosheh, Yoreh De'ah*, 11, no. 174, *anaf* 3, cites this narrative as "perhaps" reflective of a halakhic provision permitting a non-Jew to perform mercy killing if a mortal wound has already been inflicted by human hands. Cf., however, a later responsum, *Iggerot Mosheh, Ḥoshen Mishpat*, 11, no. 73, sec. 3, in which Rabbi Feinstein cites his earlier responsum as leaving the issue unresolved and declares R. Ḥananyah ben Teradion's action to have been a *hora'at sha'ah*. Cf., Ran and Rosh, *Nedarim* 22a; and R. Shlomoh Kluger, *Nidrei Zerizin, Nedarim* 22a.

41. For diverse and conflicting analyses of the halakhic import of this narrative see R. Eliezer Waldenberg, *Tzitz Eli'ezer*, IV, no. 13, chap. 2, sec. 7; R. Isaac Liebes, *Teshuvot Bet Avi*, 11, no. 153; R. Menasheh Klein, *Mishneh Halakhot*, VII, no. 282; R. Saul Israeli, *Amud ha-Yemini*, no. 32, sec. 2; R. Moshe Dov Welner, *Ha-Torah ve-ha-Medinah*, VII-VIII (5715-5717), 318; and *Yam shel Shlomoh, Bava Kamma* 8:59. See also Ya'akov Weinberger, *Diné Israel* 7 (5736), 117.

42. See *Contemporary Halakhic Problems*, 11, 341-367.

Issues of Noahide law are often extremely difficult to resolve. More significantly, the Jewish obligation with regard to *tikkun ha-olam* does not end with determination of particular points of Noahide law. It is clear that in the society in which we live there cannot be one public policy for gentiles and a different public policy for Jews. The result is that Jewish endorsement of policies, that from the Jewish perspective, are perfectly acceptable for non-Jews will inevitably lead to effects not acceptable for Jews. Support for the neutering of stray dogs will lead to transgression, knowingly or unknowingly, of a biblical prohibition by Jewish veterinarians. Support for personal autonomy and freedom of choice with regard to withholding of medical treatment will inevitably result in contrahalakhic withholding of treatment from Jewish patients. Criminalization of conduct deleterious to the moral welfare of society and increasing the severity of punishment for acts already branded as criminal will undoubtedly impact upon Jewish malfeasors. Yet, rabbinic sources are far from unequivocal in recognizing the authority of gentile authorities to impose penal sanctions upon Jewish nationals.[43] Successful Jewish advocacy of social policies pertaining to matters involving a disparity in Jewish law between Jews and non-Jews must affect members of the Jewish community. Consideration of such consequences must be judiciously factored into any analysis of Jewish obligations to promote *tikkun ha-olam*.[44]

IV.

Although non-Jews are not formally bound other than by the Seven Commandments and Jews have no obligation to impose any higher morality upon gentiles, nevertheless, there are sources indicating that the divine intent is that, at least with the passage of time, the nations of

---

43. See this writer's "Jewish Law and the State's Authority to Punish Crime," *Cardozo Law Review*, 12:3-4 (February-March, 1991): 829-857, reprinted in *Contemporary Halakhic Problems*, IV (New York, 1995), 67-91.

44. For example, I am convinced that the patently specious argument advanced by the representative of Agudath Israel in the Polish Sejm in opposition to capital punishment was not intended as declarative of principles by which Noahides should be bound but motivated by concern for execution of Jewish nationals. See *Contemporary Halakhic Problems*, II, 366, note 35.

the world will adopt the standards that are normative for Jews. The most authoritative of these sources is R. Jacob Ettlinger, who eloquently developed this thesis in his homiletic work, *Minḥat Ani, Parashat be-Midbar:*

> The Torah is therefore termed an "illuminating light" and proceeds bit by bit until it illuminates all inhabitants of the universe under all the heavens. And Israel will be the priests of God into whose hands has been given the banner of the Torah to carry unto all corners of the earth... This is explained at the conclusion of the midrashic comment[45] in the statement "'and in the waste, a howling wilderness' [Deuteronomy 32:10] – The universe was [as] night.[46] As soon as Israel accepted the Torah the world lit up, as it is said, 'For *mitzvah* is a lamp and Torah is light' [Proverbs 6:23]." This indicates that not for [Israel] alone did the Torah become a light illuminating the darkness but rather for the entire world. Therefore Israel gives thanks to its Father in Heaven saying, "He delivered me because He wanted me" [2 Samuel 22:20], [i.e., He wanted] to give the light of His Torah into my hands to illuminate the entire world through it.[47]

The comments of R. Jacob Ettlinger serve to establish two distinct points:

First, the moral principles embodied in the Sinaitic laws, although not normatively binding upon non-Jews, serve to establish a morality to which they should aspire. Moreover, this aspiration will become actualized, at least in the eschatological era. Quoting a midrashic statement underscoring the fact that the Torah was "offered" to both Esau and Jacob,[48] *Minḥat Ani* adds that, although the original offer to Esau was in vain, "nevertheless the word of God does not return empty in that in the end of times the light of Torah will illuminate even Esau and his compatriots."

---

45. *Minḥat Ani's* quotation is actually a paraphrase of *Be-Midbar Rabbah* 2:5.
46. The midrashic interpretation is based upon rendering *"yelel"* as a form of *"lel,"* meaning "night," rather than as a form of *"yelalah"* meaning "wail" or "howl."
47. These comments are advanced by *Minḥat Ani* in elucidation of *Yalkut Shim'oni,* II Samuel, no. 161.
48. See *supra,* note 4.

Secondly, the role of Israel in achieving that goal is entirely passive, at least insofar as "outreach" activity directed toward the nations of the world is concerned. There is no hint whatsoever in either *Minḥat Ani's* comments or in the midrashic source upon which they are predicated indicating that Jews have any particular obligation to assure that such a goal is achieved. Apparently, the role of Israel is to teach by example. Obviously, the greater the quality and the purity of the example, the greater the effect. The more intense the "light of Torah," the brighter the illumination that it will cast.

Noteworthy also are the comments of R. Naphtali Zevi Yehudah Berlin, popularly known as the "Netziv," in his *Kidmat ha-Emek*, introducing his commentary on the Pentateuch: "...it is the desire of the Holy One, blessed be He, that [gentiles] study Scripture and for that reason the Holy One, blessed be He, commanded that it be translated into seventy languages." An even clearer and more forceful statement of the obligations of Jews vis-à-vis non-Jews occurs in Netziv's introduction to his *Ha'amek Davar* on *Sefer Shemot*. In those comments Netziv develops the thesis that the Book of Exodus is actually the complement to the Book of Genesis in that it constitutes the concluding portion of the story of creation. As Genesis records the efficient cause of creation, Exodus records the final cause, or *takhlit*, of creation: *viz.*, the notion that the world was created on account of "*reshit*," i.e., "on behalf of Israel which is termed *reshit*." (Rashi, Genesis 1:1).[49] This goal, Netziv tells us, was not fulfilled "until Israel exited from Egypt and *achieved their telos that they be fit to be an illumination unto the nations to cause them to arrive at knowledge of the Lord of the universe*" (emphasis added).

The theme is further developed by Netziv in his commentary on Exodus 12:51. The final phrase of the verse "And it came to pass the selfsame day that God brought the children of Israel out of the land of Egypt *al tzivotam*" is generally understood as meaning "by their hosts." Netziv understands the term "*tzava*" in the sense of "service" as in the verse "Is there not a time of service to man upon earth" (Job 7:1), i.e.,

---

49. Cf., *Pesikta Zutrata* 1:1 and *Midrash Tanḥuma* (ed. S. Buber), *Parashat Bereshit* 3, where the phrase appears as "in the merit of Israel."

"every person is created for his *telos* and that is his 'service.'"[50] The *telos* for which Israel was created, continues Netziv, is "to be an illumination unto the nations to cause them to arrive at knowledge of the Lord of the universe." Only upon undergoing circumcision[51] and their subsequent exodus from Egypt "did [the children of Israel] attain their service, i.e., that for which they were created on earth."

Netziv is silent with regard to how this task is to be achieved. He neither declares that Israel's role is passive in nature nor does he take issue with the earlier published views of R. Jacob Ettlinger and demand that Israel play an active role in providing instruction to non-Jews. With regard to Netziv's remarks in *Kidmat ha-Emek* concerning translation of the Bible, it may be observed that God commanded that the Pentateuch be translated into seventy languages but not that it be taught in seventy languages. The Torah is to be made available by means of translation, but there is no obligation to establish a Jewish Gideon Society. The Torah is to be made available by means of translation, but there is no concomitant obligation actively to disseminate even the Written Law among non-Jews.

The passive nature of Israel's mission to mankind is expressed at even greater length by a disciple of R. Jacob Ettlinger, R. Samson Raphael Hirsch. R. Hirsch's comments are verbose and perhaps infelicitous to the contemporary ear, but they are entirely unequivocal. As stated by R. Hirsch:

---

50. Netziv's interpretation of this term is not as imaginative as might appear. The term "*kol yotzei tzava*," occurring in Numbers 1:21 and frequently thereafter, is translated "all that are capable of going forth to war." The term "*tzava*" in that context clearly denotes an armed force. However, an armed force is a "host" in which every individual has an assigned duty. Thus, the term "*tzava*" may well have the connotation of both "host" and "assignment" or "service." It is certainly in the latter sense that the term is used in Job 7:1. Accordingly, Netziv understands the phrase "*al tziv'otam*" as having an indentical connotation.

51. Netziv asserts that realization of this *telos* became possible only subsequent to circumcision to which reference is made in Exodus 12:44 and 12:48. Although he does not offer an explanation or rationale for the connection between circumcision and Israel's role as "an illumination unto the nations" he points to a parallel connection in the command to Abraham to circumcise himself and Abraham's role as "the father of the multitude of nations" in bringing them nigh to the service of God.

When, in the choice of Abraham, the foundation-stone of this people was laid, God, Who did it, pronounced its significance: "and in thee shall all families of the earth be blessed" [Genesis 12:3], and explained the blessing that came from this choice: "... For I know him, that he will command his children and his household after him, and they shall keep the way of the Lord, to do justice and judgment" [Genesis 18:18] – meaning that Abraham's descendants should follow with love and justice in the ways of God and by this silent example become a blessed monument to God and humanity among the peoples of the earth, so that they should be "a kingdom of priests, and a holy nation" [Exodus 19:6].

As the priest among the people, so should they among mankind uphold the vision of God and humanity and by so doing be a holy nation, raised above every injustice, profaneness and hardheartedness, as becomes the bearers of such a message. ... Let us live our Jewish life quietly and modestly, illumine and strengthen mind and soul through the teachings of the Torah; perpetuate these teachings for ourselves and others by observing our Festivals of Commemoration, fulfil them by a life of justice and love towards every creature that bears the seal of God's creating, as our religion teaches us. If, thus, we were truthful, just and holy and loving in mind and soul, in possession and enjoyment, in word and deed, if then God would let this promise of salvation grow out of our fate and our life: that the whole of mankind, awakened by its own experience, enlightened anew and uplifted by our destiny and life, should, in unity with us, turn to the One and Only – and if thus we would fulfil our vocation as priests to humanity – what bliss there would be...![52]

Despite his assertion that the mission is essentially passive in nature, R. Hirsch recognizes that it is necessary to seize opportunities to teach by example. Thus, he writes:

---

52. *Horeb: A Philosophy of Jewish Laws and Observances*, trans. I. Grunfeld (New York, 1962), no. 613, p. 465.

Do not shirk the social obligations of pulsating modern life; do not regret that today's nations, in their struggle for enlightenment, have invited also the sons of Jewish Law to participate in their social aspirations and that they have opened for the sons of Israel the gates to scientific and civil endeavors and achievements.[53]

However, carrying out these responsibilities should never result in compromise of halakhic obligations, nor should an individual seek a role or occupation which, while furthering Israel's mission to mankind, might create pitfalls with regard to the individual's own religious observance. R. Hirsch cautions, "Your only purpose in trying to acquire property... should be to... work for the advancement of your people and humanity: ...In the choice of an occupation the guiding consideration should be which one involves the least danger to your loyalty to God's law...."[54]

In defining Israel's mission as an obligation to teach by example, R. Hirsch develops at some length the corollary theme that Israel is admonished to abjure conduct that would have the opposite effect:

But because Israel has such a high and sacred vocation, because, for the working out of this destiny, every son and every daughter of Israel is obliged to contribute thereto by their behaviour in their own humble circle – how careful do we need to be in our behaviour, in particular in the way in which we conduct ourselves towards non-Jews, so that they may see in our lives really only a reflection of the Torah of truth, of justice and of love![55]

R. Hirsch further asserts that unbecoming conduct on the part of the Jews constitutes a form of profanation of the Divine Name:

Therefore, once more so urgently to *all of us goes* out the call: Do not profane My Holy Name! Do not destroy, through your way

---

53. *The Collected Writings*, VIII (New York and Jerusalem, 1995), 325.
54. *Horeb*, no. 524, pp. 392-93. See also *The Collected Writings*, VII (New York and Jerusalem, 1984), 12.
55. *Horeb*, no. 613, pp. 465-466.

of living, the recognition of the all-holy God and His word in the minds of the nations among which you live!...

Therefore our Sages say: "The crimes of stealing and injustice are greater towards a non-Jew than towards a Jew"; for towards a Jew it is the simple violation of a commandment, "Thou shalt not steal," etc. But in the case of a non-Jew, as well as being that, it is also that great crime which can only be expiated by death: The *chillul HaShem*, profanation of the Divine Name. Every Jew who deceives or cheats a non-Jew commits this greatest of all crimes, and, indeed, it is said: "and those that remain of Israel shall not commit injustice, shall not speak false things, neither shall their lips utter words of deceit!" And here, again, avoid not only real injustice, real hardheartedness, but even the semblance of them... towards your non-Jewish brethren; for the semblance is the crime as much as the actual sin, because it – as with the sin itself – breeds contempt for that very thing which it is your task to maintain as holy.... [56]

R. Hirsch's development of this thesis is paralleled and, in a sense, extended by R. Naphtali Zevi Yehudah Berlin in the preface to his *Ha'amek Davar* on the Book of Genesis. Joshua 10:23 and 2 Samuel 1:18 refer to a certain *Book of Yashar*. The Gemara, *Avodah Zarah* 25a, queries: "What is the *Book of Yashar*? R. Ḥiyya ben Abba said in the name of R. Yoḥanan, 'It is the book of Abraham, Isaac and Jacob who were called "righteous" (*yesharim*), and of whom Scripture says, "Let me die the death of the righteous and let my last end be like his." ' "

Citing this statement *Ha'amek Davar* comments:

---

56. *Loc. cit.* Cf., R. Meir Simchah ha-Kohen of Dvinsk, *Meshekh Ḥokhmah, Parashat Mishpatim*, s.v. *"ve-yetakhen,"* who finds halakhic expression for the thesis that the murder of a non-Jew is more heinous than the murder of a Jew in that it involves, in addition to the crime of homicide, a transgression in the nature of profanantion of the Divine Name.

This was the praise of the Patriarchs, that in addition to being righteous, pious and lovers of God in the greatest manner possible, in addition they were righteous (*yesharim*) that is, that they conducted themselves with the nations of the world even with repugnant idolators... with love and with concern for their benefit since that is what sustains creation. Thus we see how much our father Abraham put himself out to pray for Sodom... This is precisely as "the father of the multitude of nations" for even though the son does not tread in straight paths nevertheless he is concerned for his welfare and benefit, and our father Jacob, although he was sorely vexed by Laban who intended to eradicate him... nevertheless [Jacob] spoke soft words to him... and quickly became reconciled with him.[57]

Ha'amek Davar asserts that recognition that the nations of the world are necessary to "sustain creation" constitutes a motivating force for active concern for their welfare. Recognition that the nations of the world, too, play a significant role in actualization of the divine blueprint for human destiny renders it "righteous" for Israel to contribute to, and hasten, the actualization of the divine plan.

The function of Israel as a role model for the nations of the world is further developed by R. Hirsch in his *Nineteen Letters*. R. Hirsch describes the moral degeneration of mankind depicted in the opening chapter of Genesis as the process of abjuring a theocentric existence and supplanting service of God with a desire for material possessions and hedonistic pleasure. In the Seventh Letter, R. Hirsch asserts that "it became necessary that a people be introduced into the ranks of the nations which through its history and life should declare God the only creative cause of existence, fulfilment of His will the only aim of life;

---

57. This concept is echoed in an etymological observation advanced by R. Hirsch and applied as a categorization of Jews as a people. Deuteronomy 33:26 employs the term "*Yeshurun*" as a cognomen for the people of Israel. R. Hirsch, in his commentary on Deuteronomy 5:17, understands the term to be derived from "*yashar*," meaning "straight" or "just," and comments: "...in their intercourse with other people [Jews] are to show themselves as *yashar*, as the straightest, most honest, most upright nation amongst the nations."

and which should bear the revelation of His will... *unto all parts of the world* (emphasis added) as the motive and incentive of its coherence."[58]

In the same letter R. Hirsch makes it abundantly clear that fulfilment of the original purpose of creation is not restricted to Jews but that, at least ultimately, all of mankind will rededicate itself to fulfilment of the divine plan. In a footnote appended to the Fifteenth Letter, R. Hirsch, in what must be understood in a homiletical vein, observes that the rabbinic dictum "The pious of the nations of the world have a portion in the world-to-come" may be interpreted as meaning that "all nations will help to work out the historical destiny of humanity." In the interim, Jews, in their meticulous observance of God's commandments, keep that goal alive and serve as an exemplar for emulation by others. As a people, Israel "must remain alone and aloof, must do its work and live its life in separation, until, refined and purified by its teachings and its example, universal humanity might turn to God and acknowledge in Him the only Creator and Ruler. That attained, Israel's mission will have been accomplished."[59]

The essentially passive nature of this educative function is underscored by R. Hirsch in the Ninth Letter: "If in the midst of a world which reveres wealth and lust... if we were, if we would become, what we should be – if our lives were a perfect reflection of our laws – what a mighty engine we would constitute for propelling mankind to its final goal of all human perfection! More quietly, but more forcefully, and profoundly, would it affect mankind...."[60]

The prophet Isaiah testifies that in the end of days there will be a pervasive thirst for the word of God and, ultimately, non-Jews will turn to Jews in their quest to become familiar with the law of God: "And it shall come to pass in the end of days.... And many nations shall come and say, 'Come ye, and let us go up to the mountain of the Lord, to the house of the God of Jacob and he will teach us His ways (*derakhav*) and we will walk in his paths (*orḥotav*)'" (Isaiah 2:2-3). Malbim, in his commentary on this passage, notes that elsewhere the Hebrew term

---

58. *Nineteen Letters*, pp. 66-67.
59. See also S. R. Hirsch, *The Collected Writings*, I (New York, 1984), 175, 348, and 371.
60. *Nineteen Letters*, pp. 85-86.

"derakhav," translated as "His ways," denotes major roads or highways while the term "*orhotav*," translated as "His paths," refers to secondary roads. Thus, according to Malbim, Isaiah speaks of Jews teaching the nations the "roots and principles" of divine service and prophesies that, in the end of days, these nations will seek even greater edification and will, of their own accord, seek to discover even the byways and footpaths, i.e., the details and minutiae, of the Torah.

R. Hirsch returns both to an elucidation of the mission of Israel and its essentially passive nature in his commentary on Psalms 126:5. The verse "Those who sow in tears will reap in exultation" is understood by R. Hirsch as referring to the sowing and harvesting of a spiritual crop. The exile, declares R. Hirsch, turned Israel into "the sowers of God," i.e., those whose task was "to disseminate the seeds of truth concerning God and the destiny of mankind into the fields of man's future." This mission is apparently developed by Israel simply by virtue of its presence and example. As stated by R. Hirsch:

> And Israel has fulfilled this vocation as "God's sower" through the Divine Book which nations everywhere have accepted from its hands, as well as through the living commentary which it has given to the doctrine taught in this book by virtue of its conduct in private and public life alike. For every aspect of Israel's life was directed to all that was spiritual, humane and pure, and ran its course with self-sacrificing devotion in morality and loyalty to duty.

Those seeds are sown together with, and despite, the tears of persecution. But ultimately "the seed sowed with tears will open in the form of ever-growing homage paid on earth to truth and right, morality and mercy as the duty and destiny of mankind." Then, and apparently only then, the "'sowers of God'... will be allowed to rejoice and exult in this harvest."[61] That is so, at least in part, because we ourselves are not aware

---

61. S. R. Hirsch, *The Psalms,* trans. Gertrude Hirschler (Jerusalem and New York, 1978), commentary on Psalms 126:5, 11, 385.

of our own success in fulfilling this mission and will not fully appreciate our accomplishment until:

> our return to Zion, then we shall awaken as if from a dream. It will seem to us that we had lived through the long, long years of our exile as in a dream, a long nightmare during which, absorbed in ourselves, we had taken little notice of the changes which had gone on round about us, and of the impact which, unknown to us, our wanderings had had upon the nations with which we had come in contact during our dispersion.[62]

V.

There is yet another consideration that must inform policies adopted by the Jewish community vis-à-vis the general society. The earlier-cited rulings of Rambam address only the obligations of Jews to secure general acceptance of the Seven Commandments bestowed upon the nations of the world. They do not at all address the question of punishment for particular transgressions of the Noahide Code. However, in *Hilkhot Melakhim* 10:11, Rambam writes, "The *bet din* of Israel is obligated to establish judges for these resident strangers in order to judge them on the basis of these ordinances in order that the world not be destroyed (*she-lo yishaḥet ha-olam*)."

The nature of Rambam's ruling is somewhat problematic. According to Rambam's own formulation in *Hilkhot Melakhim* 9:14, the last of the Noahide commandments, *viz.*, *dinin*, obligates Noahides to establish a judiciary in order to enforce the Noahide Code and to punish transgressions thereof. The commandment of *dinin*, however, is addressed to Noahides, not to Jews. The commandment addressed to Jews with regard to establishment of *batei din* is couched in the words "Judges and officers shall you establish *to yourself* in all your gates" (Deuteronomy 16:18). Yet Rambam explicitly declares that there exists an obligation incumbent upon the Jewish *bet din* to establish a judicial system for Noahides. It is precisely because there is no explicit commandment

---

62. *Ibid.*, commentary on Psalms 126:1, 11, 384. See also R. Hirsch's commentary on Psalms 149:1, *ibid.*, pp. 492-93.

giving rise to such an obligation that he finds it necessary to append an explanatory comment indicating the rationale underlying this ruling, *viz.*, "so that the world not be destroyed." The ruling and its rationale are not based upon any explicit talmudic text. Rambam maintains that the obligation is self-evident and *a priori*. Lawlessness and anarchy, even if limited to non-Jews, are bound to have a deleterious effect upon Jews. Immorality is contagious and its effects are inescapable. Disintegration of the moral fabric of society affects everyone. Particularly in our age, we cannot insulate ourselves against the pervasive cultural forces that mold human conduct. Jewish self-interest requires that society not be allowed to become morally degenerate.[63]

VI.

The foregoing notwithstanding, there is no question that, historically, the Jewish community has not engaged in any concerted effort to influence non-Jews to abide by the provisions of the Noahide Code nor has it attempted to influence society to reflect the mores of the Noahide Code in its laws and institutions. The reasons, I believe, can better be elucidated by social historians than by students of Halakhah. The relevant factors, however, are not difficult to discern. Until fairly recently, Jewish influence upon the dominant society was virtually nil. No one was listening to us and certainly no one was asking us. Moreover, given the burden of a long and arduous *galut*, other internal concerns were much more pressing. Those concerns demanded commitment of time and human resources to such an extent that focus upon obligations vis-à-vis society at large was precluded.

In the twentieth century, disenchantment with the nations of the world grew as anti-Semitism reared its ugly head in the 1930s and reached its height during and after the Holocaust. The poet Uri Zevi Greenberg voiced the disillusionment of the members of his generation:

> Between us and the nations of the world lie the
> slaughtered of our family...

---

63. See also the comments of *Sefer Ḥasidim* cited *supra*, note 16.

> Deathly poison is the spirit of Europe....[64]
> We were as dreamers of a reality that is not and shall
> not ever be.
> The world of the nations is a night forest of beasts and
> they in it are wild animals.[65]

In the wake of the Holocaust he came to regard non-Jews as entirely bereft of a capacity for humaneness and declaimed:

> The time has come to examine the concept of "European culture" in the light of the furnace, in the light of reality, and to effect two departures at one time, from Europe and from its culture.... There are two types of person in the world, circumcised and uncircumcised; that is the reality.[66]

In many circles any hope of educating or refining the nations of the world was written off as a utopian endeavour incapable of realization in pre-messianic times.

Finally, in the modern age, social action became a dominant concern of the Reform movement with the result that such activity quite incorrectly became suspect within the traditionalist sectors of our community. Reform theology stressed the universal and abnegated the particular. The two paragraphs that together constitute the *Aleinu* prayer are vastly different in content. The theme of the first paragraph underscores Jewish particularism, extols Jewish chosenness and distinctiveness and expresses gratitude to the "Master of everything," who "has not made us like the nations of the lands and has not emplaced us like the families of the earth; for He has not assigned our position like theirs nor our lot like all their multitudes." In contrast, the second paragraph of the prayer outlines Judaism's universalist teachings, reiterates hope for the universal recognition of the supremacy of God, expresses the aspiration "to

---

64. *Reḥovot ha-Nahar: Sefer ha-Iliyut ve-ha-Ko'aḥ* (Jerusalem, 1950), p. 172.
65. *Ibid.*, p. 176.
66. Uri Zevi Greenberg, oral remarks cited in Aaron ben Or, *Toledot ha-Sifrut ha-Ivrit be-Doreinu* (Tel Aviv, 1958), I, 277.

perfect the universe through the sovereignty of the Almighty – *le-takken olam be-malkhut Shadai*" and heralds the dawn of an era in which "all the world's inhabitants will recognize and know that to You every knee should bend, every tongue should swear."

The first paragraph, with its unambivalent emphasis on the motif of Jewish chosenness, was profoundly disconcerting to the liturgists of Reform and Liberal Judaism. Accordingly, over the decades, several Reform rites completely omitted the comparative phrases from the *Aleinu* prayer and thereby entirely eliminated any particularist tone. Some Reform prayerbooks retained the original Hebrew but paraphrased or altered the translation. Other Liberal prayerbooks emended the Hebrew text by stating the particularist teachings in positive terms and eliminating the negative references to other nations.[67]

However, while many Reform prayerbooks include an attenuated version of the beginning of the *Aleinu* prayer, the second paragraph usually appears in its entirety and without the slightest alteration. This universalist paean was greatly beloved by the very Reform liturgists who found the opening words of the *Aleinu* so embarrassingly chauvinistic. Indeed, at times, the relative length of this Hebrew passage is striking, appearing as it does in some Reform rites in its pristine form as one of the lengthier Hebrew selections to be found in the prayerbook.

Reform teaching did indeed extol the mission of Israel "*le-takken olam* – to perfect the world."[68] But neither the predilections of our separated brethren, nor, *le-havdil*, the contemporary zealotry of Habad

---

67. For a discussion of this topic and an outline of revisions in the *Aleinu* text in thirty-six different Reform prayerbooks see Jakob J. Petuchowski, *Prayerbook Reform in Europe: The Liturgy of European Liberal and Reform Judaism* (New York, 1968), pp. 298-306.

68. It is of interest to note that, although the standard texts read, "לתקן עולם" meaning "to perfect the universe," the Yemenite prayerbook reads "לתכן עולם" meaning "to establish the universe." Meir Bar-Ilan, "Mekorah shel Tefillat 'Aleinu le-Shabeah,'" *Daat*, vol. 43 (1999), p. 20, note 72, argues that the latter was the original reading. Indeed, לתכן עולם reflects the dominant motif of the prayer. If so, the concept of perfection of the universe , important as it may be, is unrelated to the *Aleinu* prayer. For a review of the diverse readings found in various manuscripts see Mitchell First, "Aleinu: Obligation to Fix the World or the Text?" *Hakirah, the Flatbush Journal of Jewish Law and Thought*, 11 (Spring, 2011), 187-197.

emissaries with regard to teaching the Seven Commandments of Noah .
to non-Jews,[69] should serve to deter us from enunciating Jewish teaching
even if, at times, it has made the propagation of such teachings somewhat
more difficult. We are not about to abandon our belief in the coming
of the Messiah because of our embarrassment at the spate of advertise-
ments in the media erroneously announcing his advent as an already
accomplished fact. Public teaching of the subject may suffer, for the
nonce, but surely, as hallowed by tradition, no *darshan* will hesitate to
conclude his sermon with the age-old prayer for the coming of the Messiah speedily in our day!

VII.

Jews committed to Halakhah have only rarely, and only recently, taken
positions *qua* Jews on matters of public policy. Despite the democratic
institutions of this country, Jews whose roots were in a totally different
environment were apt to view themselves as living on sufferance even
on these shores. In many circles it was felt that a low profile should be
maintained lest latent anti-Semitism be aroused. Some argued that political influence should best be husbanded and held in reserve for matters
of more vital concern to the Jewish community. Nor should it be overlooked that in earlier periods of American Jewish history, the sector of
the Jewish community that was concerned with matters of Halakhah
could boast of few articulate spokesmen with a mastery of the vernacular.

In recent years, the Orthodox community has matured, but it has
still chosen to remain silent on most public issues. When it *has* spoken
it has done so not out of a desire to impose halakhic standards upon the
community at large but for entirely different reasons. Abortion legislation
is a case in point. But the fact is that no Orthodox group has mounted a
legislative campaign or lobbied for the enactment of restrictive measures.
Testimony before legislative committees and public statements were

---

69. See the censorious comments of R. Eliezer Schach, "Le-Hitraḥek me-Kat ha-Yedu'ah:
Le-Hasir Mikhshol," *Mikhtavim u-Ma'amarim*, III (Bnei Brak, 5748), 101, directed
against a sect that conducts a "campaign regarding the Seven Commandments of the
Sons of Noah as if only this is presently lacking to us." The letter originally appeared
in *Yated Ne'eman*, 7 Shevat 5747. Cf., also R. Moshe Sternbuch, *Edut*, *supra*, note 16.

forthcoming because they were specifically requested and because the teachings of classical Judaism had been distorted in public forums. But the issue simply did not cause Jews to buttonhole legislators, generate a barrage of telegrams, or march on Washington.

The gay rights bill enacted in New York City by the City Council did occasion a flutter of opposition on the part of some Jewish groups. Here, too, the expressed concern was not the desire to impose halakhic norms upon society at large. The concern focused particularly upon the presence of professed homosexuals in the classroom as authority figures whose lifestyle and mores might serve as a role model for youngsters in their formative years. Since Judaism does not view homosexuality as an acceptable alternative lifestyle, those groups perceived the proposed legislation as boding a moral danger to themselves and their families. They were hardly concerned with legislating Halakhah for society in general.

Personal liberty and the rights of the individual are strongly rooted as cardinal values of Western philosophy. Systems of thought that view the rights of individuals as paramount and inalienable find it difficult to accommodate the concept of a state that requires its citizens to surrender basic freedoms and to sublimate individual self-interest for the sake of the welfare of society. Much of Western social and political philosophy is devoted to the formulation of an intellectual matrix designed to justify extension of the powers of the body politic to spheres beyond the simple protection of its members against evildoers. Thus, eighteenth- and nineteenth-century European thought gave rise to various forms of social-contract theory. Inherent in many such theories is the concept that, at least ideally, the state should maintain a laissez-faire attitude toward its citizens insofar as possible.

Jewish thought – and law – is based upon an entirely different set of premises. Judaism views man as his brother's keeper. Man is bound by divinely imposed imperatives that oblige him to be concerned with the needs – and morals – of his fellow. Jewish law recognizes that the human condition requires that the governing authority, acting as the representative of society as a whole, be endowed with the broad powers necessary for the promotion of social welfare and moral conduct.

This is, of course, sharply at odds with the posture of contemporary Western society which, despite its abandonment of the laissez-faire doctrine in the arenas of economic and social welfare, tends to view a hands-off policy as the ideal to be pursued in areas of personal morality. Within a libertarian framework, the positions of Mill, Hart, *et al.* are eminently consistent and logical. But one can hardly use the philosophical systems of these thinkers as a backdrop for the formulation of halakhic or quasi-halakhic policies. By the same token, one must recognize that if any legislation is to pass a judicial test of constitutionality it must reflect some defensible social interest over and above the furtherance of personal morality.

It is the strong inclination of this writer that there should be a Jewish response to many of the social problems on the contemporary agenda. Any responsible response requires careful assessment of the principles herein outlined and, above all, dare not suborn violation of the Noahide Code. Advocacy in the public and political arenas should be an expression of cogent and principled positions reflecting halakhic norms applicable to non-Jews as well as to Jews. There should emerge carefully articulated policy statements regarding such topical issues as abortion, health-care plans and sexual mores as well as capital punishment and gun control legislation.

We live in an age of searching and seeking. We should certainly not hesitate to make the teachings of Judaism as they bear upon contemporary issues more readily accessible to our fellow citizens. At the very minimum, that would be one way of imparting knowledge of Torah to our fellow Jews. Beyond that, it would quite likely serve to improve the moral atmosphere in which we all live.

11

Maimonides on the Distinction between Science and Pseudoscience[1]

Maimonides does not present a systematic exposition of his understanding of the notion of causality. Nevertheless, he certainly understood and accepted the principle of causal relationships between empirical events. Causality is clearly invoked in his discussion of divine

---

1. The dichotomy of science and pseudoscience refers to Maimonides' distinction between true causality and incorrectly perceived causal relationships in particular cases. Maimonides reserves the term "*ḥazayyah*," variously translated as "senseless things" or "ravings," to describe the theories posited by the Sabians and others in presenting a purportedly scientific view of the world, i.e., nonsensical notions presented as scientific theory. Cf., J.I. Gellman, "Maimonides' 'Ravings,'" *Review of Metaphysics*, vol. 45, no. 2 (December, 1991), pp. 309-328 and Sarah Stroumsa, "'Ravings': Maimonides' Concept of Pseudo-Science," *Aleph*, I (2001), 141-163.

attributes, critique of Kalam philosophy, proof of the existence, unity, and incorporeality of God, creation, prophecy, good and evil, divine knowledge and will, and also in his philosophy of law as well as in his formulation of *ta'amei ha-mitzvot* (the purpose or rationale underlying the various divine commandments).[2]

Maimonides certainly believed that the universe is governed by a set of physical laws. To speak of the universe as governed by a set of laws is but another way of stating that physical phenomena occur in an orderly and predictable manner. That formulation, in turn, is actually a good working definition of the notion of causation, i.e., the principle that affirms that physical events are not merely isolated and discrete individual occurrences that happen to occur in a certain chronological order but that there is a certain intrinsic connection between them such that, *ceteris paribus*, the occurrence of one will necessarily and invariably lead to another. However, while the notion of causality as an intrinsic and necessary relationship between otherwise independent events may be an *a priori* concept inherent in the human intellect, specific instances of cause and effect relationships may not always be immediately discoverable; in other cases the existence of a causal relationship may be debatable. Philosophy may posit the existence of such a relationship, but it is science that must provide instantiation.

It is certainly arguable that, for Judaism, causality is not simply a philosophical construct of entirely speculative interest but is part of the axiological framework upon which Halakhah is predicated. The Jew is commanded to eat *matzah* on Passover, but *matzah* does not descend as manna from heaven. The obligation to eat *matzah* on Passover carries with it an obligation to prepare unleavened bread to be eaten on the festival. Implied in that commandment is the empirical principle that when flour is mixed with water and then kneaded and subsequently placed in a heated oven, *matzah*, rather than porridge, will emerge. Implied in all positive commandments requiring physical artifacts for their fulfilment is a notion that man is capable of producing or fashioning such artifacts. Man is not required to engage in random activity in the pious hope that

---

2.　See Arthur Hyman, "Maimonides on Causality," *Maimonides and Philosophy*, Shlomo Pines and Yirimiyahu Yovel, eds. (Boston, 1986), p. 157.

somehow his haphazard actions will yield the necessary object, much as the Golden Calf emerged from Aaron's bonfire, but to act in an orderly, purposive manner fully confident that his endeavor, properly executed, will yield the anticipated result. Man is, in effect, commanded to accept the principle of causation; otherwise he could plead impotence in failing to fulfil the *mitzvot* imposed upon him.[3]

The principle of causality is certainly reflected in Maimonides' formulation of the principle that all measures must be taken, whether in a therapeutic context or in nontherapeutic situations, for purposes of preservation of life (*Hilkhot Rotzeah* 1:14; *Commentary on the Mishnah, Nedarim* 4:4; and *Hilkhot Nedarim* 6:8) and in his ruling (*Hilkhot Yesodei ha-Torah* 5:1-2, 5:4, and 5:6) that, with the exception of the three cardinal transgressions, all provisions of Jewish law are suspended in the effort to preserve life, even if the efficacy of the endeavor is in doubt (*Hilkhot Shabbat* 2:1).

In light of these clearly enunciated principles, Maimonides' statement, *Hilkhot Shabbat* 19:14, is problematic. The issue is whether or not

---

3. The source of all causal power is, of course, the Deity. Attribution of all causal power to God may culminate in occasionalism rather than a strict notion of physical causation. Occasionalism is the doctrine that events that occur in the world are occasions for the application of God's power which produce the phenomena we perceive as effects of those events. This does not necessarily mean that God must engage in a constant series of miraculous interventions in the natural order. The concept "The Holy One, blessed be He, stipulated a condition with the works of creation" (*tenai hitneh Ha-Kadosh barukh Hu im ma'aseh bereshit*), formulated in *Pesikta Zutrata* 3:24 and *Bereshit Rabbah* 5:4, implies that *ab initio*, in the act of creation, God established a series of coordinated developments. The divinely decreed coordination between those events is perceived as causal in nature. In explaining this notion, a seventeenth-century philosopher, Arnold Geulincx, offered the example of two clocks perfectly adjusted to keep the same time. One has a dial showing the hour; the second strikes to tell the hour. It appears that the second strikes because the hand of the first has reached the hour. The appearance of a causal connection between the clocks is, in fact, the result of precise prearrangement. Volitional acts on the part of human beings and their intended results are also synchronized by God. Occasionalist theories differ from a strict notion of causality in that the latter posits an intrinsic physical factor inherent in the corporeal object which is responsible for the causal connection. No attempt is made in this discussion to adjudicate between those theories and the conventional notion of causation or to determine whether or not Jewish philosophers of the medieval period adopted one or another occasionalist theory of causation.

an amulet may be worn on *Shabbat* while passing from a private to a public domain. Maimonides rules:

> One may go out with a tested amulet. What is a tested amulet? One which has cured three persons or which has been made by a person who has cured three persons by means of other amulets.

Maimonides' codification reflects the ruling of the Mishnah, *Shabbat* 60a, and the ensuing discussion of the Gemara, *Shabbat* 61a, and is predicated upon acceptance of the curative powers of amulets when prepared by persons proficient in such matters.[4]

---

4. Elsewhere, in *Guide for the Perplexed*, Part 1, chap. 61, Maimonides writes:

> You must beware of sharing the error of those who write amulets. Whatever you hear of them or read in their works, especially in reference to the names which they form by combination, is utterly senseless; they call these combinations *shemot* [names] and believe their pronunciation demands sanctification and purification and that by using them they are able to work miracles. Rational persons ought not to listen to such men nor in any way believe their assertions.

These comments negating the efficacy of amulets seem to contradict the clear ruling of the Mishnah, *Shabbat* 60a. Indeed, Shem Tob, in his commentary on the *Guide, ad locum*, indicates that Maimonides intended to negate error that might arise on the basis of that mishnaic comment. However, Shem Tob seems to be unaware of Maimonides' own seemingly contradictory comments in the *Mishneh Torah, Hilkhot Shabbat* 19:14. See also the comments of Jacob I. Dienstag, *Talpiyot*, vol. IV, no. 1-2 (Tammuz 5709), p. 261. Maimonides' negative comment in *Hilkhot Mezuzah* 5:4, cited below, although somewhat ambiguous, seems to refer to treatment of *mezuzot* as amulets rather than to amulets themselves and is interpreted in that matter in the Hyamson translation of the passage.

This contradiction might perhaps be resolved by positing that Maimonides accepted the ruling of the Sages regarding entering a public thoroughfare on *Shabbat* while wearing the object described in the Mishnah, *Shabbat* 60a, even though he regarded them as devoid of any therapeutic efficacy. Maimonides might have assumed that the Sages ruled in this manner because, since the masses accepted their efficacy, albeit erroneously, such items acquired the status of articles of clothing or of ornaments simply by virtue of being customarily worn as a cure or prophylaxis. See Rashi, *Shabbat* 60a. Alternatively, Maimonides may have regarded the practice as being permitted because, in light of the fact that the items in question "are not carried in the usual manner," no transgression of a biblical prohibition is involved. See *Teshuvot ha-Radvaz le-Leshonot ha-Rambam*, V, nos. 63 (1,436) and 153 (1,526); and the comments of the interlocutor as reported in *Teshuvot Shemesh Tzedakah*, no.

Maimonides, to be sure, was well aware of the traumatic effect of withholding even useless remedies and the possibility that resultant

---

29. Since no biblical prohibition is entailed, and since the masses were desirous of wearing amulets because of their misplaced beliefs regarding therapeutic properties ascribed to such amulets, the Sages did not choose to disturb the practice with an interdiction against wearing them on the Sabbath.

Those explanations, however, are entirely unlikely. However, another resolution of Maimonides' conflicting comments does suggest itself. In context, Maimonides' comments in the *Guide* occur in the course of a discussion of the various names of God and indicate that only the tetragrammaton is the *nomen proprium* of the Deity, while all other appellations are simply reflective of divine attributes indicating the relationship of certain actions to Him but are in no way reflective of the divine essence. Moreover, Maimonides insists that all divine attributes are negative in nature and are designed to negate the possibility of certain actions or qualities but tell us nothing of the nature of the Deity in a positive sense. Maimonides' critical comments concerning amulets may, then, have been directed only against writers of amulets containing various divine names or various combinations of divine names and their ascription of supernatural properties to those names. Indeed, amulets written during the medieval period were of that nature. Since Maimonides denies that those divine names define the essence of the Deity, he categorically rejected the efficacy of amulets employing such names. Those names neither reflect the essential nature of the Deity nor do they reflect His qualities or attributes in any positive sense. Thus they cannot conceivably be endowed with any mystic power. It is noteworthy that in *Hilkhot Mezuzah* 5:4 Maimonides decries the practice of inscribing on the inside of the *mezuzah* "the names of angels, holy names, a biblical verse or seals… as if it were an amulet for their own benefit as has occurred to their foolish minds that this is something that yields benefit with regard to the vanities of the world." The amulets described in the Talmud, to which he refers in *Hilkhot Shabbat*, may well have been of an entirely different nature. Their nature is, of course, unknown to us. But those amulets, when demonstrated to have been efficacious, were accepted by Maimonides and their curative power acknowledged by him.

It must be noted that *Bi'ur ha-Gra, Yoreh De'ah* 179:13, asserts that Maimonides denies the efficacy of amulets and declares that Maimonides was misled by his philosophical speculations. If the foregoing analysis of Maimonides' ruling in *Hilkhot Shabbat* is correct and Maimonides did acknowledge the therapeutic powers of the amulets described in the Mishnah, *Bi'ur ha-Gra's* criticism of Maimonides must be understood as directed toward Maimonides' invective against amulets composed of divine names. Such criticism would then be based upon *Bi'ur ha-Gra's* own conviction of the efficacy of such amulets, and hence of his certainty that the amulets to which the Talmud refers were of such nature, rather than Maimonides' putative rejection of explicit talmudic attestation of their validity.

anguish might hasten death. Thus, in *Hilkhot Avodat Kokhavim* 11:11, he rules:

> One who has been bitten by a scorpion or by a snake may recite an incantation over the site of the bite, even on the Sabbath, in order to put his mind at ease and to strengthen his heart. Even though it is entirely of no avail, since he is in danger, [the Sages] permitted it to him so that his mind not become destroyed.

Even though incantations are generally forbidden, as Maimonides clearly rules in the immediately preceding paragraph, *Hilkhot Avodat Kokhavim* 11:10, he nevertheless sanctions resorting to incantations for purposes of *pikuaḥ nefesh*, i.e., preservation of life. Despite the fact that Maimonides regards incantations as intrinsically useless, he permits them because the condition of a victim of a snake bite who believes them to be of therapeutic value is such that the victim may become agitated and the danger to his life aggravated if the incantation is withheld. Maimonides does not hesitate to permit otherwise forbidden pseudoremedies when their use is indicated by virtue of psychological considerations but explicitly indicates the reason for that permissiveness. Maimonides offers no such justification with regard to the use of amulets. Moreover, as noted by *Maggid Mishneh, ad locum*, amulets are permitted even for the cure of non-life-threatening maladies on the grounds that, for the sick, they are comparable to articles of clothing.[5] Thus, Maimonides permits the wearing of amulets on *Shabbat* even in the absence of life-threatening emotional anguish. If so, why does Maimonides permit only an amulet of demonstrated efficacy or an amulet that has been fashioned by persons of demonstrated competence? At least in cases of illness posing a danger to life, even an amulet of merely possible therapeutic value should be permitted on grounds of *safek pikuaḥ nefesh*, i.e., possible preservation of life.

A similar problem arises with regard to Maimonides' comments in his *Commentary on the Mishnah, Yoma* 8:6. The Mishnah declares:

---

5. Cf., R. Meir Don Plocki, *Klei Ḥemdah, Parashat Pinḥas*, sec. 1, s.v. *ve-ra'iti*, who categorizes such an amulet as a "*takhshit*" or "ornament."

> One who has been bitten by a mad dog should not be fed of the
> lobe of its liver. But R. Mattia ben Ḥeresh permits [this practice].

The practice of prescribing the liver of the attacking dog as a prophylactic
measure against contracting rabies seems to have been fairly widespread
among physicians of antiquity[6] and appears to have survived in at least
some primitive societies until comparatively recent times.[7] An obvious and facile analysis of that controversy is presented by R. Menaḥem
ha-Me'iri, *Bet ha-Beḥirah, Yoma* 82a, who comments that R. Mattia ben
Ḥeresh permitted consumption of the liver "because he thought it to
be therapeutic," while the Sages forbade the practice "because it is not a
cure," even though it was categorized as such by the masses. According
to this analysis, R. Mattia ben Ḥeresh maintained that, since consumption of the dog's liver was an accepted treatment for the bite of a mad
dog and was commonly recommended by physicians, the prohibition
against eating the flesh of unclean animals may be disregarded. Although
the therapeutic or prophylactic efficacy of this remedy could not be
demonstrated, the victim was, nevertheless, permitted to eat the liver
of the dog because the liver was regarded as possibly, albeit doubtfully,
efficacious. The Sages, on the other hand, were convinced that the liver
was devoid of any therapeutic value. A similar analysis is independently
advanced by Maharam ben Ḥabib, *Tosafot Yom ha-Kippurim, Yoma* 83a.

Assuming that the Sages maintained that the liver of a dog is of
entirely no benefit in the treatment of rabies, their position is unexcep-
tionable. Violation of proscriptions of Jewish law for purposes of saving a
human life is sanctioned only when there exists at least a possible cause-
and-effect relationship between the violation and the desired effect. If
it is factually determined that no such relationship exists, there are no
grounds upon which violation of the prohibition might be sanctioned.

Maimonides, however, does not offer this obvious analysis of the
controversy between the Sages and R. Mattia ben Ḥeresh. According

---

6. See sources cited by Julius Preuss, *Biblical and Talmudic Medicine*, trans. Fred Rosner
    (New York, 1978), p. 196, note 90.
7. *Ibid.*, note 91. Preuss himself regards use of the liver of the rabid dog as a form of
    antitoxin treatment; see *ibid.*, p. 196.

to the Ibn Tibbon version of the *Commentary on the Mishnah*, Maimonides states:

> The law with regard to this is not in accordance with R. Mattia ben Ḥeresh who permits feeding a person the liver of a dog that bites because this does not benefit other than by way of a *segulah*. But the Sages declare that one may not transgress the commandments other than in conjunction with a therapy, i.e., with regard to things which cure in accordance with Nature. That is, a true matter derived by reason or[8] experience that approaches truth. But to treat by means of things that cure by virtue of their *segulah* is forbidden because their power is weak, not [known] by virtue of reason and its [demonstrated efficacy on the basis of] experience is far-fetched; its advocacy by one who is in error is weak.

The Kafih version of the same text reads:

> But the Sages declare that one may not transgress the law other than in conjunction with therapy that is a clear matter mandated by reason or[9] simple experience[10] but not for treatment by means of *segulot* because they are weak in nature, not mandated by reason and its [demonstrated efficacy on the basis of] experience is far-fetched but is [nevertheless] advocated by its advocate.

Here, too, Maimonides' analysis presents us with the identical problem. If the efficacy of the treatment is not dismissed out of hand, why is it not permitted for purposes of *pikuaḥ nefesh*? Maimonides' comments make it abundantly clear that, were it to be known with certainty that the dog's liver is capable of curing or preventing the occurrence of rabies, consumption of the liver by the victim of the dog bite would be sanctioned.

---

8. The *vav* appearing in the text is ambiguous. It may serve as *vav ha-ḥibbur* and mean "and" or as a *vav ha-pirud* meaning "or." I believe that it is correctly rendered "or."
9. See above, note 8.
10. The term is presumably used in the sense of "common experience."

If so, since the therapeutic or prophylactic value of that therapy has not been ruled out, consumption of the dog's liver should be permissible as a matter of *safek pikuaḥ nefesh.*

Maimonides, *Guide* 2:22, records a series of four axioms assumed by "Aristotle and all philosophers." The first axiom states that a simple element can produce only one simple thing, while a compound can produce as many things as it contains simple elements. The second of these axioms is: "Things are not produced by others at random; there must be some relation between cause and effect…." Maimonides then proceeds to ask a question: The first intellect is undoubtedly simple. "How then can the compound form of existing things come from such an intellect by fixed laws of Nature, as Aristotle assumes?" According to the laws of Nature, a compound can emanate only from a compound. Therefore, concludes Rambam, "It must now be clear that this emanation could not have taken place by the force of the laws of Nature, as Aristotle contends."

Moreover, Maimonides, *Guide* 2:19 and 2:24, observes that there exists a certain lack of order in the celestial realm. Although celestial spheres move with uniform circular motion, the varied velocities of the planets have no apparent order. In some instances a sphere moving with greater velocity is above one moving more slowly, while in other instances the reverse seems to be the case. In still other instances two spheres differing in location have the same velocity. These and other celestial irregularities cannot be explained on the basis of the Aristotelian view that the universe is totally ordered.

Maimonides concludes that although the sublunar world is governed by necessary laws, i.e., cause-and-effect relationships which are intelligible to man, nevertheless, in the translunar world causality is not necessarily operative. Maimonides, *Guide* 2:22, succinctly states:

> I hold that the theory of Aristotle is undoubtedly correct as far as the things are concerned which exist between the sphere of the moon and the center of the earth…. But what Aristotle says concerning things above the sphere of the moon is, with few exceptions, mere imagination and opinion….

Maimonides concedes that the sublunar world is governed by the laws of Nature in general and by the principle of causality in particular. But this is not the case with regard to the translunar universe. The translunar universe is not governed by the laws of Nature but, as Maimonides declares in the same chapter, by the "design and determination of a Creator in accordance with His unfathomable wisdom." Formulation of that position makes it possible to accept the doctrine of creation rather than the Aristotelian notion of the eternity of the universe.

Although Maimonides' distinction is cast in terms serving to distinguish the sublunar world from the translunar universe, the underlying distinction may well be regarded as being essentially a distinction between the physical and the metaphysical. As such, it is not at all surprising that the laws of Nature apply only to the physical universe. One should not anticipate that physical laws are applicable to any metaphysical being or power. Accordingly, translunar celestial bodies are outside the pale of the laws of Nature, simply because those laws are limited to the sublunar universe which, by virtue of its very nature, is corporeal and physical.

The categories of the metaphysical and the physical, while essentially dichotomous, are not without points of interaction. One of the problems inherent in Aristotle's view regarding the motion of the celestial bodies is how an incorporeal intelligence may serve as an efficient cause in effecting motion in a corporeal substance. Nevertheless, Aristotle maintains that metaphysical causes have physical effects. The cosmogony of the Kabbalah, in which human activity plays a focal role in *tikkun*, i.e., restoration of the world of *asiyah* to its spiritual perfection, is founded upon the premise that the correlate principle is also true, i.e., that physical causes produce metaphysical effects.

The problem is mitigated considerably if it is recognized that the interaction between the physical and the metaphysical is not governed by laws of Nature, just as the realm of the purely metaphysical is not governed by laws of Nature. Thus, categories of causality as reflected in the sublunar physical world cannot fully explain those relationships. Our understanding of particular causal relationships is the product of inductive inference based upon empirical observation which, by its very nature, is limited to situations in which both the cause and the effect are observable, i.e., physical rather than metaphysical. Nevertheless, areas of interaction between the physical and the metaphysical do exist.

An example of such interaction can be found in Nahmanides' exposition of the nature of sorcery in his *Commentary on the Bible*, Deuteronomy 18:9:

> And now, know and understand with regard to the matter of sorcery, that when the Creator, blessed be He, created everything *ex nihilo* He made the higher powers to be guides for the lower powers beneath them. He placed the power of the "earth and all things that are thereon" (Nehemiah 9:6) in stars and constellations in accordance with their rotation and position as proven by the science of astrology. Over the stars and constellations He further appointed angels and "lords" who are the soul [of the stars and constellations] as guides. Now, their behavior from the time they came into existence until eternity is according to the decree of the higher power which He placed in them. However, it was one of His mighty wonders that, within the power of the higher forces, He put configurations and capacities to alter that which is under them. Thus if the gaze of the stars towards the earth be good or bad to a certain land, people or individual, the higher powers can change by their own gaze…. Therefore, the author of the Book of the Moon, the expert in necromancy, said that when the moon, termed the sphere of the world, is, for example, at the head of Aries and the constellation thus appears in a certain position, you should make a certain picture and engrave upon it the time and the name of the angel – one of the names mentioned in that book – appointed over it and then perform a certain burning of incense in a certain specified manner and the result of the gaze [of the stars] will be for evil… and when the moon shall be in a certain constellation and a certain gaze you should make the picture and the burning in a certain manner and the result will be all manner of good…. This then is the secret of sorcery and power…. Therefore it is proper that the Torah prohibit these activities in order to let the world remain in its customary way and in its simple nature which is the desire of its Creator.

It is certainly true that Maimonides, *Hilkhot Avodat Kokhavim* 11:16, negates the efficacy of sorcery and witchcraft and, *inter alia*, dismisses such practices with the observation that "…they are all imaginary and foolishness which attract only those that are deficient in knowledge." Nevertheless, Maimonides certainly recognized that metaphysical causes may produce physical effects. Maimonides, no less than Aristotle, accepted the principle that incorporeal intelligences are the cause of motion of corporeal bodies. Maimonides' own understanding of causality and the differing role of causation in the physical and metaphysical realms may serve to illuminate his halakhic rulings regarding amulets and nonscientific remedies.

As indicated by his comments in *Hilkhot Shabbat* and in his *Commentary on the Mishnah*, Maimonides was quite prepared to accept the therapeutic efficacy of amulets and certain remedies that he describes as *segulot*. The term *"teva"* ("Nature") that appears in the Ibn Tibbon version of the *Commentary on the Mishnah* in elucidating the dichotomous nature of the two modes of therapy reveals the crucial nature of the distinction between conventional cures and *"segulot."* The distinction is between medical remedies rooted in the laws of Nature, whose efficacy is explainable in accordance with causal connections between the medicament and the disease for which it is prescribed, and other remedies whose effects can be explained only in some nonnatural or metaphysical manner.

The thesis that, according to Maimonides, violation of halakhic restrictions for purposes of preserving life is permitted only in conjunction with the use of natural remedies, but not permitted with regard to *segulot*, is certainly an inviting one. That distinction would be justified by the contention that transgression of halakhic prohibitions is permitted only in conjunction with actions designed to yield predictable effects based upon known causal relationships present in the natural order. This, indeed, seems to be the position of Maharam ben Ḥabib, *Tosafot Yom ha-Kippurim, Yoma* 83a. That authority seems to be of the opinion that transgression of a biblical prohibition can never be sanctioned for the purpose of administering therapy in the form of a *segulah*. This is also the manner in which Maimonides was understood by *Admat Kodesh*, I,

Yoreh De'ah, no. 6, as well as by *Teshuvot Pri ha-Aretz*, III, no. 3.[11] Those authorities were asked if a nonkosher chicken might be fed to a person suffering from some form of mental illness. The cure is described as a *segulah*. We are, however, informed that it was well-known that the lives of many people were saved by means of this therapy. Although those authorities permit use of the therapy in question, they indicate that Maimonides would have forbidden the use of even a tried and tested *segulah* under such circumstances but that, according to other authorities, any known therapy, even a *segulah*, may be utilized in cases of danger. R. Chaim Joseph David Azulai, *Birkei Yosef, Oraḥ Ḥayyim* 301:6, applies the same analysis to the propriety of writing an amulet on *Shabbat*, apparently even when the success of the procedure is not in doubt.[12] Similarly, R. Shlomoh Kluger, both in his *Teshuvot Tuv Ta'am va-Da'at, Mahadura Kamma*, no. 239, and in his *Teshuvot U-Vaḥarta ba-Ḥayyim*, no. 87, forbids desecration of the Sabbath in order to secure the prayer of a saint, even if it is known with certainty that the prayer will effect a cure. Prayer, while undoubtedly efficacious, can also be described as a nonnatural cause yielding a physical effect.

R. Chaim Sofer, *Teshuvot Maḥaneh Ḥayyim, Yoreh De'ah*, II, no. 60, explains that availing oneself of the ministrations of a physician is permitted only because of specific dispensation granted by the verse "and he shall cause him to be thoroughly healed" (Exodus 21:20). Permission to utilize medical remedies entails an obligation to use them in the preservation of life. The obligation to preserve life, in turn, serves to obviate strictures of religious law. However, asserts *Maḥaneh Ḥayyim*, the obligation arising out of that verse is limited to utilization of natural remedies; no similar obligation exists with regard to the use of nonnatural, occult, or metaphysical powers in effecting a cure. Infractions of Jewish law are permitted for purposes of preserving life only because such measures are demanded by Halakhah. Accordingly, *Maḥaneh Ḥayyim* concludes that, according to Maimonides, even *segulot* of demonstrated efficacy may not be employed, even in face of danger to life, if such use involves

---

11. See also *Teshuvot Shemesh Tzedakah*, no. 29.

12. See also R. Chaim Joseph David Azulai, *Ḥayyim Sha'al*, II, no. 38, sec. 81.

an infraction of a halakhic prohibition. Alternatively, the verse "It is not in heaven" (Deuteronomy 30:12) may serve to establish the principle that all human obligations are limited to employment of natural forces present in the sublunar world.

Such a principle would serve to explain why, for example, there is no absolute mandatory obligation to offer prayer on behalf of a sick person.[13] Given the phenomenon of prayer and its efficacy, it is otherwise unclear why the obligation "Nor shall you stand idly by the blood of your fellow" (Leviticus 19:16) does not establish an absolute obligation to pray on behalf of a person whose life is endangered concomitant with the obligation to administer therapeutic measures or to engage in other endeavors to preserve his life. That problem is immediately resolved if it is posited that man's obligations are limited to the physical but exclude the employment of "heavenly" or metaphysical forces.

This distinction also serves to illuminate the comment of Rema, *Yoreh De'ah* 339:1, with regard to the treatment of a *goses*.[14] Although active euthanasia is always forbidden and the hastening of death by even a matter of moments is regarded as tantamount to homicide, Rema rules that, in the case of a *goses*, "…if there is something that causes a hindrance to the departure of the soul such as a clattering noise or salt upon his tongue and these prevent the departure of the soul they may be removed for this involves no act whatsoever but only the removal of the impediment." These comments of Rema notwithstanding, *Teshuvot Shevut Ya'akov*, I, no. 13, cites *Yoma* 85a as demonstrating that *Shabbat* laws are suspended for the purpose of even marginal prolongation of life. *Shevut Ya'akov* declares that all recognized therapeutic remedies must be utilized in prolonging the life of a *goses*, regardless of how brief a period of time he may be expected to survive. This authority evidently distinguishes between natural remedies of demonstrated efficacy involving readily recognizable causal relationships and nonscientific *segulot* of undemonstrable causal efficacy, such as the placing of salt upon the

---

13. Cf., however, 2 Chronicles 16:12 and this writer's discussion of that verse in *Judaism and Healing* (New York, 1981), pp. 5-6.
14. A *goses* is a moribund patient as defined by criteria posited by Halakhah. For a fuller definition of the state of *gesisah*, see this writer's *Judaism and Healing*, pp. 141-42.

tongue. The latter, according to this analysis, is not required in the case of a *goses*, because such remedies are not recognized medical procedures and hence their utilization is never required as a matter of normative Halakhah.[15]

The rulings of the earlier cited latter-day authorities notwithstanding, the language employed by Maimonides in his *Commentary on the Mishnah, Yoma* 8:6, seems to support the view that nonnatural remedies are forbidden when their use necessitates violation of halakhic restrictions only if those *segulot* are of unconfirmed therapeutic value but that no similar restrictions are placed upon administration of tried and tested *segulot* whose value has been confirmed by experience. According to the Kafih version of the *Commentary on the Mishnah*, Maimonides distinguishes between therapy "mandated by reason or simple experience" and "*segulot*" that are "weak in nature," i.e., not mandated by reason, and whose "demonstrated efficacy on the basis of experience is far-fetched." According to the Ibn Tibbon version, one may not employ otherwise forbidden measures in attempting to cure by means of a *segulah* because "their power is weak, not [known] by virtue of reason and its [demonstrated efficacy on the basis of] experience is far-fetched."

The reference, according to both versions, to cures that are known by virtue of "reason" is clearly a reference to medicaments or procedures with regard to which there is a rational, well-understood cause-and-effect relationship between the remedy and the cure. Maimonides' reference to "experience" as an independent criterion indicates that he is willing to accept the existence of a cause-and-effect relationship on the basis of "experience" or empirical generalization, even if the underlying scientific causal relationship is not fully understood. Experience gained over a period of time indicating a chronological relationship between cause and effect is accepted for purposes of Halakhah as indicative of

---

15. This also seems to be the position of *Teshuvot Ḥatam Sofer, Yoreh De'ah*, no. 338 and *Bi'ur Halakhah, Oraḥ Ḥayyim* 329:2. However, other authorities, most notably, *Teshuvot Bet Ya'akov*, no. 59, followed by *Iggerot Mosheh, Yoreh De'ah*, 11, no. 174, apparently make no such distinction and rule that it is forbidden to prolong the life of a *goses* by any means whatsoever. Cf., R. Eliezer Waldenberg, *Tzitz Eli'ezer*, x111, no. 89, sec. 14; *ibid.*, v111, no. 15, chap. 3, sec. 16; *ibid.*, IX, no. 47; *idem, Ramat Raḥel*, no. 28; and *idem, Assia*, (Nisan 5738), p. 195.

an intrinsic relationship between the events, or at least of the possible existence of an intrinsic relationship between the events, with the result that violation of Halakhah is sanctioned, and indeed mandated, for reasons of *pikuaḥ nefesh*. Nevertheless, Maimonides distinguishes between "experience that approaches truth" (Ibn Tibbon) or "simple experience" (Kafih) and experience that is "far-fetched" (*raḥok*), i.e., between experience that is demonstrably compelling and experience that is inconclusive.

The crucial phrase in Maimonides' exposition of the position of the Sages in refusing to permit the victim of a dog bite to eat the liver of its attacker is that the ascription of curative power to this remedy on the basis of experience is far-fetched. Apparently, even putative cures attributable to such therapy were few and far between. Such experience does not serve to confirm the efficacy of the contemplated measure. Nevertheless, similar therapies may be employed, even in the absence of the evidence of experience, in situations in which use of such remedies is "mandated by reason" or known "by virtue of reason." It would appear then that, according to Maimonides, the crucial factor in suspension of halakhic restrictions in situations involving *pikuaḥ nefesh* is the presence of a causal relationship or, more precisely, the reasonably possible presence of a cause-effect relationship. Thus, suspension of halakhic proscriptions is warranted either on the basis of a cause-and-effect relationship postulated by reason or on the basis of experience. Since, in the case of *segulot*, the human intellect cannot grasp the presence of a causal relationship, the sole basis for permitting their utilization when such use involves an infraction of Jewish law is experience. Hence, when the evidence based upon experience is "far-fetched," no basis exists for permitting such use.

Assuming that what Maimonides says with regard to the translunar world is true with regard to metaphysical phenomena as well, *segulot* cannot *ipso facto* be subsumed under causal categories. This, it would appear, is the meaning of Maimonides' statement that the power of *segulot* is "weak," i.e., ordinary causal connections are not predictable as being uniformly present. It is that element of predictability that Maimonides regards as the *sine qua non* for suspension of halakhic prohibitions in the face of *pikuaḥ nefesh*. It is, of course, quite true that accepted medical remedies do not unvaryingly result in a cure. Such negative phenomena do not suggest the absence of a causal relationship since instances of failure are readily attributed to the severity or advanced state of the disease, complicating factors, or the like. However, when the putative effect is only infrequently manifested, the curative power must be ascribed, not to the causal operation of laws of nature, but to the noncausal, unpredictable operation of a metaphysical power or *segulah*.

Maimonides thus relies upon experience in establishing the existence of a causal relationship, even in situations in which no scientific explanation is discernible. The inability of the human intellect to explain the basis of a cause-and-effect relationship does not necessarily mean that no such relationship exists. Hence, if the effects of a remedy can be predicted in a reliable manner, that in and of itself is evidence that the remedy in question is efficacious because of the presence of a causal principle. Such a remedy is not to be relegated to the category of a *segulah* of unconfirmed and unsubstantiated efficacy and thus may be utilized in instances of a threat to life, even if such use would otherwise be forbidden by Jewish law.

There are, however, situations in which physical effects are generated in a manner that cannot possibly be explained in terms of the operation of laws of nature governing the physical universe. Despite the regularity and predictability of such phenomena, they are clearly the result of the operation of metaphysical causes. When there exists sufficient evidence demonstrating a regular, predictable relationship between the metaphysical cause of the physical event, e.g., in the case of a "tested amulet," the phenomenon is treated no differently than natural, i.e., physical, causal relationships.

This analysis of Maimonides' distinction is supported by *Tiferet Yisra'el, Yoma* 6:32, who cites Maimonides' comments with regard to cure by means of *segulot* in the face of halakhic strictures and concludes, "Therefore, any [such remedy] whose cure is not certain is forbidden." The threshold level of possible efficacy, and hence of *safek pikuaḥ nefesh*, is satisfied if the putative therapeutic property of the medicament in question is perceived by reason or if it has been established on the basis of experience. Since even *safek pikuaḥ nefesh*, i.e., even doubtful or possible preservation of life, is sufficient to warrant disregard of halakhic restraints, it is not necessary that reason or experience establish therapeutic efficacy beyond cavil; it is sufficient that reason or experience point to probable, or even possible, benefit.[16] Nevertheless, in the absence of experiential evidence of past success or cogent reason to assume therapeutic value, utilization of a contemplated remedy does not rise to the level of "doubtful" *pikuaḥ nefesh*. However, when therapeutic value has been demonstrated on the basis of experience, remedies in the nature of *segulot* are treated no differently than recognized and established medical cures.[17]

---

16. Maimonides, *Guide* 3:37, certainly accepts the medical efficacy of therapy "that has been verified by experiment, although it cannot be explained by analogy." Included in that category are wearing the egg of a certain species of locust, a fox's tooth, and a nail from the gallows of an impaled convict, each of which was worn as a putative remedy for a specific disorder. Those therapies are specifically permitted according to the normative opinion of R. Meir recorded in the Mishnah, *Shabbat* 67a. Maimonides, in the *Guide*, explains that "the ways of the Amorite" are forbidden "because they are not arrived at by reason, but are similar to the performances of witchcraft, which is necessarily connected with the influences of the star," but that the earlier enumerated therapies are permitted nevertheless because "these things have been considered in those days as facts established by experiment." On the basis of Maimonides' remarks in his *Commentary on the Mishnah* on *Yoma* and in the *Guide*, it might be argued that Maimonides assumes that whenever medical efficacy is confirmed by experience it must be presumed that the therapy is in accordance with the natural order even though the nature of the causal relationship between the medicament and the cure is not understood. This analysis of Maimonides' position cannot be accepted for a number of reasons: (1) Other medieval authorities clearly recognized that the items enumerated by the Mishnah in *Shabbat* had no natural therapeutic properties; see, for example, *Teshuvot ha-Rashba*, I, no. 411. (2) Maimonides, in the *Guide*, comments, "They served as cures, in the same means as the hanging of the peony over a person subject to epileptic fits, or the application of a dog's excrement to the swellings of the throat, and of the vapors of vinegar and marcasite to the swelling of tumors." The clear implication is that the enumerated remedies were recognized as nonnatural *segulot*. (3) Most significant is Maimonides' explicit categorization in his *Commentary on the Mishnah, Shabbat* 76a, of the practices referred to by the Mishnah as remedies advocated by "*ba'alei ha-segulot*." Moreover, and perhaps most significantly, Maimonides, as has been shown, maintains that when there is cogent scientific reason to believe that a proposed therapy will even possibly be effective, it must be assumed that such therapy constitutes *safek pikuaḥ nefesh* even though the hypothesis lacks experimental confirmation. See also *Teshuvot ha-Radvaz le-Leshonot ha-Rambam*, no. 63, and R. Isaac Joseph Nunez-Vaes, *Siaḥ Yitzḥak, Yoma* 83a.
17. It is quite possible that *Tosafot* espouse a position similar to that of Maimonides but require that the therapeutic power of a *segulah* be known with "certainty" in any

Although Maimonides maintains that events confined entirely to the translunar world are not at all governed by causal principles, he makes no specific reference to the nature of the relationship between metaphysical powers and physical phenomena such as are manifest, for example, in motion imparted to celestial bodies by incorporeal intelligences. It is therefore entirely possible that some metaphysical causes not only produce physical effects but do so in a uniform, patterned manner entirely similar to the manner in which causally connected physical phenomena occur. Since the cause is metaphysical, the rationality of the connection is unlikely or impossible to be grasped by the human intellect. Nevertheless, when such matters do recur with regularity, a causal relationship can be inferred from such experience on the basis of empirical generalization.[18]

---

situation in which its use involves violation of a halakhic prohibition. The Talmud declares that Elijah and Phineas were one and the same person. *Tosafot, Bava Metzi'a* 114b, question the permissibility of Elijah's conduct in resuscitating the son of the widow of Zarephath. Since Phineas was a priest, he was forbidden to defile himself through tactile contact with a corpse. How, then, was he permitted to revive the dead child? *Tosafot* answer that since Elijah was certain of the success of his endeavor, violation of the priestly code was permissible. *Tosafot's* comment is puzzling since the general principle is that halakhic strictures are suspended even on the mere chance that the procedure may succeed in saving a life. R. Abraham Jacob Neumark, *Eshel Avraham* (Tel Aviv, 5708), *Pinot Genosar*, no. 23, cites Maimonides' discussion of remedies in the nature of a *segulah* and, asserting that according to Maimonides a *segulah* may be employed in face of halakhic strictures only if its curative powers are known with certainty, explains that Elijah's use of prophetic powers was also a "non-natural" therapy and hence was justified only because of his certainty of success. See also R. Iser Yehudah Unterman, *Ha-Torah ve-ha-Medinah*, IV, 25 f., and *idem, Shevet me-Yehudah, Sha'ar Rishon*, chap. 7. For other interpretations of *Tosafot's* thesis see *Contemporary Halakhic Problems*, I (New York, 1977), 89-91.

18. It is indeed quite possible that Maimonides may have regarded physical cause-and-effect relationships as the manifestation of powers intrinsic in corporeal objects whereas metaphysical phenomena may have no intrinsic relationship to the physical effects that follow in their wake but that the effect is each time generated by divine powers. This is testament to speculating that the causal relationship between metaphysical causes and physical effects is of the nature described as occasionalism; see *supra*, note 3. On such an analysis, the distinction between a *segulah* such as the liver of a rabid dog and a tested amulet is also readily understandable on the basis of the relative likelihood of the metaphysical cause being the occasion for the manifestation of a physical effect. When the metaphysical phenomenon is only infrequently the

According to this analysis, Maimonides' sanction of the wearing of an amulet on *Shabbat*, provided that the efficacy of the amulet has been demonstrated, is readily understandable. *Segulot* in the form of metaphysical cures are treated no differently from scientifically explainable remedies in those limited situations in which the effect of the *segulah* is predictable.[19]

---

occasion for the physical effect, the relationship is not at all analogous to causality inherent in the operation of the laws of nature. However, when the metaphysical event is regularly and predictably the occasion for subsequent manifestation of a physical event, the phenomenon is treated in a manner identical to that of natural causal relationships.

19. For a further discussion of therapeutic measures of demonstrated efficacy versus those of unproven value, see this writer's "Experimental Procedures: The Concept of *Refu'ah Bedukah*," *Contemporary Halakhic Problems*, IV (New York, 1995), 203-217.

12

The Problem of Identity in Rashi, Rambam and the Tosafists

I. THE PROBLEM

Persons as well as things endure over time. People are born as infants, grow into adolescence, mature into adults and decline in senescence. An acorn takes root, a sapling emerges, a tree develops verdant foliage and eventually enters into a decline. Change is an ongoing and omnipresent phenomenon. Yet change is devoid of meaning unless understood as an accident, in the Aristotelian sense of the term, of some underlying substratum or of a Kantian *Ding-an-sich* that remains constant. The problem of identity has long been the bane of philosophers. Common sense tells us that, despite the flow of time and the assumption of different characteristics, there exists a constant element in every person or thing. What is the essence of continuity that exists despite change? Certainly, it is that elusive quintessential element that is captured in the notion of identity.

    Long before becoming aware of the fact that, from antiquity until the present, the problem of identity had engaged the intellects of foremost philosophers, I was gripped by the enormity of the problem as a result of its reflection in a seemingly frivolous legal maneuver.

Most people are familiar with the horrendous acts committed by Nathan Leopold and Richard Loeb, two Chicago playboys who abducted a child and subsequently murdered him. It was a purposeless, senseless crime. Both because of its frivolous nature and because of the fact that it was committed by wealthy, privileged young men, the incident was surrounded with notoriety. Leopold and Loeb were both sentenced to life in prison. They were extremely bright, well-educated young men. In prison they became jailhouse lawyers and continuously peppered the courts with writs and motions, petitions for retrial, etc., etc.

By chance, I came upon a report of a plea for parole filed by one of those young men.[1] Nathan Leopold sought release from prison on very, very ingenious grounds. As are most of us, he was also aware that, with perhaps the exception of the brain and the central nervous system, in the process of time every single cell of the human body is destroyed and then regenerated. To be sure, destruction and regeneration does not occur to every cell simultaneously but together they constitute a constant, ongoing process affecting the entire body. Thus, for example, every time a person claps his hands he destroys perhaps many hundreds of cells but, fortunately, others are continuously created to take their place. Cells simply outlive their usefulness and disintegrate, only to be replaced by others. It is reported that, within a period of seven years, all cells are destroyed and replaced. Apparently, it is a virtual certainty that no single cell that is present in the body at the beginning of any given seven-year period will still be present in the body at the expiration of that seven-year period. "No cell that was in my body at the time of the crime is there today," contended Leopold. Indeed, that phenomenon might have been cogently invoked as providing ample grounds for a writ of *habeas corpus* – quite literally. More than seven years had elapsed since the time of the crime. Accordingly, he might have argued, "Give us the body" because the imprisoned convict is not the perpetrator. Leopold alleged that he did not share the identity of the person who had committed the crime and therefore he was being unjustly incarcerated.

---

1. See *New York Times*, January 9, 1953, p.14.

Leopold's plea for parole was dismissed. Assuredly, a judge with a plea for *habeas corpus* on such grounds would assert that the legal system embraces the common sense notion of personal identity. The law will not allow itself to be confused by scientific facts because, at least with regard to this matter, it regards them as totally irrelevant. The notion of personhood and the notion of individual identity have nothing to do with the permanence versus the transience of the cells of a body. Identity is a reflection of some other concept—a concept that a jurist may not be responsible for apprehending, much less explicating—but one with which a philosopher, and certainly a legal philosopher, must grapple.

As stated by one contemporary writer, "People age, some trees regularly shed their leaves, ice melts with the coming of spring, and wood, when burned, gives way to fire and ash."[2] The question is whether the toddler in the pictures that a mother displays is the same individual as the grown, mature adult. If so, in what sense? By the same token, one can ask whether, when ice melts and becomes water, is there a preservation of identity? When wood is burned, and gives way to charcoal and then to ash, is there any continuum of identity between the wood that formed the tree and the ash which is the residue subsequent to combustion? The problem, for philosophical as well as legal reasons, is of course most acute with regard to the personal identity of human beings, but essentially the same problem exists with regard to the identity of members of the animal kingdom and even of inanimate objects.

II. PHILOSPHICAL RESOLUTIONS

Philosophers have dealt with this issue in a variety of different ways. David Hume, in his *Treatise of Human Nature*, concedes that the problem admits of no resolution. According to Hume, the very notion of identity is specious because human consciousness is naught but a collection, or bundle, of perceptions. The notion of identity is nothing more than a construct of the mind which it imposes upon an uninterrupted series of perceptions. Hence, Hume categorizes the notion of identity as a fic-

---

2. Avrum Stroll, "Identity," *Encyclopedia of Philosophy*, ed. Paul Edwards (New York, 1972), IV, 121.

tion and the notion of an intuitively apprehended self as not genuine. Thus, in effect, he dismisses the problem as specious and hence as not requiring a solution: there is no need to explicate the nature of personal identity because there is no personal identity.[3]

Putting aside the question of identity with regard to inorganic entities, John Locke, in *An Essay Concerning Human Understanding*, proposes a solution to the problem of personal identity by attempting to make identity contingent upon memory. Each individual possesses a unique set of memories and it is those memories that constitute his or her unique identity. In effect, it is the series of memories that constitutes the person. For Locke, the identity of person is the identity of consciousness.[4]

That categorization of personal identity has been challenged for cause. Imagine that a prince went to sleep in a royal palace. In the morning the prince awakens and utters the memory claims of a cobbler. He looks at himself and does not really believe that he is a prince since he has no memory of his royal station. The same evening, a cobbler living in his miserable abode hundreds of miles away went to sleep and wakes up believing that he is the prince. He proceeds to demand that he be taken to the royal palace and treated in a manner appropriate to his station. We are confronted with two different people—at least we would call them different people—and each one claims the retained memories of the other. If identity is nothing more than a chain of memories there are no grounds to distinguish between veridical memories and hallucinatory memories. And indeed Locke seems to be prepared to say that the prince and the cobbler are the same person.[5] In an attempt to obviate that problem, some philosophers, such as Thomas Reid, in his *Essays on the Intellectual Power of Man*,[6] and Joseph Butler, in an essay entitled "Of Personal Identity," published as an addendum to the first volume of *The Theology of Religion*, ed. W.E. Gladstone (Oxford, 1897), retain the notion

---

3. See *Treatise of Human Nature*, Book I, Part IV, sec. 6 and Appendix. See also A. J. Ayer, *Language, Truth and Logic* (New York, 1946), p. 127.
4. See *An Essay Concerning Human Understanding*, Book 2, chap. 27.
5. *Ibid.*, point 15.
6. Essay III, chap. 4.

of identity defined in terms of memory but couple it with the postulation of a mind or spiritual substance in which memories adhere. In the introduction to his *Critique of Pure Reason*, Immanuel Kant develops the thesis that empirical experiences are imposed upon an *a priori* faculty of cognition which seemingly requires a persisting subject or owner.

In more recent times, A. J. Ayer, in his *Philosophical Essays*, develops a notion that had at least been suggested in earlier philosophical writings, particularly in Locke's discussion of the identity of inanimate entities, and seeks to define identity in terms of spatio-temporal continuity.[7] I prefer the term spatio-temporal contiguity rather than spatio-temporal continuity for reasons that may become a bit more obvious later. Basically, according to Ayer's thesis, a person preserves his identity as an individual because he has succeeded in time and place to the same individual who occupied the same or contiguous space a nanosecond earlier. Identity is thus dependent upon both spatial and temporal contiguity. A person who passes out of existence and reappears at some future time would not be the same person, no matter how brief the interval between his disappearance and his reappearance. Nor, according to Ayer, would a person who disappears only to appear instantaneously in some other place be the same person.

Later, in *The Problem of Knowledge*, Ayer modifies that definition somewhat, and insists that, although spatio-temporal contiguity is essential to the definition of personal identity, it must, however, be modified by incorporating the notion of physical characteristics. When spatio-temporal contiguity exists and is also accompanied by appropriate persistent physical characteristics, Ayer is willing to recognize that the two in tandem are what we mean when we speak of personal identity.[8]

It seems to me that there is a much older solution to the problem, although it was not formulated as a solution to this particular problem. In discussing the nature of causality, Aristotle enumerates four separate notions of causality, the last of which he calls the final cause. The final cause is the *telos* or purpose of the act. Although the final cause is chronologically subsequent to the other causes in that it cannot be

---

7. *Philosophical Essays* (New York, 1963), p. 15.
8. See *The Problem of Knowledge*, chap. 5.

achieved without them, it is nevertheless logically prior. Accordingly, Aristotle informs us that the effect is really present in its cause from the very beginning.[9]

Aristotle also presents the notion of *entelechies* as an explanation of how it is, for example, that an acorn develops into an oak tree.[10] *Entelechies* are those things which have their end in themselves. If one thinks of the *enteleche* as some kind of metaphysical entity it is that entity that transforms potentiality into actuality. If the *enteleche* is identified as the mediator responsible for the actualization of the final cause, those two notions taken together represent a highly sophisticated theory of causality. Causation is the process of actualization of the potential by means of the *enteleche*. In contradistinction to Hume, who denies the reality of causality, Aristotle may be understood as formulating a very clear notion of causality.

It seems to me that Aristotle's unique notion of causality gives us not only a definition of causality but provides us with a notion of identity as well. Cause and effect are intrinsically related. As mediator of the final cause, the *enteleche* establishes an identity between the causal entity and the effect that is already present in that cause. The presence of the effect in the cause creates a nexus between them; it is that nexus of which we speak when we speak of the continuum of identity.

III. PERSONAL IDENTITY IN TALMUDIC SOURCES

The issue of identity, both individual identity as well as identity as a member of a species, was certainly a matter of concern to rabbinic scholars. Identity as a member of a species was perhaps the focal point of their

---

9. It is this understanding of the nature of causality that led both Rambam and Crescas to reject the possibility of the emergence of matter directly from God in the form of emanation. Rambam, *Guide of the Perplexed*, Part II, chap. 22, states, "Aristotle and the philosophers assume as an axiom that a simple element can only produce one simple thing." Crescas, *Or ha-Shem*, II, *klal* 3, chap. 4 (p. 68a) comments, "Inasmuch as this matter is extremely imperfect, it could not have come by necessity from God who is infinitely perfect." That argument is based upon the presumption that an effect is, in some sense, already present in the cause and hence cannot be dissimilar to the cause.

10. *Metaphysics*, Book Theta.

attention because of its relevance in determining the status of a particular animal as a member of a kosher or of a non-kosher species. Nevertheless, personal identity was also a matter of concern and an analysis of rulings formulated by the Gemara reveals that the talmudic notion of identity is even more far-reaching than its common sense counterpart.

The Gemara, *Bava Batra* 159a, states as follows:

> If a son sold property of his father during his father's lifetime and then died, his son may recover [the property] from the purchasers. And it is this that is difficult among the laws of jurisprudence for [the purchasers] ought to be able to say to him, "Your father sold and you are recovering?" But what is the difficulty? Perhaps [the grandson] might say, "I come with the rights of the father of my father as it is written, 'In place of your fathers shall be your sons [whom] you shall make princes in all the land' (Psalms 45:17)."

It is virtually axiomatic that a person cannot transfer or devise property interests that are not vested in him. If so, the son could not possibly bequest to the grandson property that he has already alienated.[11] Yet the Gemara declares that the grandson's claim to recover the alienated property presents no doctrinal difficulty because property passes directly from the grandfather to the grandson by operation of the law of inheritance thereby obviating any property interest that might have been asserted in the name of the son.

The Gemara then proceeds to formulate the difficulty in another manner:

> If a firstborn son sold [his] primogeniture share during his father's lifetime and then died during his father's lifetime, his son may recover [the property] from the purchasers. And it is this that is difficult among the laws of jurisprudence: His father sold and he recovers?

---

11. The obvious question of the invalidity in Jewish law of a transfer of a future interest is addressed by *Tosafot, ad locum.*

> If you say that in this case as well the grandson might say, "I come with the rights of the father of my father," nevertheless, what is his connection to the share of primogeniture?
> But what is the difficulty? Perhaps [the grandson] might say, "I come with the right of the father of my father but I stand in the place of my father."

In this retort the Gemara establishes not simply that the transfer of property is directly from grandfather to grandson but that the grandson literally stands in the place of the father, i.e., he has acquired the legal persona of the father with all the rights and prerogatives consequent thereto.

The Gemara herein presents a theory akin to the notion of inheritance by representation found in Roman law. In Roman law the heir succeeds not only to the estate of his progenitor but becomes liable for his debts as well. That rule follows from the notion that, juridically speaking, the two individuals are regarded as a single person. However, in Jewish law a son bears no personal responsibility for discharging a debt incurred by his father; liability of heirs is limited to recovery from the inherited assets.[12]

Nevertheless, the only cogent theory that allows for a grandson to succeed to the son's right of primogeniture without title first passing through the son is the notion that, for the limited purpose of inheritance, they are deemed to be one person. Thus, the grandson, as a sort of alter ego of the son, enjoys the positive benefit of inheritance but is not responsible for personal debts of his forebears and is also not bound by his progenitor's attempt to alienate property. That thesis flows from a literal reading of the verse "In place of your fathers shall be your sons."

This theory is unique to the case of inheritance by a son but does not pertain to inheritance by other relatives. It is not the case that this doctrine has a practical effect solely with regard to the right of primogeniture which, by definition, is limited to a son; the doctrine of filial inheritance by representation is reflected in the rule codified by Rambam,

---

12. For a detailed discussion of the liability of heirs see *Encyclopedia Talmudit*, XXIII, 516-550. For some authorities such an obligation does exist but is not jurisprudential in nature; rather, it is rooted in the son's duty to honor his father. See *ibid.*, p. 521.

Hilkhot Melakhim 1:7, providing for the inheritance of the monarchy and other communal appointments by lineal descendants. Collateral heirs enjoy no such rights. That distinction is readily understood if it is recognized that direct descendants—and only direct descendants —are not really heirs at all but are the extension of the same persona.[13] Similarly, filial inheritance of property—but only filial inheritance—is based upon a notion of representation.

This talmudic discussion of inheritance certainly reflects a doctrine of identity and, moreover, establishes that the notion of identity is not at all predicated upon the phenomenon of memory. It may be shown that early-day authorities understood identity as predicated upon spatio-temporal contiguity or in terms of a causal nexus akin to the Aristotelian notion of an *enteleche*.

IV. SPECIES IDENTITY IN JEWISH LAW

1. *The Principle of* Yotzei

Quite apart from the concept of the personal identity of a human being, identity is a significant halakhic notion with regard to animals. With regard to the dietary code and similar matters the issue is primarily that of

---

13. See R. Elchanan Wasserman, *Kovetz Shi'urim*, 11, no. 12, who invokes this theory in explaining why the posthumous issue of a proselyte succeeds to his father's property even though it has already been seized as ownerless property by another. *Kovetz Shi'urim* compares the situation of a posthumously born child to the phenomenon of a person dying only to reappear and lay claim to his property. *Kovetz Shi'urim* also invokes this theory in explaining why a son may collect certain fines due his mother even though fines cannot be inherited.

Although self-endangerment is permitted, and, according to some authorities, even mandatory in order to rescue another person from certain death, sacrifice of one's life in order to preserve the life of another is forbidden. See R. Jacob Emden, *Migdal Oz, Even ha-Bohen* 1:85, who states that the matter is self-evident; R. Jacob Ettlinger, *Teshuvot Binyan Tziyyon*, no. 165; R. Yitzchak Ya'akov Weisz, *Teshuvot Minhat Yitzhak*, V, no. 8, addendum; and R. Moshe Feinstein, *Iggerot Mosheh, Yoreh De'ah*, 11, no. 174, *anaf* 4. Nevertheless, R. Jacob Emden, *loc. cit.*, suggests that a parent may sacrifice his life in order to preserve a child from certain death. Although *Migdal Oz* does not advance this consideration, if parent and child constitute a single person, such an exception is readily fathomed. Cf. also, R. Shlomoh Kluger, *Imrei Shefer, Parashat Kedoshim*, sec. 14, who expresses a similar concept in a different context.

identity as a member of a particular species. But, as will be shown, species identity is a direct consequence of intergenerational personal identity.

The quest for a halakhic theory or theories of identity begins with an analysis of a talmudic statement presented in *Hullin* 62b and *Niddah* 50b:

> Rav Papa said: The *tarnegola de-agma* is forbidden; the *tarnegolta de-agma* is permitted. Your sign [to remember which is forbidden and which permitted is] "An Ammonite but not an Ammonitess." Meremar expounded: The *tranegolta de-agma* is forbidden: We see that it stomps [its prey] and eats it; it is the [forbidden] *giruta*.[14]

Despite the attempts of translators and scholars to identify the species that are the subject of this talmudic discussion there is no halakhically acceptable manner of determining the species to which reference is made. The fact that the classic talmudic commentators disagree with regard to the meaning of Rav Papa's statement only underscores our inability to identify any ornithological species named in the Pentateuch or in rabbinic literature other than on the basis of received tradition.

A literal reading of the text would seem to indicate that there is some species of *tarnegol* indigenous to the *agma*[15] and that the male of that species is forbidden while the female is permitted. That is certainly the impression conveyed by the use of the masculine "*tarnegol*" in juxtaposition to the feminine form "*tarnegolta*" as well as by the mnemonic supplied. *Tosafot, Hullin* 62b, regard such a literal reading to be halakhically absurd since all members of every kosher species, male as well as female, are permitted. Or, as declared in the talmudic principle quoted by *Tosafot*: "*Kol ha-yotzei min ha-tahor tahor*—All that emerges from the pure is pure." Accordingly, *Tosafot* hasten to explain that the two terms do not denote the male and female of a single species but

---

14. The Soncino translation renders "*giruta*" as "parrot." Jastrow more cautiously defines the term as "moor-hen" or "hen of the marshes."

15. The term "*agma*" or "*agamma*" is ambiguous and may denote either an uncleared field, a meadow, a marsh, stagnant water or a lake. Thus, the Soncino translation renders "*tarnegol de-agma*" as "moor-cock" and "*tarnegolta de-agma*" as "moor-hen" while Jastrow translates the latter term as "moor-hen" and as "hen of the marshes."

are the names of two distinct species, one of which is kosher and the other non-kosher. *Tosafot, Ḥullin* 62b, peremptorily dismiss any other possible interpretation of the text. It follows, of course, that, according to this analysis, in each of those species both the male and female are either kosher or non-kosher.

However, both Rashi and one opinion cited by *Tosafot* in their commentary on *Niddah* 50b understand the Gemara's distinction quite literally: the male of the species to which reference is made is forbidden whereas the female is permitted. The male is forbidden because it lacks the criteria of a kosher bird. In resolving the obvious problem posed by the dictum "All that emerges from the pure is pure," which would render the bird permissible regardless of its physical criteria, *Tosafot, Ḥullin* 62b, state that birds do not give birth to young directly; rather, they lay eggs and the gestating embryos are nurtured by putrid matter within the eggs. That putrid matter is categorized by the Gemara as having the status of "dust." Thus, since the hatchling is produced by "dust" rather than from a living creature, there is no continuity of identity between the bird and its young.

The principle cited by *Tosafot* is formulated by the Mishnah, *Bekhorot* 5b:

> . . .a clean animal that gives birth to an unclean animal [the offspring] is permitted to be eaten; an unclean animal that gives birth to a clean animal [the offspring] may not be eaten, for that which emerges from the impure is impure and that which emerges from the pure is pure.

Tosafot's statement asserting that the principle of *yotzei* does not apply to birds hatched from eggs is an application of the principle formulated by the Gemara, *Temurah* 31a, in explaining that a bird born of an egg laid by a *terefah* is permitted because the fledgling develops only when the egg becomes putrid "and upon its becoming putrid it is mere dust." The notion "*me-afra ka-gadil*—it grows from dust" is employed by *Tosafot* to explain why the female fledgling is permitted even though its male progenitor is non-kosher. *Me-afra ka-gadil* serves to establish that the principle of *yotzei* is rendered inapplicable by virtue of the destruction of the non-kosher source and its replacement by innocuous "dust." But, then, if it is "dust" that generates the new bird, why should that bird be non-kosher even if it is endowed with the characteristics of a non-kosher species? Since it is generated by "dust" which is "pure" its status should be that of a creature that "emerges from the pure" and hence it should be kosher as well. Indeed, the concept *"me-afra ka-gadil"* should be applied to all birds, including the perfectly usual cases in which both parent birds are non-kosher, and should yield the result that all their progeny are kosher since they are the product of putrid dust that is halakhically "clean": It is precisely for that reason that a bird born of an egg laid by a *terefah* is permitted. The Gemara, it should be remembered, justifies that ruling by declaring that the embryo does not begin to develop until the egg has already become putrid and hence the embryo must be regarded as having developed from "mere dust."

Rambam, *Hilkhot Ma'akhalot Assurot* 3:11, seems to be aware of this difficulty. Rambam ignores the rationale advanced by the Gemara and rules that a fledgling born of the egg of a *terefah* is permitted, not because it is generated by "dust," but because "there is no unclean [bird] in its species." Ra'avad, in a gloss to Rambam's ruling, takes Rambam to task for substituting his rationale for that of the Gemara but fails to address the underlying difficulty, *viz.*, that the same rationale should logically render all the young of unclean species permissible.

Rashi's position is further complicated by a view expressed in his comments on *Ḥullin* 9a, s.v. *alma.* The Gemara cites the statement of the Mishnah, *Nazir* 49b, declaring that a Nazarite becomes defiled through contact with "a corpse and with an olive-size [piece] of a corpse." The Gemara objects that if a Nazarite is defiled by an olive-size portion of a corpse, *a fortiori*, the Nazarite must be defiled through contact with an entire corpse and hence the initial mention of "a corpse" is superfluous. The Gemara responds by pointing to the reality of the existence of a corpse whose size in its entirety is less than the size of an olive, *viz.*, "an abortus whose limbs were not yet bound together by sinews." Having established that a human embryo can have the status of a corpse even before sinews have developed, the Gemara then deduces that, with regard to animals, the prohibition attendant upon eating the meat of consecrated animals may devolve upon the embryo before the advent of an independent prohibition against eating the sciatic sinew. In context, the Gemara is struggling with the issue of whether a second prohibition can attach itself to an already prohibited entity. *Tosafot* explain the Gemara's deduction as based upon the presumption that the sciatic sinew develops as a unique structure from already existing undifferentiated tissue. Thus, the tissue that becomes the sciatic sinew was already prohibited as sanctified meat. Rashi, however, comments that the embryo "is sanctified from the moment of creation [when] the sinew was not yet created."

Quite cogently, *Tosafot* apparently assume that the principle of *yotzei* assures that tissue "emerging" from already existing tissue has the halakhic status of the tissue from which it is produced. Rashi, in emphasizing that the sinew "was not yet created," seemingly assumes that the principle of *yotzei* is applicable even with regard to tissue that is generated *de novo* and compounds that difficulty by assuming that the chronologically prior prohibited status of the original tissue is also somehow immanent in as yet non-existent tissue as well.[16]

---

16. Immortality of the soul does not pose a serious problem for most theories of identity. Assuming that the soul has memories of terrestrial events experienced while incarnate it is readily understandable that the continuum of identity survives death. If the notion of spatio-temporal contiguity is crucial to an understanding of personal identity it must be amended to include a notion of meta-spatial and meta-temporal continuity.

Bodily resurrection presents a more formidable problem. In what sense can the physically restored body be deemed identical to the body earlier reduced to the dust? This problem has been raised by at least one philosopher, Terence Penelhum, in his essay "Personal Identity, Memory, and Survival," *Journal of Philosophy*, vol. 56, no. 22, pp. 899-903.

From the vantage point of Jewish tradition, one might dismiss the issue as lacking in theological import. Personal identity in bodily resurrection must, in any event, be understood as identity of the soul. Whether the body is the "same" or different is hardly crucial. It should be sufficient to say that the bodies in both existencies are the physical habitat of the same soul.

Yet, the question does have halakhic ramifications that are at least theoretical in nature. Laws predicated upon man's corporeal nature, e.g., matrimonial provisions and property rights, presume personal identity. The issue then is, if the resurrected body enjoys the same identity as its precursor, are earlier marital bonds reestablished and may the resurrected person reclaim property owned in a previous existence?

Such a result should not follow from either of the theories herein advanced in the explanation of the notion of personal identity. According to Rashi, retention of

There is a yet more perplexing issue with regard to the notion of *yotzei*. As noted earlier, the young of unclean species are non-kosher even if they are born with the physical characteristics of a kosher animal. Rambam, *Hilkhot Ma'akhalot Assurot* 1:5, records the prohibition against eating such an animal with the simple statement that such an animal is "forbidden with regard to eating." The implication is that the prohibition attendant upon the progeny is identical to that associated with the mother and carries the identical punishment of forty lashes.[17] The milk of a non-kosher animal and the eggs of a non-kosher species are similarly forbidden as recorded by the Gemara, *Bekhorot* 6b, with regard to milk and, *Hullin* 69b, with regard to eggs. The principle underlying those prohibitions is the notion of *yotzei*. However, as explicitly codified by Rambam, *Hilkhot Ma'akhalot Assurot* 3:6, although the prohibition is biblical in nature, the punishment of lashes is not administered for partaking of either the milk or the eggs of unclean species.

---

a single identity depends upon a causal nexus manifest in generation and regeneration of the cells of the body. That chain of causal phenomena terminates with death. Accordingly, the resurrected body does not enjoy the same halakhic persona as its predecessor. According to *Tosafot* and Rambam, personal identity is contingent upon a spatio-temporal continuum. It is quite understandable that rules and regulations governing this-worldly institutions are determined by physical, rather than metaphysical, contiguity.

Of course, since the problem is entirely halakhic rather than philosophical, it might be resolved by means of a simple halakhic concept, *viz.*, Halakhah posits death as an event that terminates marriage and extinguishes property rights.

17. See *Pri Megadim, Mishbetzot Zahav* 81:1, who questions why this is so but remarks that "not a single one among the decisors can be found" who rules otherwise. R. Chaim ha-Levi Soloveitchik, *Hiddushei ha-Grah al ha-Rambam, Hilkhot Ma'akhalot Assurot* 3:11, *Me-Ginzei ha-Grah* (Johannesburg, 5749), no. 117 and *Kuntres Ma'atikei Shemu'ah* (Jerusalem, 5756), p. 24 assumes this to be true as a matter of course. See also the numerous sources cited in *Encyclopedia Talmudit*, XXIII (Jerusalem, 5757), 325, notes 591 and 593. Cf., however, *Teshuvot Yad Eliyahu*, no. 2, cited by *Pithei Teshuvah, Yoreh De'ah* 79:2, who expresses doubt with regard to the matter. Cf., the somewhat unclear comments of the *yesh min ha-mefarshim* cited by *Maggid Mishneh, Hilkhot Ma'akhalot Assurot* 3:6.

There are, however, authorities who conflate the two types of *yotzei* and others who for various reasons do not regard the young of an animal to be encompassed within the category of *yotzei*. See *Encyclopedia Talmudit*, XXIII, 286-87 and 323-37. See also endnote.

Clearly, then, the status of *yotzei*, or the emerging entity, is not entirely identical to that from which it arises. Nevertheless, the young of the species have precisely the same status as their progenitors. Also, an adult pig, for example, possesses far greater mass than a newly-born piglet. The additional meat was not present at birth but was produced from tissue existent at birth. Logically, such additional tissue should be in the category of *yotzei*. Yet, it is abundantly clear that, unlike consumption of meat or eggs, partaking of an olive-size piece of meat derived from any portion of the animal engenders the statutory punishment of forty stripes.

Although they are closely related, the concept of *yotzei* clearly has two different facets: 1) a literal notion of *yotzei* predicated upon a causal nexus between the source and the effect, e.g., milk or eggs produced by a prohibited animal; and 2) *yotzei* in the descriptive sense which serves to transpose identity and halakhic status as a member of a particular species. The notion of identification as a member of a species is best summed up in a pithy comment attributed to R. Chaim Soloveitchik. It is reported that R. Chaim queried: Why is a horse a horse? Is it a horse because it is a horse or is it a horse because its mother was a horse? To rephrase the question: Is a horse a horse because it manifests the characteristics that are the necessary conditions for identification as a member of the equine species or is a horse a horse because its mother was a horse? R. Chaim proceeded to declare that a horse is a horse solely because its mother was a horse and explained that ancestral identity is the sole factor that determines membership in a particular species. Thus, as spelled out by the Mishnah, *Bekhorot* 5b, identity as a member of a clean or unclean species is determined by birth and not by distinguishing physical characteristics. Accordingly, a colt is a horse because its mother's persona is transposed to her young. Of course, the mother is the proximate cause of the existence of her offspring; however, the identity of the young is not rooted simply in the causative factor but in the accompanying transfer of identity. R. Chaim, *Ḥiddushei ha-Graḥ al ha-Rambam, Hilkhot Ma'akhalot Assurot* 3:11, as well as *Me-Ginzei ha-Graḥ* (Johannesburg, 5749), no. 117 and *Kuntres Ma'atikei Shemu'ah* (Jerusalem, 5756), p. 24, describes that form of *yotzei* as giving rise to the halakhic status of that which "emerges" as a status *mi-tzad atzmo*, i.e., a status intrinsic to its identity.[18] Quite obviously, then, since the offspring shares the identity of its progenitors, whatever prohibition is attendant upon partaking of the flesh of the mother is also attendant upon partaking of the flesh of the young.[19] The same principle applies with regard to added weight put on by an animal as it grows into adulthood. The young have the status and identity of the progenitors; *a fortiori*, naturally added tissue also has the status and identity of the entity to which it adheres.

R. Elchanan Wasserman remarks several times in his writings that, although the concept of *yotzei* is usually formulated with regard to the status of food products, it does not constitute a novel rule limited to determining the permitted or prohibited nature of a foodstuff for purposes of the dietary code. Rather, asserts R. Elchanan, anything that is emitted by, or proceeds from, a particular entity has the status of the entity that produced it.

In his *Kovetz Shi'urim, Pesaḥim*, sec. 120, R. Elchanan demonstrates the operation of the principle of *yotzei* with regard to the progeny of animals with whom humans have engaged in acts of bestiality. Any animal, male or female, that has participated in an act of that nature may not be offered as a sacrifice. R. Elchanan demonstrates that, at least in the case of the young born of two animals each of which has engaged in an act of that nature, their progeny may also not be utilized for sacrificial purposes. To be sure, offspring conceived subsequent to such acts has not been employed for immoral purposes; nevertheless, the status of such a newborn animal is that of an animal that has engaged in an act of that nature because it has "emerged" from an animal having that status.

In a separate discussion in his *Kovetz Inyanim, Ḥullin* 17a, R. Elchanan examines the status of milk. The Gemara, *Bekhorot* 6a, finds it necessary to adduce a biblical verse in demonstrating that the milk of a kosher species is permissible. Absent specific license, the milk produced by a living animal would have the status of an entity that "emerges" from an organ of a living animal. A limb or organ torn from a living animal is prohibited and hence the *yotzei* of such an organ is also forbidden.

---

18. Cf., however, R. Yitzchak Ze'ev Soloveitchik, *Ma'atikei Shemu'ah*, 11 (Bnei Brak, 5753), 106.

19. See endnote.

However, at least according to one opinion recorded in the Gemara, *Ḥullin* 103a, a living animal is not viewed as a mere aggregate of limbs and organs (*behemah be-ḥayyehah lav le-evarim omedet*). Hence the milk it yields is not the *yotzei* of "a limb [severed] from a living animal." Why, then, should specific dispensation be required to permit the drinking of milk? R. Elchanan explains that, although no prohibition is attendant upon a non-dismembered living animal, anything that emerges from the animal is endowed with the status of that animal. R. Elchanan explains, in effect, that the "torn" status of a limb is an "accident" that is imposed upon a limb that is integral to a living animal. Milk yielded by a cow has the same essential status as the cow but is different with regard to one crucial accident, *viz.*, it is "torn" or separated from the cow; upon milking, it becomes separated from the cow. Since the milk "emerges" from the cow it, too, has the status of a separated, and hence ostensibly forbidden, organ of the cow. Accordingly, biblical dispensation is required to render the milk permissible.

The concept of *yotzei* as reflected in these halakhic provisions is rooted in the notion that a cause remains present, either physically or metaphysically, in its effect. The notion is also reflected in the principle "*Yesh shevaḥ etzim be-pat*—The enhancement of firewood is [present] in the bread." No benefit may be derived from artifacts that have been used as objects of idolatry. Thus, for example, a deified piece of wood may not be utilized as firewood. The rule forbidding benefiting from objects of idolatry extends to bread baked by use of such firewood as fuel despite the fact that the wood has been destroyed in the process of burning and is no longer in existence. The prohibited status of the bread reflects the notion that the wood, although destroyed, remains in existence in the bread which is enhanced by its presence. Put somewhat differently, the wood is the cause and remains in existence in its effect, *viz.*, the bread.

Consequently, it is quite understandable that when multiple causes contribute to a single effect the rule does not apply. On the contrary, the applicable principle is that *zeh va-zeh gorem*, i.e., when two causes combine to yield a particular effect, the resultant entity is untainted by prohibition. Thus, for example, if forbidden wood is combined with permissible wood to provide fuel for baking bread, the bread is permitted. Rabbenu Nissim, *Avodah Zarah* 48b, goes so far as to describe this rule as an application of the notion of *bittul* or nullification, i.e., the prohibited cause is not present in the effect because it has been submerged in, or overwhelmed by, the parallel innocuous cause. In any event, whether or not the principle relies upon *bittul* it is clear that, where there are multiple causes, Halakhah does not recognize any single cause as identifiably present in the result.

2. Identity as a Member of a Species

The notion of identity as a member of a species, however, is not simply an application of the causal notion of *yotzei*. As noted earlier, the milk and eggs of non-kosher species are prohibited but the attendant prohibition is less severe than the prohibition attendant upon consumption of the meat of those species. Partaking of the meat of a colt or a piglet entails precisely the same prohibition and punishment as consuming the flesh of the mare or the sow. The prohibition upon the young of the species flows, not from its nature as a derivative or effect of a prohibited cause, but from a concept of identity transfer: The young is not simply the product of its progenitor but the continuum of the same persona. The young succeeds to the identity of its progenitor in the same manner as an adult animal of massive weight retains in every ounce of its body the identity it acquired at birth or earlier.

The notion of identity as a member of a species certainly applies only to a living entity in contradistinction to physical byproducts such as milk or eggs. But physical characteristics, even those regarded as species-distinctive such as split hooves or ruminant stomachs, are regarded as accidents—in the philosophical sense of the term—having no bearing upon determination of species identity. Accordingly, if a cow gives birth to progeny having all phenomenological characteristics of a pig such an animal is endowed with the halakhic status of a cow in every sense.

The most obvious explanation of this halakhic principle is that it reflects a spatio-temporal notion of an individual identity that is extended to identity as a member of a species. Individual identity is retained from the neonatal state through senescence and beyond by reason of spatio-temporal contiguity. That identity is also transmitted to progeny as is the literal meaning of "In place of your fathers shall be your sons." Thus, identity as a member of a species is simply a concomitant of personal identity.

Species identity is one aspect of personal identity and hence is a factor of personal identity passed on by means of a generational continuum.

The phenomenon of spatio-temporal contiguity is most obvious in the maternal-filial relationship since it is clearly manifest in the process of gestational development. The fetus is readily perceived as quite literally developing as part of the mother's body until physically separated in parturition. Transmission of paternal identity is a bit more complex. Identity as a member of a specific tribe and, as noted, the concept of representation in the operation of certain types of inheritance is predicated upon paternal identity and presumably reflects the spatial-temporal contiguity effected through seminal emission and fusion of the sperm with the ovum.[20]

Nevertheless, a fundamental controversy is recorded in the Gemara, *Ḥullin* 79a, with regard to whether or not paternal identity is transmitted to progeny in the animal kingdom. Consumption of *ḥelev*, i.e., certain fatty tissue located primarily, but not exclusively, in the hindquarters of an animal classified as a *behemah*, is prohibited; consumption of the same tissue of an animal classified as a *ḥayyah* is permitted. The commandment requiring covering with earth of a portion of the blood flowing from the slaughterer's incision is limited to the blood of birds and of any species categorized as a *ḥayyah*; the blood of an animal categorized as a *behemah* need not be covered by earth. Regardless of the status of the sire of the progeny, the status of a mother is transmitted to her young with regard to both the prohibition against consumption of *ḥelev* and the requirement for covering the blood of the slaughtered animal. The status of the offspring of a male *ḥayyah* and a female *behemah*

---

20. Nevertheless, the identity and status of a non-Jewish male who consorts with a Jewess is not passed on to the offspring of that union. The talmudic formulation of the concept underlying that principle is expressed by the Gemara, *Yevamot* 98a, as "*afkereih Raḥamana le-zareih*—God rendered his semen *res nullius*." That concept should be understood as expressing the notion that identity can be destroyed by "confiscation" of the semen thereby depriving the conceptus of paternal identity. Lacking the identity of the progenitor, the semen cannot transmit that identity to resultant offspring. Similarly, the identity of a child born to a non-Jewish woman and a Jewish father does not share in the identity or status of the father. The Gemara, *Kiddushin* 68b, bases that rule upon Deuteronomy 7:4 which is understood as declaring that "your son born of a gentile woman is not your son but her son."

or of a male *behemah* and a female *hayyah* both with regard to the prohibition against partaking of *helev* and with regard to the requirement for covering the blood is that of the mother. For these purposes transmission of maternal identity, in and of itself, is sufficient. The controversy in *Hullin* 79a is with regard to whether or not "one must [also] take account of the seed of the father" (*hosheshin le-zera ha-av*), i.e., is transferal of identity limited to transferal of maternal identity or is paternal identity transferred as well. If paternal identity is also transferred, the *helev* of the progeny of a male *behemah* is also prohibited and the blood of a male *hayyah* must also be covered.

> If the issue is that of spatial-temporal contiguity, the identical issue should arise not only with regard to identity as a member of a species but with regard to personal identity as well. And indeed it does. According to biblical law, a foal delivered after the mother has been slaughtered need not itself be slaughtered. Although slaughter of such an animal is rabbinically required, biblical law regards the act of slaughter performed upon the mother to be efficacious for its fetus as well. Moreover, if two animals delivered post-slaughter mate, their progeny are similarly exempt from slaughter. In effect, the "slaughtered" status of the progenitor is transmitted to the offspring.

Problematic, however, is the case of a foal delivered post-mortem that mates with a conventionally born animal. If the offspring shares only the persona of the mother it must be deemed to be "slaughtered." But if it also shares the persona of the father then part of its persona is "unslaughtered." If so, the animal is partially "slaughtered" and partially "unslaughtered." The rule is that an act of slaughter that is interrupted cannot be completed at a subsequent time.[21] Hence, the foal delivered post-mortem to a slaughtered mother that mates with a conventional animal, if regarded as partially unslaughtered, can never be rendered kosher.

---

21. *Shehiyah* or "interruption" is one of the five enumerated impediments to valid slaughter as transmitted orally to Moses at Sinai. See *Hullin* 28a.

3. Rambam and Tosafot: *Identity as a Product of Spatio-Temporal Contiguity*

Although the principle of *yotzei* is accepted by all, the principle of *ḥosheshin le-zera ha-av* is the subject of talmudic controversy. Clearly, then, the principle of *yotzei* is not sufficient to achieve transfer of identity. The consequence of the principle of *yotzei* with regard to the product of a causal nexus is that the cause is deemed to be present in the effect in some manner but that principle does not establish an identity of persona. The latter is the product of a much more circumscribed notion of spatio-temporal contiguity.

The distinction is most evident in Rambam's formulation of the distinction between the status of a bird hatched from the egg of a mother of a non-kosher species and a bird hatched from an egg laid by a *terefah*. The Gemara declares the latter to be kosher because the embryo is developed from "mere dust." Ra'avad criticizes Rambam for ignoring that rationale and substituting his own explanation in stating with regard to the *terefah* "for there is no unclean [bird] in its species."

R. Chaim ha-Levi Soloveitchick, *Ḥiddushei ha-Graḥ al ha-Rambam, Hilkhot Ma'akhalot Assurot* 3:11, astutely observes that Rambam seeks to underscore the distinction between the factor of *yotzei* in establishing halakhic status contingent upon "accidents" and status derived from transmission of identity. *Terefut* is an accident rather than an attribute of essence. Accidents are not integral to identity and, hence, were a single person to be divided, the accident might remain present in one of the divisions but not in the other. Since *terefut* is not an element of identity and since neither the egg laid by a *terefah* nor the hatchling born of the egg is itself a *terefah*, the bird hatched from such an egg cannot have intrinsic status as a *terefah*. Nevertheless, the egg is not kosher, but it is not kosher solely because it is the product, or *yotzei*, of a *terefah*.

However, the status of the egg as a *yotzei* of a *terefah* is not passed on to the hatchling because the hatchling is not the product of the egg but the product of the "dust" produced as the egg becomes rancid. The principle of *yotzei* reflects the ongoing presence of a cause in its effect and results in a forbidden entity only if there is constancy in the prohibited nature of its cause. Putrefaction of the egg destroys its nature as a foodstuff and transforms it into a halakhically innocuous substance.

Thus the hatchling develops from halakhically innocuous "dust." The cause present in the young bird is not the prohibited egg but the resultant "dust." Accordingly, the hatched bird is not regarded as the stigmatized effect of a prohibited *yotzei*.

Rambam assumes that, unlike *yotzei*, species identity, and individual identity upon which species identity is predicated, is not rooted in the existence of a causal nexus. Rather, identity is predicated upon spatio-temporal contiguity. Spatio-temporal contiguity does exist between a female bird that lays an egg and the hatchling that emerges from that egg. It is the "dust," rather than the egg, that is the proximate cause of the hatchling but there is a clear uninterrupted continuum connecting the bird, the egg, the dust and the hatchling. It is that continuum of spatio-temporal contiguity that establishes the identity of the hatched bird.[22]

Rambam's statement declaring that "there is no unclean [bird] in its species" is designed to indicate that *terefut* is a mere accident and hence to explain why the hatchling does not succeed to the status of the mother as an intrinsic *terefah*. The Gemara's statement that the hatchling is the product of "dust" rather than of an edible egg explains only why the lesser prohibition of *yotzei* of a *terefah* is not attendant upon the bird born of an egg laid by a *terefah*.[23]

As noted earlier, *Tosafot, Ḥullin* 62b, posit the *tarnegola de-agma* and the *tarnegolta de-agma* as two separate and distinct species. In doing so *Tosafot* declare that were they a single species, the male would be permissible despite the lack of the physical criteria of a kosher species since it is perforce the progeny of a kosher mother and "the *yotzei* of the pure is pure." In that statement *Tosafot* invoke the notion of *yotzei* as the principle applicable to establishing species identity and clearly assume that transmission of species identity in birds is no different from transmission of species identity in animals despite the fact that birds develop from putrid eggs. Thus *Tosafot*, as well as Rambam, regard identity as a product of spatio-temporal contiguity rather than of a causal nexus.

---

22. Cf., however, the interpretation of Rambam presented by R. Natan Gestetner, *Le-Horot Natan*, VII, no. 58, sec. 8.
23. See the comment of R. Shlomoh Zalman Auerbach, cited by Abraham S. Abraham, *Nishmat Avraham*, III, (Jerusalem, 5751), 217.

4. Rashi: Identity as the Result of Causality

Rashi, *Niddah* 50b, does identify the two birds as members of the same species and understands the Gemara as declaring the male to be permitted. To the challenge that "the *yotzei* of the pure is pure," *Tosafot, ad locum*, respond on behalf of Rashi that birds do not give birth to their young; their young are born of eggs in which the embryo develops from "dust." *Tosafot* clearly imply that, for Rashi, putrefaction of the egg is an impediment to transmission of species identity. In the absence of identity derived from a progenitor, identity is established *sui generis* on the basis of physical criteria and hence the distinction between the male which possesses the characteristics of a non-kosher bird and the female which possesses those of a kosher bird.[24]

Although, as R. Chaim so eloquently phrased it, a horse is a horse because its mother was a horse, the primordial horse did not have a mother. If so, how could any horse be forbidden? Assuredly, the answer is that the prohibition against partaking of equine flesh is predicated upon a prohibition devolving upon a specific horse or group of horses at the time of its promulgation. The Torah refers to a specific horse or class of horses and declares them prohibited. Once prohibited, their progeny are also prohibited by virtue of generational transmission of identity as templates of the original horses. The animals originally banned are identified by means of physical criteria, *viz.*, non-rumination and absence of split hoofs. One may, of course, argue that the horses denoted in this manner are not the animals contemporaneously extant at the time of Revelation at Sinai but the primordial horse that came into existence on the fifth day of creation.

More than a semantic quibble lies in this speculation. Consider the hypothetical phenomenon of a mutation or a series of mutations that occurred some time after creation but before Revelation and yielded a cud-chewing split-hooved colt. Is this animal, and hence also its progeny, kosher or non-kosher?[25] If only non-ruminants possessing cloven

---

24. Cf. the comments of R. Elchanan Wasserman, *Kovetz Shemu'ot, Ḥullin*, sec. 27.
25. Were the barbarusa a pig that mutated into a ruminant after Sinai it would be a kosher animal. See this writer's *Contemporary Halakhic Problems*, iii (New York, 1989), 66-77.

hooves alive at the time of Sinaitic Revelation were proscribed the pre-existing mutation would be kosher. However, if God declared at Sinai that the descendants of primordial non-ruminant, cloven-hooved animals are forbidden then the ruminant split-hoof mutation in existence at the time of Revelation was also forbidden.

Noteworthy in this context is Rashi's remark in his commentary on Genesis 7:2. Rashi is puzzled by Noah's distinction between "clean" and "unclean" animals in an epoch in which no animal was, as yet, forbidden. Rashi explains that the appellations "clean" and "unclean" were assigned to animals that were destined to be declared clean and unclean at a future time. A simple, but by no means certain, reading of that comment would indicate that the import of Rashi's remark is that the very animals then depicted as "unclean" were retroactively declared to be members of an unclean species.

The foregoing serves to illuminate *Tosafot's* analysis of Rashi's position. Identity as a member of a particular species is transmitted on the basis of a cause and effect relationship. But when there is no ancestral cause, e.g., when a bird develops from mere "dust," the bird is regarded as *sui generis* insofar as species identity is concerned. The halakhic status of the bird is similar to the primordial bird or the bird extant at the time of Sinai; in effect, the bird becomes the founder and sole member of a species whose species identity is established on the basis of its own physical criteria.

Thus, for Rashi, identity must be defined as a causal concept rather than as a spatio-temporal continuum.[26] In the case of a bird, even

---

26. The notion of identity as a reflection of a causal nexus is perhaps taken to an extreme by R. Zevi Ashkenazi, *Teshuvot Ḥakham Tzevi*, no. 93, who suggests that a *golem* created by a Jew is to be regarded not only as a human being but as having the status of a Jew as well by virtue of the fact that it was created by a Jew for "the works of the righteous are their progeny." Such a conclusion certainly cannot be entertained if identity is the result of a spatio-temporal continuum. If personal and species identity is understood on the basis of a causal nexus in which the cause is transposed and becomes immanent in its effect, a *golem*, which is a living entity, might well be considered as being endowed with the identity of its human—and Jewish—creator.

It is not necessary to dwell upon the point that Ḥakham Tzevi's line of reasoning provides insight into the concept of the immanence of the divine nature within man as simply one aspect of the notion that every cause is present in its effect.

though the "dust" is the material successor of the mother, the mother is not present in the "dust" in an essential sense since the mother's essential nature has been destroyed.[27] In explaining Rashi's position, *Tosafot* regard the concept of *yotzei* governing the permissibility or impermissibility of "emitted" products such as milk and eggs and the concept of *yotzei* governing transmission of species identity as one and the same. The sole difference is that, although the principle of *yotzei* applies to any "emission," the identity of a living organism can be transmitted only to another living organism which then is, in effect, a template of the first.[28]

5. The Halakhic Ramifications of the Controversy

Let us consider the entirely hypothetical possibility of an egg laid by a non-kosher bird from which an embryo develops and emerges manifesting a phenotype typical of members of a kosher species. Application of the rule "that which emerges from the impure is impure" would lead to the conclusion that such a hatchling is not kosher. That principle, however, is formulated explicitly by the Mishnah only with regard to mammals. Its applicability to avian species is not addressed in any talmudic text.

Birds "emerge" from the body of mother birds through the intermediacy of eggs that have become putrid; as a result the fledgling is regarded by Halakhah as having risen from "mere dust." Nevertheless,

---

27. For Rashi it is no accident that the aggadic report recorded in *Yalkut Shim'oni*, Job 29:18, regarding a bird that is periodically consumed in a conflagration only to be rejuvenated subsequently differs from the Phoenix myth in one salient detail: the Midrash describes the bird as restored from one remaining egg-size bit of tissue; the Phoenix arises entirely from ashes. Cf., Amos Hakham, *Da'at Mikra*, Job 28:18, note 21. According to Rashi, the bird's identity would be lost were it to arise from ashes; its identity is preserved by virtue of the residual glob of tissue from which it is revivified.

28. Indeed, *Tosafot, ad locum*, contrast the two aspects of *yotzei* by questioning why it is, according to the opinion that *zeh va-zeh gorem* is forbidden, that the female (despite possession of kosher characteristics) is not forbidden by virtue of the fact that the father was non-kosher. In posing the question, *Tosafot* are asking simply why the father's status as a cause is ignored. *Tosafot* respond by noting that the male's contribution is also rendered nugatory by virtue of the putrefaction of the egg, i.e., putrefaction negates the prohibited nature of any and all causes.

the normal-looking progeny of a non-kosher avian mother are certainly forbidden. As explained earlier, according to Rambam and *Tosafot, Ḥullin* 52b, identification as a member of a particular species is determined not by physical characteristics, but by spacio-temporal contiguity. If so, a chicken hatched from the egg of an eagle, regardless of its physical characteristics, would have the halakhic status of an eagle. Conversely, an eaglet, hatched from the egg of a chicken would enjoy the status of the hen that laid the egg and would be kosher. If so, the principle formulated by the Mishnah in *Bekhorot* is also applicable to avian species.

Not so according to Rashi. As explained earlier, according to Rashi as elucidated by *Tosafot, Niddah* 50b, the young of a species do not acquire the species identity of the mother on the basis of spacio-temporal contiguity, but on the basis of the causal nexus between them coupled with the notion that a cause remains present in its effect. In birds the causal nexus is severed by virtue of the fact that the egg becomes putrid and turns into "mere dust" and it is the dust that is the cause of the generation of the developing embryo. Since the hatchling's progenitor is "mere dust," it does not acquire the status of its mother by virtue of a causal connection between them but is accorded the status of the primordial member of the species simply on the basis of its physical characteristics.[29] If so, in normal situations, a duckling emerging from an egg laid by a duck is kosher solely by virtue of its physical characteristics.[30] Unlike the rule posited with regard to mammals, the rule applicable to

---

29. Cf., *Ḥazon Ish, Yoreh De'ah* 14(a):12. *Ḥazon Ish* formulates a novel thesis explaining how the male of the species to which the Gemara, *Ḥullin* 62b, refers may be pure and the female impure. He regards the male and female eggs as constituting separate and distinct species. *Ḥazon Ish* describes the egg in which the male gestates as impure "from the six days of creation" and, conversely, the egg from which the female develops as pure "from the six days of creation." See also *Ḥazon Ish, Yoreh De'ah* 13:11.

30. Identification of the particular physical characteristics that define any specific avian species is beyond the scope of this enterprise. Suffice it to say: 1) Only the specified impure species are prohibited. Hence, the characteristics of the twenty-four non-kosher species enumerated by Scripture need be identified; all other species are kosher. 2) The physical characteristics enumerated by the Sages as associated with non-kosher species and recorded in *Shulḥan Arukh, Yoreh De'ah* 86:1, e.g., the bird feeds by means of *derasah*, may be necessary physical attributes of those species but do not necessarily exhaust the physical characteristics that define a phenotype.

birds would be "If it quacks like a duck and waddles like a duck, it is a duck." Conversely, an eaglet that emerges from the egg of a duck is non-kosher because it exhibits the physical characteristics of an eagle. *Ba'al Halakhot Gedolot*, as cited and endorsed by Ramban, *Bekhorot* 6b, declares that a bird having the characteristics of a non-kosher species that hatches from an egg laid by a kosher species is non-kosher.[31] *Bet Me'ir, Yoreh De'ah* 86 and *Imrei Binah, Hilkhot Terefot*, no. 11, assert that this is also the view of Ran, *Ḥullin* 64b.[32] The hatchling, then, is, in effect, regarded by these authorities as arising *sui generis* with a status identical to that of its primordial progenitor. Hence, according to Rashi, in the opposite case of a duck hatched from an egg laid by an eagle, the duck would be regarded as kosher while an eaglet hatched from the egg of a duck would be non-kosher. *Or Zaru'a, Hilkhot Terefot*, no. 436, apparently espouses Rashi's view in maintaining that a forbidden bird is not prohibited because its progenitor was a member of an impure species. *Or Zaru'a* declares, "An impure bird is forbidden even though it develops from dust because such is the decree of the King."

Aristotle has been paraphrased as declaring, "Metaphysics is the most divine of all sciences because it is the least practical."[33] And, indeed, for students of philosophy, adjudication between diverse theories of identity is of scant practical consequence. For students of Halakhah, however, that investigation is divine in the most literal sense of the term: It contributes to a deeper understanding of divine mysteries encoded and revealed in Halakhah.

They may merely be indicators or "markers" of membership in an impure species but irrelevant when other physical characteristics of a known impure species are clearly manifest.

31. See R. Natan Gestetner, *Le-Horot Natan*, VII, no. 58.
32. Ran is understood differently by *Pri Ḥadash, Yoreh De'ah* 86:18.
33. Cf., *Metaphysics*, 973a.

ENDNOTE

The principle that species identity is determined on the basis of parentage is contradicted by a literal reading of several midrashic sources declaring that the pig will one day be a permitted animal because it will become a ruminant. The published version of *Va-Yikra Rabbah* 13:5 reads:

> The swine is an allusion to Edom [Rome]; "Which does not do *gerah*," i.e., which will not bring in its train (*garar*) another empire to follow it. And why is the last-named called "*ḥazir*" [i.e., swine or boar] — Because it will yet restore (*ḥazar*) the crown to its [rightful] owner. This is indicated by what is written, "And saviors shall come up on Mount Zion to judge the mount of Esau; and the kingdom shall be the Lord's" (Obadiah 1:21).

A variant version of that text reads: "Why is it called '*ḥazir*?' Because it will be restored to Israel in the eschatological era." Various versions of the text are cited by Ritva, *Kiddushin* 49b; R. David ibn Zimra, *Teshuvot Radvaz*, II, no. 828; Recanti, Leviticus 23:2 on the basis of *Midrash Tanḥuma* [see *Midrash Tanḥuma*, ed. R. Chanoch Zundel (Jerusalem, 5720), *Parashat Shemini*, sec. 7 and *Midrash Tanḥuma*, ed. Solomon Buber, *Parashat Shemini*, sec. 12, note 75]; R. Isaac Abarbanel, *Rosh Amanah* chap. 3; R. Jacob Emden, commentary on *Perek Shirah*, chap 4; and R. Moses Sofer, *Torat Mosheh*, *Parashat Re'eh*.

A similar statement appears in *Midrash Shoḥar Tov*, no. 146:4: "'God loosest the bound (*matir assurim*)' What is the meaning of '*matir assurim*?' Some say that every animal that is unclean in the present era the Holy One, blessed be He, will purify in the world-to-come." For an entirely different midrashic statement with an even broader connotation regarding abrogation of halakhic prohibitions see *Va-Yikra Rabbah* 13:3 and its reconciliation with halakhic norms by R. Moses Sofer, *Teshuvot Ḥatam Sofer, Yoreh De'ah*, no. 19.

The obvious halakhic implication of these statements is drawn by Rema of Panu, *Ma'amar Ḥakor Din*, II, chap. 17, and R. Chaim ben Attar, *Or ha-Ḥayyim*, Leviticus 11:7. In his comment on the phrase "*vehu gerah lo yigar*" – and it does not chew its cud," *Or ha-Ḥayyim* states: "This constitutes a condition — so long as it does not chew [it is forbidden] but in the eschatological era it will chew its cud and return to a permitted state; not that it will remain without a cud, for the Torah does not change."

These versions of the midrashic text are dismissed by R. Isaac Abarbanel, *Yeshu'ot Malko, ha-iyyun ha-revi'i,* chap. 3, as unauthoritative and possibly an intentional forgery on the part of a Christian polemicist. See also *Midrash Shoḥar Tov,* ed. Solomon Buber, no. 146, note 4. Earlier, Rabbenu Bahya, *Commentary on the Bible,* Leviticus 11:7, reported that "the multitude" understand the Midrash as declaring that the pig will one day become a permitted animal. Rabbenu Bahya himself, however, rigorously dismissed that contention.

The problem posed by the popular reading of the Midrash is that even if the swine, either miraculously or by means of genetic evolution, were to become a ruminant it would nevertheless retain the status of a pig and remain forbidden on the basis of the principle of *yotzei.* That problem is raised by R. Joseph Patzanovsky, *Pardes Yosef,* Leviticus 11:7. *Pardes Yosef* notes that, as recorded by Rambam, *Hilkhot Ma'akhalot Assurot* 2:3, and *Shakh, Yoreh De'ah* 79:4, the prohibited status of *yotzei,* e.g., milk of a forbidden animal, is not identical to the prohibited status concerning the forbidden animal that is its source. Prohibited species are expressly forbidden by Scripture; the prohibition against *yotzei* is derived exegetically and its violation carries a less severe punishment than violation of the commandment against eating the flesh of the animal itself. Accordingly, *Pardes Yosef* suggests that, although the *yotzei* of a proscribed animal is indeed forbidden, the *yotzei* of a *yotzei* may be entirely permissible. If so, he argues, although an animal born to a non-kosher mother that manifests the physical criteria indicative of a kosher species is forbidden as *yotzei,* the next generation, i.e., the progeny of the animal prohibited only as a *yotzei,* are entirely permissible. Nevertheless, *Pardes Yosef* cites *Pri Megadim, Yoreh De'ah, Mishbetzot Zahav* 81:1 and *Yavin Da'at, Yoreh De'ah* 81:1, who rule that the *yotzei* of *yotzei,* i.e., that which is the product of a forbidden entity, is also forbidden. Thus, declares *Pri Megadim,* the "milk of a cow born of a camel" is forbidden.

According to the herein formulated distinction between *yotzei* as categorization of the status of the product of a forbidden entity and *yotzei* in the sense of identification as a member of a species, progeny of an animal must be regarded as entirely identical to their progenitors with regard to species identification regardless of differences in phenotype. According to that thesis *Pardes Yosef*'s distinction between *yotzei* and *yotzei* of a *yotzei* could not be accepted.

Various interpretations of the popular version of this midrashic statement regarding future permissibility of the animal have been advanced in an endeavor to reconcile its import with the principle that commandments will not be abrogated in the messianic era. The most intriguing is that of *Pardes Yosef, loc cit.* The Gemara, Ḥullin 109b, records that, although the swine is forbidden, there exists a counterpart having an identical taste that is permitted, *viz.*, a fish known as the *"shibuta."* In another reference to the *shibuta* that occurs in the introduction to *Eikhah Rabbah*, the Midrash declares that fish were exiled from the Promised Land together with the people of Israel and upon culmination of the Babylonian exile returned to the Land of Israel together with them. The sole exception was the *shibuta* which did not return from exile but will eventually be restored to its proper habitat in the messianic era. *Pardes Yosef* suggests that the reference to future permissibility of the *ḥazir* is actually not a reference to the swine but to the permitted fish having an identical taste, i.e., the *shibuta*.

Radvaz understands the midrashic statement in a figurative manner as referring to foods that are "fat" and delectable as is the pig. Accordingly, Radvaz interprets the Midrash as declaring that during the messianic era those foods will be available in abundance and will be enjoyed "as if" the pig were rendered permissible. Abarbanel, in his *Rosh Amanah*, chap. 13, suggests that the pig may be permitted during the period of reconquest of the Land of Israel just as non-kosher foods, including "sides of swine" were permitted in the days of Joshua during the original war of conquest. See Ḥullin 17a. Recanti interprets the statement as a kabbalisitic reference to the accusing angel Ḥazri'-el who, in the eschatological era, will no longer denounce Israel but become its defender. A rather similar interpretation is advanced by Rabbenu Bahya. For a fuller discussion of the various interpretations of the popular version of these midrashic statements see R. Abraham Israel Rosenthal, *Ke-Motzei Shalal Rav* (Jerusalem, 5760), *Va-Yikra*, pp. 118-120 and R. Matis Blum, *Torah la-Da'at*, VIII (Kew Garden Hills, N.Y., 5769), 44-45.

13

Resurrection and Personal Identity

I.

The notion of preservation of personal identity in face of physical change as well as identity as a member of a particular species was discussed in the previous chapter in an endeavor to elucidate the principles that serve to regulate the *kashrut* status of the offspring of members of kosher and non-kosher species. That discussion demonstrated that, according to Rashi, personal identity is the product of a cause and effect relationship. Change certainly does occur in the course of human development and maturation but, were there no baby, there would be no adolescent; were there no adolescent there would be no adult. The baby, in a very significant sense, is the cause of the adolescent and the adolescent is the cause of the adult. That causal nexus gives rise both to personal identity and to identity as a member of a species because, despite any physical change that may occur, the cause is always present in its effect. Accordingly, the mother is present in her offspring and hence the offspring shares in the species identity of its progenitor.

The Gemara, *Temurah* 31a, declares that in the course of gestation the fertilized egg becomes putrid with the result that the hatchling that is produced arises from mere dust *("me-afra ka gadil")*. According to Rashi, in birds, with decomposition of the egg and its reduction into dust, the causal nexus between the mother bird and its young is broken. It is "dust" rather than the mother that gives rise to the nascent bird. Accordingly, the status of every newly-born fledgling is that of a primordial bird and its species identity is determined by physical characteristics rather than by the identity of its progenitor.

Rambam, it was contended, maintains that, despite ongoing change, personal identity as well as identity as a member of a particular species is an epiphenomenon of spatio-temporal contiguity. Hence, although the egg degenerates and becomes "dust," the resultant dust is also part of the continuum of mother bird to egg, egg to dust and dust to hatchling. "Dust" is part of that spatio-temporal continuum and hence the fledging is endowed with the same species identity enjoyed by its mother.

Neither theory serves to explain why, or in what sense, upon resurrection of the dead, the reconstituted body should in all circumstances be regarded as the same person who died years or centuries earlier. According to the thesis ascribed to Rashi, sexual reproduction is certainly a causal phenomenon. The progenitor is the cause of the offspring and is present in the effect. Causality in the physical universe is a natural phenomenon. Natural processes deploy themselves in a manner such that the causal nature of the nexus is readily apprehended. Resurrection, on the other hand, is entirely miraculous, and, as such, involves no element of physical causality. God is the sole cause of that phenomenon. He may choose to use the residual substance of an earlier existing person as the material from which the resurrected individual will be formed but, since He is the sole and complete author of that process, continuity of identity between the deceased and the resurrected person cannot be established on the basis of a causal relationship between the two bodies. In no sense is the original body even a contributing cause of the existence of the resurrected body. In no way is the role of the original body comparable to that of the adolescent who, as the cause of the adult, remains present in the adult.

According to Rambam, it was argued, identity is associated with the phenomenon of spatio-temporal contiguity. That which occupies contiguous points in space during the course of successive moments of time is a single entity endowed with a single identity. Ostensively, then, resurrection poses no problem: a person dies; the corpse is interred and turns into dust; at the time of resurrection, the dust is reassembled and reconstituted as a living person. The material substance of the original body and of the newly-resurrected body is one and the same. The substance occupies contiguous points in space during the course of its journey from deathbed to grave to site of resurrection.

However, what of the body that is not buried but is consumed by fire and vaporized leaving no residual substance? There can be no question that those consigned to crematoria during the Holocaust were not thereby deprived of an opportunity for resurrection.[1]

The problem is hardly novel. It was first raised by R. Saadia Ga'on in his *Book of Beliefs and Opinions*, Treatise VII, chap. 7,[2] Saadia poses the question in a highly complex form:

> But suppose a lion were to eat a man, and then the lion would drown and a fish would eat him up, and then the fish would be caught and a man would eat him, and then the man would be burned and turn into ashes. Whence would the Creator restore the first man? Would He do it from the lion or the fish or the second man or the fire or the ashes?

Saadia presents a scientifically sophisticated response. He propounds a thesis that today would be described as the notion of conservation of matter. According to Saadia, matter can be converted to other forms of matter but cannot be destroyed since "it is not conceivable that anyone should have the power to annihilate anything to the point at which it

---

1. Folk wisdom has it that Judaism abjures cremation because of its belief that the body must be preserved for resurrection. That notion is simply inaccurate. Cremation is forbidden by virtue of the commandment "for you shall surely bury him" (Deuteronomy 21:23), but not because cremation precludes resurrection. It may be the case that a person who eschews burial in favor of cremation will not merit resurrection but that is so only because such a choice reflects renunciation of a biblical commandment, not because there is no body available for resurrection.

2. All proceeding quotations from R. Saadia Ga'on are from his *Book of Beliefs and Opinions*, Treatise VII, chap. 7.

would vanish completely except its Creator who produced it *ex nihilo*." Fire, declares Saadia, "merely effects a separation of the parts of a thing and a reunion between each part and its original element, causing the dust part to turn into ashes." Vaporization, Saadia would surely have said, is merely the conversion of a solid into a gas but does not signify annihilation of matter. No matter what happens to a corpse "none of the constituent parts ... could have been annihilated; they must all have been set aside, wheresoever they may have been taken up, ... until such time as they are to be restored in their entirety." For Saadia, incineration of a body does not affect spatio-temporal contiguity and hence does not negate that concept as the defining criterion of preservation of identity despite ongoing change.

R. Hasdai ibn Crescas, however, did not find it necessary to resort to a doctrine of conservation of matter in order to account for bodily resurrection. For Crescas, the manner in which the decomposed body will be reconstituted is not at all a problem since it is not necessarily the original body that will be reassigned to the soul at the time of resurrection. In his *Or ha-Shem, ma'amar gimmel, kelal daled*, chap. 4, Crescas writes:

> there is no benefit in those [original] components coming together, and all the more so if it would be necessary to separate them [from other animals]. Rather, divine justice would be manifest in them even if God creates a creation [endowed] with the temperament and characteristics possessed by Reuben, for example, such that "not one hair of his head fall to the ground," ... and were [Reuben's] soul, which is a substance enduring *per se*, to unite with this creation, there is no doubt that this soul and its faculties would use this body, upon its union with it, identically as it had used the body of Reuben.
>
> ...
>
> ... just as there is no special care taken with regard to the clothing that it be from the same components of that in which he was buried, as long as it is in its likeness, as if he were sleeping in his clothing, for in this there is some indication of the individuality of the man, so there is no special care taken concerning the

body, that the components of the elements be those which had been separated from it, as long as they be in the same relation ...

One may restate Crecas' position by saying that the human body is analogous to a suit of clothes. A person wears one suit one day and another suit the next day but the essence of the individual is in no way affected. In an ontological sense, clothes do not make the man. Identity of appearance is preserved when an individual wears different suits of the same measure, style, and color. Similarly, a person is not defined in terms of his body. Therefore, the particular body assigned to an individual upon resurrection is of no more significance to definition of his identity than is the suit he may choose to wear on any given day. If so, spatio-temporal contiguity cannot be the defining factor of personal identity. In what sense, then, can it be said that the individual who died and the individual who had been resurrected are one and the same person?

II.

The question "In what sense can it be said that the individual who died and the individual who has been resurrected are one and the same person?" may well be an example of the fallacy of the compound question. What evidence is there that the two bodies share a single identity?

To the extent that there are philosophical considerations supporting the notion of physical resurrection, those considerations demonstrate that the corpse and the resurrected body must share a common identity. As cited by R. Joseph Albo, *Sefer ha-Ikkarim*, Book IV, chap. 30, the 13th-century rabbinic scholar R. Aaron ha-Levi maintained that reward and punishment must be experienced both by the body and the soul. R. Aaron ha-Levi maintained that the soul itself is "incomplete" and requires a body for its perfection. Accordingly, divine justice requires resurrection of the body so that it may be accorded reward for its physical participation in the service of the Deity. It would stand to reason that, according to R. Aaron ha-Levi, in order to satisfy that notion of divine justice, the resurrected body would have to be identical in its material substance to the body that earned the reward.[3]

---

3. Albo, *Sefer ha-Ikkarim*, Book 4, chap. 35, counters that view with the argument that

Crescas, *Or ha-Shem*, Third Treatise, First Section, Part 3, chap. 3, makes much the same point in asserting that, since man, in either serving God or rebelling against Him, does so as an entity in which body and soul are conjoined, it is proper that both should participate in the reward. Resurrection, for Crescas, is designed to provide for reward in that guise.[4]

In Part 4, chap. 4, Crescas asserts that, upon resurrection, the reconstituted body need not consist of the body's original components and indeed "there is no advantage in those [original components] coming together." Divine justice requires only that a body endowed with the same temperament and characteristics be created. Crescas' thesis concerning the notion of personal identity will be discussed presently, but it is clear that his understanding of divine theodicy requires that the resurrected person have the same identity as the individual who died since, as he stated earlier in Part 3, chap. 1, "reward cannot be given to Reuben as compensation for the services of Simeon."[5]

III.

The issue of identity at the time of resurrection is not merely a matter of philosophical speculation; it is a matter having significant halakhic ramifications. Granted that the body in its original existence is the template for the resurrected body, the question of circumcision is moot. Since

---

such a doctrine would entail that a large number of bodies belonging to different periods of the deceased's life would have to be resurrected so that each would experience reward. Thus, Albo clearly rejects both the notion of spatio-temporal contiguity and the presence of a cause and effect relationship as the defining factor of human identity.

4. See also *Or ha-Shem*, Third Treatise, First Section, Part 4, chap. 2.
5. *Tosafot, Bekhorot* 8a, s.v. *tarnegolet*, cite an interpretation of "and the almond-tree shall blossom" (Ecclesiastes 12:5) as describing the function of an almond-shaped bone known as the *luz* located in the spinal column in inaugurating the process of resurrection. *Eliyahu Rabbah* 300:2-3 describes the bone as indestructible under all circumstances. *Eliyahu Rabbah* states that the *luz* derives sustenance only from the post-Sabbath *melaveh malveh* repast. The *luz* is sternal because it did not benefit from the fruit of the Tree of Knowledge that was consumed by Adam on Friday. See *Mishnah Berurah* 300:2 who refers to the bone as "*neskuy*." See also *Sha'ar ha-Tziyyun* 300:7 as well as *Arukh ha-Shulḥan* 300:2. Saadia and Crescas, even if they were aware of such a tradition, did not take it literally.

a circumcised male is resurrected without a foreskin, there is nothing to excise. But a male who at birth lacks a foreskin over his glans nevertheless requires *hatafat dam brit*, i.e., letting of a minuscule amount of blood signifying the "blood of the covenant." If the resurrected body does indeed share a common identity with the body prior to its demise, there will be no need for such blood-letting. But if the two bodies do not share a single identity, it would stand to reason that the resurrected individual would be subject to that requirement since the resurrected male endowed with a new identity has not previously fulfilled the commandment concerning circumcision.[6] For that matter, if his identity is newly acquired his status as a Jew cannot arise from matrilineal succession and hence, logically, he should require conversion to Judaism.[7]

Perhaps of even greater import is the question of whether a resurrected couple are deemed to be husband and wife or whether, as persons arising *sua sponte*, there are no preexisting marital bonds between them.[8]

The latter question was first posed by R. Saadia Ga'on in his previously cited discussion of resurrection. Saadia regards the question in the

---

6. Ramban, in his commentary on Rambam's *Sefer ha-Mitzvot, shoresh* 3, sec.7, rules that, upon resurrection, Aaron and his progeny will require consecration as priests in a manner comparable to the original consecration of Aaron and his sons because they will be "*anashim mehudashim* --renewed individuals." Taken literally, Ramban seems to assert that the original identity of resurrected priests is not preserved. However, *Sifra, Parashat Tzav* 18:1, records a controversy with regard to this matter. If no renewed consecration is required, priestly identity must be regarded as having been preserved. Perhaps Ramban employs the term "*anashim mehudashim*," i.e. "renewed individuals," rather than "*anashim hadashim*," i.e. "new people," in order to indicate that it is only priestly status that requires renewal because such status lapses upon death but that individual identity is unaffected.

7. See R. Chaim Kanievski, *Siah ha-Sadeh*, 11, *Likkutim*, no. 4.

8. Another possible ramification might arise in a situation in which a homicide victim is restored to life by a prophet. It is arguable that, if the resurrected victim is the same person who was murdered, the murderer should not be liable to the death penalty. Nevertheless, R. Abraham Kahana-Shapiro, *Dvar Avraham*, I, no. 5, sec. 3, takes it for granted that the murderer would nevertheless be culpable. Indeed, were it not the case, no homicide could be punished since it may be anticipated that the victim will be restored to life with the advent of the eschatological era. Cf., however, R. Meir Don Plocki, *Klei hemdah, Kuntres ha-Milu'im, Parashat Mishpatim*, who expresses doubt with regard to this notion. See also the note appended *ibid.* by the author's son in which the latter asserts that there is no culpability in such circumstances. It

same light as the query of the Gemara, *Niddah* 70a, regarding whether or not those who will be resurrected will be required to have "water of purification" sprinkled upon them as is required for those who come into contact with a corpse. The Gemara responds, "Our teacher Moses will be with them," i.e., since Moses will be present and available to resolve the matter, the answer can abide the event. Similarly, declares Saadia, we need not concern ourselves with the marital status of a resurrected couple but can leave the matter for clarification by Moses.

Saadia's comparison is not apropos. The issue of persistence of personal identity is attendant not only upon general resurrection but becomes germane in individual cases of resurrection that may occur long before that time. Unlike questions of ritual defilement that have no ramifications during the present era, the marital status of any deceased person who might merit earlier resurrection would immediately become a practical problem.

Indeed, apart from the instances of resurrection at the hands of a prophet recorded in biblical narratives, the Gemara reports two such events that occurred during the talmudic period. The Gemara, *Megillah* 7a, records that Rabbah and R. Zeira shared a Purim feast. Rabbah became inebriated and slit R. Zeira's throat. On the morrow Rabbah prayed on behalf of R. Zeira and restored him to life.[9] Similarly, the Gemara, *Ketubot* 62b, recounts that R. Ḥananyah ben Ḥakhinai left his family and spent twelve years at the academy. When he returned to his home he found his wife sitting and sifting flour. Upon seeing her husband she became overcome with joy and "her spirit flew away."[10] R.

---

may, however, be the case that culpability for homicide has no bearing upon identity or personhood because "*retziḥah*," or homicide, is a technical concept and defined in its own categories for purposes of culpability.

9. See, however, Maharsha, in his commentary *ad locum*, who interprets the narrative in a non-literal manner.

10. The Gemara, *Shabbat* 88b, reports that as each of the Ten Commandments was uttered by God "the souls of Israel departed." R. Akiva Joseph Schlesinger, in his responsa, *Oraḥ Ḥayyim*, no. 231, understands that statement as declaring that the people of Israel did not actually die but merely fainted. The statement of the Gemara, *Ketubot* 62b, may well be understood in a similar vein.

R. Menasheh Klein, *Mishneh Halakhot*, IX, no. 401, cites a statement of *Pirkei de-Rabbi Eli'ezer*, chap. 31, establishing the same point. *Pirkei de-Rabbi Eli'ezer*

Ḥananyah prayed on her behalf and she was restored to life. There is no hint in those sources with regard to whether either R. Zeira or R. Ḥananyah were required to remarry their respective wives in a new ceremony in order to reestablish a marital relationship. [11] Indeed, *Knesset*

states that as the knife was placed upon the throat of Isaac "his soul flew away and exited." As soon as God commanded Abraham, "Do not put your hand upon the lad" Isaac's soul returned to his body. Nevertheless, Isaac remained Abraham's heir and certainly did not require a second act of circumcision or of "letting of the blood of the covenant."

Far more striking is the aggadic source cited by *Shibbolei ha-Leket* and *Tanya Rabbati* that declares that Isaac actually "became ash and his ashes were cast on Mount Moriah. The Holy One, blessed be He, brought dew upon him by means of which the Holy One, blessed be He, resurrected Isaac. The ministering angels immediately exclaimed, "Blessed art Thou, Lord, who resurrects the dead." That aggadic statement contradicts the position of *Ḥatam Sofer* and *Rav Pe'alim*, cited *infra*, note 11, to the effect that personal identity is lost upon decomposition of the body and that identity is established *de novo* upon resurrection.

11. Probably the most widely-cited discussion of those two incidents in this context is that of R. Chaim Joseph David Azulai, *Birkei Yosef, Even ha-Ezer* 17:1. *Birkei Yosef* assumes that no marriage ceremony was necessary, but *Birkei Yosef* does not treat the matter as establishing the principle that personal identity survives death and continues upon resurrection. *Birkei Yosef* declares that the marital union remained intact in the cases described by the Gemara because the bodies had yet not been interred. It is generally agreed that death occurs only upon irreversible cessation of the bodily functions that constitute the criteria of life. Thus, successful resuscitation indicates that death has not yet occurred. If so, *Birkei Yosef* apparently regards revivication up to the time of burial as resuscitation rather than as resurrection. Rather than affirming that personal identity is preserved in resurrection, *Birkei Yosef* seems to affirm precisely the opposite: identity (and hence marital bonds) survives resuscitation and hence revivication prior to burial, but does not survive resurrection after burial has occurred; accordingly, upon resurrection, the parties will not be regarded as married to one another.

Ḥatam Sofer, Niddah 70b, distinguishes between revivication prior to decomposition of the body and resurrection. *Ḥatam Sofer* suggests that personal identity is lost, at least for purposes of Halakhah, only when the body turns to dust. Cf., *infra*, note 25. See also *Rav Pe'alim*, 11, *Sod Yesharim*, no. 2. See *Temurah* 31a where the Gemara explains that a bird hatched from an egg laid by a *terefah* is permitted because the fledgling develops only when the egg becomes putrid "and upon its becoming putrid it is mere dust." Rashi as well as one opinion cited by *Tosafot, Niddah* 50b, s.v. *tarnegolta*, employ that concept in their analysis of determination of identity as a member of an avarian species. Rambam, on the other hand, maintains that identity as a member of a species remains intact. See section I.

ha-Gedolah, Hagahot ha-Tur, Even ha-Ezer 17:2, rules that the marriage of a person restored to life by a prophet remains intact.

The earliest authority to discuss a related issue was R. Israel Isserlein, *Terumat ha-Deshen, Pesakim u-Ketavim*, no. 102. *Terumat ha-Deshen* discusses the status of the wife of the prophet Elijah subsequent to Elijah's bodily ascent to heaven and focuses upon the terminology employed by Scripture in formulating the prohibition against adultery. Levitcus 20:10 describes a married woman as the "wife of his fellow." *Terumat ha-Deshen* infers that "'the wife of your fellow is forbidden,' but not the wife of an angel." The term *"re'a"* connotes a peer, i.e., a corporeal being, and hence excludes metaphysical entities such as angels. Elijah, while in heaven, has no body and hence is not "your fellow" and, accordingly, his wife is permitted to others. By the same token, it would appear that, according to *Terumat ha-Deshen,* upon death of the husband, entailing as it does separation of the soul from the body, the wife is no longer the wife of "your fellow" and hence there is no longer a marriage.

R. Joseph Babad, *Minḥat Ḥinnukh*, no. 206, challenges *Terumat ha-Deshen*'s conclusions. *Minḥat Ḥinnukh* readily agrees that an angel lacks capacity to contract a marriage. However, he points out that, as stated by the Gemara, *Kiddushin* 13b, a widow would forever be precluded from remarriage but for the principle that death of the husband severs marital bonds. That rule is established on the basis of hermeneutic principles. Accordingly, *Minḥat Ḥinnukh* objects that those principles establish only that marriage is terminated by the death of the husband; there is no parallel derivation establishing that bodily ascent to heaven or transmutation into an angelic state similarly serves to dissolve the marriage.[12]

Ḥatam Sofer's view that original identity is lost upon decomposition and later identity upon resurrection is established *de novo* seems to be contradicted by the earlier-cited opinion found in *Sifra, Parshat Tzav* 18:1. *Sifra* records a controversy with regard to whether the original anointment of Aaron and his sons serves to consecrate resurrected priests or whether priests must be newly anointed upon resurrection. If their original identity is lost upon decomposition it is difficult to fathom why a new act of consecration should not be required.

12. *Minḥat Ḥinnukh* himself postulates a theory to the effect that, according to some authorities, if circumstances arise making it impossible to contract a marriage, e.g.,

Terumat ha-Deshen presumably understood the hermeneutic principle applied, not as establishing that death is a *"mattir,"* i.e., an event that dissolves a marriage with finality comparable to the dissolution of marriage by divorce, but as establishing that only the existence of a living husband prevents a woman from contracting a new marriage. Death is then simply the most obvious, but not necessarily the only, example of non-existence of a living husband.[13] Bodily ascent to heaven might be another. If so, even according to *Terumat ha-Deshen,* upon resurrection, the physical presence of the husband might serve to reestablish the marital relationship.[14] [It is certainly arguable that, even according to this analysis of *Terumat ha-Deshen,* should a woman contract a new marriage during the period of her husband's physical non-existence, that marriage would prevent reinstatement of her earlier marriage upon the physical reconstitution of her first husband. The principle with regard to sanctified animals is that, once sanctification has occurred, it does not become abrogated. Similarly, the second marriage, once validly contracted, does not terminate other than upon divorce or death of the new partner.[15]] *Teshuvot Avnei Nezer, Even ha-Ezer,* no. 56, and R. Elchanan

apostasy of the husband, an already existing marriage also becomes nullified. Accordingly, since neither a corpse nor an angel can contract a marriage, death serves to abrogate marriage.

13. Cf., R. Elchanan Wasserman, *Kovetz Shi'urim,* II, no. 28. Reb Elchanan posits this conceptual dispute as the basis of a controversy between Ramah and *Bet Yosef, Yoreh De'ah* 267, regarding the status of slaves of a convert who are minors at the time of the convert's demise.

14. See R. Chaim Eleazar Wachs, *Nefesh Ḥayyah, Even ha-Ezer,* no. 3, s.v. *u-be-vad'ai,* who tentatively suggests, but later rejects, the notion that a woman having been permitted to marry, cannot later be forbidden to do so. See *infra,* note 15. *Nefesh Ḥayyah* speaks only of individual resurrection but does not address issues pertaining to resurrection in the eschatological era.

15. R. Isaac Schmelkes, *Teshuvot Bet Yitzḥak,* I, no. 6, sec. 14, invokes the concept "Her ways are ways of pleasantness" (Proverbs 3:17) in arguing that, having entered into a legitimate union, the woman cannot subsequently be prohibited to her new husband. That principle is formulated by the Gemara, *Yevamot* 87b, in establishing that a woman who is not subject to levirate obligations upon death of her husband cannot subsequently become forbidden to marry freely. Hence, that principle should be equally applicable even if the wife has not actually contracted a new marriage. See *supra,* note 14.

Wasserman assert that death of the husband, like divorce, is an event that severs all marital bonds. If so, capacity to contract a new marriage upon resurrection is not at all germane to the issue of personal identity.

IV.

Although there is less reason to assume that bodily ascent to heaven terminates personal identity than there is for such a determination with regard to death, one authority seems to adopt that position with regard to bodily ascent as well.

As a qualification for serving as a member of a court qualified to administer capital or corporal punishment, Jewish law requires ordination transmitted in an unbroken chain beginning with the individuals ordained as judges by Moses in the wilderness. That chain of transmission was interrupted during the Roman persecution and ordination has lapsed. The problem then is, how will ordination be restored and a Sanhedrin reestablished with the coming of the Messiah? One solution offered by R. Levi ben Haviv in his *Kuntres ha-Semikhah* is that since Elijah did not die but ascended bodily to heaven, he will return to earth and use his authority to ordain others.

R. Jacob Berav takes exception to that suggestion. R. Jacob Berav asserts that Elijah's qualification to bestow ordination was abrogated when he rose to heaven. R. Jacob Berav clearly understands that the Elijah who will return is, for purposes of Halakhah, not the same person who was taken from earth. The clear implication is that the two personae do not share a single identity.

V.

Crescas himself advances a theory that both explains the need for bodily resurrection as a matter of divine justice and also serves to explain continuity of personal identity. An individual possesses a single identity before death and subsequent to resurrection of the body because his soul remains unchanged. The problem of identity arises only because of change; the adult is so markedly different from the neonate that it is difficult to recognize them as one and the same person. When constancy is preserved throughout existence the problem does not arise. Thus, for example, philosophers do not question why a rock is regarded as remaining the same rock over an extended period of time; the rock is durable and undergoes no perceived change. Similarly, the soul is constant and undergoes no change in leaving the body for a transcendental existence or in its restoration to a corporeal body. Accordingly, it is the unchanging soul that accounts for constancy of personal identity.

Crescas sees no problem with regard to divine justice apparently because he does not regard divine justice as requiring that the particular inanimate material substance of the body be rewarded. To return to the analogy of suits of clothes: divine justice does not require that a person receiving reward for a good deed be attired in the suit he wore while performing that deed. By the same token, the soul receiving reward need not inhabit the same body in which it was present while earning such reward. Nevertheless, divine justice demands that reward must be accorded the soul while united with a body because the qualitative nature of the reward experienced by a soul inhabiting a body is different in nature from the reward that might be experienced by a disembodied soul. Hence:

> If God were to create a creation of the temperament and characteristics possessed by Reuben, for example, ... and his soul which is a substance *per se* were to unite with this creation, there is no doubt that this soul and its faculties would use this body, upon its union with it, identically as it had used the body of Reuben.[16]

It is the temperament and characteristics of Reuben in his original incarnation that must share in the reward rather than the molecules of his previous body. "Temperament and characteristics" are matter-dependent, but do not depend upon particular particles of matter.

Crescas develops his thesis by first pointing to the phenomenon of growth of a person during the course of his life. The person possesses a single identity during the course of his lifetime despite the fact that the material substance of which the body is composed undergoes significant change. That is readily understandable once it is recognized

---

16. *Or ha-Shem*, Third Treatise, First Section, Part 4, chap. 4.

that personhood is determined by the unique soul possessed by each individual and recognition that the soul is constant and unchanging:

> Behold, Reuben, for example, who was born slight of stature together with a vegetative soul and subsequently grew. If it is [the case] that the parts of his body came into existence from the food which descends through the organs of his body -- and it is clear with regard to every part of the parts of his body that it came into existence from the food that was outside the body -- if within the body it is a different entity, similarly, the soul then unites with this body whose characteristics are just like Reuben's. Although the part[s] of his body are from exterior places, upon becoming united with this soul they are one entity. Since the soul is the essential form of the possessor of the soul and gives him his essence, the soul gives form to the body and gives it its essence. Because the essence of the soul does not change it is necessarily the case that the body which becomes united with it be carried along with it just as the food is carried along with the recipient of the food and is converted to become his body.

In this exposition Crescas has resolved the problem of personal identity -- at least as the concept pertains to human beings. Human personhood depends upon the soul. Since, unlike the body, the soul is unchanging it is by reference to the soul that continuity of human identity can be understood. It then follows that, since the soul is immortal, identity survives death of the body.

VI.

Further evidence that individual identity is preserved even after death is found in various sources indicating that some deceased individuals returned to terrestrial existence for brief periods and assumed their earlier corporeal identity. The Gemara, *Ketubot* 113a, relates that, at least for a limited time after his death, R. Judah the Prince returned to his home every Friday evening. *Sefer Ḥasidim,* no. 1129, amplifies that narrative in indicating that R. Judah was not present as a mere apparition but that he also recited *kiddush* on behalf of the assembled. R. Chaim Joseph

David Azulai, *Shem ha-Gedolim*, I, *Ma'arekhet Gedolim*, s.v. *Rabbenu Eli'ezer bar Natan*, cites earlier sources indicating that, on one occasion, the Patriarch Abraham returned to earth and was counted as a member of a *minyan*. It is not conceivable that a metaphysical entity is qualified either to recite *kiddush* on behalf of others or to serve as a member of the quorum necessary for public prayer. The individuals in question must, then, not only have been physically present but must have been present in their earlier identities; they could not have appeared *sui generis* because a spontaneously arising individual would have no obligation with regard to commandments. Those narratives are meaningful only if the previous corporeal identity of those individuals is regarded as having been preserved.[17]

VII.

If death of the husband severs matrimonial bonds in a manner similar to divorce then quite obviously at the time of resurrection a deceased couple, although they may retain their earlier personae, will no longer be married.[18] The situation of a deceased wife who returns to life is significantly different. There is no biblical source from which it may be

---

17. A further problem, however, remains. R. Yechiel Michel Tucatzinsky, *Gesher ha-Ḥayyim*, II, chap. 26, sec. 3, notes that death relieves a person from obligations *vis-à-vis* commandments. Accordingly, if, after death, such an individual does fulfill commandments, he would do so as an "uncommanded" person. The rule is that an "uncommanded" person cannot enable a "commanded" person to discharge his obligation with regard to a *mizvah* by acting on his behalf. *Gesher ha-Hayyim* finds himself forced to conclude that the dead, even if temporarily restored to life, are fully obligated to fulfill all commandments. See the aggadic narrative recorded in *Bava Metzi'a* 114b indicating that Elijah, as a *kohen*, would not have been permitted to defile himself through contact with a corpse. In talmudic sources Elijah is identified as Pinhas the son of Eleazar. Cf., however, R. Elchanan Wasserman, *Kovetz Shi'urim*, II, no. 29, who maintains that obligations with regard to fulfillment of commandments are entirely terminated by death with the result that individuals who are resurrected are free from all such obligations.

18. See the discussion in *Kovetz Shi'urim*, II, no. 28. Having contracted a second marriage, the woman would be forbidden to all others, including her resuscitated first husband. Cf., *Rav Pe'alim*, II, *Sod Yesharim*, no. 2, who cites *Zohar, Bereshit* 21b, which declares that upon her death a woman returns to her first husband in Paradise. *Rav Pe'alim* asserts that, upon resurrection, a widow who had contracted a second marriage may

derived that death of a wife dissolves a marriage. Hence, if inherited identity survives death and resurrection, it should follow that a woman restored to life during the lifetime of her husband remains married to him[19] and lacks capacity to contract a second marriage.[20] Such a conclusion is not contradicted by the authorities who entertain the possibility that the wives of Elijah and of R. Zeira were free to remarry; it is the death of the husband that severs marital bonds, not the death of the wife.

The notion that marriage is not terminated by death of the wife is not as bizarre as it may seem. R. Elchanan Wasserman, *Kovetz Shi'urim, Ketubot*, sec. 314, asserts that, to a limited extent, property may remain vested in the deceased.[21] Citing the principle enunciated by the Gemara, *Sanhedrin* 48a, to the effect that unexpended funds raised to defray the burial expenses of a particular person must be distributed to

---

return to her first husband on the grounds that, at least for purposes of Halakhah, personal identity is not preserved after death and decomposition. See *infra*, notes 19 and 25.

19. An intriguing issue would arise with regard to reestablishment of marital bonds between a husband and his resurrected wife in the event that the husband had married the sister of his deceased wife. Since a person cannot be married to two sisters simultaneously, does a valid marriage to the second sister have the effect of nullifying the marriage to the first sister? See *Tosafot, Yevamot* 49b, s.v. *sotah* and R. Joseph Aryeh Lorentz, *Pela'ot Edotekha* (n.p., 5768), 11, 33-44. *Rav Pe'alim*, 11, *Sod Yesharim* 2, asserts that, upon resurrection, entirely new personae are acquired and hence the women do not have the halakhic status of sisters. According to *Rav Pe'alim*, it follows that, subsequent to resurrection, a formal marriage ceremony will be required in order to reestablish a marital relationship and that there will be no prohibitions based upon consanguinity. See *Pela'ot Edotekha*, 11, 42, and *supra*, note 18.

20. In the event that the husband remarried in the interim the applicability of Rabbenu Gershom's edict prohibiting polygamy may or may not compel him to divorce one of the wives. It is certainly arguable that Rabbenu Gershom's ban did not encompass such extraordinary circumstances.

21. Thus, explains Reb Elchanan, heirs who succeed to an estate must satisfy certain debts of their progenitor because of their obligation to honor their deceased father despite the fact that the commandment to honor one's parents does not mandate expenditure of a child's own funds. Reb Elchanan contends that title to inherited property remains vested in the father to the extent that he has need for such property. Nevertheless, absent a duty of filial honor, or in the case of minor heirs who have no such duty, creditors cannot seize the property upon the claim that the property remains vested in the debtor himself. The explanation is that, upon death, the *sh'ibud*,

his heirs, *Teshuvot ha-Rashba*, I, no. 375, rules that funds raised to erect a tombstone on the grave of the decedent cannot be diverted for purposes other than enhancing the honor of the deceased. Reb Elchanan regards the underlying principle as predicated upon the generation of a property interest vested in the decedent even though the funds were conveyed after his demise.[22] In *Kovetz Shi'urim*, II, no. 11, Reb Elchanan expands upon that thesis in explaining why, as stated in *Bava Batra* 142a, the estate of a proselyte who dies leaving a pregnant wife is inherited by his posthumously born child. Generally, the estate of a proselyte who dies without issue is *res nullius*. According to the talmudic opinion that maintains that inherited property does not vest in a fetus, it would logically follow that title should vest in anyone who seizes the property since the fetus has not yet succeeded to the estate. Reb Elchanan explains that the decedent retains title to his property, and can even acquire title to property, to the extent that he has need for use of such property. Passing property to an heir, argues Reb Elchanan, represents such a need.[23] Reb Elchanan further asserts that upon restoration to life the proselyte may reclaim his property from anyone who seized it.[24] It would then

---

or lien, upon the debtor's person becomes extinguished. The remaining "need," then, is the honor that must be accorded the decedent by his children in repaying the outstanding debt rather than the repayment *per se*. Cf., *Pela'ot Edotekha*, II, 34.

22. See also Rashba cited by *Shitah Mekubbetzet, Bava Batra* 8b. Cf., however *Yad Ramah, Sanhedrin* 48a and *Maḥaneh Efrayim, Hilkhot Zekhiyah u-Mattanah*, no. 3. *Maḥaneh Efrayim* rejects the notion of a property interest vested in a corpse and explains *Bava Batra* 48a and *Teshuvot ha-Rashba* as predicated upon considerations of honor that must be accorded the deceased.

23. In *Kovetz Shi'urim, Bava Batra*, sec. 489, Reb Elchanan states that the neonate does not acquire title retroactively. He then questions how, in the case of an inherited slave, the slave can acquire freedom while the fetus is yet in the womb and subsequently return to his original status as a slave upon birth of the child. Similar issues arise in situations in which the person who has seized an animal of the deceased proselyte later consecrates the animal or uses the seized object to acquire a bride. Upon birth of the child does the animal return to its earlier non-sanctified state? Does the bride return to her earlier status as an unmarried woman? See *Pela'ot Edotekha*, II, 33-34.

24. It seems to this writer that Reb Elchanan's thesis is inherent in the distinction drawn by *Tosafot, Bava Batra* 154b, s.v. *be-ḥezkat*, between heirs and purchasers of property with regard to a demand for exhumation of a corpse in order to establish a financial claim. Purchasers have the right to demand such exhumation in order to examine

stand to reason that the deceased, upon resurrection, should be able to reclaim their property.[25]

---

the corpse for the presence of pubic hair in order to establish the decedent's capacity to convey property. Heirs may not make such a demand in order to demonstrate the absence of pubic hair in order to substantiate lack of such capacity and hence to invalidate the sale. *Tosafot*, in one explanation, explain the discrepancy on the basis of the fact that heirs are "relatives." The conventional explanation is that relatives have an obligation of burial and that *Tosafot* assert that prevention of other forms of ignominy *vis-á-vis* the deceased is also part of their duty. But, if so, why are they not also obligated to expend their own funds in refunding the purchase price in order to grant the purchaser's claim for exhumation? See R. Moshe Feinstein, *Iggerot Mosheh, Yoreh De'ah*, II, no. 151.

It also seems to this writer that further evidence in support of Reb Elchanan's thesis may be found in a ruling recorded in the Gemara, *Menahot* 51b. The High Priest was obligated to sacrifice a meal offering termed a *minhat havitin* each day. In the event of the death of the High Priest, the offering is purchased with funds supplied by the heirs of the High Priest. Although that regulation is derived from the verse "and the priest anointed in his place from among his sons" (Leviticus 6:15), the Gemara does not posit an obligation limited to the son of the High Priest nor does it use the expression "relatives." The implication is that the obligation devolves only upon heirs of the High Priest who succeed to his estate. Rambam, *Hilkhot Temidin u-Musafin* 3:22, declares that the offering is made for the "atonement" of the deceased High Priest. If only "heirs," rather than relatives, are liable, the most plausible explanation is that the decedent retains a property interest in his estate to the extent that he has need of those assets for his own benefit. Posthumous atonement in the form of the *minhat havitin* is such a need.

In light of the foregoing, it may be explained that the financial obligation of heirs to bury the deceased is limited to use of funds of the estate of the deceased for that purpose. The decedent retains title to his property to the extent that such property is necessary to defray burial expenses. The heirs, however, have no obligation to expend their own funds for such purposes and hence need not use their own funds in order to prevent desecration of the body of their relative by others.

25. That position is contradicted by *Hatam Sofer, Bava Batra* 38b. *Hatam Sofer* rejects the notion that personal identity survives death and decomposition and hence a resurrected person has not claim to recover property owned during his previous lifetime. *Hatam Sofer* further offers a novel insight into the narrative recorded in II Kings 8:3-6. That is also the position of *Rav Pe'alim* discussed *supra*, notes 17-18. *Hatam Sofer* asserts that the property of the child restored to life by Elijah was seized by heirs of the child's deceased father on the claim that the resurrected child was a "new person" and not entitled to inherit as a son. The King and Gehazi restored the property to the son, asserts *Hatam Sofer*, only because they did not believe that the child had actually died and been resurrected.

It might then be assumed that, upon resurrection of his wife, a yet living husband might reclaim marital privileges just as he may recover property interests. Nevertheless, *Tosafot, Bava Batra* 114b s.v. *mah*, cites the opinion of Rivan who maintains that the "relationship (*she'erut*) is dissolved by death just as [it is dissolved] by divorce." *Tosafot* employs that concept in explaining why a deceased husband does not inherit his wife's estate "in the grave" in order to pass her estate to his own heirs. *Tosafot* reject Rivan's thesis on the basis of a text indicating that a wife is deemed to be the husband's *she'er* or relative even subsequent to death. In context, *Tosafot* apparently assumed that Rivan regarded death of either the husband or the wife as severing the relationship.[26] If so, Rivan regarded death of a wife as similar to divorce and hence it would follow that, according to Rivan, the marital relationship is not reestablished upon resurrection of the wife. Indeed, for Rivan it would be impossible to contend that death of the husband -- unlike divorce -- is merely the absence of the husband and that if he is restored to life the marriage persists. Rivan's position, however, does not contradict the notion that personal identity is preserved during death and resurrection.

The comments of *Ḥatam Sofer* seem to be contradicted by *Ḥatam Sofer*'s own comments on *Niddah* 70b cited *supra*, note 10. In his comments on *Niddah, Ḥatam Sofer* maintains that personal identity is extinguished only upon decomposition of the body.

26. Cf., *Ḥiddushei Reshash, loc. cit.*, and R. Eliezer Waldenberg *Teshuvot Tzitz Eli'ezer*, XVI, no. 24, sec. 6.

14

The Metaphysics of Property Interests in Jewish Law: An Analysis of Kinyan

Virtually every first year law student has heard property defined as "a bundle of rights." That notion is seminal to an understanding of the notion of property in its various guises as reflected in common law. That which is bundled can be unbundled. Reversionary interests, remainders, life estates, riparian rights, mineral rights, air rights, servitudes, and much more, are easy to grasp once it is understood that just as light waves can be beamed through a prism and emerge as a spectrum of waves of different length and hence as distinct colors represented by the letters ROYGBIV, so is a fee simple absolute divisible into a wide spectrum of discrete rights. A light wave is a coalesced amalgam consisting of waves, each of which, when refracted, is perceived as a different color of the rainbow. A fee simple absolute is a bundled conglomeration of the sum total of rights recognized by the legal system. Those rights are separable in a manner analogous to separation of light waves into waves of different color.

Rights are vested in people. They serve as a legal and moral basis for the exercise of prerogatives, dominion, and even exploitation. To speak of property as a bundle of rights is somewhat of an oxymoron. It is not property that is a bundle of rights in the same sense that light is a bundle of waves each a different length or color. Property is that which may be utilized as an instrument in assertion of rights and in securing compliance with such rights. More accurately, property is that with regard to which those separate and distinct rights may be bundled and exercised. The focus of the proprietor-property relationship is entirely upon the proprietor. The intrinsic nature of property is in no way changed or modified by its status as property.

Not so in Jewish law. In Jewish law the concept of property reflects not rights but ontology. To be sure, there are rights that flow from the proprietor-property relationship, but those rights flow from – and indeed are simply an epiphenomenon of – an ontological state, that is, a state of being having existence independent of those rights. The concept is metaphysical. To say that the metaphysical is not subject to perception by the physical senses may be a tautology. But a metaphysician would have no problem understanding the proposition that metaphysical causes may have physical effects.[1] A metaphysician would certainly have no problem with the assertion that metaphysical reality may give rise to rights and duties in the natural world.

An imprecise parallel lies in the institution of matrimony. In some primitive societies a wife was the property of her husband – or at least such is the common perception. But in no society was the husband the property of the wife. Yet in every society a wife had rights *vis-à-vis* her husband. Those rights did not arise from a property interest; they were

---

This material was originally presented at a conference convened by the DePaul University College of Law Center for Jewish Law and Judaic Studies under the sponsorship of the Jack Miller Center for Teaching America's Founding Principles and History. The author wishes to thank Mr. Jack Adelman and Mr. Mark Lekarew for their meticulous reading of an earlier draft and for their valuable comments.

1. See, for example Plato, *Phaedo*, 100c-101d and 100e5-6.

the product of the state of matrimony. That is not to say that there cannot be rights without either a property interest or a particular ontological state. But in the marital relationship those rights arise from the state of matrimony and to talk of rights arising from the state of matrimony is to reify matrimony in a manner than can only be metaphysical. To be sure, modern man may have denuded marriage and reduced it to a collection of reciprocal rights and duties. But, traditionally, matrimony has been spoken of as an ontological state that comes into being with the union of bride and groom, a concept that explains, *inter alia*, the indestructibility and inseverability of the marital relationship in some traditions.

The notion that matrimony is an ontological state may be no more than a myth. But myths, whether or not they are literally true, serve as an aid in simplifying and comprehending difficult concepts. The abstract is difficult to comprehend precisely because it is abstract; the tangible is more readily appreciated. Reification – even of the metaphysical— serves to transform the abstract into the tangible.

The most celebrated example of such an exercise is Plato's Theory of Ideas. I doubt that anyone, including Plato, accepted the Theory of Ideas literally. Nevertheless, Plato did believe that a transcendental realm does exist and that there is some type of relationship between our physical world and that transcendental reality. Hence, Plato's reification of that transcendental world in the Theory of Ideas and his explanation of our imperfect ability to understand the relationship between our world and that transcendental world by means of the Allegory of the Cave.

The notion of property as reflected in Jewish law must be understood as a reflection of an ontological relationship binding property to its proprietor. The relationship, and its effect upon property, is no more subject to sensory perception than is the state of matrimony; nevertheless, the metaphysical nature of that relationship does not diminish its ontological reality.

Additionally, although the status of a tangible object as property is metaphysical, that status comes into being in a very physical manner—a very clear example of a physical act having a metaphysical effect.

The Uniform Commercial Code §2-207 provides that property conveyed by a seller to a purchaser is transferred at whatever point in time or place at which the parties agree that such transfer shall occur.

A meeting of minds is not merely a necessary condition of vesting of title but constitutes the essence of the conveyance. An owner of wheat in Chicago may contract for the delivery of a carload of wheat to a customer in New York City. The wheat is then shipped by train from Chicago to New York. While traversing the Horseshoe Curve in the vicinity of Pittsburgh, the train overturns and the wheat is irretrievably lost. Which party bears the loss, the seller or the purchaser? The answer depends upon the particular point in time or place the parties agreed that title was to pass. That understanding can be spelled out in the sales contract, thereby providing clear evidence of determination reached by a meeting of minds, or it can be left for the legal system to puzzle out constructively, or by application of statute. Be that as it may, the global answer is that title passes when and where the parties wish it to pass.

Not so in Jewish law. Jewish law provides that no transfer or acquisition of property (save by inheritance) takes place other than by means of *kinyan*, i.e., an overt act that gives effect to the transfer. Certainly, Jewish law requires a meeting of minds. In its own terms, Jewish law defines meeting of minds as *gemirat da'at*, firm determination to convey on the part of the conveyor, and *semikhat da'at*, reliance and acceptance of transfer on the part of the conveyee. We need not now explore the theory underlying the efficacy of *kinyan*. Suffice it to say that, in Jewish law, *kinyan* is the *sine qua non* of (virtually) all conveyances. For our purpose, concentration upon the function and *telos* of *kinyan* will be sufficient.[2]

The function of *kinyan* – and with it the notion of property in Jewish law – can best be understood on the basis of a "myth" that, feeble as it assuredly is, is inspired by Plato's Allegory of the Cave.[3] Imagine

---

2. There are indeed scholars who regard "meeting of minds" as the sole operative factor in transfer of title. For them, *kinyan* serves either as evidence of a meeting of minds or is generative in nature in the sense that it creates firm determination and reliance. See R. Yechezkel Abramsky, *Dinei Mammonot*, 2nd ed. (Bnei Brak, 5729), pp. 10f. See also Rashbam, *Bava Batra* 88a, s.v. *Rav Safra* and R. Shlomoh Kluger, *Teshuvot Tuv Ta'am va-Da'at, Mahadurah Kamma*, no. 270. However, those theories of *kinyan* do not serve to explain why, for example, future interests cannot be conveyed or why inchoate interests are not recognized.
3. See Plato, *Republic* 514a–520e.

that we possess metaphysical spectacles with which we may observe the metaphysical entities that permeate the physical world. We would see that every non-human physical entity is endowed with tentacles attached to it by suction cups. The opposite side of each tentacle also sports one or more suction cups. The tentacles of many, and probably most, of those physical entities are attached to the shoulders of human beings by this second set of suction cups. The term "property" is nothing more than the term we use to indicate that the object to which reference is made is attached to a human being through the intermediacy of those tentacles. Although phenomenologically invisible, the attachment is real and ontologically tangible.

A law enacted as a conservation measure forbidding taking an ax in hand and cutting down an ancient redwood tree is readily comprehensible to the human mind. Quite similarly, the law forbids us to take a knife and sever the tentacles connecting a tangible physical object from the human being to which it is attached. The law also forbids seizing the tentacle from the shoulder to which it is secured and attaching it to one's own shoulder. The term we use for that act is "theft." The act is forbidden; the act is illegal, but it is efficacious. The act creates a new ontological reality: The property is no longer attached to its rightful owner and it is precisely the *kinyan geneivah*, or *kinyan* of theft, i.e., the severance of the ontological relation between the property and its rightful owner and the establishment of a new relationship between the property and the seizing intruder that constitutes the essence of theft. Kant described at length the metaphysics of morals. Jewish law always recognized the moral implications of the metaphysics of property.

Kinyan is nothing more and nothing less than removal of the tentacles from the shoulder of the person to whom it is attached and its reattachment to the shoulder of another. The act of *kinyan* is the physical means of accomplishing that metaphysical end and it varies with the nature of the property being conveyed. Depending upon the nature of the surface to which a physical object adheres, different types of solvent are necessary to dissolve the glue binding the items to that surface. In the case of real property, payment of the purchase price, delivery of a deed or *ḥazakah*, the progenitor of livery of seisin enshrined in common law, has that effect. Dislocating and moving a chattel and delivering the reins of a domestic animal have the same effect as do various other modes of *kinyan*.

In *ḥalipin*, i.e., exchange or barter, there is no requirement that each party perform a separate act of *kinyan*. Consummation of *kinyan* by one party automatically results in reciprocal vesting of *kinyan* in the other. Attachment of tentacles of the newly-acquired property by operation of *kinyan* has the effect of also dislodging the tentacles attaching the property that is to be conveyed in exchange and forcing their attachment to the party whose property has been divested by means of overt *kinyan*.[4]

It is of interest that in some few cases, e.g., the obligation of the father of a bride or groom, the obligation to deliver the stipulated dowry becomes binding without a formal, overt *kinyan*. The obligation is in the form of a *shi'bud* instituted in exchange for receiving an object of value, i.e., the delight experienced by a parent in the marriage of his child. Although described as a verbal *kinyan*, it is actually a form of *ḥalipin*: the father receives pleasure provided by the prospective son-in-law or daughter-in-law and, in turn, becomes obligated to the value of the dowry.[5] The experience of pleasure provided by the bride

---

4. Not all persons are qualified to perform a *kinyan*. A minor, for example, lacks such capacity. On this analysis, such an individual lacks capacity to transfer the tentacles to another person. R. Abraham Kahana Shapiro, *Dvar Avraham*, I, no. 1, sec. 16, asserts that, although the Sages had the power to expropriate property and such expropriation is biblically effective, they lacked authority to cause property to vest in a person who cannot be seized of property; or, for purposes of biblical law, to divest property from a person lacking capacity to transfer property; or to cause property to be transferred without a physical act of *kinyan*. On the basis of the thesis herein presented, the explanation is that the Sages lacked power to effect changes in ontological reality just as they lacked power to effect changes in the physical universe. According to *Teshuvot R. Akiva Eger*, no. 226, sec. 6, the Sages had authority to expropriate property but lacked authority to vest property in any person in a manner that would be effective for purposes of biblical law.

5. Rashi, *Kiddushin* 9b, describes the pleasure as giving rise to a form of *ḥalipin*. R. Joseph of Posen, son-in-law of R. Ezekiel Landau, *Noda bi-Yehudah, Mahadurah Tinyana, Ḥoshen Mishpat*, no. 27, s.v. *u-mah she-katav adoni*, infers from Rashi that the *kinyan* is "as every other *kinyan*, biblical in nature." See also *Ḥazon Ish, Ḥoshen Mishpat: Nezikin, Bava Kamma* 21:5. Me'iri, *Kiddushin* 9b, similarly understands the *kinyan* to be of that nature but as a rabbinic, rather than biblical, *kinyan*. *Noda bi-Yehudah, Mahadurah Kamma, Ḥoshen Mishpat*, no. 26, s.v. *hineh* and no. 28, s.v. *od*

or groom to his or her father-in-law is itself reified and raised to the equivalent of conveyance of chattel. If *kinyan* is essentially a manipulation of metaphysical entities, it should not be surprising that emotional gratification provided by one person to another is equated with transfer of a physical object.

The owner of property may also renounce ownership by simply detaching the tentacles from his shoulder and casting them upon the ground, thereby rendering the physical object *res nullius*. That process does not require any great effort; the property can be abandoned by means of a mere verbal declaration renouncing ownership, in effect, by "blowing" the tentacles off one's shoulder. The abandoned property is then available for seizure by any person who wishes to acquire title. Acquisition of title, even of an item that is *res nullius*, requires a physical act, i.e., a formal *kinyan*. This description of abandonment of property explains why property cannot be abandoned in favor of a particular individual or group of individuals to the exclusion of all others: abandonment requires removal of tentacles; unattached property is then available to everyone. Items of property that never had an owner are also endowed with tentacles. The virgin suction cups of those tentacles are available to all and sundry who then acquire title by affixing those suction cups to their shoulders.

As earlier noted, a thief also acquires a particular form of title, i.e., a *kinyan geneivah*, or "title of theft." If property is a bundle of rights, it includes "negative rights" as well. I do not know whether Bill Gates or Warren Buffet suffers from insomnia. I do know that if either does have sleepless nights he is entitled to them. He has the "right" to worry about his property. A pauper, on the other hand, sleeps like a baby. He has no property worth worrying about and hence has no "right" to sleepless nights. The owner of property has the "right" to suffer the loss of that property. To say that a thief has acquired a *kinyan geneivah* is to say that

<hr />

ahuvi, maintains that the obligation does not arise by virtue of *kinyan* but is nevertheless enforceable by rabbinic decree. Me'iri, *loc. cit.*, cites earlier authorities who maintained a position similar to that espoused by *Noda bi-Yehudah* and explained that the rabbinic legislation was designed to prevent a claim that it was the intention to make the validity of the marriage contingent upon fulfillment of the financial promise.

he has acquired the right to bear the financial consequence of the loss of the stolen object even if such loss results from *force majeure* or an act of God. Accordingly, despite the fact that the property would have been rendered valueless even if the thief had not stolen the property, he will be liable of payment of its full value at the time of the theft. That "negative interest" is acquired only by means of *kinyan*.

To be sure, a thief does not acquire absolute title to his ill-gotten gains. Primarily, he is vested with one of a bundle of rights, *viz.*, the right to suffer loss if the object is destroyed. The rightful owner retains the right to the return of his property *in rem* and the thief may return the stolen property and suffer no further liability. But if the object cannot be restored, even as a result of an "act of God," the thief, through the act of theft, acquires the "right" to suffer the loss and, accordingly, he must compensate his victim by payment of the value of the property at the time of theft.

The metaphysical analysis of the negative right to suffer the financial consequences of loss or destruction of the stolen property is identical to the analysis of the conveyance of a particular positive right: At the time of theft, only the tentacle representing the negative right to suffer loss in the event of destruction is detached from the victim and attached to the thief. All other tentacles, or parts of the tentacles, remain firmly attached to the rightful owner.

Nevertheless, the thief's title may ripen into a more comprehensive property interest. If a person steals flour and bakes it into bread or steals lumber and fashions it into a piece of furniture, the rightful owner no longer has a claim for restoration of the stolen property. The reason does not lie in a theory involving recognition that value reflecting expended labor has been added by the thief. Were that the case, the victim would at least be entitled to the option of recovering the stolen property and compensating the thief for the value added. The explanation is that conversion of a raw material into a finished product serves as a further *kinyan*, i.e., it serves to vest additional property interests in the thief. The thief, in converting the raw material, succeeds in plucking off all remaining tentacles binding the property to its prior owner and attaching those tentacles to himself. He remains liable for the value of the property at the time of theft in much the same manner as a debtor is liable for repayment of a loan. A *shi'bud* or servitude in the person is generated at the time of theft. Cast in the context of the Myth of the Tentacles, this means that the tentacles attaching property to its rightful owner cannot be removed from the rightful owner in any way without the owner's tentacles becoming attached to the person of the thief. Put somewhat differently, the thief may succeed in detaching the owner's tentacles from his property in whole or in part and replace them with his own but the owner's tentacles are "sticky" in nature and adhere themselves to the person of the thief. Consequently, the thief is liable to compensate his victim by virtue of the *shi'bud ha-guf* he has acquired in the body of the thief.

The liability of a bailee is of the same nature and arises in the same manner. The obligations of a bailee arise not from some abstract duty of care but from a *kinyan*. That *kinyan* serves to convey a negative right upon the bailee, *viz.*, the right to be held liable for loss of the bailed property in accordance with the nature of the bailment: negligence in the case of a gratuitous bailee; theft and loss in the case of a bailee for hire; and even more extensive liability in the case of a borrower. In each case the *kinyan* serves to transfer that negative right from bailor to bailee.

The Myth of the Tentacles serves to explain why Jewish law does not recognize a property interest in intangible, inchoate property or the efficacy of the transfer of a future interest. Such property interests do not exist because *kinyan* cannot be performed with regard to that which does not exist or with regard to that which is not tangible. The usual form of *kinyan* involves a physical act performed upon the item transferred, i.e., *meshikhah*, or dislocating and causing the movement of the item conveyed, signifying its exit from the domain of the grantor and entry into the domain of the grantee, or *mesirah*, i.e., delivery of the reins of an animal. But there are other forms of *kinyan* that do not require the act to be performed upon the property conveyed, e.g., *agav karka*, transfer by accession, in which the *kinyan* is made on real property and "moveables," i.e., chattels, are automatically conveyed as well when such is the intent of the parties. Chattels need not be located on the real property in order to be transferred by accession. If it is understood that *kinyan* is more than meets the eye, *viz.*, that it is designed to effect detachment and reattachment of tentacles, it becomes obvious that, although that phenomenon can be accomplished without contiguous tactile contact, it can nevertheless not occur unless the object is "real."[6] Tentacles cannot attach to property that does not yet exist or to property in which one does not yet have an interest. Future interests cannot adhere to one's shoulder in the present by means of suction cups.[7] For a similar reason property cannot be conveyed to a person not yet in existence.

---

6. Thus, Rema, *Ḥoshen Mishpat* 276:6, rules that a *davar she-ein bo mammash*, i.e., something that is not tangible including the right to choose the recipients of charitable funds, cannot pass by means of inheritance. *Shakh, Ḥoshen Mishpat* 264:4, further rules that such rights cannot be transferred nor can such rights be reclaimed if another person is in possession. For the discussion of the rights of an heir who is in possession see *Ketzot ha-Ḥoshen* 276:2 and *Netivot ha-Mishpat* 276:4.

Similarly, the right to perform a *mitzvah* cannot be alienated. For example, a father is obligated to circumcise his own son. Another person who preempts the *mitzvah* is liable to payment of a fine. However, in the case of a father who has designated a *mohel* to perform the circumcision but another individual frustrates that intention by seizing the opportunity to do so himself, *Shiltei Gibborim, Ḥullin* 87a, cites Rosh who rules that there is no recovery. The reason is clearly that, since such a right is not tangible, it is not subject to transfer by means of *kinyan*. Nevertheless, *Shiltei Gibborim* himself, *Bava Kamma* 91b and *Berakhot* 47a, rules that if a host designates a person to lead in *Birkat ha-Mazon* but another person preempts that prerogative the fine is assessed. See R. Naphtali Zevi Judah Berlin, *Teshuvot Meshiv Davar*, 11, no. 14.

7. This exposition readily reflects the position of the early-day authorities who maintain that future interests (*davar she-lo ba le-olam*) are intrinsically unconveyable. See *Teshuvot Rivash*, no. 328 and *Tashbatz*, IV, no. 13. See also *Levush, Ḥoshen Mishpat* 209:4; *Kiryat Sefer, Hilkhot Mekhirah*, chap. 22; *Noda bi-Yehuda, Mahadura Tinyana, Even ha-Ezer*, no. 54, sec. 12; *Netivot ha-Mishpat* 207:18; *Imrei Binah, Hilkhot Halva'ah*, no. 63; and *Ḥazon Ish, Dema'i*, no. 17. Cf., however, *Nemukei Yosef, Bava Metzi'a* 66b; *Sefer ha-Yashar*, no. 592; *Rashba, Bava Metzi'a* 66b; *Teshuvot Maharam Mintz*, no. 35; *Teshuvot Mabit*, 11, no. 137; *Derishah, Ḥoshen Mishpat* 209:3; *Sema, Ḥoshen Mishpat* 203:19; *Teshuvat Mahari Basan*, no. 19; and *Teshuvot R. Alexander Sender Margoliyot, Even ha-Ezer* no. 37, sec. 14, who maintain that such conveyances fail because of a lack of a "meeting of minds." Cf., *Tosafei ha-Rosh*, cited in *Shittah Mekubbetzet, Bava Batra* 142b. See also R. Elchanan Wasserman, *Kovetz Shi'urim, Bava Batra*, sec. 276, who asserts that these conflicting views are reflected in the controversy with regard to whether *situmta*, i.e., a non-statutory *kinyan* born of trade practice, is effective as a conveyance of a future interest. Thus, for example, *Ketzot ha-Ḥoshen* 201:1, peremptorily dismisses the notion that *situmta* is valid for effecting such conveyances. However, even according to the authorities who recognize the efficacy of *situmta* with regard to future interests, the conveyance is not consummated until the future

This perspective regarding a *shi'bud nekhasim* serves to resolve yet another perplexity. That a person's property may be seized in satisfaction of a debt is readily understandable. The concomitant of the debtor's duty to repay a debt is the creditor's right to seize the debtor's property. The right to claim property from a successor in title is less

interest is actualized or, in the terms of the Myth of the Tentacles, until the separated tentacles can attach themselves to a concrete object. See also R. Shalom Mordecai Schwadron, *Teshuvot Maharsham*, IV, no. 66.

Teshuvot Rivash cites and rebuts an earlier scholar who allegedly asserted that conveyance of a future interest fails simply because there is no "meeting of minds" with regard to what lies in the future. Accordingly, that scholar argued, if another factor is present that does serve to generate determination, e.g., an oath to honor the conveyance, the *kinyan* is effective. In accordance with his thesis, that scholar justified the validity of Esau's sale of his birthright, a future interest, on the basis of the fact that it was accompanied by an oath. R. Chaim ibn Attar, *Commentary on the Bible*, Genesis 25:33, declares that, although future interests can be transferred, nevertheless, inchoate interests cannot be conveyed and that Esau's oath was designed to assure that he would not assert inchoate rights associated with his birthright.

[It may be of interest to note that the earlier scholar was identified by Rivash's interlocutor as R. Jacob ben ha-Rosh, the author of *Tur Shulḥan Arukh* who, in turn, proffered his comments in the name of Rosh. Rivash peremptorily derides the thesis advanced and its attribution to R. Jacob ben ha-Rosh or his father. Those comments now appear in the published biblical commentary of the *Ba'al ha-Turim, Peirush ha-Tur he-Arukh al ha-Torah*. R. Joseph Saul Nathanson, *Sho'el u-Meshiv, Mahadura Telita'ah*, II, no. 163, asserts that had Rivash been aware of that work he would have accepted the view conveyed to him.

Contrary to the view of *Sho'el u-Meshiv*, it seems to this writer that the flavor of Rivash's dismissive comment, "Neither the Rosh nor Rabbenu Ya'akov are signatories to it," reflects Rivash's awareness of a manuscript ascribed to R. Jacob and it is precisely the authenticity of that attribution that Rivash challenges. Rivash disputes the provenance of the manuscript precisely because he is convinced that it contradicts at least one clearly evident matter of Halakhah. Rivash's skeptical reaction to attribution of authorship of previously unknown manuscripts to luminaries of an earlier generation is reflected in the attitude of more recent authorities, particularly Ḥazon Ish and R. Moshe Feinstein to newly-discovered rabbinic manuscripts. See R. Moshe Bleich, "The Role of Manuscripts in Halakhic Decision-Making: Ḥazon Ish, His Precursors and Contemporaries," *Tradition*, Winter 1993.

Parenthetically, *Sho'el u-Meshiv's* acceptance of the view presented in this source parallels his espousal of the concept of a proprietary interest in intellectual property. See *infra*, note 10. Each of those positions can be entertained only upon rejection of the notion that property interests are the product of ontology.]

readily understandable. The debtor's title to the land is extinguished with transfer of the property to a third party. What causes the claim against the purchaser to give rise to a lien that travels with the land? Of course, it might be argued that the funds advanced serve as a *kinyan* conferring a limited property interest that vests in the creditor immediately, i.e., the right to seize the property in the event of non-payment of the debt. If so, having conveyed that right to the creditor, the debtor cannot assign absolute title to the purchaser of that property. But what of property acquired by the debtor only subsequent to contracting the debt? No interest can be conveyed in after-acquired property. How then does the creditor acquire the right to prevent conveyance of absolute title in after-acquired property?

The matter is entirely resolved upon recognition that a *shi'bud nekhasim* is a derivative of a *shi'bud ha-guf*, i.e., that the lien against property flows from a lien *in personam*. The creditor's tentacles attach themselves to the person of the debtor. All of the debtor's property is attached to his person by similar suction cups. Accordingly, that property is also attached to the creditor, albeit indirectly, through the intermediacy of the debtor's *shi'bud ha-guf* binding the debtor to the creditor. Hence, any after-acquired property becomes attached not only to the debtor but also to the creditor by means of the debtor's act of acquisition.

Underlying this analysis is the notion that a *shi'bud nekhasim* arises from a *shi'bud ha-guf* and that no *shi'bud nekhasim* in after-acquired property could possibly arise in the absence of a *shi'bud ha-guf*.[8] But it does seem apparent that a *shi'bud nekhasim* cannot ever arise other than as the product of a *shi'bud ha-guf*. Even hypothecation does not eliminate the *shi'bud ha-guf* by creating a *shi'bud nekhasim* exclusively. Rather, hypothecation is a limitation upon the ambit of the tentacles constituting the *shi'bud ha-guf* allowing them to extend only to the hypothecated property through the mediation of a *shi'bud ha-guf*.[9]

---

8. For evidence supporting that thesis see this writer's *Be-Netivot ha-Halakhah*, II (New York, 5759), 191-194.

9. These comments serve to support the conceptual basis for the rejection of the view of R. Shimon Grunwald, *Teshuvot Maharshag*, I, *Yoreh De'ah*, no. 5 and *No'am*, II (5719), 33-37, and of R. Moshe Feinstein, *Iggerot Mosheh*, I, *Yoreh De'ah*, no. 5 and *Iggerot Mosheh*, *Yoreh De'ah*, II, nos. 62-63, regarding payment of interest by corporations.

Despite the contrary opinion of some authorities, it seems to me that Jewish law does not recognize inchoate rights such as those reflected in intellectual property for the simple reason that tentacles, even though they are metaphysical, cannot attach themselves other than to physical entities.[10] Tentacles may be metaphysical but they can link only that which is tangibly present in the physical world.

The notion that property is a concept associated with that which is concrete but does not encompass the ephemeral or the inchoate is poignantly reflected in a German case regarding electrical power. In the early years of electricity, a German citizen was accused of having stolen electricity. The facts were firmly established but the case was nevertheless dismissed. The facts of the 1899 case are as follows: A man rented an apartment that was furnished with electricity. A meter measured the amount of current that was consumed; however, the tenant, a clever handyman, withdrew the current before it reached the meter. Criminal proceedings for theft were eventually brought against him and the accused tenant was found guilty. On appeal, however, the Reichsgericht, the highest German court at the time,[11] acquitted the accused.[12] The

---

See R. Ya'akov Yitzchak Weisz, *Teshuvot Minḥat Yitzḥak*, III, no. 1, sec. 3. Since every debt generates a *shi'bud ha-guf*, hypothecation does not serve to avoid a prohibition against payment of interest on the grounds that the obligation to make such payment does not devolve upon the person of the debtor, but only upon property. That assertion is devoid of halakhic import if there cannot exist a *shi'bud nekhasim* in the absence of a juridically prior *shi'bud ha-guf*.

10. See R. Isaac Shmelkes, *Teshuvot Bet Yitzḥak, Ḥoshen Mishpat*, no. 80. See also R. Zevi Spitz, *Minḥat Tzevi*, I, no. 18, secs. 5-10; R. Yehudah Silman, *Darkei Ḥoshen* (Kiryat Sefer, 5759), p. 257; R. Avraham Levy, *Lo Kol ha-Zekhuyot Shemurot* (Kiryat Sefer, 5761); and R. Samuel Baruch Genut, *Or Yisra'el*, no. 59 (Nisan, 5770). Cf., the view of R. Joseph Saul Nathanson, *Teshuvot Sho'el u-Meshiv, Mahadura Kamma*, I, no. 44. The extensive earlier rabbinic literature devoted to this topic focuses primarily upon the rights of a publisher and upon issues of unfair competition rather than the rights of the author in his intellectual property. Cf., however, R. Moshe Feinstein, *Iggerot Mosheh, Oraḥ Ḥayyim*, IV, no. 40, sec. 19, and R. Zalman Nehemiah Goldberg, *Teḥumin*, VI (5745), 186-207. It is probably precisely because rights to intellectual property were not recognized that the *ḥerem* was harnessed as a device to achieve the desired effect.

11. The Reichsgericht was the highest German court between 1879 and 1945.

12. Judgment of May 1, 1899, Reichsgericht, Ger., 32 Entscheidungen des Reichsgerichts

court, in a careful and rather formal opinion, wrote that theft, according to the text of section 242 of the Criminal Code in force in Germany at the time, can be perpetrated only upon "*Sache*," i.e., "things" or "objects." The concept of a *Sache*, according to the court, was subject to interpretation and interpretation required an exploration of prior linguistic usage in legal settings. The court found that "things," according to the concept of German and Roman law, are physical objects which occupy a given space. Since case law was bound to this historical juristic meaning of the word, electricity could not be conceived of as a "thing" but only as a *Kraft* or force. In effect, the court ruled that property interests are limited to concrete physical objects and not to electricity, which is a power rather than an object.

The remedy, of course, was the enactment of a new statute specifically criminalizing the theft of electricity.[13] This gap in the law was filled by a statute of April 9, 1900, which expressly made punishable the theft of electricity by means of a "*Leiter*," or a conductor attached to a power line.[14] Nevertheless, in a decision of December 8, 1933, the *Reichsgericht* held that the operation of an automatic telephone by means of altered coins did not constitute an offense under this law, since it was accomplished by technical means not contemplated therein.[15] The laws of June 28, 1935, are designed to prevent the recurrence of such decisions and to bring the jurisprudence of the courts into harmony with the "German legal conscience."[16]

---

in Strafsachen [RGST] 165.

13. In Jewish law there might be recovery for theft of electricity on the basis that the person appropriating electricity generated by another has derived financial benefit at the expense of another. The party generating electricity has expended funds for the purchase of fuel in order to generate electricity; the user of electricity has directly benefited from the expenditure of those funds. However, in Jewish law that is a cause of action entirely different from theft.

14. RGBL, II, 228

15. *Entscheidungen in Strafsachen*, 165.

16. By the "Gesetz zur Anderung des Strafgesetzbuchs" of June 28, 1935, Art. 8, a provision on the "misuse of automats," designed to correct this decision, is inserted in the *Reichsstrafgesetzbuch* as 265a.

In Jewish law as well there is always the possibility of plugging the lacunae by means of rabbinic legislation provided that there is a properly constituted body enjoying such legislative power.

The Myth of the Tentacles does not require the conclusion that a conveyance can be only of a fee simple absolute but that particular rights cannot be conveyed. Property is indeed a "bundle of rights" but only in the sense that property is a kind of substratum or *Ding an Sich* in which multiple interests coalesce. Each of those interests can be teased out of the bundle and separately conveyed. Examples of conveyance of only a particular right abound.

An object can also be conveyed for a particular use to the exclusion of all other uses. A "use" itself is inchoate and cannot be transferred. But the physical component of an item of property that makes such a use possible *can* be conveyed. That factor is distinct from factors that make other uses possible. Hence, that factor may be isolated and conveyed to the exclusion of all others. Thus, servitudes exist in Jewish law. A servitude, in Jewish law, is the transfer of an interest in the underlying property and it is termed a *shi'bud*. A revocable servitude is generally termed a license. The notion of a servitude reflects the concept of some interest inherent in the property whereas a license has the flavor of a right or privilege that is personal in nature. In Jewish law, a license is certainly revocable because it conveys no property interest. It merely allows for acts to be performed on sufferance. If no right vests, there exists at most a mere promise of ongoing sufferance. Even if the license is granted in return for valuable consideration, a cause of action will arise only for recovery of funds expended, but not for specific performance. A servitude, on the other hand, is the conveyance of a particular aspect of the property and vests in the recipient immediately.

Jewish law could not recognize the sale of commodity futures in a conventional sense. Nevertheless, it is quite possible, at least in some cases, to transfer a future interest by means of utilizing a device making it possible to alienate a particular present interest. The "fruits of a tree" (*peirot dekel*) do not exist until they are grown. Hence, as "a thing that has as yet not come into the world" (*davar she-lo ba le-olam*), no present property interest has vested and, consequently, title to the fruit cannot be alienated. But, it is entirely possible to transfer title to the physical component of a tree that is responsible for the production of fruit. Transfer of *dekel le-peirotav*, i.e., "the tree for its fruits," is not the conveyance of a future interest; it is the conveyance of a particular, presently existing, component of the tree.

The owner of a tree becomes the owner of fruit yielded by the tree because it is the issue or *yotzei* of his property, just as the owner of a cow becomes the owner of its calf simply because the calf is the progeny of the cow. True, the proprietor of the tree becomes the owner of the fruit only when the fruit comes into existence. But, it is not necessary to acquire all the rights that coalesce in the ownership of a tree in the conventional sense in order to acquire title to its emerging fruit. Inherent in a fruit tree is a "power" that causes fruit to grow. Title to the power to produce fruit that is resident in the tree is sufficient to vest title to the fruit in the owner of that power at such time as the fruit comes into existence, since the fruit is the issue of that power. Students of philosophy are familiar with the Aristotelian notion of an entelechy. For Aristotle, all future acorns are present in an oak tree in minuscule form from the moment of the tree's inception, even though they cannot be perceived by the naked eye, just as all ova produced in a woman's lifetime are present in the *corpora lutea* present in a female child's ovaries at birth. Aristotle's entelechy may be metaphysical rather than physical but it is certainly located within the confines of a physical entity. Jewish law reifies that entelechy and regards it as a presently existing, tangible entity.

The basic concept is eloquently expressed in an anecdote well-known among rabbinic scholars. In European communities of not so long ago, householders often owned cows that were kept in the backyard so that milk, butter and cheese would be readily and cheaply available. Rabbinic appointments came with certain emoluments, usually including a parsonage and often a cow. It happened that a wagon driver in the city of Brest-Litovsk, known among Jews as Brisk, suffered the loss of his horse upon which he depended to eke out a meager livelihood. He approached the rabbi of the city, the famed R. Chaim of Brisk, with his woe. The rabbi responded by telling him that he did not have sufficient money to purchase a replacement for the deceased horse and would find it difficult to raise the requisite funds. Instead, he offered the wagoner his cow and advised him to sell the cow and buy a horse with the funds realized from the sale. He added a wry comment to the effect that "although the householders of Brisk may not be sufficiently charitable to provide a horse so that a poor man might earn a livelihood, they will not allow their rabbi to remain without a cow."

As the rabbi correctly foresaw, he was promptly provided with a replacement for his cow. A delegation presented the cow to the rabbi with the declaration: "Rabbi, we are not giving you absolute title to the cow. We give you the *parah le-ḥelbah*, the cow for its milk." Rabbi Chaim accepted in good humor with the comment, "The householders of Brisk are not only consummate scholars they are also charitable individuals. They did not give me absolute title because of their quite cogent fear that I might give away this cow as well and they would be forced to provide yet another cow. Now, since I do not have title to the cow, they have effectively prevented me from doing so. However, they did not have to give me title to the cow for its milk; they could simply have granted me the right to consume the milk! That would have been a personal, non-transferable right of use with the result that I would have no right to share the milk with others. But they are charitable people and so they enabled me to acquire absolute title to the milk. Now, if a poor man comes to my door begging for food, I can at least give him a glass of milk and a piece of cheese."

Rights in real property extend *ad infernos et ad coelum*. But air rights standing alone are inchoate and cannot be transferred. Nevertheless, the Talmud and the Codes entertain the notion of a condominium which, above the first floor, essentially constitutes ownership of space between certain altitudes, but they carefully distinguish between the sale of mere air and the conveyance of a servitude to erect a structure, on stilts if necessary, on the land. The former is inchoate; the latter a servitude on the land itself and is not at all inchoate.

As a practical matter, rights are divisible; some can be conveyed while others are reserved. Thus, Jewish law recognizes a right of usufruct, life estates, servitudes that run with the land and various other property rights. Servitudes in particular, as is the case with other conveyances, can be for a specific term or made defeasible by a condition subsequent. Applying the Myth of the Tentacles, we may say that the tentacles are composed of a variety of strands or tendrils, each one identified with a particular property right. The tentacle may be unraveled and each tendril separately attached, detached and reattached.

But, this is not a matter of logical necessity; it is simply a description of an ontological universe we cannot observe. In an alternative universe, all or some of the strands of which the tentacle is composed might be irreversibly fused. There might also exist a universe in which such strands, or some such strands, once divided and separately attached, cannot again be detached. Such an alternative universe does exist. The Gemara, *Bava Kamma* 90a, records an opinion to the effect that real property brought by a bride to a marriage cannot be conveyed to a third party even if both husband and wife join in the conveyance. Jewish law knows nothing of tenancy by the entirety. Hence, real property brought by a wife to the marriage remains vested in the bride. The husband acquires a right of usufruct for the duration of the marriage with the use of proceeds restricted to enhancing the family's standard of living. The husband also acquires a right of inheritance with regard to the underlying estate. As a result, for the duration of the marriage, the wife retains ownership of the underlying estate while the husband enjoys a life estate coupled with an irrevocable right of inheritance should his wife predecease him. As cited by the Gemara, Rabbi Eliezer maintained that those rights, once separated, cannot be conveyed to a third party either individually by either party or jointly by both entering into the conveyance. In effect, in this case, the separated strands bundled in the tentacles cannot be made to adhere to the shoulders of a third party. Only when the two rights again become merged, either by termination of the life estate by divorce or by the husband's inheritance of the underlying estate, which is automatic and requires no *kinyan*, can they be transferred.

There are no wills in Jewish law in the conventional legal sense of the term because devised property vests only upon the death of the testator. A corpse cannot be seized of property: death of the physical body causes detachment of the attached metaphysical tentacles. Nevertheless, an identical effect can be achieved by means of an *inter vivos* transfer given effect a moment before death or by utilization of some other device. Intestate inheritance can also be explained by the Myth of the Tentacles. In *inter vivos* transfers, the suction cup must, by operation of *kinyan*, be removed from the shoulder of the proprietor and attached to the shoulder of another. Inheritance takes place *nolens volens* and is entirely automatic. When life no longer exists, the seal attaching the suction cup to the body is broken; the tentacle detaches itself from the body and seeks out the heir or heirs to whom it reattaches itself without need of a physical act in the form of *kinyan*. Although, according to the opinion cited above, individual property rights of husband or wife in property brought to the marriage by a bride, or the strands of the tentacle representing them, cannot be detached, and transferred to a third party, upon death of the husband, his property interests (i.e., his life estate and right of inheritance) become extinguished. If the wife predeceases her husband, title to the underlying fee passes to the husband by inheritance, which requires no *kinyan*, and merges with his right of usufruct.

The Myth of the Tentacles is no more and no less a myth than is the notion of a magnetic field. If iron filings are placed on a piece of paper and a magnet is passed under the paper, the filings will align themselves in the shape of the magnet. We speak of the existence of a magnetic field that causes this phenomenon to occur. But we cannot see, feel, touch, smell or hear the magnetic field. We can only see the effect of this invisible, unperceivable entity. We might just as readily speak of the angel of magnetism that resides in magnetized iron and stretches out its tentacles to grasp iron filings. Indeed, we might say that iron is magnetized precisely because a particular angel has taken up residence within its confines. The angel of magnetism has a voracious, insatiable desire for iron filings. When brought into proximity with iron filings it stretches out angelic tentacles in an attempt to seize such filings. A magnetic field is either a metaphysical construct endowed with ontological reality – not materially different from an angel — or a convenient myth employed to explain certain physical phenomena in a manner that renders them more comprehensible to the human intellect. The Myth of the Tentacles is similarly either a depiction of ontological reality or a myth designed to explain legal phenomena in a manner that makes them more comprehensible to the human mind.

This analysis of the notion of property in Jewish law is also relevant to the understanding of contracts in Jewish law. The distinction between words of promise and words of contract is known to all who are familiar with the legal system. Only words of contract have the power to create enforceable obligations; words of promise are vacuous platitudes. There is a certain symmetry between conveyance of property and entry into a contract in the common law system. Transfer of title requires a meeting of minds. A binding contract arises only when there is seriousness of intent and reliance on the part of the contracting parties. Words of contract reflect deliberative determination; words of promise are not indicative of seriousness of purpose. As a general rule, in Jewish law, mere words are of no impact and are dismissed as frivolous. Consequently, words of contract are no different than words of promise.

Little wonder, then, that there are no contracts in Jewish law. But, of course, there are contracts in Jewish law. Contracts, to be binding, must be accompanied by a very particular form of conveyance. The simplest and most paradigmatic form of contract is one that arises between a debtor and a creditor. Acceptance of a loan creates a *shi'bud ha-guf*, or obligation *in personam*. That obligation is not simply a personal obligation but, literally, a servitude upon the body. Acceptance of a loan serves to convey a property interest in the body of the debtor. The loan is "guaranteed" by the body, not as a Shylockean entitlement to a pound of flesh, but as a servitude upon the body that serves to establish a property interest in the property of the debtor and hence in any handiwork he may produce. The biblical phrase "the debtor is the slave of the creditor" (Proverbs 22:7) is understood in a quasi-literal manner: A slave is the property of his master; a creditor has a property interest in the debtor. That property interest cannot give rise to peonage only because such exercise of a property interest is barred by Scripture other than as governed by the institution of *eved ivri* or indentured servant. Thus, the debtor cannot be forced to seek employment in order to satisfy his debt since that would be tantamount to involuntary servitude. Nevertheless, the creditor's "property interest" in the person of the debtor creates a servitude against any property the latter may own or acquire just as title to property acquired by a slave vests in the master of the slave. Similarly, the creditor's "property interest" gives rise to a servitude upon the handiwork of the debtor just as the property interest of the master extends to the handiwork of his slave.

Accordingly, as might be anticipated, contracts for specific performance are generally void. Contracts for future sale of real property, as well as whether such a contract can render a subsequent sale to a third party nugatory, is the subject of significant discussion. Such contracts are generally regarded as void because the contract itself does not serve as a conveyance of a tangible property interest. An inchoate obligation to engage in a future conveyance cannot be established by contract precisely because it is not a conveyance.[17]

Examined through the prism of the Myth of the Tentacles, the matter is readily understandable. A contract to repay a loan is nothing other than the conveyance of a servitude upon the person of the debtor. The tentacles binding the debtor to the creditor do not attach themselves to all aspects of the debtor's body, as is the case with regard to a slave, but they do attach themselves "to the body for its usufruct." Those tentacles attach themselves to the elements within the debtor's body capable of producing handiwork. The creditor cannot compel the debtor to actualize those elements by seeking employment solely because of scriptural constraints against peonage. Also conveyed in the contract is an interest in property presently owned by the debtor as well as property subsequently acquired by him. Through the intermediacy of the debtor's body the creditor's tentacles become superimposed upon all property attached to the debtor; similarly, later-acquired property becomes attached to the creditor in a like manner.

---

17. See *Ketzot ha-Ḥoshen* 206:1; *Netivot ha-Mishpat* 206:2; and *Imrei Binah, Dinei Halva'ah*, no. 21. See also R. Pinchas Scheinberg, *Taba'at ha-Ḥoshen* 203, as well as the much earlier and more extensive discussion of R. Aaron Sasson, *Teshuvot Torat Emet*, no. 133. Both authorities focus upon the particular formula employed in such a contract and regard the validity of such contracts as predicated upon conveyance of a lien upon the person for future performance as distinct from a mere undertaking to perform an act. In effect, they concede the doctrinal point regarding the unenforceability of contracts but interpret the rulings of earlier authorities who upheld such contracts as based upon language generating an immediately conveyed *shi'bud*. Similarly, the conveyance of a reciprocal *shi'bud* is imputed to partners who bind themselves by contract to share the future earnings of either partner. See Rema, *Ḥoshen Mishpat* 176:3.

The Philosophical Quest

Since "a laborer may withdraw even in the middle of the day" (*Bava Metzi'a* 10a), there are no oral employment contracts in the sense of a contract that can serve as a basis for enforcement of specific performance. That is not at all surprising since "mere words" do not constitute a conveyance. Early-day authorities disagree with regard to whether *kinyan* is effective in generating an enforceable obligation for specific performance. If not, the reason is that because, with the exception of the institution of *eved ivri*, a person has no power to convey his body. As expressed in the talmudic dictum: "For unto Me are the children of Israel slaves and not slaves to slaves" (*Bava Kamma* 116b).

Latter-day scholars had difficulty explaining the position of those authorities who maintain that *kinyan* renders employment contracts enforceable. Some reasoned that the *kinyan* does indeed generate a *kinyan ha-guf*, i.e., a conveyance of the body, but one that is limited in scope and duration and hence permissible since it does not rise to the level of peonage. Others regard it as giving rise to a mere servitude, i.e., a qualitatively more limited type of conveyance analogous to the conveyance of a right of usufruct.

The status of *mammon she-ein lahem tove'im* — "money that has no claimants" — is also illuminated by this thesis. Various tithes and other gifts must be presented to priests and Levites. The obligation is incumbent upon the owner who must designate the portion of the produce or the items that must be presented and who enjoys the prerogative of choosing a particular priest or Levite as the recipient. Nevertheless, should the owner fail to deliver the gift, no individual priest or Levite has standing to advance a claim against him. Nor can a group of potential recipients join in a "class action." Hence, the property is described as "money that has no claimants." Effectively, the obligation to deliver the gifts to a member of the class of potential recipients is reduced to a personal obligation rather than a concomitant of a right enjoyed by the recipient.

Applying the Myth of the Tentacles, the status of such property is readily explainable. Designation of produce or other required gifts serves a sacerdotal purpose but has no effect upon property interests because the tentacles binding the property to the proprietor remain undisturbed. Since the donor has the option of choosing the particular recipient, no member of the class of potential recipients enjoys the prerogative of establishing a property interest by attaching his own tentacles to the designated property; nor, for the same reason, does a potential recipient acquire a *shi'bud ha-guf* that could enable his tentacles to seize the body of the owner of such property. A financial obligation or an obligation to deliver property that is unaccompanied by a *shi'bud* is nothing more than a personal obligation unaccompanied by the transfer of any property interest. That state of affairs reflects ontological reality, i.e., it reflects the fact that no property interest of any kind can vest in any potential recipient because of the ontological reality that no such recipient has the capacity to apply his tentacles to either the property in question or to the person of the proprietor.

Law is not metaphysics; nor is Halakhah. By the same token, legal scholars are not metaphysicians. Nevertheless, metaphysical constructs serve to make legal concepts more readily grasped by the human mind much in the same way that Kant's categories impose a structure upon the universe and thereby make it comprehensible to us. Such is the function of the Myth of the Tentacles.

15

Is There a Right to Physician-Assisted Suicide?

We hold these truths to be self-evident, that all men are created equal, they are endowed by their Creator with certain unalienable Rights, that among these, are Life, Liberty, and the Pursuit of Happiness.[1]

I. THE DILEMMA

The opening section of the Declaration of Independence is couched in terms of human rights or immunities from state intervention. Those rights are born of recognition of fundamental moral values that dare not be suppressed. The formulation of the sentiments expressed in this historic document were prompted by the moral theory of John Locke who believed that moral laws are derivable "by the light of nature," i.e., by reason alone.[2]

It is doubtful, to say the least, that anyone would quarrel with the notion that life, liberty and pursuit of happiness represent fundamental

---

1. Declaration of Independence, para. 2 (U.S. 1776).
2. John Locke, *An Essay on Human Understanding*, Book II, chap. 28, sec. 8. *See also* Book IV, chap. 3, sec. 18.

349

human values. Standing alone, each of those values should be promoted; standing alone, none of those rights should be abrogated. But what should be done when one of the members of this triad of values comes into conflict with another?

Life would be so much easier for ethicists as well as for ordinary mortals if all issues were black and white. The ethicist may resort to the expedient of creating his own universe of discourse by positing a *ceteris paribus* clause asserting that "all things being equal" the moral judgment is thus and so. Real life however, is, quite different. "Honor thy father and thy mother"[3] is a moral maxim that obligates one to provide for the physical comfort of one's parents. But what if one's father suffers from chronic emphysema and wishes to be supplied with cigarettes? How does a moral individual react when confronted by a situation that imposes two conflicting moral imperatives? On the one hand, he is obliged to honor his father's wishes; on the other hand, by virtue of the commandment, "Thou shalt not kill,"[4] he is constrained not to aid and abet the wanton destruction of human life. How does a person escape from between the horns of a moral dilemma of such a nature while preserving intact ethical commitments?

Physicists are well aware of the phenomenon of antagonistic vector forces which, when totally equal, cancel each other out. When one force is stronger than the other, the prevailing force is equal to that of the greater minus that of the lesser. When the velocity of an object hurled into space is greater than the force of gravity, it escapes the earth's gravitational pull; when weaker, it falls back to earth; when velocity and the force of gravitational attraction are exactly equal, the object remains suspended in orbit.

Ethical systems operate in much the same manner. Ethical conduct often requires adjudicating between competing moral claims. Every ethical system must, of necessity, not only posit a set of ethical values but must also either arrange those values in a hierarchical order or develop a system of rules to be applied in resolving conflicts between values. Moral vectors operate in a manner which parallels the behavior

3. Exodus 20:12.
4. Exodus 20:13.

of physical vector forces. The weaker moral value must give way to the stronger. The ethicist is charged not only with identification and labeling of moral values but also with assessing and determining the relative weight to be assigned to each moral value *vis-a-vis* all others.

An excellent, although perhaps seldom recognized, example of this process is presented in the Robin Hood[5] narrative. Preservation of human life is certainly a moral goal and so is preservation of property rights. Robin Hood finds himself confronted with a moral dilemma arising from two conflicting and irreconcilable moral claims. His obligation to preserve human life compels him to do whatever is necessary to assuage the hunger of starving widows and orphans; his obligation to respect the property rights of others restrains him from expropriating any object of material value under the jurisdiction of the Sheriff of Nottingham. What is required is a ranking of values so that the moral agent may be guided in his conduct and enabled to preserve or promote the higher moral value. Robin Hood's conduct is predicated upon a determination that the sanctity of human life represents a higher moral value than preservation of property. Presumably, the Sheriff of Nottingham recognizes a different order of moral priorities. Perhaps the most significant aspect of the Robin Hood tale is the role of Friar Tuck who, as a "professor of moral theology," gives ecclesiastic sanction to Robin Hood's value judgment (as opposed to that of the Sheriff of Nottingham) and the course of action that flows therefrom.

The crucial problem is not identification of values. Regardless of our ethical orientation we are all fairly well agreed on the nature and definition of those values. A problem arises only when one value comes into conflict with another. The crucial questions arise in attempting to order those values in a hierarchical series or in attempting to devise rules for purposes of establishing conditions under which one value supersedes another.

John Locke posited the right of enjoyment of one's property as a fundamental moral value.[6] The dilemma faced both by Robin Hood

---

5. James Clarke Holt, *Robin Hood* (1982).
6. In his *Second Treatise of Government*, chap. 2, sec. 4, Locke declares that "all men are naturally in ... a state of perfect freedom to order their actions and dispose of their

and the Sheriff of Nottingham arose from collision of that value with the value inherent in preservation of life. The tension between those values recurs in the ongoing debates with regard to many current bioethical dilemmas, including universal health care, managed care, treatment of the terminally ill, and many other topical concerns, which, to a significant extent, center upon allocation of societal resources, i.e., conservation of property belonging to the commonweal. Many of those issues can be reduced to a simple and straightforward question: To what extent shall society be compelled to dedicate its material resources to the goal of preserving or prolonging human life?

The debate concerning physician-assisted suicide is not an issue of preservation of life versus enjoyment of property. It does, however, center upon a closely related moral dilemma. In the Declaration of Independence, Locke's enjoyment of property becomes transmuted into happiness. Apparently, to the American mind, both then and now, enjoyment of property and happiness are, if not synonymous, at least closely related concepts. Elimination of pain and happiness are indeed two sides of the same coin. Clearly, pain and happiness cannot coexist. Pain is the antithesis of happiness; removal of pain is itself accompanied by a form of pleasure that may be described as a rudimentary form of happiness. Suicide on the part of the terminally ill is usually motivated by a desire for freedom from pain. But the dilemma that is posed lies in the fact that, although elimination of pain is clearly a moral *desideratum,* when suicide is the instrument for achieving that goal it perforce entails sacrifice of another moral value, namely, preservation of human life.

The right to choose between conflicting values is inherent in liberty, the third member of the triad of values posited by the Founding Fathers. But in such situations, liberty itself is in conflict with the fundamental value inherent in life. Life and liberty are posited as specific rights discernible by reason. But it is not always possible to pursue both.

---

possessions and persons as they think fit, within the bounds of the law of nature, without asking leave or depending upon the will of any other man." In sec. 6 of that chapter he enumerates "life, health liberty and possessions." Noteworthy is Locke's inclusion of health. In chap. 11, sec. 135, he speaks of "lives and fortunes," life or property" and "life, liberty or possession."

The inability to enjoy both prompted Patrick Henry to exclaim, "Give me liberty or give me death!"[7]

The question which we are asked to address is not that of self-preservation versus martyrdom in the name of liberty from oppression. Rather, it is the conflict between preservation of life and individual autonomy that is the fulcrum of much of current bioethical debate. In the bioethical context the question is which of those two values should be promoted over the other. In its most extreme formulation the question is: Does commitment to the preservation of life preclude the liberty to commit suicide or does a person enjoy absolute autonomy to the extent that preservation of life is subservient to the principle of liberty? In the context of the ongoing assisted-suicide debate, the libertarian motto has now become "Give me liberty *and* give me death." It is precisely adjudication between the conflicting claims of individual liberty, personal autonomy and self-determination versus preservation of life as a societal value that is at the core of the issue posed by physician-assisted suicide.

II. THE CASE AGAINST SUICIDE

The "unalienability" of which the Founding Fathers of this country spoke[8] refers, not simply to a lack of capacity on the part of any person or power to deprive man of any of these fundamental rights, but also to self-alienation of such rights by the individual himself. Those rights are inherent in the moral condition of mankind and hence man can no more divest himself of those rights than he can divest himself of his humanity. Since freedom is inalienable, a contract providing for the enslavement of an individual is null and void *ab initio*. The British philosopher Thomas Hobbes similarly argued that a contract requiring an individual not to thwart the taking of his life even when that life becomes forfeit through due process of law, i.e., by means of execution as punishment for a crime,

---

7. Patrick Henry, "Give Me Liberty or Give Me Death," in 2 *The Annals of America* 323 (1976) (reprinted from William Wirt, *Sketches of the Life and Character of Patrick Henry* 137-42 (1841)).

8. *See supra* note 1 and accompanying text.

is devoid of either legal or moral significance.[9] The right to life is of paramount moral significance and simply cannot be limited or encumbered.

Common law categorized alienation of the right to life as a crime—the crime of homicide. Criminalization of *felo-de-se*, i.e., suicide, was formalized in England by King Edgar in the year 967.[10] In the middle of the thirteenth century, Henry de Brackton, the first English legal writer to discuss suicide, wrote that self-destruction is analogous to murder.[11] Thus, abnegation of one's own right to life (suicide) was regarded as indistinguishable from murder at common law. Since execution was impossible (and even if feasible, execution would hardly have been regarded as an appropriate punishment or have served as a deterrent) the prescribed punishment consisted of 1) denial of burial rites and of interment in consecrated ground; 2) branding the body with "marks of ignominy," e.g., a stake driven through the body and a stone placed on the corpse which was then buried at a cross-roads; and 3) forfeiture of goods and chattels.[12] Although comparable sanctions were never widely adopted in this country, at least three states still consider suicide a crime or an immoral act.[13] Some states forbid attempted suicide[14] while criminal sanctions under case or statutory law for aiding and abetting suicide are widespread and exist in the vast majority of states.[15]

---

9. Thomas Hobbes, *Leviathan* 209-10 (1963).
10. Norman St. John-Stevas, *Life, Death and the Law: Law and Christian Morals in England and the United States* 233 (1961); Hon. Sir John Vincent Barry, *Suicide and the Law*, 5 Melb. U. L. Rev. 1, 2 (1965).
11. Barry, *supra* note 10, at 2-3.
12. Keith Burgess-Jackson, *The Legal Status of Suicide in Early America; A Comparison with the English Experience*, 29 Wayne L. Rev. 57, 61, 64, 76-80 (1982).
13. Alabama, Oregon and South Carolina have each held suicide to be a crime. *See* Southern Life & Health Ins. Co. v. Wynn, 194 So. 421, 423 (Ala. Ct. App. 1940); Wyckoff v. Mutual Life Ins. Co., 147 P.2d 227, 229-30 (Ore. 1944); State v. Levelle, 13 S.E. 319, 321 (S.C. 1891).
14. *See* Royal Circle v. Achterrath, 68 N.E. 492, 498 (Ill. 1903) (citing Darrow v. Family Fund Society, 116 N.Y. 537 (1889)); Wallace v. State, 116 N.E.2d 100,101 (Ind. 1953); State v. Carney, 55 A. 44,45 (N.J. 1903); cf. D.C. Code Ann. §§ 22-103 (1981); *see also* 40 Am. Jur. 2d Homicide § 583 (1968 & Supp. 1997). But *see* Commonwealth v. Dennis, 105 Mass. 162,163 (1870).
15. Alaska Stat. § 11.41.120 (Michie 1996); Ariz. Rev. Stat. Ann. § 13-1103 (West 1989 & Supp. 1997); Ark. Code Ann. § 5-10-104 (Michie 1993); Cal. Penal Code § 401 (West

The law ascribes criminal liability for causing the death of another not only when an overt act of aggression is involved but also when death is the result of withholding the necessities of life, e.g., food, drink, or medication. Thus, in *Commonwealth* v. *Konz*,[16] a woman was held criminally liable for removing insulin from a refrigerator, hiding it, and thereby causing the death of her diabetic husband. Similarly, suicide, although primarily a crime of commission, can at times be committed by means of an act of omission. This principle was clearly affirmed by a New Hampshire court a number of years ago.[17] It follows that suicide, the crime of *felo-de- se,* is attendant upon causing one's own death by starvation or

---

1987); Colo. Rev. Stat. § 18-3-104 (1997); Conn. Gen. Stat. § 53a-56 (1994); Del. Code Ann. tit. 11, § 645 (1995); Fla. Stat. Ann. 782.08 (West 1992); Hawaii Rev. Stat. § 707-702 (1993 & Supp. 1996); Kan. Stat. Ann. § 21-3406 (1995); Me. Rev. Stat. Ann. Tit. 17-A, § 204 (West 1983); Minn. Stat. Ann. § 609.215 (West 1987 & Supp. 1996); Miss. Code Ann. § 97-3-49 (1994); Mo. Ann. Stat. § 565.021 (West 1979); Mont. Code Ann. § 45-5-105 (1997); Neb. Rev. Stat. § 28-307 (1995); N.J. Stat. Ann. 2C; LL-6 (West 1995); N.M. Stat. Ann. § 30-2-4 (Michie 1997); N.Y. Penal Law § 120.30 (McKinney 1987); Okla. Stat. Ann. tit. 21 §§ 813-818 (West 1983 & Supp. 1998); Or. Rev. Stat. § 163.125 (1990); 18 Pa. Cons. Stat. Ann. § 2505 (West 1983); P.R. Laws Ann. tit. 33, § 1385 (1969); S.D. Codified Laws Ann. § 22-16-37 (Michie 1988); Tex. Penal Code Ann. § 22.08 (West 1994); Wash. Rev. Code Ann. § 9A.36.060 (West 1988); Wis. Stat. Ann. § 940.12 (West 1982); *see also* 40 Am. Jur. 2d *Homicide* § 585 (1968 & Supp. 1997); Commonwealth v. Hicks, 82 S.W. 265 (Mass. 1904); Commonwealth v. Mink, 123 Mass. 422 (1877); Blackburn v. State, 23 Ohio St. 146 (1872); Tlirner v. State, 108 S.W. 1139 (Tenn. 1908).

16. 402 A.2d 692 (Pa. Super. Ct. 1979), rev'd on other grounds, 450 A.2d 638 (Pa. 1982). When there exists a legal duty to care for or to protect another, any act of omission results in criminal liability when failure to act proximately causes death and the omission occurs with knowledge of the consequences or through negligence. *See* Wayne R. Lafave & Austin W. Scott, Jr., *Handbook of Criminal Law* 182-91 (1st ed. 1972); J. Turner, *Russell on Crime* 402 (12th ed. 1964); G. Williams, *Criminal Law: The General Part* (2d ed. 1978); Lionel H. Frankel, Criminal Omissions: A Legal Microcosm, 11 Wayne L. Rev. 367 (1965); P.R. Glazebrook, Criminal Omissions: The Duty Requirement in Offenses Against the Person, 76 L.Q. Rev. 386 (1960); Graham Hughes, Criminal Omissions, 67 Yale L.J. 590 (1958); Rollin M. Perkins, Negative Acts in Criminal Law, 22 Iowa L. Rev. 659 (1937); Wallace M. Rudolph, The Duty to Act: A Proposed Rule, 44 Neb. L. Rev. 499 (1965).

17. *See* In re Caulk, 480 A.2d 93, 94, 96-97 (N.H. 1984) (refusing to permit suicide by starvation).

dehydration. Criminal sanctions provided by law for aiding and abetting a suicide should similarly apply in instances of passive suicide.

The classification of suicide as a felony in common law may appear to be antithetical to the common law right to bodily self-determination as well as to the recently developed notion of a constitutionally protected right to privacy. The classic and frequently quoted formulation of the self-determination doctrine is that of Justice Benjamin N. Cardozo in *Schloendorff* v. *Society of New York Hospital*:[18]

> In the case at hand, the wrong complained of is not merely negligence. It is trespass. Every human being of adult years and sound mind has a right to determine what shall be done with his own body, a surgeon who performs an operation without his patient's consent commits an assault, for which he is liable in damages.[19]

There is, to be sure, a fundamental tension between an individual's right to liberty and the denial of his right to terminate his own life. Perhaps the simplest resolution of that dilemma is suggested by the philosopher most intimately associated with advocacy of liberty and personal autonomy, John Stewart Mill. In his essay *On Liberty,* Mill argues that commission of an act which forecloses any future enjoyment of liberty beyond that single act cannot be justified on libertarian grounds.[20] In selling himself as a slave a person abdicates his liberty. Hence, argues Mill, the principle of freedom cannot require that a person should be free not to be free: "It is not freedom to be allowed to alienate . . . freedom."[21] A person cannot invoke a right to liberty as justification for being permitted to dispose of his own life. Liberty cannot exist as a transcendental ideal; liberty is meaningful only as an attribute of a subject. Destruction of a human life is *ipso facto* destruction of all the attributes of that life. Hence, to uphold the right to suicide in the name of liberty is illusory and even self-contradictory for it assimilates into an argument for the

---

18. 211 N.Y. 125, 105 N.E. 92 (1914).
19. *Id.* at 129-30, 105 N.E. at 93.
20. C.L. Ten, *Mill on Liberty* 124 (1980).
21. *Id.* at 117 (internal citation omitted).

right to invoke liberty the means to abrogate and extinguish that very same liberty. There is indeed an inherent irony in a claim of a right to destroy the life from which all rights flow and in which all rights adhere.[22]

Of direct legal significance is the fact that the liberty given constitutional protection by the Fourteenth Amendment[23] is by no means absolute. Governments retain powers of sovereignty vaguely termed "police powers" relating to the safety, health, morals and general welfare of the public. Enjoyment of both property and liberty are subject to such reasonable conditions as may be imposed by the State in the exercise of its police powers. Courts have long recognized that the Fourteenth Amendment was not designed to interfere with the exercise of such powers.[24]

The interest of the State in preventing suicide was first articulated in the sixteenth-century British case, *Hales v. Petit.*[25] In *Hales,* Justice Dyer enumerated a number of different and diverse objections to suicide. For purposes of later jurisprudence one crucial consideration is that suicide is a crime "[a]gainst the King in that hereby he has lost a subject . . . one of his mystical members."[26] Suicide may be prevented – and punished – by the King because it constitutes interference with his rights as monarch. The notion that suicide constitutes interference with the prerogatives of the monarch was accepted by Blackstone who, in his *Commentaries,* states that "[T]he suicide is guilty of a double offense; one spiritual in

---

22. *See* Robert M. Byrn, Compulsory Life Saving Treatment for the Competent Adult, 44 Fordham L. Rev. 1, 20 (1975); cf. Furman v. Georgia, 408 U.S. 238, 290 (1972) (Brennan, J. concurring) ("An executed person has indeed 'lost the right to have rights.'"). At the other end of life, the contradiction has been noted in actions brought by a child for "wrongful birth." *See* Gleitman v. Cosgrove, 227 A.2d 689 (N.J. 1967); Williams v. State, 18 N.Y.2d 481, 223 N.E.2d 343, 276 N.Y.S.2d 885 (1966).

23. U.S. Const. amend XIV, § 1.

24. As stated in Barbier v. Connolly, 113 U.S. 27, 31 (1884), "neither the [Fourteenth] amendment—broad and comprehensive as it is—nor any other fix was designed to interfere with the power of the State, sometimes termed its police power, to prescribe regulations to promote the health, peace, morals, education, and good order of the people. . . ." See also, Lochner v. New York, 198 U.S. 45 (1905); Mugler v. Kansas, 123 U.S. 623 (1887); In re Kemmler, 136 U.S. 436 (1890); Crowley v. Christensen, 137 U.S. 86 (1890); Ex parte Converse, 137 U.S. 624 (1891).

25. Hales v. Petit, 75 Eng. Rep. 387 (1562).

26. *Id.* at 400.

evading the prerogative of the Almighty, and rushing into his immediate presence uncalled for; the other temporal, against the king, who hath an interest in the preservation of all his subjects...."[27] The common law notion of preservation of life as a monarchical prerogative has been transformed in American legal theory law into an inherent function of government. Thus Thomas Jefferson wrote, "[T]he care of human life and happiness, and not their destruction, is the first and only legitimate object of good government."[28] As an early Massachusetts court noted, "[t]he life of every human being is under the protection of the law and cannot be lawfully taken by himself, or by another with his consent, except by legal authority."[29]

The government's function and purpose is the ordering of a social structure in which individuals may maximally achieve their desires and aspirations. In order to exercise their rights in achieving those goals, members of society permit other rights to be limited or curtailed to the extent that it becomes necessary to do so in order to preserve the social fabric without which all rights are rendered meaningless and nugatory. Prevention of suicide, even by force if necessary, is rooted in the firmly established doctrine that individual rights, whether rooted in common law or constitutionally guaranteed, may be abrogated in the face of a countervailing State interest.

The State interest in prevention of suicide is multi-faceted but clearly definable. The decision in *Hales* posited a monarchial interest in not being deprived of an economically functioning individual. To phrase the same concept in other terms: A suicide has already taken full advantage of the benefits bestowed by the community but seeks to shirk his own duties to the same community. The State enjoys an interest in the productivity of each of its citizens; only by assuring his or her life and well-being can the State reap the benefits of that person's labor. A close parallel is the State's interest for healthy citizens to assure its security and defense. Although earlier common law sources fail to declare explicitly that the King's interest is a need for citizens to serve in

---

27. William Blackstone, 4 *Blackstone's Commentaries* 189 (1871).
28. Thomas Jefferson, *Writings of Thomas Jefferson* 310 (Lipscomb & Bergh eds. 1903).
29. Commonwealth v. Mink, 123 Mass. 422, 425 (1877).

his armies or a need for procreators of soldiers to defend the realm, one New York decision declares that the State interest in preserving the life of each of its citizens is associated, *inter alia*, with its need for citizens capable of bearing arms. Thus, in *People* v. *Carmichael*,[30] the court noted that "[i]t is [in] the interest of the State to have strong, robust, healthy citizens, capable of self-support, of bearing arms, and of adding to the resources of the country."[31] Accordingly, the court held that legislation requiring motorcycle drivers to wear a protective helmet was a valid purpose of legislative action under the police power of the State. In *State* v. *Congdon*,[32] a New Jersey court held that the state could impose criminal sanctions on individuals who refuse to take cover during an air raid drill, declaring that "the basis of the State's police power is the protection of its citizens. This protection must be granted irrespective of the fact that certain individuals may not wish to be saved or protected."[33]

III. SUICIDE AND WITHDRAWAL OF TREATMENT

The State's interest in preserving the life of each of its citizens, to the extent that it is rooted in the individual's real or potential economic contribution, the State's need for military manpower, the individual's social contribution as a citizen, or any other benefit to the State, diminishes as the individual ages, becomes feeble and approaches death. Those as well as other interests[34] may well be balanced against both a right to privacy

---

30. 288 N.Y.S.2d 931; 56 Misc. 2d 388 (Genessee County Ct. 1968).
31. *Id.* at 935, 56 Misc. 2d 390 (quoting People v. Havner, 43 N.E. 541, 543-44,149 N.Y. 195, 203-204 (1896)).
32. 185 A.2d 21 (1963).
33. *Id.* at 31. Similarly, in Bisenius v. Karns, 165 N.W.2d 377 (Wisc.), appeal dismissed, 395 U.S. 709 (1969), a Wisconsin court declared that if it is deemed fatal to a statute that it *seeks* only to protect a person against his own actions, many statutes would be suspect, including laws requiring hunters to wear bright jackets, prohibiting riders on motor-driven cycles from attaching same to any other vehicle on the highway, requiring lifeboats to be equipped with life preservers, prohibiting aerial performances without a net, requiring water skiers to wear life preservers, requiring tunnel workers to wear protective helmets and other industrial employees to wear protective goggles.
34. Although the State can derive no "benefit" from a non-sapient patient in a terminal condition, it nevertheless does maintain an interest in: 1) preserving respect for all

and a liberty interest. Such a balancing doctrine was first enunciated by the New Jersey Supreme Court in *In re Quinlan*:[35]

> We think that the State's interest *contra* weakens and the individual's right to privacy grows as the bodily invasion increases and prognosis dims. Ultimately there comes a point at which the individual's rights overcome the State interest.

Although in *Cruzan* v. *Director, Missouri Department of Health*[36] the U.S. Supreme Court pointedly refrained from doing so,[37] a balancing test

---

human life and 2) preventing health care professionals from assisting in the demise of their patients lest their professional and ethical sensitivities be dulled with resulting deleterious effects upon their ministration to other patients entrusted to their care. These concerns, which apply so strongly in cases of attempted suicide on the part of competent adult patients, have even greater force when related to the terminally ill because of the latter's vulnerability and helplessness. The concern for the interest of the physicians and the hospital were clearly recognized in John F. Kennedy Memorial Hospital v. Heston, 279 A.2d 670 (N.J. 1971). Similarly, in United States v. George, 239 F. Supp. 752 (D. Conn. 1965), the Court declared that "the doctor's conscience and professional oath must be respected" and accordingly refused to permit the withholding of a blood transfusion labeling such a course of action as "amounting to medical malpractice." *Id.* at 754.

35. 355 A.2d 647 (N.J. 1976).
36. 497 U.S. 261 (1990).
37. The Cruzan decision should not be construed as affirming an absolute liberty interest in refusing medical treatment. Quite to the contrary, the Court took pains to note that "the dramatic consequences involved in such a refusal" would have a bearing upon constitutional permissibility. *Id.* at 279. The decision was apparently based upon a determination that, because of the facts of that particular case, the State's interests could not overcome the rights of the individual. Thus, the Court declared:
> But determining that a person has a "liberty interest" under the Due Process Clause does not end the inquiry; "whether respondent's constitutional rights have been isolated must be determined be balancing his liberty interest against the relevant state interests." Youngberg v. Romeo, 457 U.S. 307, 321 (1982). See also Mills v. Rogers, 457 U.S. 291, 299 (1982).
> Petitioners insist that under the general holding of our cases, the forced administration of life-sustaining medical treatment, and even of artificially delivered food and water essential to life, would implicate a competent person's liberty interest. Although we think the logic of the cases discussed above would embrace such a liberty interest, the dramatic consequences involved in refusal

taken to its extreme may arguably yield the conclusion that the State's interests are never so great as to require unwanted medical intervention. Indeed, at least one commentator has stated that "The right of a competent person to refuse medical treatment is virtually absolute."[38] Although the American legal system may be moving in the direction of recognizing such a "virtually absolute right," existing case law falls short of establishing that principle. The vast majority of relevant cases deals with terminally ill patients. The few cases involving a non-terminally ill person, of which *Bouvia v. Superior Court* (Glenchur),[39] is the most significant, affirm such a right only for individuals affected with burdensome, debilitating and degenerative conditions. Two New York decisions that followed closely in the wake of *Bouvia* were similarly limited in application. In *Matter of Delio*,[40] the Appellate Division ruled that termination of artificial nutrition and hydration in accordance with the known wishes of the patient may be sanctioned "in cases involving a person existing in a chronic vegetative state with no hope of recovery."[41] This decision was rapidly followed by a somewhat more permissive ruling by Justice Edward Conway in *Matter of Brooks*.[42] Justice Conway felt "bound" by the *Delio* decision to permit a mentally competent nursing

---

of such treatment would inform the inquiry as to whether the deprivation of that interest is constitutionally permissible. But for purposes of this case, we assume that the United States Constitution would grant a competent person a constitutionally protected right to refuse lifesaving hydration and nutrition. *Id.* In a non-medical context the Cruzan court explicitly recognized the right of the State to prevent a physically able adult from starving himself to death. Id. at 280; see *infra*, note 75 and accompanying text.

38. Alan Meisel, *The Right to Die* 470 (2d ed. 1995). *See also* The New York State Task Force on Life and the Law, *When Death is Sought: Assisted Suicide and Euthanasia in the Medical Context* 50 (1994) [hereinafter "New York State Task Force Report"]; George J. Annas, The Promised End – Constitutional Aspects of Physician-Assisted Suicide, 335 New Eng. J. Med. 683, 684 (1996); Sandra Johnson, Setting Limits on Death, 2 BioLaw §§ 149-51 (July-Aug. 1996); Susan M. Wolf, Holding the Line on Euthanasia, 19 Hastings Center Rep. 13 (Jan.-Feb. 1989)

39. 179 Cal. App. 3d 1127, 225 Cal. Rptr. 297 (Cal. Ct. App. 1986).

40. 129 A.D.2d 1, 516 N.Y.S.2d 677 (N.Y. App. Div. 1987).

41. *Id.* at 4, 516 N.Y.S.2d at 680.

42. N.Y.L.J., June 16, 1987, at 1 (Sup. Ct. 1987).

home patient not afflicted by a terminal illness to refuse food in order to starve herself to death.

It is indeed true that in two New York cases the courts have refused to order treatment on behalf of competent adult patients who refused life-saving medical intervention despite the fact that, if successfully undertaken, the patients would have been restored to normal, healthy and productive lives. In *Erickson* v. *Dilgard*,[43] the court refused to compel a patient to undergo a blood transfusion in conjunction with an operation for gastrointestinal bleeding, stating that "it is the individual who is the subject of a medical decision who has the final say and that this must necessarily be so in a system of government which gives the greatest possible protection to the individual in the furtherance of his own desire."[44] *Erickson* involved' a situation in which a competent, conscious, adult patient was admitted to a county hospital suffering from intestinal bleeding. An operation was suggested, to be accompanied by a transfusion designed to replace lost blood. The transfusion was deemed necessary in order "to offer the best chance of recovery" in that "there was a very great chance that the patient would have little opportunity to recover without the blood."[45] The patient consented to the operation but refused the transfusion. In seeking an order to compel the transfusion, the superintendent of the hospital stated that the refusal represented the patient's calculated decision. The court noted:

> The county argues that it is in violation of Penal law to take one's own life and that as a practical matter the patient's decision not to accept blood is just about the taking of his own life. The court [does not] agree ... because it is always a question of judgment whether the medical decision is correct.... [I]t is the individual who is the subject of a medical decision who has the final say.... [46]

Erickson has been heralded by some as guaranteeing a competent patient

---

43. 44 Misc. 2d 27, 252 N.Y.S.2d 705 (N.Y. Sup. Ct. 1962).
44. *Id.* at 28, 252 N.Y.S.2d at 706.
45. *Id.*
46. *Id.*

the right to die under any and all circumstances.[47] That, however, is a gross misreading of the *Erickson* decision. *Erickson* is not a "right to die" case; it is a case regarding the patient's right to determine the efficacy and appropriateness of a proposed protocol of treatment. A careful reading of *Erickson* leads to a recognition of three points which make this conclusion inescapable. The court explicitly denied that the patient was unquestionably *in extremis.*[48] It was the *county's* contention that the patient's decision not to accept blood was tantamount to a decision to take his own life but "the court [does not] agree . . . *because it is always a question of judgment whether the medical decision is correct,*" i.e., the court did not agree that refusal of blood represented an imminent danger of death.[49] Although the odds for survival of the operation without a transfusion were poor and transfusing the patient offered the "best chance" for recovery, the procedure might indeed have been successful without a transfusion. Thus, refusal of a blood transfusion was not the functional equivalent of acceptance of death. Finally, and most significantly, every blood transfusion represents a trade-off between the risk inherent in loss of blood against the novel risks introduced by the transfusion itself, as well as the possibility that the transfusion might prove to be totally inefficacious. The balancing of these risks is also part of the "judgment whether the medical decision is correct."[50] Whenever such risks must be weighed, whenever such decisions must be made, "it is the individual who is the subject of a medical decision who has the final say."[51] As one legal scholar has categorized this decision: "Whether these conclusions of the court were medically correct is irrelevant. They are the premises of the opinion."[52] Since the patient was not *in extremis* and the proposed treatment was not regarded as absolutely necessary and, in addition, carried with it no guarantee of success, a question of

47. *See,* David H. Bamberger, Mercy Hospital Inc. v. Jackson: A Recurring Dilemma for Health Care Providers in the Treatment of Jehovah's Witnesses, 46 Md. L. Rev. 514 (1987).

48. *Id.*

49. *Id.* (emphasis added).

50. *Id.*

51. *Id.*

52. Byrn, *supra* note 22, at 3.

"a right to die" does not arise.[53] The case was resolved on the basis of the firmly established principle that the patient has the right to make all necessary decisions regarding the efficacy, wisdom and choice of his own treatment. It is this principle – and only this principle – that was definitively enunciated in *Erickson.*

Another case frequently cited in this context is *In re Melideo.*[54] In *Melideo,* the court refused to compel a life-saving transfusion necessitated by a uterine hemorrhage subsequent to a diagnostic dilation and curettage. The court stated: "[T]he patient is fully competent, is not pregnant, and has no children. Her refusal to submit to a blood transfusion even though it may be necessary to save her life, must be upheld."[55] However, in *Melideo,* the patient sought to decline the transfusion on religious grounds. Thus, the issue was not simply that of a right to privacy, but of a First Amendment right of free exercise.[56]

Neither the constitutionally protected right to privacy nor the right to Free Exercise as applied to religious practices is absolute. Even the privacies explicitly protected by the Constitution are not absolute. The public good permits searches and seizure with a warrant and, "if reasonable," on probable cause even in the absence of a warrant. Self-incriminating testimony can be compelled if the witness is given immunity from prosecution.[57] However, a far more stringent standard is imposed for the setting aside of a free exercise privilege than for overcoming a right to privacy.

It is a well established principle of constitutional law that not all rights are equally protected. At least prior to the U.S. Supreme Court's 1996 decision in *Department of Human Resources of Oregon v. Smith,*[58] constitutionally protected rights guaranteed by the First Amendment

53. *Id.* at 3, n.12.
54. 88 Misc. 2d 974, 390 N.Y.S.2d 523 (Sup. Ct. 1976).
55. *Id.* at 975, 390 N.Y.S.2d at 524.
56. *Id.*
57. *See* Kastigar v. United States, 406 U.S. 441, 443 (1972).
58. 494 U.S. 872 (1990).

occupied a "preferred position."[59] As later stated by Judge Simons in his concurring opinion in *Fosmire v. Nicoleau*:[60]

> [D]efendants' right to relief is manifest. Although her right of self-determination, standing alone, may be restricted if it is outweighed in any degree by cognizable State interests, when the State requires her to undergo treatment which violates her religious beliefs it interferes with her fundamental constitutional rights. Before doing so, it must demonstrate under the 'strict scrutiny' test that the treatment pursues an unusually important or compelling goal and that permitting her to avoid the treatment will hinder the fulfillment of that goal.[61]

The doctrine in place at the time of the *Melideo* decision was that free exercise of religion might be compromised only in the face of a compelling state interest. Although there is as yet no definitive standard for justifying the abrogation of a right to privacy, it seems clear that the right to privacy is subservient to the realization of legitimate state interests that fall short of the compelling interest standard.[62] In a long series of decisions, courts have refused to order blood transfusions save in cases

---

59. *See* Marsh v. Alabama, 326 U.S. 501, 509 (1946) ("When we balance the Constitutional rights of owners of property against those of the people to enjoy freedom of press and religion ... we remain mindful of the fact that the latter occupy a preferred position."). Although rights secured by the First Amendment are for the first time accorded a preferred position vis-a vis other rights in the Marsh decision, the phrase "preferred position" has long been used to describe the freedom specified by the First Amendment. *See* Jones v. Opelika, 316 U.S. 584, 608 (1942) (using "preferred position" for the first time in Chief Justice Stone's dissent); Murdock v. Pennsylvania, 319 U.S. 105, 115 (1943) (employing "preferred position"); Prince v. Massachusetts, 321 U.S. 158,164,167 (1944) (same); Saia v. New York, 334 U.S. 558, 562 (1948) (same); Kovacs v. Cooper, 336 U.S. 77, 88 (1949) (same); Kovacs, 336 U.S. at 90, 93, 95, 96 (Frankfurter, J., concurring) (same); Kovacs, 336 U.S. at 106 (Rutledge, J., dissenting) (same).
60. 75 N.Y.2d 218, 551 N.Y.S.2d 876, 551 N.E.2d 77 (1990).
61. *Id.* at 234, 551 N.Y.S.2d at 885, 551 N.E.2d at 86.
62. *See*, e.g., Wyman v. James, 400 U.S. 309 (1971) (holding that a home visit by caseworker in conjunction with dispensation of AFCD program is not an unwarranted invasion of personal privacy).

involving the state's compelling interest as *parens patriae* in order to safe-guard the welfare of children, or to save the life of a mother of young children or of a pregnant woman. Accordingly, the Court in *Melidio* carefully predicated its decision upon the consideration that "where there is not a compelling state interest which justifies overriding an adult patient's decision not to receive a blood transfusion *because of religious beliefs,* such transfusions should not be ordered."[63] Absent such a belief and the concomitant assertion of a free exercise claim, the court would have had no hesitation in ordering the transfusion.[64]

---

63. Melideo, 88 Misc. 2d at 975, 390 N.Y.S.2d at 524 (emphasis added). This statement should not be construed as conferring legal sanction upon all forms of suicide when based upon an assertion of a Free Exercise claim. The Supreme Court in Reynolds v. United States, 98 U.S. 145 (1878), in an early formulation of the notion of a compel-ling state interest, queried rhetorically, "if a wife religiously believed it was her duty to burn herself upon the funeral pile of her dead husband, would it be beyond the power of the civil government to prevent her carrying her belief into practice?" *Id.* at 166. Presumably, the Melideo court regarded the benign neglect of not ordering a blood transfusion as below the threshold that would compromise a compelling state interest, perhaps because of the passive nature by which the life would be lost, perhaps because the patient might have died in any event either because of blood incompatibility or because of the underlying medical problem, possibly because, in the court's estimation, omission of a procedure of such nature would not be perceived as a blatant denigration of the value of life, or possibly because of a combination of these considerations. But *see* Morrison v. State, 252 S.W.2d 97,103 (Mo. App. 1952) (entertaining the possibility that a "religious zealot" may have the right to fast until death). Nevertheless other courts have ruled that the State may prohibit the handling of poisonous snakes in religious ceremonies even though the danger is limited to only the willing participants. *See* Hill v. State, 88 So. 2d 880 (Ala. Ct. App.), cert, denied, 88 So. 2d 887 (1956); Lawson v. Commonwealth, 164 S.W.2d 972 (Ky. 1942). Similarly, in People v. Woody, 394 P.2d 813 (Cal. 1964) (en banc), although a state statute prohibiting the use of peyote was held to be unconstitutional as applied to members of a religious sect which used the drug in its ceremonies, the court implied that had the State shown the substance to be injurious to the morals and health of the practitioners, curtailment of the religious practice would have been justified. In Quinlan, the court rejected the plaintiff's argument that the right to die is a religious belief protected by the Free Exercise Clause by drawing the familiar distinction between religious belief and religious practice. *See* Quinlan, 355 A.2d at 661.

64. Nor does People v. Robbins, 83 A.D.2d 271, 443 N.Y.S.2d 1016 (N.Y. App. Div. 1981), support the proposition that a patient is always free to refuse life-saving intervention. In Robbins, the court ruled that a husband was not guilty of criminally negligent

It is also quite clear that *Fosmire v. Nicoleau*[65] does not support a doctrine of an absolute right to refuse medical treatment. Although the patient was not terminally or hopelessly ill, her refusal to consent to blood transfusions was motivated in part by her concern "for the dangers associated with transfusion, particularly the risk of contracting a communicable disease such as AIDS."[66] Nor was there proof in the record "that non-blood medical treatments would have been successful."[67] In essence, although not decided on those grounds, *Fosmire* could have been construed as a choice of treatment case. However, the Court explicitly took cognizance of the religious objection expressed by the defendant albeit with recognition that the right to refuse treatment even in such cases is not absolute. The Court was, in principle,[68] quite prepared to apply a balancing test but found that "the hospital has not identified any State interest which would override the patient's rights under these circumstances."[69]

---

homicide in not summoning medical attention for his wife who declined such assistance. *Id.* at 274, 443 N.Y.S.2d at 1018. The court did indeed cite *In re Storar*, 420 N.E.2d 64, 52 N.Y.2d 363, 438 N.Y.S 2d 266 (1981), in such a context without acknowledgment of the fact that Storar involved a terminally ill patient but only in support of its holding that "[I]t would be an unwarranted extension of the spousal duty of care to impose criminal liability for failure to summon medical aid for a competent adult spouse who had made a rational decision to eschew medical assistance." Robbins, 83 A.D.2d at 275, 443 N.Y.S.2d at 1018. Although not emphasized in the court's holding, Mrs. Robbins declined treatment on religious grounds and, presumably, the court would have had little difficulty in affirming her right to do so on Free Exercise grounds. Nevertheless, even if the patient were incapable of asserting a right against which state interest would not prevail, refusal of treatment is certainly recognized in Robbins as extinguishing the spousal duty of care. That holding is entirely cogent and does not mitigate the State's right to compel treatment. The State's interest and right in preserving life does not generate a concomitant duty to the spouse rather than to the State.

65. 551 N.E.2d 77, 551 N.Y.S.2d 876, 75 N.Y.2d 218 (1990).

66. Fosmire, 551 N.E.2d at 79, 551 N.Y.S.2d at 878, 75 N.Y.2d at 223.

67. *Id.*

68. "In these and similar cases the courts have to weigh the interest of the individual against the interests asserted on behalf of the State to strike an appropriate balance." *Id.* at 81, 551 N.Y.S.2d at 880, 75 N.Y.2d at 227.

69. *Id.* at 80, 75 N.Y.2d at 225, 551 N.Y.S.2d at 879.

IV. ACTIVE SUICIDE AS DISTINGUISHED
FROM PASSIVE SUICIDE

Although it may be appropriate to recognize a balancing test, or even an absolute liberty interest, with regard to refusal of medical treatment, the State's interest in preventing overt acts of suicide is far more compelling. In addition to identifying the King's interest in preservation of the life of each of his subjects, *Hales* identifies a further State interest in prohibiting suicide in declaring that suicide is an offense against the King in that "the King, who has the government of the people, [takes] care that no evil example be given them."[70] Killing invites imitation; therefore, self-destruction serves as an "evil example" encouraging emulation by other susceptible members of society. Suicide "infringe[s] upon the King's peace" because a suicide is not an isolated individual act.[71] The harm is not really to the King as an individual but constitutes an offense against society because of potential harm to others. If openly permitted, suicide diminishes commitment to the preservation of life and compromises the State's interest in preserving respect for life which constitutes the fundamental underpinning of the social fabric.

---

70. 1 Plowden 255, 75 Eng. Rep. 387, 400 (1562).
71. In a study of what has been labeled the Werther Syndrome – the tendency of people to imitate a publicized suicide – Dr. David Phillips, a sociologist at the University of California at San Diego, has found that a significant rise in suicides occurs after every publicized case of suicide. A nationally publicized suicide, he found, increases the suicide rate by approximately 2% and by 7% among teenagers, who are highly imitative. According to Dr. Phillips, "hearing about a suicide seems to make those who are vulnerable feel they have permission to do it." *See also* Alvarez, *The Savage God* 58, 109 (1970). It is of topical interest to note that a recent study by Dr. David Shaffer, a professor of child psychiatry at Columbia University, has demonstrated that the effect of media reports concerning teenage suicide is a significant increase in both successful suicide and suicide attempts among young people. Professor Shaffer notes that there exists considerable imitation or "contagion" with regard to the phenomenon of youth suicide. *See* The New York Times, March 12,1987, at B6. That item appeared in conjunction with news reports of a suicide pact in which four Bergenfield, N.J. teenagers died. Less than a week later, on March 18, 1987, the Times reported the rescue by police of two other teenagers who had almost succeeded in committing suicide in the same place in an identical manner. *See* The New York Times, March 18,1987, at Al. Another similar incident is reported in The New York Times, March 14, 1987, at 30.

There are indeed many limits upon an individual's right to privacy and bodily autonomy based upon potential harm to others. The right to an abortion ceases at the beginning of the third trimester when the fetus becomes independently viable.[72] Despite the right of every individual to control his own person, there may be an exemption for intimate examination of a condemned woman to determine if she is pregnant in order to guard against the taking of the life of an unborn child for the crime of the mother.[73] A stop and frisk by policemen on the street may be reasonable despite the severe intrusion upon bodily security.[74] Similarly, a person may be forced to submit to a vaccination in order to protect the community from disease.[75] Likewise, a blood sample may be forcibly extracted from a person for drunken driving.[76] Accordingly,

> it is self-evident that the right to privacy does not include the right to commit suicide.... "[O]nly personal rights that can be deemed 'fundamental' or 'implicit in the concept of ordered liberty'... are included in this guarantee of personal privacy." ... To characterize a person's self-destructive acts as entitled to that constitutional protection would be ludicrous.[77]

That it is within the State's power to prevent an overt act of suicide is beyond question. Indeed, one federal court dismissed a constitutional challenge to an attempted suicide statute for want of a substantial federal question.[78] More recently, the U. S. Supreme Court in *Cruzan* recognized the authority of the State to prevent suicide even by passive means: "[T]he majority of States in this country have laws imposing criminal penalties on one who assists another to commit suicide. We do

---

72. Roe. v. Wade, 410 U.S. 113 (1973).

73. *See* Union Pacific Ry. v. Botsford, 141 U.S. 250 (1891).

74. *See* Terry v. Ohio, 392 U.S. 1 (1968).

75. *See* Jacobson v. Massachusetts, 197 U.S. 11 (1905).

76. *See* Schmerber v. California, 384 U.S. 757, 770-72 (1966).

77. Matter of Von Holden v. Chapman, 87 A.D.2d 66, 68, 450 N.Y.S.2d 623, 625 (4th Dept. 1982) (citations omitted).

78. Penney v. Mun. Ct. of Cherry Hill, 312 F. Supp. 938, 940-41 (D.N.J. 1970).

not think a State is required to remain neutral in the face of an informed and voluntary decision by a physically able adult to starve to death."[79]

In a concurring opinion, Justice Scalia affirmed the right of the state to use force, if necessary, in order to restrain a person from committing suicide:

> It is not even reasonable, much less required by the Constitution, to maintain that although the State has the right to prevent a person from slashing his wrists, it does not have the power to apply physical force to prevent him from doing so, nor the power, should he succeed, to apply, coercively if necessary, medical measures to stop the flow of blood. The state-run hospital, I am certain, is not liable under 42 U.S.C. § 1983 for violation of constitutional rights, nor the private hospital liable under general tort law, if, in a State where suicide is unlawful, it pumps out the stomach of a person who has intentionally taken an overdose of barbiturates, despite that person's wishes to the contrary.[80]

Nevertheless, the Court did not identify any inconsistency between a prohibition against suicide and a constitutionally protected liberty interest in refusing unwanted medical treatment.[81] In her concurring opinion, Justice O'Connor further found that refusal of artificially delivered food and water is encompassed within that liberty interest.[82] Whether the Court recognized an absolute right to refuse treatment[83] or, as noted earlier,[84] a more limited right involving a balancing of a liberty interest against countervailing state interests is not relevant to the crucial point, namely that liberty interests, even when recognized, do not extend to acts of suicide.

Cruzan does pose a problem in legal logic. If the state has the authority to ban suicide under all circumstances, and if both

---

79. Cruzan, 497 U.S. at 280.
80. *Id.* at 298-99.
81. *See id.* at 278.
82. *See id.* at 287, 289 (O'Connor, J. concurring).
83. *See id.* at 278-79.
84. *See supra* notes 67-69 and accompanying text.

manslaughter and *felo-de-se* may be committed by acts of omission, how is it possible to assert a liberty interest with regard to unwanted medical treatment including artificial nutrition and hydration?

Reflection upon the doctrine enunciated in *Hales* serves to dispel the problem. As previously noted, in *Hales,* Justice Dyer identified several distinct state interests in the banning of suicide, primarily, (1) the King's interest in being deprived of an economically functioning individual, and (2) restraining an act of violence that infringes upon "the King's peace."

As noted earlier, the benefits that the State derives from its citizens are commensurate with the contributions the individual is capable of making. Those contributions certainly decrease in a manner directly related to declining health and physical prowess. It is thus arguable that, at some point, the State's interests become not only less than compelling, but may even become non-existent, whereas the individual's right to privacy or liberty interest remains undiminished.

Such a balancing test is cogent when it is the State's positive interest in the potential services or contributions of a citizen that is placed in balance. That is indeed the nature of the State's interest as formulated in the first consideration enunciated in *Hales.* However, when an individual's liberty interest in committing an overt act of suicide is examined in light of the second consideration posited in *Hales,* i.e., the State's interest in eliminating violence, an entirely different and unambiguous conclusion emerges. Since violence is a *malum per se,* the State's interest in preventing violence is well-nigh absolute. Against that interest, an individual's liberty interest fades into insignificance. Acts of violence do lead to emulation. Moreover, violence is violence, whether the victim is a terminally ill, barely competent patient or a vigorous and robust young adult. Abhorrence of violence is absolute and admits of no exception. It is precisely because *felo-de-se* is a violation of "the King's peace" that a balancing test is of no avail. As stated by Justice Nolan in his dissenting opinion in *Brophy* v. *New England Sinai Hospital,*[85] "Suicide is direct self-destruction and is intrinsically evil. No set of circumstances can make it moral."[86]

---

85. 497 N.E.2d 626, 640 (Mass. 1986).
86. *Id.* at 640.

If the State cannot countenance violence to oneself, *a fortiori,* it cannot countenance violence to another or assistance to another in an act of violence to the self.[87] Furthermore, a right to self-violence, even if it were discovered, does not entail a similar right to assist or to be assisted in that violence.[88] Even if one were to maintain that the right to privacy or an individual's liberty interest is, in certain circumstances, stronger than the State's interest in preventing violence to oneself, it does not at all follow that the right to render assistance to others in committing such an act or the right to the assistance of others is equally strong. Surely, no one would argue that a liberty interest might be invoked as justification for consensual murder or as sanction for engaging in the practice of dueling. Violence to another is far more likely to be emulated than violence to the self. By virtue both of its nature and the involvement of more than just the effected person such an act constitutes a far more egregious violation of "the King's peace."

Contra the position of the Ninth Circuit Court of Appeals in *Compassion in Dying v. Washington,*[89] recognition of suicide as an act of violence negates the conclusion that the State's "interest in preventing suicide in general. .. like the state's interest in preserving life, is substantially diminished in the case of terminally ill competent adults who want to die" and hence violates the Due Process Clause of the Fourteenth Amendment.[90] On the contrary, although the state's interest in preserving life may be diminished in the case of a terminally ill, incapacitated patient, its interest in preventing an act of violence directed

---

87. The Ninth Circuit's observation, "[W]e *see* no ethical or constitutionally cognizable difference between a doctor's pulling the plug on a respirator and his prescribing drugs which will permit a terminally ill patient to end his own life," Compassion in Dying v. Washington, 79 F.3d 790, 824 (9th Cir. 1996), rev'd sub nom., Washington v. Glucksberg, 117 S. Ct. 2258 (1997), reflects a failure to recognize that administering a lethal potion is an act of violence against a person, whereas pulling a plug, which simply restrains further delivery of oxygen, is an act of violence against a machine.

88. Cf. Brophy, 497 N.E.2d at 639(accepting hospital's argument "that it ha[d] no... right to deny nutrition and hydration to Brophy so as to bring about his death.").

89. 79 F.3d 790 (9th Cir. 1996), rev'd sub nom., Washington v. Glucksberg, 117 S. Ct. 2258 (1997).

90. *Id.* at 820.

against such a person is substantially enhanced.[91] The more vulnerable the victim of violence, the more likely that countenancing such an act will result in emulation in the form of further acts of violence against others similarly situated.[92]

Such recognition also serves totally to dispel the notion advanced by the Second Circuit Court of Appeals in *Quill v. Vacco*[93] to the effect that, in violation of the Equal Protection Clause,

> New York does not treat similarly circumstanced persons alike: those in the final stages of illness who are on life support systems are allowed to hasten their death by directing the removal of such systems; but those who are similarly situated, except for the previous attachment of life-sustaining equipment, are not allowed to hasten death by self-administering prescribed drugs.[94]

Quite to the contrary, all persons are treated alike in their assertion of a liberty interest against forcible medical treatment and all are treated alike in being denied the right to commit violence. Assuredly, the Equal Protection Clause could not be invoked by "those in the final stages of illness" who might direct the removal of life support systems, were they previously attached to such systems, to demand overt termination of their lives by means of euthanasia.[95] The distinction lies entirely in the fact that active euthanasia entails an act of violence and that all persons are treated alike in being legally restrained from committing acts of violence. *Mutatis mutandis,* all persons are treated alike in being denied the right to commit violence inherent in *felo-de-se.*

---

91. *See* Cruzan v. Director, Missouri Department of Health, 497 U.S. 261 (1990).
92. *Id.*
93. 80 F.3d 716 (2d Cir. 1996), rev'd, 117 S. Ct. 2293 (1997).
94. *Id.* at 729.
95. Compassion in Dying, 79 F.3d at 840 (Beezer, J. dissenting).

16

The Physician as Conscientious Objector

I. ACCOMMODATION OF THE CONSCIENTIOUS OBJECTOR

Rabbinic lore relates an anecdote, probably apocryphal, portraying a lively student who flits from person to person in the study hall. To each one he says, *I have an answer. Ask me a question!* I do not claim to have a resolution to the dilemma posed when a conflict arises between a patient's rights and a physician's conscience, certainly not a facile one. My real task is to convince those in a position to implement a solution that a problem exists and that it merits serious consideration. Patient autonomy certainly deserves both moral respect and legal protection, but to demand of a physician that she act in a manner she deems to be morally unpalatable not only compromises the physician's ethical integrity, but is also likely to have a corrosive effect upon the dedication and zeal with which she ministers to patients.

Society has long recognized and been forced to come to grips with the conflict arising from a woman's right to terminate a pregnancy as announced by the United States Supreme Court in *Roe v. Wade*[1] and the moral convictions of a health care practitioner that constrain her to refuse to participate in the extinguishing of nascent human life. A physician's belief that certain forms of assisted reproduction constitute a violation of natural law does not impact an infertile couple's right of procreation for the simple reason that a physician who espouses such views will choose another area of specialization. Yet, the issue of whether an employer who finds such forms of procreation to be morally offensive, but who must nevertheless include coverage of such forms of fertility treatment in health care insurance provided to employees represents an unresolved moral dilemma as evidenced by a recent debate in the New York legislature.[2] Finally, the courts in *Tarasoff v. Regents of the University of California*[3] and its progeny have long since recognized and addressed the issue of maintaining professional confidentiality in the face of imminent criminal activity.

II. CONSCIENTIOUS OBJECTION
VS. PATIENT AUTHORITY

There remain two areas in which conflicts do exist, but are largely ignored. First, is the treatment of the terminally ill, in both the broad sense of the term and the more narrow sense, the determination of the time of death at which continued treatment is regarded as inappropriate. The second is in the field of neonatology with regard to the institution of measures designed to assure the survival of an unborn infant suffering from a serious congenital anomaly. Contemporary society has long conscientiously subscribed to the tongue-in-cheek adage formulated by Arthur Clough: "Thou shalt not kill; but needs't not strive

---

1. 410 U.S. 113, 153 (1973).
2. S. 936, 224th Ann. Leg. Sess. (N.Y. 2001); S. 7359, 225th Ann. Leg. Sess. (N.Y. 2002) (discussing acts to amend the insurance and health law in relation to health insurance and conscience clauses).
3. Tarasoff v. Regents of the Univ. of Cal., 551 P.2d 334, 340 (Cal. 1976) (holding that therapist's special relationship to patient also applied to plaintiff, and that therapist had a duty to exercise reasonable care when he was aware that patient was going to harm victim).

officiously to keep alive."[4] However, there are individuals who sincerely believe that the preservation of life is a paramount value, and that the quality of life preserved is irrelevant to fulfillment of the moral imperative generated by that value. For these individuals, failure to provide aggressive treatment for even the most premature neonate, for instance the infant afflicted with spina bifida,[5] or a severe chromosomal defect,[6] is the moral equivalent of infanticide. Likewise, failure to intubate[7] a terminally comatose patient, or even to administer cardiopulmonary resuscitation,[8] when there is a realistic possibility of clinical success, constitutes passive euthanasia. These individuals would also consider employment of neurological criteria in pronouncing death nothing but a deceptive subterfuge designed to disguise an immoral act by means of semantic sleight of hand.

There have been a number of instances where hospitals have declined to honor a request for discontinuance of a feeding tube and other life supporting technology.[9] However, such occurrences have been few and far between and have involved matters of institutional policy

---

4. Arthur Hugh Clough, *The Latest Decalogue*, in *The Oxford Book of Nineteenth-Century English Verse* 205 (3d ed. 1974). These words, when quoted, are almost invariably cited in a literal sense. In actuality, the poet was not endorsing the moral position expressed in this couplet, but was engaging in irony. *See* Maurice Benjamin Strauss, *Familiar Medical Quotations* 159b n.1 (1968).

5. Spina bifida is a condition, which results from defective development of the posterior wall of the spinal canal (neural arches) causing one or more vertebrae to remain incomplete. *The Oxford Medical Companion* 918 (John Nicholas Walton et al. eds., 1994).

6. A chromosome is a thread-shaped structure consisting largely of deoxyribonucleic acid ("DNA") and protein. *Id.* at 138.

7. Intubation is the introduction and maintenance of a tube within part of the body, particularly an endo-tracheal tube to maintain an airway for artificial ventilation and administration of general anesthesia. *Id.* at 435.

8. Cardiopulmonary resuscitation ("CPR") is the "restoration of cardiac output and pulmonary ventilation following cardiac arrest and apnea, using artificial respiration and manual closed chest compression or open chest cardiac massage." *Stedman's Concise Medical Dictionary for the Health Professions* 760 (John. H. Dirckx, M.D. ed., 3rd ed. 1997).

9. *See, e.g.*, Cruzan v. Dir., Mo. Dep't. of Health, 497 U.S. 261,268 (1990) (denying a court order for a third party to force a hospital to remove a patient's feeding tube and hydration equipment).

rather than an expression of the qualms of an individual physician or nurse. Solo practitioners are also confronted with this dilemma. A solo practitioner's isolation aggravates her dilemma because she must make a principled decision without the moral support of like-minded colleagues, and without the benefit of institutional legal talent or informational resources.

The first difficulty in generating awareness of the problem apparently lies in the relatively small number of health care practitioners who find themselves morally conflicted. The problems of the few seldom become the concern of the many. A more serious hurdle lies in the unwillingness of many medical institutions, as well as society, to recognize the existence of a genuine moral dilemma.

Law and morality occupy quite different arenas; nevertheless, law frequently gives expression to the moral values of society. Ostensibly, the decision handed down in *Employment Division, Department of Human Resources of Oregon v. Smith* was designed to establish the parameters of the Free Exercise Clause of the First Amendment.[10] *Smith* establishes the principle that only religious worship enjoys absolute constitutional protection.[11] According to *Smith*, religious conduct does not enjoy any particular constitutional protection so long as the religious practice is not singled out in a discriminating fashion.[12] The result of this principle is that, even in the absence of a compelling state interest, statutes of general applicability can be enforced against an individual even when conformity with the law compels compromise of religious scruples.[13] Prior to *Smith*, religious practice was accorded deference on constitutional grounds so long as there was no countervailing compelling state interest.[14] The *volte face* in constitutional law represented by *Smith* can only be explained by changing societal attitudes vis-à-vis religion in general and religious practice in particular.

---

10. Emp. Div., Dep't of Human Res. of Or. v. Smith, 494 U.S. 872, 890 (1990).
11. *Id.* at 877-78.
12. *Id.*
13. *Id.* at 889.
14. *Id.* at 883; *see also* Scherbert v. Verner, 374 U.S. 398, 402-03 (1963) (holding that the conditions used for unemployment benefits infringed on the party's free exercise of religion).

While continuing to pay at least lip service to the role of religion in society, society simply does not take religion and religious scruples as seriously as it did in days gone by. The prevailing notion seems to be that religious preferences are precisely that, namely, preferences, but not mandates. Thus, just as recreational, aesthetic, or gastronomical preferences must bow to laws of general applicability, it is assumed that religious preferences must bow to the demands of the dominant culture that are enshrined in statute.

Such a socio-political stance not only fails to respect the role of religion in the life and value system of the religionist, but also fails to recognize the historical and pragmatic basis from which the principle of religious freedom developed. Indeed, although often overlooked, the Free Exercise Clause of the First Amendment[15] was rooted, at least in part, on practical considerations.

The Framers of the Constitution of the United States made extensive use of the writings of John Locke, whose influence was most direct upon the First Amendment.[16] Locke recognized that religious intolerance was inconsistent with both public peace and good government, and deemed religious rivalry and intolerance to be among the most severe political problems of his day.[17] Civil strife and lawlessness, not to speak of war between nations, were regarded by Locke as the product of religious turmoil.[18] In an essay written in 1689, Locke stated:

> It is not the diversity of opinions, which cannot be avoided; but the refusal of toleration to those that are of different opinions, which might have been granted, that has produced all the bustles and wars, that have been in the Christian world, upon account of religion.[19]

---

15. U.S. Const. amend. I.
16. Michael W. McConnell, The Origins and Historical Understanding of Free Exercise of Religion, *103 Harv. L. Rev. 1409*, 1430-31 n.7 (1990).
17. *Id.* at 1431.
18. *Id.*
19. *Id.* at 1432 (quoting VI John Locke, *Letters on Toleration*, in *The Works of John Locke* 53 (Scientia Verlag 1963) (1823)).

Elsewhere, decrying the futility of religious coercion, Locke wrote, "let divines preach duty as long as they will, 'twas never known that men lay down quietly under the oppression and submitted their backs to the blows of others, when they thought they had strength enough to defend themselves."[20]

The way to avoid such strife is by assuring toleration and liberty of religious practice for all. Freedom of religious practice also enables a government to govern effectively. A populace that perceives its religious principles to be thwarted by the government will harbor deep resentment and disrespect for the ruling authority. Consequently, the government will be delegitimized in the eyes of those whose religious liberties are denied, thereby compromising respect for the government and its laws. Such considerations apply to matters of religious practice no less so than to matters of belief and worship.

There has been at least one case where a physician has testified that he would feel morally compelled to disobey a court order that would result in hastening the death of a patient[21] In *Grace Plaza of Great Neck, Inc.* v. *Elbaum,* Dr. Lester Corn, the medical director of Grace Plaza, testified that he would not remove artificial nutrition or hydration from a patient, even under court order.[22] Dr. Corn testified that not only would he refuse to disconnect the patient from a feeding tube, but also that he would not allow access for that purpose to a physician not connected with Grace Plaza.[23] Dr. Corn apparently adopted that stance, not on the basis of religious conviction, but because of his perception of the ethical commitment of a medical practitioner.[24] Dr. Corn "further testified that he would not disconnect a patient from a feeding tube because to

---

20. *See* I H.R. Fox Bourne, *The Life of John Locke* 190 (1876).
21. *See generally* Bouvia v. Super. Ct. of L.A. County, 225 Cal. Rptr. 297 (Ct. App. 1983). *See also* George J. Annas, When Suicide Prevention Becomes Brutality: The Case of Elizabeth Bouvia, 14 Hastings Center Rep. 20, 20 (1984). Although not cited in the decision, Dr. Donald E. Fish, chief of psychiatry at Riverside County General Hospital, "testified that he would have force-fed the patient with a nasogastric tube even if the court ordered him not to." *Id.*
22. Grace Plaza of Great Neck, Inc. v. Elbaum, 588 N.Y.S.2d 853, 859 (App. Div. 1992).
23. *Id.* at 863.
24. *Id.* at 858.

do so would be condemning the patient 'to death, which is in essence contrary to the dedication of medicine [to] the preservation of life and not the discontinuance of life.'"[25] A physician who internalizes such values because of an objective to fulfill the divine mandate, "nor shall you stand idly by the blood of your fellow,"[26] rather than based on a subjective perception of the ethical commitment of a medical practitioner, can hardly be expected to be less tenacious.

Civil disobedience, if tolerated, can rapidly degenerate into anarchy. Yet, even upon taking note of that concern as a moral consideration, a person of abiding religious conviction may find that her conscience demands that she disregard the fiat of a secular state when she finds it to be in conflict with divine law. Locke sagaciously recognized that when such a conflict arises the state is inevitably the loser, regardless of how the conflict is resolved.[27] Civil disobedience, even in the name of religion, undermines respect for the law; coerced obedience to laws deemed to be repugnant to religious scruples breeds disdain for the state and its institutions. Locke's solution was to prevent such conflicts from arising in the first place.[28] The authors of the First Amendment were prompted by the recognition that strategic retreat in the face of a religious claim redounds to the interest of the state, at least in the absence of a countervailing state interest.

III. THE CONFLICT BETWEEN INDIVIDUAL AUTONOMY AND PRESERVATION OF LIFE

Both the religionist and the secular humanist regard individual autonomy and preservation of life as moral values. The problem occurs when the two come into conflict, i.e., when one cannot preserve one value other than by compromising another. When this conflict exists, it is not the case that the secular humanist always gives preference to individual autonomy over preservation of life. No one has argued that either consensual homicide or dueling is, or ought to be, constitutionally protected.

---

25. *Id.* at 863.

26. Leviticus 19:16.

27. McConnell, *supra* note 16, at 1496-97 n.7.

28. *Id.* at 1445.

At least to that extent, society recognizes the state's paramount interest in restraining conduct designed to compromise the value of human life even at the cost of curtailing individual liberty.

Indeed, recent debate concerning a constitutional right to suicide, with or without physician assistance, has been limited to suicide on the part of the terminally ill or the seriously debilitated. The plaintiffs in *Washington v. Glucksberg* did not claim an untrammeled right to commit suicide, much less to assistance in doing so.[29] In a previous suit against the state of Washington, the plaintiffs asserted their right to "the existence of a liberty interest protected by the Fourteenth Amendment which extends to a personal choice by a *mentally competent, terminally ill* adult to commit physician-assisted suicide."[30] In arguing that "the constitutional principal behind recognizing the patient's liberty to direct the withdrawal of artificial life support applies at least as strongly to the choice of *impending death* by consuming lethal medication,"[31] the plaintiffs narrowed the issue to the determination of whether such rights could be advanced by a terminally ill patient. The district court and the court of appeals, relying on *Planned Parenthood of Southeastern Pennsylvania v. Casey,*[32] took the same position when "determining 'what liberty interest may inhere in a *terminally ill* person's choice to commit suicide.'"[33]

Despite an early decision in *John F. Kennedy Memorial Hospital v. Heston,* it is now well-established that even an otherwise healthy competent adult has the right to refuse medical intervention, even in life-threatening situations.[34] In *In re Quinlan,* the New Jersey Supreme Court determined that this right is based upon the constitutionally protected right to privacy as well as the common law right to bodily integrity.[35] Later, in *In re Conroy,* the court relied upon the common law right of

---

29. Wash. v. Glucksburg, 521 U.S. 702, 707-08 (1997).
30. Compassion in Dying v. State, 850 F. Supp. 1454, 1459 (W.D. Wash. 1994) (emphasis added).
31. *Glucksberg,* 521 U.S. at 725 (emphasis added).
32. 505 U.S. 833 (1992).
33. *Glucksberg,* 521 U.S. at 726 (emphasis added).
34. John F. Kennedy Mem'l Hosp. v. Heston, 279 A.2d 670, 674 (N.J. 1971), *overruled by In re* Conroy, 486 A.2d 1209, 1226 (N.J. 1985).
35. *In re* Quinlan, 355 A.2d 647, 663 (N.J. 1976).

self-determination.[36] Although *Quinlan's* emphasis on the constitutional privilege has been criticized by Justice Handler in *In re Jobes*,[37] as well as by Professor Laurence Tribe,[38] the existence of both a constitutional and a common law basis for such a right has been acknowledged in numerous cases.[39]

Less clear, and certainly debatable, is whether a healthy adult of clear mind has a constitutional right passively to commit suicide by refusing food and water.[40] The issue with regard to passive suicide is whether the state's interest in preventing the death of one of its healthy citizens trumps not only the would-be suicide's liberty interest, but also his right to bodily integrity. Although the courts consider the insertion and even the continued use of a feeding tube to be a medical procedure, which as such, may be refused by any person, they nevertheless appear to be willing to countenance such intervention in the face of refusal of food and water that might be ingested in a normal manner.[41] The court's statement in *Superintendent of Belchertown State School* v. *Saikewicz* implies that declining life sustaining medical treatment may not properly be viewed as an attempt to commit suicide.[42] Refusing

---

36. *Conroy*, 486 A.2d at 1222-23.

37. 529 A.2d 434, 454 n.3 (N.J. 1987) ("The *Quinlan* court may have been mistaken in its choice to base the decision on constitutional grounds.").

38. Laurence H. Tribe, *American Constitutional Law* § 15-11, at 937 (1978).

39. *See, e.g.,* Cruzan v. Dir., Mo. Dep't of Health, 497 U.S. 261, 278 (1990) (holding that a competent person has a constitutionally protected liberty interest in refusing unwanted medical treatment); Foody v. Manchester Mem'l Hosp., 482 A.2d 713, 717-18 (Conn. Super. Ct. 1984) (acknowledging that "[a]part from constitutional considerations, the individual right to self-determination has long been recognized at common law," and, "includes the right of a competent adult to refuse life-sustaining medical treatment." (citations omitted)).

40. *See, e.g.,* Bouvia v. Super. Ct. of L.A. County, 225 Cal. Rptr. 297 (Cal. Ct. App. 1983) (holding that patient who was mentally competent had a fundamental right to refuse such treatment). For a summary and analysis of that case, *see* Annas, *supra* note 21, at 20-21, 46.

41. *Cruzan*, 497 U.S. at 279 (finding that "forced administration of life-sustaining medical treatment, and even of artificially delivered food and water essential to life, would implicate a competent person's liberty interest").

42. Superintendent of Belchertown State Sch. v. Saikewicz, 370 N.E.2d 417, 423 (Mass. 1977).

medical intervention merely allows the disease to take its natural course.[43] Even more explicit is Chief Justice Rehnquist's emphatic statement in *Cruzan:* "We do not think a state is required to remain neutral in the face of an informed and voluntary decision by a physically able adult to starve to death. "[44]

It should then hardly be surprising that some members of society subscribe to a value system in which preservation of life is accorded virtually unqualified supremacy over other values. The problem is further compounded when the health care practitioner asserts not only that she regards preservation of life to be a more compelling interest than preservation of patient autonomy, but also advances her own liberty interest in the form of a claim to free exercise of religion.

It might be thought that one person's liberty interest, including the right to free exercise of religion, ends when it impinges upon the liberty interest of another. This notion is particularly compelling when that liberty interest is not only grounded in a common law right to be free from any unwanted intrusion, but also in an equally protected constitutional right of privacy. Nevertheless, in *Brophy v. New England Sinai Hospital, Inc.,* the Massachusetts Supreme Court ordered artificial maintenance of nutrition and hydration to be discontinued, and held that a medical facility must honor the substituted judgment of a patient in a persistent vegetative state.[45] However, the court also held that the medical facility treating the patient was fully entitled to remain loyal to its own moral convictions that constrained it from honoring the patient's wishes.[46] The remedy offered by the court was to authorize the patient's guardian to remove the patient from that hospital to the care

---

43. *Id.*
44. *Cruzan*, 497 U.S. at 280. Earlier, IN *Heston,* albeit in the context of a decision denying the patient's right to refuse certain forms of intervention, the New Jersey Supreme Court, in addressing the distinction between passively submitting to death and actively seeking it, declared, "[t]he distinction may be merely verbal, as it would be if an adult sought death by starvation instead of a drug. If the State may interrupt one mode of self-destruction, it may with equal authority interfere with the others." John F. Kennedy Mem'l Hosp. v. Heston, 279 A.2d 670, 672-73 (N.J. 1971).
45. Brophy v. New England Sinai Hosp., Inc., 497 N.E.2d 626, 633 (Mass. 1986).
46. *Id.* at 639.

of other physicians who were prepared to honor the patient's wishes.[47] Citing earlier cases where "maintenance of the ethical integrity of the medical profession" was recognized over a countervailing state interest,[48] the court agreed that the hospital and the medical staff "should not be compelled to withhold food and water to a patient, contrary to its moral and ethical principles, when such principles are recognized and accepted within a significant segment of the medical profession and the hospital community."[49] At the same time, the court found that so long as the hospital was itself not forced to participate in removing the gastrostomy tube, there was no violation of the integrity of the medical profession.[50]

However, it should not be assumed that the *Brophy* court established a clear hierarchy of values in which the need to maintain the integrity of the medical profession serves to establish the primacy of the individual physician's ethical sensitivity. The court pointed to the existence of "substantial disagreement in the medical community" with regard to the propriety of withdrawal of nutrition and hydration as well as to the hospital's willingness to assist in a transfer of the patient to another facility where the desired effect could be achieved.[51] The court emphasized that "[it] would be particularly inappropriate to force the hospital, which is willing to assist in a transfer of the patient, to take affirmative steps to

---

47. *Id.* at 640.
48. The earliest formulation of this consideration of a compelling state interest is in *Saikewicz*, 370 N.E.2d at 425. *See also In re* Conroy, 486 A.2d 1209, 1223-24 (N.J. 1985) (noting the state's interest in the preservation of life). In *Quinlan*, the court referred to the claimed interest of the state in the "defense of the right of the physician to administer medical treatment according to his best judgment." *In re* Quinlan, 355 A.2d 647, 663 (N.J. 1976). That concept may or may not be identical with the concept of the ethical integrity of the medical profession *Id.* at 668-69. IN *Quinlan*, the court, in effect, rejected that argument by substituting its own judgment regarding a proper medical response for that of the physician who did not wish to remove the respirator. *Id.* at 665-67. It would have been more forthright for the court to have declared that the state has no interest in preserving a physician's autonomous judgment with regard to proper practice of medicine. *Id.* at 668. In any event, the court treated "the right of the physician" as being predicated upon medical practice rather than upon ethical principles. *Id.* at 668-69.
49. *Brophy*, 497 N.E.2d at 639.
50. *Id.* at 638.
51. *Id.* at 639.

end the provision of nutrition and hydration to him."[52] Apparently for those reasons, and only because of those reasons, "[a] patient's right to refuse medical treatment does not warrant an *unnecessary intrusion* upon the hospital's ethical integrity in *this case.*"[53]

Less than a fortnight later, in *In re Requena,* a New Jersey court ruled that the right of a patient dying of amyotrophic lateral sclerosis to refuse feeding by nasogastric tube had priority over the hospital's policy against participating in the withholding of food or fluids from the patient.[54] The court ordered St. Clare's/Riverside Medical Center to remove the patient's feeding tube despite the Medical Center's willingness, and even demand, to transfer the patient to St. Barnabas Hospital for that purpose.[55] Nevertheless, the court conceded the Medical Center's proposal to be "a realistic alternative,"[56] and indeed an expedient one that "would seem to be an ideal solution to the problem presented by this case."[57]

Requena is distinguishable from, and hence consistent with, *Brophy* by virtue of the fact that Beverly Requena was conscious of her surroundings, while Patricia Brophy was in a permanent vegetative state.[58] This distinction is significant because the *Requena* court declined to honor St. Clare's demand of transfer despite the fact that Beverly Requena's physician was also a member of the St. Barnabas' staff; that, as the court acknowledged, the facilities and treatment skills available at St. Barnabas were equal to those of St. Clare; and that the transfer to St. Barnabas located in the same geographical area could be safely and easily accomplished.[59] Rather, the court based its decision on its finding that it would be "emotionally and psychologically upsetting"[60] for the

---

52. *Id.; see also* Childs v. Abramovice, 253 Cal. Rptr. 530, 535 (Ct. App.) (finding that no further right may be asserted when medical facility is willing to effect a transfer).

53. *Brophy,* 497 N.E.2d at 639 (emphasis added).

54. *In re* Requena, 517 A.2d 886, 893 (N.J. Super. Ct. Ch. Div. 1986).

55. *Id.* at 890.

56. *Id.*

57. *Id.* at 889.

58. *Compare id., with Brophy,* 497 N.E.2d at 627.

59. *Requena,* 517 A.2d at 889.

60. *Id.*

patient to be forced to leave the facility in which she was being treated, and that her removal "would also have significant elements of rejection and casting out, which would be burdensome for Ms. Requena."[61]

Nevertheless, it would be extremely naïve to assume that these two decisions do not fundamentally disagree. One can accept the assertion of the presence of an emotional and psychological burden at face value, and still question how such a burden borne for a short time could overcome and negate a state interest in maintaining the integrity of the medical profession. Quite clearly, the *Requena* court recognized no such state interest; indeed, it did not deign to acknowledge that other courts have recognized such an interest. Hence, absent acknowledgment of such an interest, the court should not have had mixed feelings in reaching its decision. Every moment that a court allows a feeding tube to remain in place represents a bodily intrusion and the invasion of a constitutionally protected right to privacy, as earlier defined by the United States Supreme Court in *Cruzan*.[62] Accordingly, the court should have forthwith issued an order directing removal of the feeding tube.

Although the court did not label it as such, St. Clare's hospital asserted that preservation of the medical facility's ethical integrity was a matter of constitutional concern.[63] The Hospital spoke of "the wrongness of denying food or water to a patient,"[64] and of "the need for all patients and potential patients of the Hospital to be absolutely assured that they would not be harmed by the Hospital or any of its personnel while undergoing care."[65] That assertion was contemptuously rejected by the court with the rejoinder that honoring the patient's request "is not denying her anything," and that, "*[p]roperly understood* it has no adverse implication for general patient care or for public confidence in the Hospital and its staff."[66]

61. *Id.*
62. Cruzan v. Dir., Mo. Dept. of Health, 497 U.S. 261, 279 (1990).
63. *Requena, 511 A2d at 892.*
64. *Id.* at 891.
65. *Id.*
66. *Id.* at 892 (emphasis added).

The issue requiring clarification is the meaning of the "maintenance of the ethical integrity of the medical profession"[67] as constituting a state interest sufficiently compelling to overcome a patient's right of privacy. The *Brophy* court found that asserting a claim of an obligation to treat a patient gives rise to a state interest in supporting that claim despite "substantial disagreement" among members of the profession with regard to the existence of such a claim under that case's circumstances.[68] In *Brophy*, the interest is treated as an ethical consideration in the classic sense of the term, i.e., as an assertion of a value, and hence a matter that might be individual or subjective in nature.[69] The *Saikewicz* court, which first enumerated "maintaining the ethical integrity of the medical profession" as one of four "countervailing state interests" that might serve to negate a right to refuse medical treatment, apparently took a diametrically opposed position?[70] That court categorized the "force and impact" of the state's interest in the maintenance of the profession's ethical integrity as "lessened by the prevailing medical ethical standards."[71] Accordingly, since "[r]ecognition of the right to refuse necessary treatment in appropriate circumstances is consistent with existing mores,"[72] it follows that in withholding such measures there is no threat to the integrity of the medical profession. As stated by the *Saikewicz* court, a state interest lies only in supporting a practitioner's judgment that is "in accord with the generally accepted views of the medical profession."[73] Thus, the expressed interest appears to be preservation of the integrity of medical *practice,* rather than of the ethics of the profession. However, if that statement is understood as meaning that the state's interest does indeed lie in maintaining ethical integrity, it is nevertheless clear that the

---

67. Brophy v. New England Sinai Hosp., Inc., 497 N.E.2d 626, 634 (Mass. 1986).
68. *Id.* at 639.
69. *Id.* (arguing that the state should not force medical professionals to take active measures "contrary to their view of their ethical duty toward their patients.").
70. Superintendent of Belchertown State Sch. v. Saikewicz, 370 N.E.2d 417, 425 (Mass. 1977).
71. *Id.* at 426.
72. *Id.*
73. *Id.* at 427.

Saikewicz court would limit that interest to preservation of only those ethical judgments that garner a consensus of medical opinion.

It is remarkable that both the *Brophy* and the *Saikewicz* courts (assuming that the *Saikewicz* court was also concerned with *ethical* integrity) focus upon the ethical integrity of the medical profession rather than of the practitioner. Both courts were willing to allow the medical profession's own practice *ipso facto* to serve as the standard for establishing an ethical norm. Such deference to the medical profession is misplaced. Physicians are not and should not be required, or even permitted, to become arbiters of ethical standards. Physicians, by virtue of training and experience, are acknowledged experts in medical science and clinical practice; they are also uniquely qualified to determine the prognosis of a malady and to assess the efficiency of alternative therapies. However, there. is nothing in their training or experience that qualifies them as ethicists. As an individual, the physician's ethical values are entitled to the same respect as any other citizen, but also to no more deference than those of any other citizen. Moreover, even the cumulative ethical values of all members of the profession are not entitled to greater protection than those of any other aggregate of individuals.

If the "maintenance of ethical integrity of the medical profession" constitutes a compelling state interest, it must be because society has a pragmatic interest in maintaining the norms that have historically been the hallmark of the medical profession. Society has a need for physicians who are healers, not "thanatologists."[74] Physicians can best protect society if their conduct is in the nature of a Pavlovian response and they intuitively and instinctively seek actively to prolong the life of a patient. Permitting a physician to withdraw a feeding tube—particularly when she does not wish to do so—serves to interfere with what hopefully is an instinctive reflex and desensitizes the physician's compelling urge to preserve life. St. Clare's Hospital well understood the meaning of, and the need for, "public confidence in [its] Hospital and its staff."[75] It also had a

---

74. Thanatology, from the Greek word for death, is the "branch of science concerned with the study of death and dying." *Stedman's Medical Dictionary* 1793 (26th ed. 1995).

75. *In re* Requena, 517 A.2d 886, 892 (N.J. Super. Ct. Ch. Div. 1986).

firm grasp of the meaning of "ethical integrity of the medical profession"[76] as a cognizable consideration in constitutional jurisprudence.

Requena is rather unique in that St. Clare's Hospital explicitly presented what was, in effect, a First Amendment argument.[77] A Roman Catholic religious order of nuns controlled St. Clare's Hospital which refused to accede to the withholding of artificial feeding because such conduct would conflict with its "pro-life" values. The court could quite well have entered into an analysis of the limitations of the rights conferred by the Free Exercise Clause and, most particularly, upon the availability of a free exercise claim in face of a countervailing constitutionally protected right to privacy. Instead, it inappropriately proceeded to correct the good sisters' "mistaken"[78] assessment of Catholic teaching:

> I suspect that part of the Hospital's insistence on what it perceives as a pro-life position in this case is a mistaken fall-out from the abortion controversy which is ongoing in our society. The Hospital, whose values are premised as they are on the loving care of people, naturally (and, I think, properly) views abortion as a terrible evil. But abortion involves the active, direct, intentional termination of life by interfering in the processes of nature. The life taken is usually perfectly healthy. The fetus does not in any sense consent to what is done to it. None of those elements are present in Mrs. Requena's case. There is no sensible comparison to be drawn between the two situations.[79]

Catholic morality is for Catholic moralists, not secular courts, to decide. Moreover, it is well-settled that not only are courts precluded from inquiring into the basis of doctrinal matters, but that the First Amendment protection extends to matters that are erroneous, inconsistent, or even illogical. In *Thomas v. Review Board of the Indiana Employment*

---

76. *Saikewicz*, 370 N.E.2d at 427.

77. *Requena*, 517 A.2d at 892 (noting the impact of the hospital's affiliation with the Roman Catholic Church).

78. *Id.*

79. *Id.*

Security Division, the Supreme Court declared that "religious beliefs need not be acceptable, logical, consistent, or comprehensible to others in order to merit First Amendment protection.[80]

Neither is unanimity among Catholics a prerequisite for assertion of a Free Exercise claim by a Catholic or by Catholic institution because "[i]ntrafaith differences . . . are not uncommon among followers of a particular creed . . . and the guarantee of free exercise is not limited to beliefs which are shared by all of the members of a religious sect."[81]

In a concluding homily that strikes as offensive to both the letter and spirit of the First Amendment, the court noted that the Hospital "rejoices in its specifically Christian heritage,"[82] and admonishes its health care workers "to recall the beautiful words of Jesus: 'Come to me, all you who are weary and find life burdensome, and I will refresh you.'"[83] The fact that ecclesiastic officials of the order responsible for the administration of St. Clare's Hospital—as well as other scholars whose moral views are more consistent with those of the court—would find this an egregious misinterpretation of Scripture is irrelevant. The Devil may or may not have divine license to quote Scripture to suit his own purpose; a judge most assuredly does not have constitutional license to do so.

Pursuant to an accelerated appeal, the appellate division affirmed the lower court's decision, but apparently only on the basis of a supplemental consideration. The appellate court declared:

> An equitable consideration here is that Beverly Requena had no notice of St. Clare's policy against withholding artificial feeding or fluids until July of 1986. The balance to be struck here is between the hospital's right to enforce its regulation and fundamental rights of the patient. Under the circumstances we find no waiver or estoppel against Beverly Requena who had no notice of the regulation prior to her admission or for 15 months thereafter.

---

80. Thomas vs. Review Bd. of Ind. Employment Sec. Div., 450 U.S. 707, 714 (1981).

81. *Id.* at 715-16.

82. *Requena,* 517 A.2d at 893.

83. *Id.* (quoting Matthew 11:28).

Viewed in this light, it is clear that Judge Stanton has not made a legal decision invalidating the hospital regulation but rather has relied upon factual findings that have substantial support in the record and he has balanced the equities in not applying that regulation to Mrs. Requena.[84]

It may certainly be argued that the appellate court chose to misread Judge Stanton's decision, but, if so, the appellate court was assisted by Judge Stanton in that misreading of his opinion. Ostensibly, Judge Stanton totally negated the hospital's claim and did not at all predicate his decision upon the absence of prior notice to Mrs. Requena.[85] Nevertheless, if St. Clare could not assert a right to continue treatment under any circumstances, there was no reason for the lower court to engage in a balancing of relevant considerations. Be that as it may, the appellate court's decision certainly affirms the principle that, at least in some circumstances, i.e., upon proper notice to the patient of the existence of such a policy, a medical facility may persist in keeping a patient alive against her wishes.[86]

Some months later, the finding of the appellate division was adopted, albeit somewhat equivocally, by the Supreme Court of New Jersey in *In re Jobes*.[87] The issue in *Jobes* was similar to that in *Requena* in that Nancy Jobes's husband brought suit seeking removal of a life sustaining nutrition system from his comatose wife who was a patient in a nursing home.[88] Yet, unlike the situation in *Requena*, there was no other readily identifiable facility that was willing to admit the patient for that purpose.[89] Hence, the court ruled that the nursing home could not refuse to participate in the withdrawal of the patient's feeding tube.[90] Regardless of the decision, it is of crucial significance that

---

84. *Id.* at 870.

85. *Id.*

86. *Id.* (suggesting that upon proper notice to the patient of a hospital's policy against withholding life sustaining treatment the court might balance the equities in favor of the hospital).

87. *In re* Jobes, 529 A.2d 434, 451 (N.J. 1987).

88. *Compare id.* at 438, *with Requena*, 517 A.2d at 888.

89. *See Jobes*, 529 A.2d at 450 (finding that "[t]he evidence indicates that at this point it would be extremely difficult, perhaps impossible, to find another facility that would accept Mrs. Jobes as a patient.").

90. *Id.* at 451.

the court's judgment was predicated upon the absence of prior notice. This is most explicitly illustrated in the court's statement that, "[w]e do not decide the case in which a nursing home gave notice of its policy not to participate in the withdrawal of artificial feeding at the time of a patient's admission. Thus we do not hold that such a policy is never enforceable."[91] Accordingly, the decision of the *Jobes'* court is consistent with that of *Requena* in recognizing a hospital's right to adhere to such a policy subject to a requirement that hospitals provide proper notice to the patient.

It should be noted that, in a dissenting opinion, Justice O'Hern implicitly accepted the existence of a countervailing state interest that should in all instances take priority over a patient's right to self-determination. Justice O'Hern found "it difficult to understand how one can order nursing professionals with an abiding respect for their patients to cease to furnish the most basic of human needs to a patient in their care."[92] However, he immediately tempered that assertion with the tantalizing suggestion that, presumably, because the patient has not explicitly issued an advance directive, the physician is entitled to make a determination of the patient's interests on the basis of her own value judgment?[93] Of course, the majority adopted a doctrine of substituted judgment rather than a best interest standard.

The position of the New Jersey Supreme Court as enunciated in *Jobes* was adopted by the United States District Court for the District of Rhode Island in *Gray v. Romeo.*[94] The health care professionals associated with Rhode Island Medical Center were "unanimous in their adamant opposition to the [removal of] nutrition and hydration" from Mrs. Gray.[95] These individuals opposed such action for various reasons. They regarded such removal as "tantamount to euthanasia, inconsistent with

---

91. *Id.* at 450.
92. *Id.* at 464 (O'Hern, J., dissenting).
93. *Id.* (O'Hern, J., dissenting). Justice O'Hern stated, "I do not believe that such an order is essential to the Court's decision, and it may impinge upon the privacy rights of those nursing professionals.... [This] is a case in which the health care providers firmly believe the treatment is adverse to the patient." *Id.* (O'Hern, J., dissenting).
94. 697 F. Supp. 580, 585 (D.R.I. 1988).
95. *Id.* at 583.

the physician's role as safekeeper of his or her patient's [well-being]," and they were concerned for the reputation of the hospital.[96]

The district court found that Mrs. Gray had a constitutional right to forego artificial nutrition and hydration. In addition, the court, citing *Jobes* as precedent, held that "Marcia Gray and her family had no reason to believe that they were giving up her right to determine her course of care by entering the Rhode Island Medical Center."[97] Accordingly, the court ruled that Rhode Island Medical Center must "accede to her request" unless she could be "promptly transferred to a health care facility that would respect her wishes."[98]

Moreover, the district court's decision in *Gray* is significant for an entirely different reason. Unlike the argument presented in *Jobes,* the healthcare facility in *Gray* raised a religious objection that the court seriously entertained.[99] Although the court's formulation of the argument can hardly be described as a model of clarity, it apparently distinguishes between providing unwanted care by means of initiation of an act of bodily intrusion and mere failure to withdraw a foreign object already in place.[100] If so, the underlying assumption must be that refusal to allow the introduction of nutrients and liquids into the feeding tube is not constitutionally protected, but that refusal of the tube itself is protected. Such a distinction would be consistent with the care the court exercises in an earlier section of its decision to categorize use of a gastrointestinal tube as a medical procedure entirely analogous to use of a respirator.[101] The *Gray* court would apparently refuse to recognize a constitutional

96. *Id.*

97. *Id.* at 590.

98. *Id.* at 591 (noting that unless she could be promptly transferred the hospital would have to respect her wishes).

99. *Id.* at 590 (stating that if 42 U.S.C. § 300 (1994) applies, then "a person associated with a health care facility may refuse on moral or religious grounds to participate in an abortion or sterilization procedure," but holding that this did not apply because the health care facility in question was not funded by the Secretary of Health and Human Services).

100. *See id.* (asserting that "the Constitution rarely commands an affirmative obligation on the government's part.").

101. *Id.* at 587 (finding that "if a person has the right to decline life on a respirator," then a person has the equal right to decline a gastrostomy tube) (citations omitted).

right enabling even a patient *in extremis,* but capable of normal inges-
tion of food, to commit suicide by starvation.[102] Thus, it reasons that,
although a patient may make medical decisions affecting himself free
from unwarranted governmental intrusion, "the government is under
no *constitutional* obligation to provide resources to enable an individual
to take full advantage of his or her rights."[103]

Thus, absent legislation, a physician has no obligation to assist
a patient in asserting her right to have the feeding tube removed. The
court then proceeds to note that Rhode Island legislation explicitly
guarantees a patient the right to refuse medical care, which the Court
impliedly assumes includes the right to forego use of an existing feeding
tube to provide life-sustaining nutrition and hydration.[104] The right to
refuse delivery of certified nutrients through an existing feeding tube is
apparently regarded as suicide, and is not constitutionally protected, but
at least in Rhode Island, the right to such refusal is guaranteed by statute.

In that context, the court proceeded to address the religious
objection, not from the perspective of a Free Exercise claim, but from
the vantage point of Rhode Island statutory law.[105] The defendant argued
that the principle reflected in Rhode Island General Laws section 23-17-
11 (1985), which states that a person associated with a health care facility
may refuse on moral or religious grounds to participate in an abortion
procedure, should apply for withdrawal of treatment as well.[106] The
extension of that statutory provision to withdrawal of a feeding tube
is summarily dismissed by the court on the grounds that the "statute is
clearly limited to procedures involving abortion and sterilization [and
as such] does not apply to the circumstances of this action."[107] Fair

---

102. *Id.* at 589 (noting the "distinction between deliberately ending a life by artificial
means and allowing nature to take its course") (citations omitted).

103. *Id.* at 590 (citing Harris v. McCrae, 448 u.s. 297, 317-18 (1990)) (holding that freedom
from government interference in abortion decisions does not include the facilitation
of funds necessary to exercise that right)).

104. *Id.* (stating that Rhode Island legislation guarantees a patient the right to refuse
medical care).

105. *Id.* (dismissing the constitutional argument in favor of a statutory and Canon law
approach).

106. *Id.*

107. *Id.*

enough—at least insofar as disposition of the case before the United States District Court for the District of Rhode Island is concerned.

Nevertheless, the district court has provided a mechanism for assuring that religious objection to withdrawal of treatment will be honored. The legislature of any state may simply enact legislation to that effect.[108] Since the court declared that, had notice been given of the hospital's policy prior to the admission of Mrs. Gray to that facility, the court would not have ordered withdrawal of the feeding tube, the purpose of such legislation would be to obviate the need for explicit notice.[109] It may also be presumed that such legislation would create a right of refusal affecting even already admitted patients. Since, according to the *Gray* court, the government has no constitutional obligation to assist the patient in asserting a right to have the tube removed, all peripheral issues are subject to statutory regulation.[110]

At present, Indiana's Health Code, Title 16, Article 36, chapter 4, section 13, provides that, "[i]f the attending physician, after reasonable investigation, finds no other physician willing to honor the patient's declaration, the attending physician may refuse to withhold or withdraw life-prolonging procedures."[111] In light of existing federal case law, assertion of a right of refusal to withhold life-prolonging procedures in the sense of refusal to withhold a respirator, or refusal to refrain from insertion

---

108. *Id.* (noting that the Rhode Island legislature enacted similar legislation with respect to abortions and sterilization procedures; specifically the right of health care facilities to refuse to participate on moral or religious grounds).

109. *See id.* at 590-91.

110. Indeed, in a footnote the court refers to the applicability of 42 U.S.C. § 300a-7(d) (1994), which provides that:

> [N]o individual shall be required to perform or assist in the performance of any part of a health service program . . . funded in whole or in part under a program administered by the Secretary of Health and Human Services if his performance or assistance in the performance of such part of such program would be contrary to his religious beliefs or moral convictions.

Id. at 590 n.6 (emphasis ommited). The court found that provision inapplicable because Marcia Gray was not receiving treatment through a federally funded health service program or in conjunction with a federally funded research activity. *Id.* The court thus acknowledged that, when treatment is provided in connection with such federally funded programs or activities, such a statutory right does indeed exist. *Id.*

111. *Ind. Code* § 1-36-4-13 (1993).

of a feeding tube, is of dubious constitutional validity (unless, as will be noted later, the patient had been given prior notice). However, refusal to withdraw a respirator or a feeding tube seems to be fully consistent with the decision issued in *Gray*.[112]

Despite the federal district court's endorsement of the doctrine formulated in *Jobes*, at least one New York court has ruled that a medical facility has no duty to participate in the removal of a feeding tube in violation of its medical-ethical judgment despite the apparent absence of prior notice of such a policy. However, in that case, *Elbaum v. Grace Plaza of Great Neck, Inc.*, the court did rule that the medical facility might be required to permit a physician retained by the patient or by the patient's family to enter its premises in order to remove the tube.[113] In a related action, the court in *Grace Plaza of Great Neck, Inc. v. Elbaum* declared that, "[t]here never has been a court order issued in this State commanding a particular physician to do an act which is directly contrary to the physician's own medical ethics."[114] In the latter decision, the court found that "[a] patient who wishes to abstain from life-saving medical treatment may have the right to do so, but he has no right to force a physician to assist, actively or passively, in what the physician himself might regard as the equivalent of suicide."[115] In addition, they unequivocally declared, "we do not recognize any right to force a health provider to render treatment which is contrary to his or her own conscience."[116]

Medical institutions or individual physicians who, for reasons of conscience, do not wish to withdraw a ventilator, nutrition, or hydration from a patient in situations where such withdrawal would otherwise be required by law would be well advised to make sure that patients are informed of such a policy. Although the matter is not explicitly addressed in *Gray*, such notice should logically establish a physician's right not only

112. *See supra* notes 103-110 and accompanying text. The Indiana statute does not require that the physician's referral be predicated upon religious or moral grounds. *Ind. Code* § 1-36-4-13 . Based on the analysis presented herein no such claim should be required in order to protect the statute from constitutional challenge.

113. Elbaum v. Grace Plaza of Great Neck, Inc., 544 N.Y.S.2d 840, 848 (App. Div. 1989).

114. Grace Plaza of Great Neck, Inc. v. Elbaum, 588 N.Y.S.2d 853, 859 (App. Div. 1992).

115. *Id.* at 858.

116. *Id.* at 859.

to refuse to remove a ventilator or feeding tube, but even to introduce such life-preserving mechanisms contrary to the wishes of the patient. Of course, the patient retains the right to seek transfer to another facility; thereby, terminating her contract with the physician. The patient may also accomplish the same end by seeking the ministration of another physician within the same facility, but prior notice would then have the effect of protecting the new physician for the duration of the existence of a contractual relationship. Although the patient has a constitutionally protected right to refuse treatment, agreement to be treated pursuant to such notice would constitute a waiver of that right, and perhaps even a contractual undertaking to permit the physician to fulfill her perceived duty to treat even in such circumstances.

Jobes and *Gray* certainly serve as precedents for protection of the moral integrity of a physician who cannot in good conscience accede to the wishes of her patient. Nevertheless, in *Childs v. Abramovice*, despite its incorporation of a reference to *Gray*, the California Appellate Court remarked that, "[the] issue of whether a court could compel physicians to act contrary to their ethical views is too profound for gratuitous discussion in a dictum. Its resolution must await an appropriate case."[117]

Legislative action would certainly be beneficial in removing lingering legal doubt and in reassuring conflicted physicians. Moreover, legislation would afford an opportunity either to enshrine a notice requirement or, alternatively, to adopt the policy enunciated by the *Grace Plaza* court and reflected in the Indiana statute, and to accord a physician greater protection by omitting such a requirement.

---

117. Childs v. Abramovice, 206 Cal. App. 3d 304, 312 (1988).

17

Godtalk: Should Religion Inform Public Debate?

As a child, knee-high to a grasshopper, I heard a Yiddish maxim from my grandmother. It wasn't really a maxim but an admonition, and in translation it runs as follows: "If, when traveling in a coach and wagon, the coachman drives past the door of a church and fails to cross himself, get out immediately!" My grandmother, and others of a bygone age to whom this rule was virtually self-evident, were not making a pronouncement of theological significance. That admonition had nothing to do with theology and everything to do with safety and survival. They simply did not trust a person who was irreligious and that distrust was well founded. Voltaire, a doctrinaire atheist himself, believed that atheism was safe only for intellectuals. He is reported to have said, "I want my lawyer, tailor, valet, even my wife, to believe in God. I think that if they do I shall be robbed less and cheated less."

My problem: As I ride in a bus passing the National Cathedral in Washington, the bus driver does not cross herself. Indeed, were she to cross herself, I am sure that on the morrow a suit would be filed by the American Civil Liberties Union accompanied by an amicus brief by the

American Jewish Congress claiming that the driver's conduct constitutes an infringement of the Establishment Clause of the First Amendment because the bus driver is, after all, a government employee, and the bus is indeed government property.

But the driver's failure to cross herself is not really my problem. After all, I could refrain from using public transportation; indeed in New York City, many residents have rejected public transportation, albeit for other reasons. My problem is much more basic. My problem is that of the man who takes a fall and proceeds to consult a physician. The doctor examines him, ascertains that there are no broken bones, and tells the gentleman, "Forget about the fall. I want to know why you fell." I am not so much concerned about the fact that the bus driver does not cross herself. I am concerned about *why* the driver would consider crossing herself to constitute inappropriate behavior.

Why is the introduction of religion into the public square regarded as inappropriate and almost an embarrassment? Our society tends to equate legality with morality. That which is legal is *ipso facto* moral; only that which is illegal is immoral. Moreover, we live in a society in which any constitutionally protected liberty is regarded as a social imperative. The exercise of that liberty becomes, if I may use the term, a *mitzvah* in the religion of secular humanism.

Examples: Friends serving in the pulpit rabbinate have told me that, on occasion, when they have wished to deny their pulpits to individuals such as the late Meir Kahane, they have been told by congregants that, in the United States, there is an absolute right to freedom of speech. Those well-meaning but misguided individuals are not totally ignorant of the fact that the First Amendment serves only as an impediment to government action but neither mandates nor bars action in the private sphere. They are, however, convinced that any form of expression that is immune from governmental interference is deserving of encouragement.

The same type of confusion manifests itself in the abortion debate. Abortion, in many circles, is regarded as an entitlement. The line of reasoning seems to be as follows: The Supreme Court has ruled that legal barriers to abortion constitute a violation of a woman's right to privacy and has affirmed a woman's right to do with her body as she chooses. Ergo, public policy should encourage her to regard termination of a pregnancy as a morally neutral act and society ought to facilitate her ability to secure an abortion. The liberties and constraints enshrined in the Bill of Rights become not simply limitations of governmental authority but societal mandates. The elementary distinction between governmental interference in personal freedoms and societal promotion of moral values has, in the minds of many, become blurred beyond recognition.

Assuredly, history has taught us much regarding the danger of permitting religion to dictate public mores. The nature of religion is such that adherents of any particular religion often feel that they are privy to absolute truth not only regarding matters of theology, but also concerning standards of morality and even mundane aspects of human conduct. Historically, the result has not infrequently been discrimination against, and persecution of, individuals and sects who dissented from the teachings of the politically dominant religious group. This country was founded as a haven for victims of religious persecution. Tolerance is quite properly a cardinal virtue of democratic society. But tolerance should extend to all who, in practice, are willing to reciprocate; it should not translate itself into intolerance of some persons or ideologies because of fear based upon historical experience. Long and deeply rooted traditions of freedom and individual liberty serve as a powerful shield against domination of any stripe.

Religion is a powerful force in shaping the tastes, desires, and aspirations of many—and indeed it should be. Needs and desires driven by religious conviction are no less real than those born of other impulses; indeed they are likely to be much more intense. Precisely because they are intense, they ought to be regarded as privileged rather than dismissed as suspect. "To each according to his needs" is firmly rooted in utilitarian principles. Maximization of the greatest happiness for the greatest number necessitates recognition of intensity of individual needs and desires. Individuals intuitively govern their actions by such notions without necessarily formulating them as rules. A person will instinctively give a spare concert ticket to a friend who is a lover of music rather than to one who is simply curious to see the inside of the concert hall. Taking the same principle one step further, I am perfectly willing to forego a piece of chocolate cake in favor of giving it to a child who will relish it far more than I. An employer who willingly allows an employee an absence from work because of religious observance, but is unsympathetic to a request for an afternoon off to attend a ballgame, is not necessarily manifesting respect for religion. If astute, the employer recognizes that those desires are qualitatively different and call for different responses. In the public arena, identification of religious concerns should serve as a marker indicating that, even from the vantage point of a utilitarian calculus, those concerns deserve enhanced weight.

Somewhat quixotically, admission of religious debate in the public square might serve to mitigate the force of nonreligious arguments advanced by religionists. The requirement that it is necessary to establish a "secular purpose" in order to justify government action results in situations in which the announced secular purpose is, at times, an excuse rather than a reason. The religionist will argue the merits of the secular purpose with far more rigor than he can accept in good conscience, all the while hiding his real concern *in pectore*. Thus, for example, the debate concerning welfare reform is restricted to the mundane, secular pros and cons. There certainly must be human beings who simply believe that it is a sin to allow human beings to go hungry. I strongly suspect that people opposed to welfare reform on grounds that can best be described as theological have not remained silent but have chosen to argue their case on grounds of social well-being. Pragmatically speaking, that is probably the more effective course; for my part, however, I would prefer a full and frank dialogue.

Just a bit more than one hundred years ago, in *Church of the Holy Trinity v. United States*,[1] Justice Brewer declared that "this is a Christian nation."[2] Today students of constitutional law find that statement, if not embarrassing, at least quixotic. But at the time it was written, the learned author found no contradiction between that pronouncement and the (anti-) Establishment Clause of the First Amendment. At issue before the Court was an anti-immigration statute. The declaration supported a finding that "[t]he common understanding of the terms labor

---

1.   143 U.S. 457 (1892).
2.   *Id.* at 471.

and laborers does not include preaching and preachers."[3] Lest anyone assume that members of the clergy actually work, the Court found it necessary to add that it would be unthinkable to assume that Congress, in enacting an anti-immigration statute, intended to bar an invitation to Anglican clergy to minister to the religious needs of u.s. citizens.

But the declaration resonates with a more profound meaning. It clearly reflects a literal interpretation of the Establishment Clause as prohibiting only an established state church but in no way precluding governmental preference of religion and religious values. The framers of the Constitution certainly envisioned a Christian nation, *de facto* if not *de jure*. Indeed, the Bill of Rights did not at all interfere in the ongoing relationship with established religions that then existed in nine of the thirteen states. The last of these states disestablished religion in 1833. Quite to the contrary, the First Amendment was designed to prevent the establishment of a *national* church that would effectively supplant the churches established by the various states. As a matter of historical fact, the Bill of Rights was made binding upon the individual states, rather than upon the federal government exclusively, only after the various state churches had long been disestablished.

In the cultural milieu that we have created, conduct or action that would violate constitutional norms if governmental activity were involved becomes a violation of socially accepted mores when displayed in the public square. Thus the (anti-) Establishment Clause in the Bill of Rights is no longer simply a restriction upon government conduct but comes to be regarded as a restraint upon public debate, ultimately a *de facto* constraint upon individual conduct.

I do not at all pretend that the First Amendment is the only reason, or even the principal reason, for the lack of religiosity, if I may call it such, in American society. Certainly it is not. But it seems to me that the First Amendment has made its small contribution to the creation of an *areligious* society. I frankly regard the First Amendment as a failed experiment. Yet, I hasten to add that I would not want to live in a society that does not boast of a First Amendment or a functional equivalent

3. *Id.* at 463.

thereof. But the desire for the protection afforded by the First Amendment should not prevent us from recognizing that neither of its clauses always achieved the effect we want.

The constitutional separation of church and state has clearly given rise to a certain embarrassment about the recognition of religion and religious values in public affairs. As a result, if a religious denomination has strong views on a particular public issue, it may be sure that its position will be dismissed as sectarian and hence unworthy of serious attention. Values nurtured by religious conviction are to be left at the church or synagogue door; they are not to influence or even inform public debate. To paraphrase a Jewish writer of the Enlightenment: Be God-fearing in private, but an agnostic in public.[4]

My own reaction to Justice Brewer's declaration in *Church of the Holy Trinity* is: "Amen. Would that the United States were indeed a Christian nation!"[5] However, as a Jew who is also a member of a law school faculty, I find it necessary to append an "oral law" interpretation. The interpretation may be found in the last scene of the play *Nathan the Wise* by the German poet Lessing in which Nathan is told: "Nathan, Nathan, indeed you are a Christian." To this Nathan responds by saying, "That which you call a Christian in me, I call a Jew in you." [6] Or, as Justice Douglas put it succinctly in *Zorach v. Clausen*,[7] "We are a religious people whose institutions presuppose a Supreme Being."[8] To be effective in the public square, religion need not, and should not, be sectarian in nature.

In some sectors of our community, to engage in activity that can be regarded, even remotely, as an encroachment upon separation of church and state is regarded as sacrilegious; to question the wisdom of maintaining a hermetically sealed wall is nothing less than heresy. Indeed, at times it would appear that the covenant of Philadelphia has supplanted the covenant of Sinai as the credo of American society and

---

4. Judah Leib Gordon, "*Hakitzah Ami*," in *Kitvei Yehudah Leib Gordon: Shirah* 17 (1959).
5. *Holy Trinity*, 143 U.S. at 471.
6. Gotthold Ephraim Lessing, *Nathan the Wise*, Act IV, Scene 7.
7. 343 U.S. 306 (1952).
8. *Id.* at 313.

that the first ten amendments command a devotion far in excess of that paid to the Ten Commandments. Modern-day devotees of the Constitution would erect impregnable fences around this wall just as the Jewish sages of old erected fences around the Law of Moses.

There is no gainsaying the fact that Jefferson's "wall of separation" has contributed to an erosion of religious awareness in the public life in our country. This was certainly not the intention of the Framers of the Constitution.

> The First Amendment... does not say that in every and all respects there shall be a separation of Church and State.... [W]e find no constitutional requirement which makes it necessary for government to be hostile to religion and to throw its weight against efforts to widen the effective scope of religious influence.[9]

Thus spake a Supreme Court Justice whose credentials as a liberal are unimpeachable—Justice William Douglas writing for the majority in *Zorach*.

It is sometimes forgotten that the First Amendment was intended to be binding only upon the federal government, not upon the individual states. Matters of religion were to be dealt with by the individual states as they saw fit. Indeed, as noted earlier, at the time that the First Amendment was inscribed to all eternity upon tablets of constitutional stone, established churches existed in nine of the original states. It was not until a Supreme Court decision handed down in 1940, *Cantwell* v. *Connecticut*,[10] that the Bill of Rights was held to be binding upon state governments by virtue of the Due Process Clause of the Fourteenth Amendment[11] and not until 1947 in *Everson* v. *Board of Education*[12] that the Court declared that the Establishment Clause applies with equal force to state governments.[13]

---

9. *Id.* at 312, 314.
10. 310 U.S. 296 (1940).
11. *Id.* at 303.
12. 330 U.S. 1 (1947).
13. *Id.* at 14-16.

Let us put questions of constitutional jurisprudence aside for a moment. Do we want Johnny to pray? Do we want teenagers to be exposed to the concept of a personal God? Do we want the coachman to make the sign of the cross when passing a church? "Yes!" comes the response, "but not in school and not on public property." Fair enough, until one realizes that (1) Far too many parents are unconcerned with such matters with the result that their children do not receive even minimal exposure to experiences that might be even remotely categorized as religious; and (2) Studied avoidance of all things religious in public contexts may become tantamount to the public negation of all religion. In the words of Justice Douglas such a result "would be preferring those who believe in no religion over those who do believe,"[14] a state of affairs quite antithetical to the goal the First Amendment was designed to achieve.

Heaven forfend that these comments be in any way construed as advocating the states' right either to engage in religious indoctrination or to interfere in the slightest with religious freedom. But we must recognize, as did former Chief Justice Burger in *Walz* v. *Tax Commission*,[15] that "[n]o perfect or absolute separation is really possible; the very existence of the Religion Clauses is an involvement of sorts—one that seeks to mark boundaries to avoid excessive entanglement."[16]

The First Amendment provides that "Congress shall make no law respecting an establishment of religion, or prohibiting the free exercise thereof...."[17] The Free Exercise Clause prohibits any form of religious coercion; the Establishment Clause proscribes government endorsement or overt assistance to religious endeavors even were there to be unanimous consent on the part of the populace. Everyone agrees that free exercise is, and must remain, an absolute. The alternative is the loss of religious liberty.

But it is not at all clear that religious liberty is incompatible with even a formal establishment of religion. The religious liberty of Jews,

---

14. *Zorach*, 343 U.S. at 314.
15. 397 U.S. 664 (1970).
16. *Id.* at 670.
17. U.S. Const. amend. I.

Moslems, Hindus, Sikhs, and members of various cults and sundry is in no way diminished—at least today—in Great Britain by virtue of the unique position of the Church of England as the established church of the realm. On the contrary, establishment serves to mitigate only the freedom of the established church and its communicants which, by virtue of its establishment, is technically subject to the whims of Parliament.

In our country, establishment is unthinkable, not simply because of the constitutional prohibition, but because establishment is regarded as carrying with it an aura bordering at least on the mildly coercive. But there is no need to throw out the baby with the bath water. The Supreme Court has wisely drawn repeated distinctions between "establishment" and "accommodation." The former is anathema; the latter commendable. The problem is where to draw the line.

It is certainly difficult to draw a line that will permit the desired result but not yield logical inconsistencies that can ultimately obliterate the line entirely. Nor should it be forgotten that denial of services and benefits for fear of violating the Establishment Clause is itself a diminution of the free exercise of religion. In *Walz* the Court sagaciously observed that there is an inherent tension between the Establishment and the Free Exercise Clauses, "both of which are cast in absolute terms, and either of which, if expanded to a logical extreme, would tend to clash with the other."[18] We may *wish* Johnny to pray in school but nevertheless recognize that such a goal is constitutionally unattainable. That should not automatically lead us to reject moments of silence as, constitutionally speaking, equally odious. The challenge is to recognize the goal and to fashion the means. The goal should be nondiscriminatory encouragement of religious activity to the fullest extent possible within the parameters of the First Amendment.

Odd as it may sound, such a policy need not be regarded as at variance from the tripartite test of constitutionality adopted by the Supreme Court in *Lemon* v. *Kurtzman*.[19] Encouragement of religious awareness serves a very tangible secular purpose. Let us put aside the very real denominational interest in financial support of parochial school

---

18. *Walz*, 397 U.S. at 668-69.

19. 403 U.S. 602 (1971). "First, the statute must have a secular legislative purpose; sec-

education. Is it not in the interests of all Americans to foster parochial school education for all citizens who wish to avail themselves of such an opportunity? Juvenile delinquency and drug use are demonstrably far less prevalent among students of those schools than among the general teenage population. That represents a tangible secular benefit to all Americans.

In *Everson* v. *Board of Education* the Supreme Court declared assistance to parochial schools in the form of bus transportation to be constitutional on the somewhat tenuous ground that the program was designed to assure the safety of children rather than to promote religious education.[20] In *Board of Education* v. *Allen*[21] the Court permitted the state to provide textbooks of a secular nature for use in parochial schools on the grounds that the benefit was to parents and children, not to schools.[22] Is not a tuition subsidy to defray the cost of hiring a teacher of mathematics but the logical and functional equivalent of the purchase of secular textbooks? Here, too, the benefit is to parents and children, not to religion. As Justice Powell stated in *Hunt* v. *McNair*,[23] "[T]he Court has not accepted the recurrent argument that all aid is forbidden because aid to one aspect of an institution frees it to spend its other resources on religious ends."[24]

The Supreme Court has indeed long struggled with attempts to determine when permissible accommodation rises to the level of proscribed establishment. Perhaps at least a partial resolution lies in an understanding of the history of the development of First Amendment protection of religion. The originally proposed text of the First Amendment, a text not promulgated, read: "The civil rights of none shall be abridged on account of religious belief or worship, nor shall any *national*

ond, its principal or primary effect must be one that neither advances nor inhibits religion; finally, the statute must not foster an excessive government entanglement with religion.'" *Id.* at 612-13.

20. *Everson,* 330 U.S. 1, 17-18 (1947).
21. 392 U.S. 236 (1968).
22. *Id.* at 243-44.
23. 413 U.S. 734 (1973).
24. *Id.* at 743.

religion be established."[25] The function of the latter clause was explicitly limited to prevention of the rise of an institution in the nature of a national established church to the prejudice of denominations not accorded that recognition. The right to institute an Established Church—or not to do so—was a right jealously preserved to the individual states. The thrust of the proposed text was not to bar aid to religion but to bar the preference of one denomination over others. Assuredly, it was not designed to render the federal government and its institutions areligious in nature. Quite apart from original intent, the phrase "establishment of religion" as it appears in the text actually adopted, could readily be interpreted as referring to religious worship, public adoration, ritual, ceremony, and the like. In that context, one could readily understand that all forms of aid to religion are interdicted by the First Amendment. Even Justice Black's formulation in *Everson* prohibiting "aid [to] one religion... [or] all religions"[26] and "aid," understood—contra Douglas—as connoting not simply financial aid but as encompassing other forms of aid as well, is sound doctrine with regard to establishment of religion in the sense of worship and other forms of public adoration. However, the policy concerns that bar establishment of religion in that sense are not directly relevant to the values, principles, morals, or even the basic teachings of religion which, in a significant sense, are so much more fundamental and so much more important.

It should also be noted that it was only with some degree of reluctance that the Supreme Court came to recognize that religious practices other than prayer and similar acts of divine service are protected by the First Amendment. Religion for a Protestant, after all, is not centered upon ritual observances and restrictions, but is fairly well circumscribed by prayer, church attendance, and Bible reading.

Perhaps we should recognize that such a limited understanding of the connotation of the term "religion" is not entirely incorrect. Accordingly, it may be argued that religion should be understood, constitutionally speaking, as a homonym employed with diverse connotations in the Free Exercise and Establishment Clauses. We must insist

25. 1 *Annals of Cong.* 434 (Joseph Gales ed., 1789) (emphasis added).
26. *Everson,* 330 U.S. at 15.

that the Free Exercise Clause is designed to protect religious practice in the broadest sense of that term but urge that the parallel clause prohibiting establishment of religion be regarded as limiting governmental entanglement with religion in the narrow sense of the term "religion," worship and overt profession of a creed. This semantic point serves to bolster Professor Laurence Tribe's argument that anything "arguably nonreligious" should not be considered religious in applying the Establishment Clause.[27]

Recognition that the ambit of "religion" proscribed by the Establishment Clause is far less encompassing than the ambit protected by the Free Exercise Clause certainly comes closer to capturing the spirit of the First Amendment than other attempts to resolve the tension between the two clauses. In the words of former Chief Justice Burger: "[F]or the men who wrote the Religion Clause of the First Amendment the 'establishment' of a religion connoted sponsorship, financial support, and active involvement of the sovereign in religious activity."[28] It did not connote a mandate for neutrality between religion and the absence thereof. Nor, as Chief Justice Rehnquist has stated, is there anything in the Establishment Clause which requires government to be strictly neutral between religion and irreligion. On the contrary, as Justice Douglas remarked, "When the state encourages religious instruction or cooperates with religious authorities... it follows the best of our traditions."[29]

Strange as it may seem to many lay people, but as students of constitutional law would readily concede, the development of First Amendment doctrine over the past two hundred years is rooted, not in transcendental truth or in the application of esoteric hermeneutical principles, but in what the Court perceives to be good for our society—surely a matter over which reasonable people may differ. The policy that reflects a view of societal welfare that recognizes the singular contribution of religion to the betterment of society was perhaps best expressed by Chief Justice Burger in *Walz*:

---

27. Laurence H. Tribe, *American Constitutional Law* § 14-6, at 828 (1978).
28. *Walz*, 397 U.S. at 668.
29. *Zorach*, 343 U.S. at 313-14.

The general principle deducible from the First Amendment and all that has been said by the Court is this: that we will not tolerate either governmentally established religion or governmental interference with religion. Short of those expressly proscribed governmental acts there is room for play in the joints productive of a benevolent neutrality which will permit religious exercise to exist without sponsorship and without interference.[30]

Read in the manner herein proposed, the First Amendment—or better, the Establishment Clause of the First Amendment—acquires a meaning entirely different from its broad interpretation in scores of judicial decisions. Of course, this line of argument will hardly be regarded as respectable in academic circles, certainly not within legal academic circles. And recognition that this type of advocacy is not respectable becomes a self-fulfilling prophecy. If one regards a certain position as somewhat less than respectable, one does not engage in discourse advocating that position. Failure to engage in that type of conversation confirms its lack of respectability and the wall of separation is thereby reinforced not only as a wall between church and state but as a wall between religion and the public square. Accordingly, religious concerns, even when introduced into the public square, lose their validity. But the converse is also true: Religious concerns presented in public discourse again and again dispel embarrassment and become self-validating. But in order for religion to become present in the public square we must first overcome the reticence from which we all suffer. Who knows? Maybe if we succeed in overcoming these inhibitions the course of First Amendment jurisprudence might even be reversed or at least modified.

---

30. *Walz*, 397 U.S. at 669.

Index

A

Aaron, 255, 311, 314

Aaron ha-Levi, R., 309

Abarbanel, R. Isaac
  on Albo, 190
  on evil spirits, 145 n. 3
  on the pig in the end of days,
    300-302
  on principles of faith, 24
  on prophecy, 68, 71, 73-74

Abba Sha'ul, 109 n. 46

Abbaye, 28

Abel, 216

Abigail, 203

abortion, 120, 250, 252, 369, 390, 394-
  396, 400-401

Abraham
  binding of Isaac by, 181, 313 n. 10
  choice of, 187, 240
  and circumcision, 114, 226, 239
    n.5
  covenant with, 185, 255
  God appears to, 47
  Lot saved for the sake of, 204
  oath with, 87 n. 6
  returned to earth, 319
  and *Sefer ha-Yashar*, 242-243

  unique qualities of, 216

Abraham ben David of Posquieres.
  See Ra'avad.

Abramsky, R. Yechezkel, 328 n. 2

Abravanel, R. Isaac. *See* Abarbanel,
  R. Isaac.

Active Intellect, 66, 70-74, 83, 155, 162,
  173-177, 201

Adam
  commandments to, 101, 121
  physical and intellectual traits
    of, 216
  revelation to, 114, 116
  sin and punishment of, 103, 186-
    187, 207, 310 n. 5

Admat Kodesh, 264-265

Adoptionism, 49-51

Adret, R. Solomon ben Abraham. *See*
  Rashba.

adultery, 93-94, 107, 213, 314

Aggadah, 141, 215, 297 n. 27, 313 n. 10,
  319 n. 17

Ahab, 203

Ahaz, 204

on *kinyan*, 334 n. 7

on reason, 113 n. 52

on *yotzei*, 288

Weinberger, Ya'akov, 235 n. 41

Weisz, R. Yitzchak Ya'akov, 223 n. 16, 281 n. 13, 337 n. 9

Welner, R. Moshe Dov, 235 n. 41

Werner, R. Samuel Baruch, 235 n. 40

Werther Syndrome, 368 n. 71

witchcraft, 264, 270 n. 16

Wolf, Susan M., 361 n. 38

Wolfsohn, Julius, 160 n. 3

Wolfson, Harry A., 40 n. 17, 46 n. 31, 47, 161 n. 4

Wollheim, Richard, 105 n. 42, 136-137

world-to-come

animals in, 300

R. Hananyah ben Teradion and, 234

heretics and, 14

intellect and, 27-30, 144-145

karet in, 175

non-Jews and, 29-30, 43, 88-89, 115-118, 244

reward in, 147, 180, 182, 206

Woszner, R. Samuel ha-Levi, 87 n. 6

Written Law, 6, 239

Y

Ya'avets, R. Barzilai Baruch, 94

Yad Eliyahu, 286 n. 17

Yad Ramah, 321

Yalkut Re'uveni. See Midrash.

Yalkut Shim'oni. See Midrash.

Yam shel Shlomoh. See Luria, R. Shlomo.

Yashar, Book of. *See Sefer ha-Yashar.*

Yavin Da'at, 301

Yeruham, Rabbenu, 36 n. 5, 223 n. 17-18

Yeshurun, 243 n. 57. *See also* Jeshurun.

Yigdal, 23

R. Yohanan, 126, 214, 242

Yosef Da'at, 87 n. 6

Yosef, R. Ovadiah, 232 n. 37

yotzei (emerging), 281-290, 293-297, 301-302, 340

Z

Zalcman, Lawrence, 41 n. 20

Zalman of Volozhin, R., 115

Zarephath, 271

Zeira, R., 312-313, 320

Zeller, Eduard, 196 n. 85

Zeno, 108

Zerah, 203

Zigabenus, Euthymius, 50

Zimra, R. David ibn. *See* Radvaz.

Zion, 246, 300

Zoar, 204

Zodiac, 215 n. 4

Zohar, 146 n. 4, 217 n. 9, 319 n. 18

The fonts used in this book are from the Arno family

Maggid Books
The best of contemporary Jewish thought from
Koren Publishers Jerusalem